SOVIET AGRICULTURAL TRADE UNIONS, 1917–70

PETER J. POTICHNYJ

Soviet Agricultural Trade Unions, 1917-70

UNIVERSITY OF TORONTO PRESS

© University of Toronto Press 1972
Toronto and Buffalo
Printed in Canada

ISBN 0-8020-5258-4
Microfiche ISBN 0-8020-0092-4
LC 70-163810

In memoriam

Eugene P. Sydoryk

Preface

In the context of the trade union movement, agricultural trade unions occupy a unique position. Outside the USSR they have emerged only sporadically, and migratory workers are only now being organized in some of the agricultural countries of the West. Why, then, at the time of the revolution in 1917 when only the industrial workers in Russia were pressing for organizations to protect their rights did Lenin set out to establish agricultural trade unions? What function could they perform in a society where leadership was to be centred in the Communist party and where Western pluralism was not desired? These issues have been relatively neglected by Western scholars, including even those who have sought to understand the forces at work in Soviet agricultural organizations. No comprehensive study has yet been made in the West, where at most a few pages of the standard texts dealing with Soviet trade unions are devoted to agricultural unions. But the subject is not without importance. Indeed, the agricultural unions hold key positions in Soviet social organization. This study was undertaken in order to illustrate the role of agricultural trade unions in Soviet society.

A number of general questions helped to focus it. One is the extent to which overall changes in Soviet society were parallelled by developments in the more limited sphere of agricultural labour relations. More specifically, in what ways can policy changes affecting agricultural trade unions be correlated to shifts in the party line? Still another involves relations between town and countryside. In particular, it was hoped that light could be shed upon the party leadership's perception of social stratification among the peasantry and upon the ways in which leaders have attempted, for political and economic purposes, to foster and manipulate cleavages between these various strata.

Other problems with which this study was concerned deal more specifically with the agricultural trade unions as an institution. One line of inquiry is directed towards problems common to all large organizations, such as the extent of bureaucratization, centre-local relations, communication processes, budgetary procedures, and personnel matters. A problem peculiar to the Communist political system is the relationship between bureaucratic organizations and the party. It was, therefore, necessary to investigate the organizational ties between the party and the agricultural trade unions.

The concerns, interests, worries, and needs of the workers, such as wages, conditions of work, social security and social insurance, and vacations, are to a great extent the same throughout the world. A major consideration of this study was to examine the functions actually performed by the agricultural trade unions. To what extent has the union, under conditions of one-party rule, been able to defend the interests of agricultural labourers? Have changes occurred in this 'defence' role of the union? What role has been assigned to the union as a mechanism for social mobilization at different periods of Soviet history?

It is clear enough that the present Soviet leaders are following the ideas of their predecessors in regarding trade unions in general, and agricultural trade unions in particular, essentially as devices for increasing production. However, in the early days of the Soviet system there was a wide-ranging debate among trade unionists, who were also members of the Communist party, over the question of the form to be taken by trade union activity and the kind of control which the party should exert over the unions. Since the capitalist system was being destroyed and the new government was the 'dictatorship of the proletariat,' some argued not only that the economic and political struggle ceased to have any rationale, but also that the organizing and guiding role of the party within the labour movement had become superfluous. Lenin countered this argument by asserting that there must be a link between the party, which was to remain comparatively small and difficult to enter, and the masses. The trade unions were to become this link, since their membership greatly exceeded that of the party and they were open to all workers. This was the basis of Lenin's famous definition of the trade union as a 'transmission belt' and a 'school of communism,' to be used by the party for the purposes of drawing the non-party masses into the building of a socialist state. The agricultural trade unions, which served as one of many links between the party and the peasantry, provide the best example of the Leninist notion of 'transmission belts.'

A more fundamental question that has come to interest students of Soviet affairs is whether the so-called mass organizations have in recent times served as defenders of workers' interests. It should be remembered that the right of trade unions to further workers' interests was specified in the 1922 Labour

Code. Later the emphasis was on production, and only at present do we see again a very slow and cautious recognition that the unions are representatives of the workers and have the right to defend workers' interests. This new development has been especially noticeable in the period since 1956, and in 1961 the duty of the unions 'to protect the material interests and rights of the working people' was incorporated into the new party program. The 1963 trade union statute explicitly stated that the 'trade unions defend the interests of workers and employees' and that they 'possess the right to legislative initiative, share in planning the economy, [and] protect the material interests and rights of the workers.' There is no doubt in my mind that the statements reflect a shift, however slight, in party policy concerning the place and functions of trade unions in Soviet society. Throughout this study an attempt is made to analyse, within permissible limits, the extent to which the unions in general, and in particular the unions in agriculture, use their powers for the benefit of the workers.

The situation of the workers continues to be difficult, however, because conflicts are not viewed as the prime moving force for further social change but as elements of trouble. In such a situation even a suggestion of conflict is perceived as a major danger, even though in reality it might not threaten the existence of the system as a whole. To this day strikes are forbidden, and if they should occur they are put down with great determination and force. In short, the possibility of trade unions playing a key role in the articulation and implementation of social needs has not yet been realized in the Soviet Union or in the countries closely allied with it.

It need hardly be said that a large amount of material on agriculture is available in the Soviet press and other publications. Pure quantity, naturally, does not necessarily imply quality, particularly in Soviet publications. However, there can be no doubt that much of what has appeared in print about the agricultural trade unions is extremely revealing if read with care. Of course, anyone who attempts to study either the history of trade unions or their role in contemporary Soviet society cannot limit himself to the contemporary literature on these organizations. One must delve at least into those studies of the trade unions which appeared prior to the general hardening of Soviet society under Stalinist rule. I have gone through all Soviet weekly bibliographies of books, journal articles, major newspaper articles, and book reviews for the years 1920–70, selecting the most obviously relevant material.

Among the several thousands of books and pamphlets that deal with various aspects of trade union activities I found the most useful the various stenographic reports of trade union congresses and such handbooks as *Spravochnik profsoiuznogo rabotnika, Spravochnik profgruporga, Voprosy profsoiuznoi raboty, V pomoshch profsoiuznomu aktivu,* and a series of pamphlets under the general titles of *Bibliotechka profsoiuznogo aktivista* and *Bibliotechka sel'skogo profsoiuznogo aktivista*.

The largest single source of information is the official publications of trade unions, such as the union daily newspaper *Trud* or the Ukrainian *Robitnycha hazeta*, the journals *Sovetskie profsoiuzy*, *Okhrana truda i sotsial'noe strakhovanie*, *Vsemirnoe profdvizhenie*, and *Novoe Vremia*. The newspapers, *Sel'skaia zhizn'* as well as *Pravda* and *Izvestiia*, also contain a large amount of material dealing with the problems in the Soviet countryside. Such party journals as *Kommunist* and *Partiinaia zhizn'* also deal with trade union matters periodically. In addition, there is much material in a number of readily available specialized publications, such as *Sel'skoe khoziaistvo*, *Ekonomicheskaia gazeta*, and others.

Several important publications relevant for this study were, unfortunately, not accessible to me. Early magazines and newspapers such as *Rabotnik zemli i lesa*, *Batrak*, *Sovkhoznaia gazeta*, and *Sel'skokhoziaistvennyi rabochii* are, generally speaking, unavailable in the libraries of the Western world.

There are a large number of professional publications which are easy to come by. In addition to books dealing with labour, law, and labour economics, there also exists a large collection of publications by sociologists on various aspects of rural life. These books and articles are important for their analytical value and the extensive information they contain and will provide a careful researcher with further insights into the problems of the large rural population of the USSR.

Many statistical handbooks are also available, a number of which are listed in the bibliography attached to this study. Unfortunately, however, the statistics for the agricultural trade unions specifically are still quite inadequate. For example, there are at best only partial data for the regional distribution of agricultural trade unions, and this is as true for the early period of the Soviet regime as it is now, although in the twenties some important publications did fill in this gap.

Other sources of information on the problems facing agricultural trade unions are the letters to the editor which contain criticisms, complaints, and suggestions and as such are of inestimable value. Especially during periods of officially sanctioned public debates the Soviet press is usually full of such letters or summaries of correspondence with the editor, and these quite often provide an insight into the problems which are being discussed.

An initial and important consideration in this study is the attitude of Lenin and his successors to the formation of agricultural trade unions, and their views on the eventual use of these organizations in controlling the generally hostile non-industrial masses of the country. Consequently, the first chapter sets forth the Soviet view of the role and function of the agricultural trade union. Also requiring treatment is the evolution of the organizational structure of the unions and a description of how the activities of central and local union organs evolved. Because the Union of Agricultural Workers, in its many forms, had a large central apparatus with multiple bureaus and committees and an enormous field network at various levels, any description had necessarily to be discriminately selective. Nevertheless, an attempt has been made in the second chapter to cover these topics as fully as possible. The third chapter attempts to cover, again as fully as the available sources permit, the composition of agricultural trade union membership from 1919 to 1970, and the political purposes reflected by changes in the membership. Agricultural trade union finances are discussed in the following chapter, while trade union functions in the spheres of labour protection and regulation of working conditions are covered in the fifth chapter. Finally, union activities in social security and social insurance programs are outlined in the sixth chapter. The last chapter summarizes major points of the study. Statistical data from various sources on trade union membership, the jurisdictional framework of the union, and a chart of its organizational evolution are contained in several appendices. A selected bibliography and a glossary of important terms and abbreviations are also provided.

Acknowledgements

I am indebted to a large number of persons for their assistance. To Professors John N. Hazard and Peter H. Juviler of Columbia University I would like to express my sincere appreciation for their encouragement and counsel during the final stages in the preparation of this study. At all stages of the work from original thoughts through investigation and refinement of ideas to the final summation, Professor Grey Hodnett of York University was a wise counsellor and a generator of purpose when that was needed. To him must go my deepest appreciation and thanks. I also owe gratitude to Harris Coulter of Washington, DC, and to Professor F.C. Barghoorn of Yale University for suggestions which led to improvements. Though I have learned from each of them, the responsibility for the material in this text is of course entirely my own.

For a research grant, I want to thank E.T. Salmon, Vice-President Arts, McMaster University, and the chairmen of the Departments of Political Economy and Political Science, Professor R.C. McIvor, FRSC, and Professor G.R. Davy respectively. This study has been published with the aid of a grant from the Social Science Research Council of Canada using funds provided by the Canada Council, and with the assistance of the Publications Fund of the University of Toronto Press.

These acknowledgements would not be complete without a mention of Lawrence H. Chamberlain, formerly the Vice-President Academic of Columbia University, whose warm friendship helped to overcome many doubts. Lastly, but importantly, I wish to thank my wife, Tamara, for her patience, sacrifice, and understanding.

PJP
Dundas, Ontario
August 1970

Glossary

ACCTU *All-Union Central Council of Trade Unions*
Aktiv, aktivist(s) *Activist(s), action group*
Apparatchiki *Functionaries*
ASSR *Autonomous Soviet Socialist Republic*
Batrachkom(s) *Batrak committee(s)*
Batrak(s) *Landless peasant(s)*
Brigada *Brigade*
Brigadir *Brigade leader*
Dal'vostbiuro *Bureau for the Far East,* ACCTU
Dal'vostsovprof *Trade Union Council of the Far East*
Dvadtsiatipiatitisiachniki *Group of 25,000*
Fabzavkom *Factory and local committee*
FZMK *Factory and local committee*
FZU *Factory training school*
Gorsovprof(s) *City trade union council(s)*
Grupporg *Group organizer*
Grupprabochkom(s) *District organization of workers' committees*
Gruzchiki *Trade Union of Loading Workers*
Gubernia(s) *Province(s)*
Gubotdel(s) *Gubernia section(s)*
ITS *Engineering and Technical Section*
Iugvostbureau *Bureau for the Southeast,* ACCTU
Iuzbiuro *Bureau for the South,* ACCTU
Kavbiuro *Bureau for the Caucasus,* ACCTU
Khozrashchet *Business accounting*

Kirgizbiuro   *Bureau for Kirgizia,* ACCTU
Kirgizsovprof   *Trade Union Council of Kirgizia*
KKOV(s)   *Committees of the poor*
KNS(s)   *Committees of the poor*
Kodeks Zakonov O Trude   *Labour code*
Kolkhoz(s)   *Collective farm(s)*
Kolkhoznik(s)   *Collective farmer(s)*
Kombedy   *Committees of the poor*
Kombinat(s)   *Combinat(s)*
Komissiia Po Trudovym Sporam   *Commission on labour disputes*
Komnezam(s)   *Committees of the poor*
Komsomol   *Communist Youth League*
Konevodtrest   *Horse-breeding Trust*
Koshchi   *Union of Small Landowners*
Krai(s)   *Province(s)*
Kraikom(s)   *Provincial committee(s)*
Kraisovprof   *Krai Council of Trade Unions*
KTS   *Commission on Labour Disputes*
Kulak(s)   *Rich peasant(s)*
KZOT   *Labour code*
Lespromkhoz   *Lumber industry*
MBIT   *Inter-Trade Union Bureau of Engineers and Technicians*
Mestkom(s)   *Local committee(s)*
MOPR   *International Organization for Aid to Fighters for Revolution*
MTM   *Machine and Tractor Shop*
MTS   *Machine Tractor Stations*
Narkom prizreniia   *People's Commissariat of Charity*
Narkomsobes   *People's Commissariat of Social Security*
Narpit   *Trade Union of Workers of Public Eating Places*
NEP   *New Economic Policy*
Obkom(s)   *Oblast committee*
Oblast   *Region*
Oblispolkom(s)   *Oblast executive committee(s)*
ODVF   *Society of Friends of the Air Fleet*
Okrug   *County*
Okruzhotdel   *County section*
Otdelencheskie komitety   *Subdivision committees*
Otdelenie(a)   *Section(s)*
Partiinost   *Party loyalty*
Peredovik(s)   *Leading worker(s)*
Plenum(s)   *Plenary session(s)*

Politotdel(s)   *Political section(s)*
Pravlenie(a)   *Administration(s)*
Pripisnye   *Attached sovkhozes*
Profgruporg   *Trade union organizer*
Profgruppa   *Trade union group*
Profintern   *Red International of Trade Unions*
Profizdat   *Trade union publishing house*
Promyshlenno-podsolnykh   *Employees of industrial enterprises*
Rabkor(s)   *Workers' correspondents*
Rabochkom(s)   *Workers committee(s)*
Rabotnikov sela profsoiuz   *Union of Village Workers*
Raikom   *Raion committee*
Raimestkom(s)   *Trade Union Committees of Raion Experimental Stations*
Raion   *District*
Raiotdel(s)   *District section(s)*
Raipravlenie(a)   *District administration(s)*
Raiprofbiuro   *Raion trade union bureau*
Raiprofsovet   *Raisovprof*
Raisekretariat(s)   *District secretariat(s)*
Raisovprof(s)   *District trade union council(s)*
Raizo   *Raion land department*
Rastsenochno-Konfliktnaia Kommisiia   *Rates and Conflict Commission*
Repkom(s)   *Republic committee(s)*
Revizionnaia Kommissiia   *Auditing commission*
RKK   *Rates and Conflict Commission*
RKP(b)   *Russian Communist party (Bolsheviks)*
RSDRP   *Russian Social Democratic Labour party*
RSFSR   *Russian Soviet Socialist Republic*
RTS   *Repair Tractor Stations*
Sel'kom(s)   *Village committees*
Selrabochkom(s)   *Village workers committee(s)*
Seredniak(s)   *Middle peasant(s)*
Sevzapadbiuro   *Bureau for the North West,* ACCTU
Sevzapsovprof   *Trade Union Council of the North West*
Shefskie obshchestva   *Patronage associations*
Shefstvo   *Supervision, patronage*
Shefstvo associations   *Patronage associations*
Shefstvo brigades   *Patronage brigades*
Sibbiuro   *Bureau for Siberia,* ACCTU
Sibsovprof   *Siberian Trade Union Council*
SKHU   *Agricultural training school*

Smychka   *Alliance, cultural unity*
Sotsial'noe Obespechenie   *Social security*
Sotsstrakh   *Social insurance*
Sovkhoz(es)   *State farm(s)*
Sovkhoznik(s)   *State farm worker(s)*
Sovprof(s)   *Trade union council(s)*
Stakhanovets   *Stakhanovite*
Strakhovye delegaty   *Social insurance agents*
Teknikum(s)   *Technical educational institutions*
Tsekh   *Shop*
Tsekhkom(s)   *Shop committee(s)*
Tselevoi profsoiuznyi upolnomochenyi   *Trade union representatives for special purposes*
Tsentral'noe(ye) pravlenie(ia)   *Central administration(s)*
Turkbiuro   *Bureau for Turkestan*, ACCTU
Uchastkom(s)   *Subdivision committee(s)*
Uezd   *District*
Uezd otdel   *District section*
Ukrbiuro   *Bureau for the Ukraine*, ACCTU
Upolnomochenyi   *Authorized agent*
Uprofbiuro   *Uezd bureau*
Uralbiuro   *Bureau for the Urals*, ACCTU
VMBIT   *All-Union Inter-Union Bureau for Engineers and Technicians*
Volost(i)   *Village district(s)*
Volsekretariat   *Village district secretariat*
Vsekokhotsoiuz   *All-Russian Hunting Association*
Vsekopromrybaksoiuz   *All-Russian Fisheries Association*
Vserabotzem   *All-Russian Agricultural Workers' Union*
Vserabotzemles   *All-Russian Agricultural and Forestry Workers' Union*
Vsesoiuzsel'khoztekhnika   *All-Union Farm Machinery Association*
VTSSPS   ACCTU
VTUZ   *Higher Technical Educational Institution*
VUSPS   *All-Ukrainian Union of Trade Unions*
Zakavbiuro   *Bureau for Transcaucasus*, ACCTU
Zakavsovprof   *Transcaucasian Trade Union Council*
Zampolit   *Deputy Chairman for Political Affairs*
Zemel'nye organy   *Land organs*
Zemliachestvo(a)   *Native region fraternal society(ies)*

Contents

PREFACE vii

ACKNOWLEDGEMENTS xii

GLOSSARY xiii

1
The development of Soviet agricultural trade unions 3
2
Organization and structure 45
3
Agricultural trade union membership 96
4
Finances 132
5
Conditions of labour 149
6
Social insurance 168
7
Conclusions 193

APPENDICES (see overleaf) 202
SELECTED BIBLIOGRAPHY 222
INDEX 249

APPENDICES

  I Organizational evolution of Soviet agricultural trade unions   202

 II Total membership in agricultural unions, 1917–70   204

III Jurisdiction of Soviet agricultural trade union in 1921   208

 IV Jurisdiction of Soviet agricultural trade unions in 1920   209

  V Jurisdiction of Soviet agricultural trade unions in 1931   212

 VI Jurisdiction of Soviet agricultural trade union in 1968   215

VII Distribution of the Group of 25,000 according to age, sex, party membership, and years as hired worker   216

VIII Distribution of new members of selected agricultural trade unions in republics according to nationality, July–December 1931   217

 IX Characteristics of agricultural membership in selected republics, based upon sample data, July–December 1931   218

  X Membership in the Agricultural and Forestry Workers' Union in various Central Asian republics, 1 April 1925   221

TABLES

2–1 Growth in membership of the Agricultural and Forestry Workers' Union drawn from native groups in Central Asia, January to October 1924   50

2–2 Membership of the Agricultural and Forestry Workers' Union drawn from native groups of Central Asia as a per cent of total Central Asian membership, January to October 1924   51

2–3 Higher organs of the union, 1921–4   52

2–4 Oblast structure of the agricultural trade unions, February 1931   59

3–1 Territorial distribution and unionization of batraks in selected areas, October 1923 to October 1924   100

3–2 Distribution of total membership of the Agricultural and Forestry Workers' Union and of batrak members by selected areas, October 1924   100

3–3 Distribution of total membership of the Agricultural and Forestry Workers' Union and batrak members in Central Asian region, January to October 1924   101

3–4 Percentage distribution of membership in the Agricultural and Forestry Workers' Union by type of enterprise and selected other categories, January and July 1924   102

3–5 Distribution of membership in the Agricultural and Forestry Workers' Union by republics and oblasts, 1 April 1925   104

3–6 Trade union membership as a percentage of total eligible agricultural labour force, 1 January 1923 to 1 January 1936   105

3–7 Trade union membership as a percentage of eligible labour force on state farms and Machine Tractor Stations, 20 April 1932 and September 1934   105

3–8 Workers and employees in sovkhozes, 1928 to 1931   109

3–9 Workers and employees in agricultural sovkhozes, August 1930 to August 1931   109

3–10 Distribution of workers and trade union members among agricultural unions from October 1931 to January 1932   113

3–11 Membership in agricultural trade unions, 1932 and 1934   115

3–12 Changes in membership of agricultural trade unions, January 1932 to April 1934   116

4–1 Expenditures by the Agricultural and Forestry Workers' Union per member, 1927   141

4–2 Scale of trade union membership dues, 1933–61   143

4–3 Scale of trade union membership dues, 1961–70   143

5–1 Average length of working day in selected sovkhozes, 1923, in hours and minutes   151

5–2 Average length of working day in selected private agricultural enterprises, 1923, in hours and minutes   151

FIGURES

1 Structure of inter-trade union organs, 1962–4   90

2 Structures of the Union of Workers and Employees in Agriculture and State Procurement, 1962–4   91

SOVIET AGRICULTURAL TRADE UNIONS, 1917–70

1
The development of
Soviet agricultural trade unions

REVOLUTION AND CIVIL WAR

Before the collapse of the tsarist government in 1917 no strong agricultural trade union movement existed. There had been efforts to organize agricultural workers, none of which was entirely successful. Of the isolated attempts made during the revolutionary movement of 1904–5, the union on the Butirsky Farm in Moscow was, perhaps, the most famous example.[1] In 1905 a Union of Gardeners was also created, but it was dissolved in 1906 by the tsarist administration. The Union of Land Surveyors was organized in 1912, died soon after, and re-emerged after the February revolution of 1917; yet it remained small and of only local importance. These initial organizing attempts were scattered, improvised, and without serious influence upon later developments, with the exception to some degree of those in Latvia.[2]

After February 1917 small unions of agricultural workers were started, chiefly in the neighbourhood of the capital and nearby industrial centres.[3] The first local cells mentioned as existing in 1917 were those of Petrograd, Mos-

---

1 *Trade Unions in Soviet Russia* (London: Independent Labour party, 1920), p. 79; VTsSPS, *Otchet za 1919 god* (Moscow: Izdatel'stvo VTsSPS, 1920), p. 389 ff.

2 Altmorov, 'Piatiletie leningradskogo gubotdela vserabotzemlesa,' *Trud*, 27 March 1924.

3 The peasant co-operatives, however, had been gaining ground even before the 1917 revolutions, in contrast to the slight progress of the trade unions. But unlike the union, which hoped to unite the village proletariat, the co-operative movement united land-owning peasantry. Sergei Pushkarev, *The Emergence of Modern Russia, 1801–1917* (New York: Holt, Rinehart and Winston, 1963), pp. 273–5.

cow, Tver, and Vladimir gubernias (provinces), and were primarily organizations uniting individual gardeners and workers on horse-breeding farms.[4] There were not many of these unions, their organizational structure was primitive, and they attracted few members. It is estimated that in 1917 the total membership of these unions was approximately 577.[5] In 1918 only two gubernias – Moscow and Petrograd – had gubernia-wide union organizations of which the former (because of Menshevik interference) was organized in November.[6] Indeed, the numerical weakness of the unions is the best indication of their insignificance.

An important fact – and one quite often overlooked in present-day discussions of agricultural trade unions – is that these unions were not at the time led by the Bolsheviks. One contemporary account clearly coloured by Bolshevik influence stated that they were under the influence of 'compromising leaders, who were mostly of the Socialist Revolutionary party with narrow bourgeois ideals and an agrarian program full of contradictions and omissions,' and that in the early period of their development after the February revolution they 'aimed mainly at protecting their craft interests, and did not realize that the problem confronting agricultural workers was the ownership and organization of production.'[7] Although the evidence suggests that the leadership of the Socialist Revolutionary party never fully grasped the importance of an organized rural proletariat, their half-hearted efforts in the countryside probably alarmed Lenin, who was aware of the threat such attempts would pose with respect to his own political ambitions.[8]

Lenin had always been avidly interested in organizing labourers in rural areas as a means of mobilizing the peasants for the impending revolution. One of the significant features in the development of his revolutionary strategy was his early realization that in Russia it would be impossible for the small urban proletariat to carry out a socialist revolution unless it could enlist the aid of at least part of the numerically preponderant peasantry. This was the basis of the slogan, first proclaimed in April 1905, of 'the revolutionary democratic dic-

4 *Profsoiuz rabochikh sel'skogo khoziaistva: Kratkii istoricheskii ocherk* (Moscow: Profizdat, 1961), p. 6. Other sources erroneously give 16 June 1919 as the date of the First Congress. Cf. *Trade Unions in Soviet Russia*, p. 79; VTsSPS, *Otchet za 1919 god*, p. 389.
5 International Labour Office, *The Trade Union Movement in Soviet Russia* (Geneva 1927), p. 67.
6 VTsSPS, *Otchet za 1919 god*, p. 389.
7 *Trade Unions in Soviet Russia*, p. 78.
8 Cf. speech of V. Chernov, then minister of agriculture and the leading SR at the Third All-Russian Conference of Trade Unions, in which he termed 'utopian' the attempts to organize agricultural workers.

tatorship of the proletariat and peasantry.'[9] In 1917 he was faced with the practical problem of bringing this alliance of proletariat and peasantry into being. One of the solutions he offered was the formation of unions for agricultural wage workers.

Lenin took advantage of the Third All-Russian Conference of Trade Unions in Petrograd at the end of June 1917 to make this proposal, although it is unlikely that he seriously hoped to influence this assembly in which Menshevik and Socialist Revolutionary delegates held a majority. The conference, he said, should assume the task of establishing an 'All-Russian Union of Agricultural Workers.' Appealing to the sympathy of the assembled delegates, he pointed out that 'every class in Russia is organizing. Yet the class that is more exploited than any other class, that is poorer, more divided, and more crushed than any other – the class of agricultural wage labourers – has, it seems, been forgotten.' He called on the 'vanguard of the Russian proletariat, the trade union of industrial workers, to come to the aid of their brothers, the village workers.' The difficulties of organizing village workers were enormous, as Lenin was well aware. He himself pointed out that only in Latvia were they organized into trade unions, while in the rest of the Russian empire such bodies did not exist. Nevertheless, he said, the factory wage workers should 'take the initiative in utilizing the cells, groups, and branches of trade unions which are scattered all over Russia in order to awaken the agricultural worker to an independent life.'[10]

A policy of organizing the village proletariat at the very moment land was being redistributed was not self-contradictory, he asserted, because 'for all those who hold fast to the class proletarian views' there should be no doubt that the Stockholm Congress of the RSDRP (Russian Social-Democratic Labour party) of 1906 was right when it resolved that

the party at all times and under all situations of democratic agrarian transformation takes upon itself the task of struggling without letup for the creation of an independent class organization of the village proletariat; of pointing out to it the irreconcilably contradictory nature of its interest as against the interests of the peasant bourgeoisie; of warning it against being deluded by the system of petty proprietorship, because this system under conditions of commodity production is ever incapable of ridding the masses of their misery ... and, finally, of pointing out the inevi-

9 V.I. Lenin, 'Revoliutsionnaia demokraticheskaia diktatura proletariata i krestianstva,' *Sochineniia* (4th ed.; Moscow 1941–50), VII, pp. 196–202. The idea was elaborated in his 'Dve taktiki sotsial-demokratii v demokraticheskoi revoliutsii,' *ibid.*, VIII, pp. 27–126.
10 V.I. Lenin, 'O neobkhodimosti osnovat' soiuz sel'skikh rabochikh Rossii,' *Lenin o profsoiuzakh, 1895–1923* (Moscow: Profizdat, 1957), pp. 360–3.

tability of a full socialist transformation as the only possible means of destroying all misery and all exploitation.[11]

Lenin felt that 'everyone who is exclusively, or mainly, or even partly engaged as a hired worker in any agricultural enterprise' should have the right to belong to a union, but he was not sure whether these three distinct types of hired workers should all be grouped together in a single union.[12] The essential consideration was simply that the fundamental class interests of all persons who sold their labour were alike, and that these people should in some way be organized. Both in 1903 and in 1917 Lenin spoke of trade unions only for agricultural labourers, that is, hired workers and not peasant cultivators working full-time for themselves.[13] But in 1917 he also stated that it would be a good policy to keep the door to agricultural trade unions open to anyone 'even partly engaged as a hired worker in any agricultural enterprise.' A peasant who worked part time as a hired hand could join, even though he might also work some of the time for himself.[14] These statements in *Pravda* in June and July 1917 were the only ones published before the October revolution in which Lenin reflected on the subject of trade unions in agriculture. It was some time before he again deemed it necessary to outline his views on this matter.

11 *Chetvertyi (ob'edinitel'nyi) s'ezd RSDRP aprel' (aprel-mai) 1906 goda: Protokoly* (Moscow: Gospolitizdat, 1959), p. 523.
12 Lenin, *Lenin o profsoiuzakh*, p. 361.
13 Lenin, 'K derevenskoi bednote,' *Sochineniia*, v, p. 296.
14 Lenin, *Lenin o profsoiuzakh*, p. 361. In *The Development of Capitalism in Russia*, written in 1899, Lenin defined the 'proletarian' and 'semi-proletarian' strata of the agricultural population as those sections which earn their livelihood mainly or halfway by the sale of labour power' (*Sochineniia*, III, p. 392). He stated further that to 'calculate that the proletarian and semi-proletarian population taken together comprise one-half of the peasantry is to underestimate and not to exaggerate their numbers' (*ibid.*). Thus according to Lenin's own definition more than half of the peasantry would have been eligible for membership in the unions. In effect, Lenin would have opened the unions not only to the 'proletarian and semi-proletarian strata' but also to many peasants who were relatively better off. Lenin narrowed this position somewhat when he came to power, as reflected in his pronouncements on class division in the village. Yet he never did define precisely the difference between a peasant and a proletarian. Apparently he was interested above all else in distinguishing what it was that brought the interests of a large segment of the peasantry into line with those of the urban working class, and his answer was the sale by a peasant of his labour. 'The fundamental class interests of all who sell their labour power are alike,' and this included 'all those who earn even a part of their livelihood by hiring themselves out to others.' On the other hand one should not be surprised to find that Lenin's definitions were vague and varied from time to time. The advantages of defining the proletariat as broadly as possible did not escape such an intensely political man as Lenin.

After the events of October 1917 the Bolsheviks vigorously pushed for the creation of an agricultural trade union.[15] Under their relentless pressure, the First All-Russian Congress of Trade Unions met in January 1918. It declared that the organization of such a union was of primary importance, and that 'it would be inconceivable to fight hunger without the aid of the toiling peasantry, without a unified All-Russian Union of Agricultural Workers.'[16] When the Second Congress met in January 1919 M.P. Tomsky, who was responsible for the unions, admitted that nothing had yet been done and explained that all energy had had to be spent on the organization of industrial trade unions so 'that no resources could have been spent on organizing agricultural workers.'[17]

The struggle for control of the existing agricultural unions among the Bolsheviks, Socialist Revolutionaries, and Mensheviks continued through 1918 and most of 1919. No side had a majority in the leadership of these unions, although it seems that in 1918 non-Bolsheviks had a greater voice in the affairs of some of them. Apparently the Lithuanian and Belorussian agricultural workers' unions were comparatively well organized and under strong Bolshevik influence.[18] Other unions which were Bolshevik dominated or strongly influenced by them were the Petrograd, Tver, and Vladimir organizations.[19] Any provincial agricultural trade union organizations elsewhere, it was said, 'were completely in the hands of specialists and petit-bourgeois elements.'[20] The important agricultural areas of the Ukraine, Volga, North Caucasus, and Siberia were outside the sphere of Bolshevik control during this period and

15 *Profsoiuz rabochikh sel'skogo khoziaistva*, p. 4.
16 *Ibid.*, p. 5. See also VTsSPS, *Vtoroi s'ezd profsoiuzov: Stenograficheskii otchet* (Moscow), p. 20.
17 The Kombedy (Committees of the Poor) were organized after June 1918, principally to carry the class war to the village and to requisition grain held by the more affluent peasants. In addition they were to overcome the influence of anti-Bolshevik elements in local soviets where they still dominated. They also were given the task of organizing collectives of poor peasants. Specifically, the instructions were for collective plowing and harvesting but, according to R.G. Wesson, the result seems to have been mostly the establishment of communes. It is probably no accident that the acceleration in the organizational advances of the union came after the law of 14 February 1919 gave state farms, not communes, the privilege of preparing for communistic agriculture. Robert G. Wesson, *Soviet Communes* (New Brunswick: Rutgers University Press, 1963), pp. 34–5, 106. See also Thomas T. Hammond, *Lenin on Trade Unions and Revolution, 1893–1917* (New York: Columbia University Press, 1957), pp. 86–9. See chapters 2 and 3 for a discussion of the relations between Kombedy and the union in Central Asia.
18 *Trade Unions in Soviet Russia*, p. 79.
19 *Ibid.*; *Profsoiuz rabochikh sel'skogo khoziaistva*, p. 6.
20 VTsSPS, *Otchet za 1919 god*, p. 389.

exercised almost no influence on the organization and early development of the future Agricultural Workers' Union. In these areas all trade union organizations developed almost independently of the centre, and only later were they gradually incorporated into the structure of the All-Russian Central Council of Trade Unions (ACCTU).

The struggle that was taking place between the Bolsheviks and other groups over control of the agricultural workers' unions came to a head in 1919. In December 1918 the Temporary Central Committee of the future All-Russian Agricultural Workers' Union had been organized, largely on the initiative of the land surveyors who had their own national union but who decided to unite with the mass of agricultural workers as well as with groups of other agricultural specialists and experts in peasant affairs. The committee agreed to convene a constituent congress, which in fact was destined to be no more than an organizing conference. This Conference of Agricultural Workers, which met in Moscow on 20 February 1919, was not a complete success, for only approximately sixty-nine delegates attended, of whom forty-nine were specialists, land surveyors, and agriculturalists, while only twenty could be classified as representing the agricultural proletariat. Of the twenty, only three were actually delegates from agricultural workers' unions (Elets, Tula, and Shuisk), while the rest came from the Moscow Landowners' Union.[21] The conference did manage to work out rules for the embryonic organization and to elect an expanded Temporary Central Committee, but an attempt at registering the new body as an existing union failed. The Bolshevik dominated ACCTU did not accept the conference's claim to be a 'congress' and would not register the union, 'owning to [its] non-proletarian character and the presence of only a small membership.'[22] However, it was recognized by the ACCTU as a preliminary conference of the executive and also as the initial organizing bureau that would convene a full-fledged congress.

The respite they had won (the date of the constituent congress was postponed to June 1919) was not wasted by the Bolsheviks. During this period they initiated an intensive organizational drive, and in March 1919 the largest agricultural workers' organization up to that time came into existence – the Agricultural Workers' Union of Petrograd gubernia, whose first congress was held from 11 to 13 March 1919.[23] In his speech to the congress Lenin expressed pleasure at seeing that steps were being taken to organize agricultural labour. He referred to his past concern over this matter and alluded to talks with 'Com-

---

21 *Trade Unions in Soviet Russia*, p. 79.
22 *Ibid.*
23 VTsSPS, *Professional'noe dvizhenie SSSR, 1917–1927* (Moscow: Izdatel'stvo VTsSPS, 1927), p. 40.

rade Shmidt, the Commissar of Labour, and with the members of the ACCTU and others' on how best to organize the rural proletariat. A marked shift in tone and emphasis distinguished this speech from his earlier ones, where he had stressed the influence such an organization might have on improving the labour conditions of rural wage workers. The important point in this particular speech was the task of preventing the emergence of a capitalist class from the richer strata of peasantry:

The soviet government will do all in its power, immediately and unconditionally, to help this [Vserasbotzem] organization to remake life in the village, so that no place will remain for the kulak, so that no speculation can exist, so that comradely public work will be the general rule in the village ... Only such a union, for the construction of which you are laying the foundations, can bring about this basic change.[24]

He expressed the hope that an All-Russian Union of Agricultural Workers would come into being in the near future, and that it would be 'the real support of the Soviet government in the village ... a foundation and advance army for the transformation of the entire life of the villages.'[25] Never had Lenin so forcefully spoken of the need to organize the village poor.[26] Nor did he later lose interest in the matter, securing financial assistance and contributing his moral support to launch this organization successfully.

Soon after the Petrograd gubernia congress the Presidium of the ACCTU issued a statement on 24 March 1919 that said in part that the ACCTU recognized the need of organizing the type of union suggested by Lenin to unite agricultural and forestry workers. It recommended that the Temporary Central Committee of the Agricultural Workers' Union be reinforced with a representative from the ACCTU and with one representative from the Union of Foresters and be formally reconstituted as a bureau charged with the task of convening an 'authoritative' First Congress of the Agricultural and Forestry Workers' Union.[27] Until the bureau was created the Temporary Central Committee had the right to delegate one of its members to the ACCTU, but only with an advisory vote. The statement noted with satisfaction that the Temporary Central Committee had already agreed to follow the instructions and recom-

24 *Lenin o profsoiuzakh*, pp. 497–500.
25 *Ibid.*, p. 500.
26 *Ibid.*, pp. 374, 432–7, 441, 465–7.
27 The Bolsheviks were eager to amalgamate the foresters with the agricultural workers at this time because the Union of Foresters was apparently in their own hands. The Land and Forestry Workers' Union was renamed Agricultural and Forestry Workers' Union at the Fifth Congress of the union in January 1926.

mendations of the ACCTU. Soon after the publication of this statement the ACCTU sent two representatives, Golubev and Levman, to the Temporary Central Committee.[28] In short order the Temporary Central Committee reconstituted itself into an Organizing Bureau (with the help of still another representative from the ACCTU named Brumberg), and together with the Organization and Instruction Section of the ACCTU issued a proclamation which read as follows:

The ACCTU which, since the fall of last year [1918] took upon itself the task of organizing such a union, warmly invites all trade union organs and trade union activists for whom the interests of the proletariat are dear to start organizing in the localities – on the gubernia and local level – cells of the new industrial union of agricultural workers, which is to unite all workers in agriculture and forestry ...

All newly established cells should immediately get in touch with the Organizing Bureau which exists in Moscow and functions as a central committee and which, under instructions from the ACCTU, is to convene on June 15 of this year in Moscow the first fully authoritative Congress of Agricultural Workers, so as to lay the foundations for one of the strongest and most important industrial associations in Russia.[29]

When threatened, the Bolsheviks moved swiftly and did everything in their power not to permit the organization of a potentially dangerous group.

On 15 June 1919 the long-awaited First All-Russian Congress of Agricultural Workers convened in Moscow. The foresters at this time chose to remain independent. Although absent from the congress, Lenin kept in touch with the proceedings and made sure that its leadership was in the hands of his lieutenants.[30] His concern was thoroughly justified as the sessions were, in the words of a Bolshevik source, quite 'stormy.'[31] The Bolsheviks' attempt to take over the leadership of the union, although successful in the end, encountered serious resistance both from the floor of the congress and from the Organizing Bureau, which was surprising in view of the fact that the bureau had been well infiltrated by Bolsheviks from the ACCTU. The strength of the opposition was impressive, as the 'petit-bourgeois elements,' so it was said, 'tried to ram through their own resolutions.' In the absence of a stenographic report of the congress, it is difficult to reconstruct who these petit-bourgeois elements were, but all available information points to the so-called agricultural experts, who were overrepre-

28 VTsSPS, *Otchet za 1919 god*, p. 22.
29 *Ibid.*
30 *Profsoiuz rabochikh sel'skogo khoziaistva*, p. 7.
31 *Ibid.*, p. 6.

sented at the congress. Indeed, the agricultural experts and land surveyors, who numbered 5,000 members in all, were represented by just a few less than one-half of the 142 delegates; the remainder of the delegates supposedly represented the rural proletariat.[32] The delegates to the congress came from thirty gubernias and represented some 48,000 organized members.[33] The Petrograd organization did not send delegates to the congress 'partly because of lack of confidence in the organization that was to be set up, and partly because of the advance of Iudenich.'[34]

Out of 142 delegates only ten were Communists and twenty-two were 'sympathizers,' yet the influence they wielded was out of proportion to their number for two reasons: they were well organized, and they had firm backing from Lenin and the ACCTU.[35] Lenin himself wrote instructions to the ACCTU that a party member be appointed secretary of the union, that it be given financial support, and that other measures of 'assistance' be taken.[36] On the initiative of the Lithuanian and Belorussian delegates a Bolshevik faction was organized at the congress and S.Ia. Babinskii placed at its head. This tightly knit group carried on the fight for five days and finally triumphed. In spite of the large number of non-party delegates, the faction succeeded in getting all its proposals carried, including its slate of candidates for the Central Committee of the union.

The newly elected Central Committee was composed of eleven members, of whom nine were Communists or sympathizers and two were non-party people who represented the agricultural experts.[37] In other words, almost all of the Communists present at the congress were elected to the Central Committee, although six of the eleven were supposedly 'workers.' Babinskii was elected the first chairman of the Central Committee, while a 'sympathizer,' K.L. Rozov (who later joined the Communist party), became secretary.[38] The

---

32 *Trade Unions in Soviet Russia*, p. 79.
33 This number is repeated by several sources. See *Profsoiuz rabochikh sel'skogo khoziaistva*, p. 6; *Trade Unions in Soviet Russia*, p. 6. Further discussion of the membership of the union appears elsewhere in this study.
34 VTsSPS, *Otchet za 1919 god*, p. 389.
35 'Tak sozdavalsia profsoiuz rabotnikov zemli,' *Trud*, 7 July 1959, p. 3. Some sources say eight Bolsheviks were able to organize a 'Batrak Faction' at the Congress and finally to take it over. K. Rozov, 'Pravil'nyi put'; k desiatiletiiu pervogo vserosiiskogo sezda soiuza s. kh. rabochikh,' *Trud*, 22 June 1929, p. 2.
36 This note is partly reproduced in *Profsoiuz rabochikh sel'skogo khoziastva*, p. 7. A more complete text reads as follows: 'O dvukh veshchakh s vami rado pogovorit'! Soiuz rabotnikov semli (vserabotzem) pomoch den'gami. Obratit' suguboe vnimanie dat' sekretaria kommunista ...'
37 *Trade Unions in Soviet Russia*, p. 80.
38 *Profsoiuz rabochikh sel'skogo khoziaistva*, p. 8.

two non-Bolsheviks were either unwilling to participate in the work of the executive or were prevented from doing so by the Bolsheviks. In any case, one of them 'did not attend meetings [of the Central Committee],' while the other 'abandoned his job after two months.'[39] Thus, a little over two years after Lenin first expressed a desire to organize the Agricultural Workers' Union, such a union had come into existence, and the Bolsheviks were in full control of its central apparatus.[40]

The degree of Communist control over local branches of the union varied. The situation even in regions close to the capital or in areas under Bolshevik control depended greatly on how entrenched the opposition was and on how far the organization of the Agricultural Workers' Union had progressed. The task of the Bolsheviks was simpler in those regions and gubernias where there were no pre-existing agricultural trade unions because they were able to establish branches on their own and prevent anyone else from seriously challenging their grasp on the union.[41] In the areas where such organizations already existed they were either taken over forcibly, dissolved, or completely by-passed. In some gubernias two or more conferences were called if the first happened to be controlled by elements hostile to the Bolsheviks.[42] This problem arose particularly in such important agricultural areas as the Ukraine, the Volga region, the North Caucasus, and Siberia, none of which was dominated by the Bolsheviks until at least 1920.

The growth of the union was directly related to the spreading of Bolshevik power. In the spring of 1920 the Agricultural Workers' Union was organized in Turkestan and in the Omsk, Kubano-Chernomorsk, and Kherson gubernias. In the summer of 1920 branches were established in Poltava, Ekaterinoslav, Chernigov, Ekaterinburg, and Odessa gubernias as well as in Bashkiriia, and the Don oblast. During the fall of 1920 the union was set up in the Terek oblast and in Dagestan and Azerbajdzhan.[43] In January 1920 sections of the union were organized in the following gubernias: Vitebsk, Vladimir, Vologda,

---

39 *Trade Unions in Soviet Russia*, p. 80; VTsSPS, *Otchet za 1919 god*, p. 390.

40 Additional proof of Bolshevik influence is provided by the composition of the First All-Russian Conference of the Agricultural Workers' Union, which was convened at the end of January and the beginning of February 1920. Out of the sixty-four delegates in attendance forty-four were Bolsheviks, and the majority of participants were agricultural workers. *Profsoiuz rabochikh sel'skogo khoziaistva*, pp. 10–11.

41 *Ibid.*, p. 8.

42 VTsSPS, *Otchet za 1919 god*, p. 390; VTsSPS, *Tretii s'ezd profsoiuzov: Stenograficheskii otchet* (Moscow 1920), p. 40; VTsSPS, *Vtoroi s'ezd profsoiuzov: Stenograficheskii otchet* (Moscow 1919), pp. 28, 32, 34–5, 65.

43 *Profsoiuz rabochikh sel'skogo khoziaistva*, p. 11.

Viatka, Belorussia, Gomel, Kostroma, Kazan, Kaluga, Moscow, Nizhegorod, Novgorod, Penza, Perm, Petrograd, Riazan, Samara, Simbirsk, Saratov, Smolensk, Tambov, Tver, Tula, Ufa, Cherepovets, Iaroslavl, Pskov, Ural, and Orenburg. In addition there were organizations of the union in Voronezh, Ivano-Voznesensk, Kursk, and Orel.[44] The process of organizing branches was extremely rapid. In the Ukraine, for example, by September 1920 committees of the Agricultural Workers' Union existed in eleven gubernias, all of them elected at gubernia congresses of the union.[45]

In some areas (e.g., Central Asia), the Bolsheviks were forced to restrict their early efforts to organizing European immigrants. Hence the Agricultural Workers' Union in Central Asia had only 3,155 members as late as January 1924. Efforts to broaden its popular base by including natives within its ranks were bitterly opposed even by Koshchi, the Bolshevik-influenced Union of Small Landowners.[46] The predominance of non-natives is also evident in the Caucasus. In July 1924 there were only 275 native trade union functionaries among a total membership of 3,498 in the entire Caucasus, while on 1 January 1925 this number had grown to only 632 out of 4,333. Although concentrated efforts to raise the number of native bureaucrats resulted in almost a three-fold increase, the overall size of the army of trade union bureaucrats rose correspondingly.[47] In many areas the affairs of the Agricultural Workers' Union were conducted directly by the party or Komsomol (Communist Youth League) and only in 1923 was some kind of union hierarchy created and the work transferred to it. In other localities gubernia sovprofs (trade union councils) carried on the work through special agents before transferring it to the union.[48]

While the First Congress and the First Conference of the union demonstrated Bolshevik control in the centre, the Second Congress, held in Moscow in December 1920, showed that the Bolsheviks had managed to extend their power to the provinces. Out of 442 delegates, 217 were members of the Communist party, while 33 were 'sympathizers.'[49] Statistics indicate that their

44 VTsSPS, *Otchet za 1919 god*, p. 391.
45 *Ibid.*, p. 12; see also A. Slutsky and V. Sydorenko, *Profsoiuzy Ukrainy posle pobedy velikogo oktiabria* (Moscow: Profizdat, 1961), p. 45.
46 VTsSPS, Sredneaziatskoe biuro, *Professional'nye soiuzy v srednei azii, 1924–1925* (Tashkent 1925), p. 13.
47 *Ibid.*, pp. 19, 49; Vserosiiskii Tsentral'nyi Sovet Profsoiuzov, Zakavkazskoe biuro, *Pervyi zakavkazskii s'ezd professional'nykh soiuzov 6–9 marta 1922* (Tiflis 1922), p. 206 ff.
48 I.I. Grafov, 'Neobkhodim vykhod,' *Trud*, 14 December 1923, p. 1.
49 *Profsoiuz rabochikh sel'skogo khoziaistva*, p. 16.

strength grew steadily until 1923. At the All-Russian Conference of the union held in September 1923, out of 440 delegates representing 70 gubernia sections, members of the Communist party numbered 239 and Komsomol members 7, together constituting a majority of 246 against the non-party membership of 154. A majority of the delegates represented the trade union hierarchy, whereas only 55 were classified as workers from the gubernia level, 122 from the uezd (district) level, and only 49 from primary trade union organizations. There were 54 deputies representing managers and administrators and 77 representing employees.[50]

NEW ECONOMIC POLICY

With the victory in the Civil War close at hand, Lenin became more and more outspoken about the tasks in the villages and the role there of the trade unions. They were to be the main support of the Soviet system in the countryside. Such support was needed because 'the more we win, the more of such areas as Siberia, the Kuban, and the Ukraine come into our hands ... regions in which the rich peasantry predominate' and because 'the more we find ourselves encircled by the peasantry and the Kuban Cossacks the more difficult our situation, the situation of the dictatorship of the proletariat, becomes.'[51] The question of the party's relationship with the peasantry once the victory had been achieved was discussed at length by Lenin in his speech to the Third All-Russian Congress of Trade Unions on 7 April 1920, in which he said:

We are conducting a class struggle and our aim is to abolish classes; so long as there still exist two classes, those of peasants and workers, socialism cannot be realized, and an irreconcilable struggle will go on incessantly. The chief problem now is how, when one class is carrying on the struggle, to attract the labouring peasantry, to defeat or neutralize it, or to crush its resistance with the aid of a strong government apparatus involving all the measures of compulsion.[52]

Lenin realized the limits of terror and quite readily admitted that 'methods of state compulsion alone will not enable us to attract to our side the labouring peasantry against the peasant owners.'[53] To achieve this goal one would also have to exert 'moral influence' on the peasantry. Lenin foresaw a long

50 'Vserosiiskaia konferentsiia vserabotzemlesa,' *Trud*, 25 September 1923, p. 3.
51 *Lenin o profsoiuzakh*, p. 569, 572.
52 *Ibid.*, p. 589.
53 This passage is omitted in *Lenin o profsoiuzakh*, p. 590. It is taken from the translation of his speech published in *Trade Unions in Soviet Russia*, p. 59.

and bitter struggle in the villages, a fight in which all means at the disposal of the Bolsheviks had to be used if they were to achieve victory.

But the struggle was not hopeless from Lenin's point of view because of the transformation that was taking place in the countryside:

The solution of the question is taking place through the eruption of divisions in the ranks of the peasantry. In the struggle following the overthrow of the capitalists, in the two years of civil war, the workers formed a single body welded into a unity; the very opposite is observed amidst the peasantry; they are undergoing gradual internal disintegration ... Various classes of the peasantry diverge widely, with the result that the peasantry is not united ... the truth is that the peasants are half workers, half owners.[54]

Therefore, the lesson was simple: keep the peasants fighting among themselves so that the class would be divided and could offer no obstruction to the 'vanguard of the proletariat' in securing its hegemony in the name of the urban workers. To do this the Bolsheviks had to bring to their side the most radical element of the peasantry – the village paupers and wage workers, who were inclined to be enthusiastically pro-Bolshevik.[55] It was the task of the Soviet trade unions, guided by the Communist party, to promote this form of social engineering.

The most comprehensive statement on the work of party and trade unions

54 *Lenin o profsoiuzakh*, pp. 592–3.
55 This fact is admitted not only by the Bolsheviks but by the SR leadership as well. For example Bykhovskii identifies the SR strength in the village as coming from the kulaks and from among the middle peasantry, while he points out that Bolshevik strength and power lay with the agricultural labour and pauper elements. See his *Vserossiiskii Sovet krestianskikh deputatov 1917 goda* (Moscow 1929). For the Bolshevik view on this problem, see M. Gaisinskii, *Bor'ba bol'shevikov za krestianstvo v 1917: Vserosiiskie s'ezdy sovetov krestianskikh deputatov* (Moscow 1933). He claims that the middle and poor peasantry were supporters of the Bolsheviks. For a more objective analysis of this problem see Oliver H. Radkey, *The Sickle Under the Hammer: The Russian Socialist Revolutionaries in the Early Months of Soviet Rule* (New York: Columbia University Press, 1963). Radkey feels that the richer stratum of the peasantry was indeed SR-oriented; the middle peasantry was split between SR and left SR, depending on the region; while the poor peasantry was overwhelmingly pro-Bolshevik. He accurately points out that 'it served the purpose of the Bolsheviks in 1917 to have the peasantry divided vertically, along political lines, just as later, in 1918 and the years following, it would serve their purpose to cleave it horizontally, along social lines, into those who had more and those who had little or nothing. The line of division did not matter so much as long as the class was paralyzed. The Bolsheviks always had the peasantry on the operating table undergoing dissection, until they devised the strait-jacket of collectivization.' *Ibid.*, p. 232.

in the countryside appeared in a resolution of the Tenth Party Congress.[56] Having pointed out that the most important task for the party and trade unions at the moment was strengthening the influence of the city proletariat over the working masses in the countryside both in the realm of ideas and in the organizational sphere, the resolution called for the creation in the villages of organizations sufficiently broad to encompass the strata of the peasantry closest to the proletariat, and to 'educate them in the spirit of the proletarian discipline.' The resolution was referring in this instance to the establishment of inter-trade union secretariats in volosti (village districts), smaller towns, and in villages. But the main stress was on the already existing Agricultural and Forestry Workers' Union and its local organs. While the inter-trade union secretariats were to 'reveal' and assemble former factory workers who were dispersed over the countryside, the Agricultural and Forestry Workers' Union was charged with finding 'practical and sufficiently flexible forms' of organizing within itself the wide semi-proletarian strata of the villages, and in this way of bringing them 'into the sphere of the overall class interests of the proletariat.'[57]

The role of the trade unions in the new agricutural setting was emphasized at the Tenth Party Conference (26–8 May 1921) – which initiated the retreat known as the New Economic Policy – at the Eleventh Party Conference (19–22 December 1921), and at the plenary session of the party's Central Committee held 28 December 1921. This Central Committee meeting adopted theses drafted by Lenin which were his last writings on the trade unions and were to provide the party with a trade union policy for the duration of the New Economic Policy. The theses stressed that membership in trade unions should be voluntary, that unreliable officials in the trade union hierarchy should be replaced, and that party control over the unions should be intensified in order to combat petit-bourgeois elements who would worm their way into the trade unions under NEP conditions.[58]

Lenin's proposals were amplified in the resolutions of the Eleventh Party Congress (March–April 1922), especially with respect to party and trade union activities in the countryside. The resolutions called for greater control by the party over volosti trade union organizations, to be achieved by flooding them with a large number of party men. In addition the party was to give the Agricultural and Forestry Workers' Union a greater measure of support so as to

---

56 Held in Moscow from 8–16 March 1921. *KPSS v rezoliutsiiakh i resheniiakh s'ezdov, konferentsii i plenumov TsK* (7th ed.; Moscow: Gospolitizdat, 1954), I, pp. 534–50.
57 *Ibid.*; *KPSS o profsoiuzakh* (3rd ed.; Moscow: Profizdat, 1957), p. 102.
58 Lenin, *Sochineniia*, XXXIII, p. 170.

enable it to carry on with 'the economic organization of the proletarianized and poor peasantry.' The resolutions, although calling for intensification of party and trade union activities in the villages, warned against an overly administrative-compulsory approach and stressed the 'economic-organizational' and 'culture-enlightenment' approaches. The importance of women labourers in the countryside was recognized in the resolutions, and the party and trade unions were called upon to make the necessary preparations to attract them by training special organizers and dispatching them to the countryside.[59]

Stalin no less than Lenin distrusted the peasant masses, talked about the superiority of the urban workers, and spoke of carrying the class struggle to the countryside. In 1921, while writing about the party's tasks in the non-Russian areas of the country, Stalin (who was commissar for nationalities) revealed an appreciation of the 'class war' possibilities of setting non-Russian labourers not only against the 'rapacious Great Russian kulaks' (rich peasants), but also against their non-Russian class brothers.[60] At the same time Stalin indicated that the tasks of the party had changed. Whereas in the past it had 'rallied the revolutionary elements of the peasantry for the purpose of overthrowing the landlord, now it was recruiting them for the purpose of improving agriculture, of consolidating the alliance between the labouring elements of the peasantry and the proletariat which is in power.'[61] Stalin returned to this theme time and again in his speeches to the congresses of the Communist party and in his later writings. No obstacles to this 'bond between town and country' were to be tolerated. Every possible form of assistance, he felt, had to be given to the rural labouring masses to strengthen their own social position in opposition to the exploiting upper strata which were 'growing as a consequence of the NEP.'[62]

At the Twelfth Party Congress, held in April 1923, the difficult problem of providing for labour hired by individual farmers was discussed, and the unenviable living conditions of workers in the socialized sector of the economy (which included sovkhozes, forestry stations, and agricultural institutions) were admitted. In its resolutions the congress stated that 'with the increasing use of hired labour drawn from among the poorer elements of the village, under conditions of a greater labour supply, the role of the Agricultural and Forestry Workers' Union as an organizer and protector of the worker would of necessity grow in importance.'[63] The Agricultural and Forestry Workers' Union was, as

59 KPSS v rezoliutsiiakh, I, p. 619; KPSS o profsoiuzakh, p. 125.
60 I.V. Stalin, Works (Moscow: Foreign Languages Publishing House, 1952–1955), V, p. 27.
61 I.V. Stalin, 'Partiia do i posle vziatiia vlasti,' Pravda, 28 August 1921, pp. 2–3; and his Works, V, pp. 109, 125, 129.
62 Ibid., p. 277.
63 KPSS v rezoliutsiiakh, I, pp. 749–50; KPSS o profsoiuzakh, p. 140.

it had often been before, referred to as the transmission belt to the peasants and particularly to the party's proletarian and semi-proletarian strata. In short, the resolutions of the Twelfth Party Congress echoed those of the Eleventh Congress in calling for greater control by the party over the union, and those of the Twelfth Party Conference (4–7 August 1922) which insisted on improvement in the work of the local trade unions organs.[64] The Thirteenth Party Conference (16–18 January 1924) again demanded improvement in the work of party organizations in the villages and admitted that if the party was going to be at all successful it would need the support of the village poor. In addition, the resolutions recommended recruitment of batraks (landless peasants) into the party and the Agricultural and Forestry Workers' Union.[65]

Only a few days after the conference, Stalin again indicated his concern over the situation in the countryside and called for a strengthening of the bond between the cities and the villages. He now stated that 'the alliance of workers and peasants must assume the form of economic co-operation between town and country, between workers and peasants, because it is directed against the merchant and the kulak, and its aim is the mutual supply by peasants and workers of all they require.'[66]

In contrast to comments made at previous congresses, the past year's work of the Agricultural and Forestry Workers' Union was praised at the Thirteenth Party Congress held from 23 to 31 May 1924. In its resolutions the congress affirmed that 'the work of the Vserabotzemles in the period of one year has been characterized by a number of successes – especially in the Ukraine, the Southeastern Region, the Volga Region, Kirgizia, and in other areas.'[67] Positive evaluation of the work of the union and its leadership provided an obvious contrast to the picture of conditions in the countryside painted by Stalin in his speech to the congress, in which he indicated that out of some 800,000 eligible workers in the countryside, only about 3 per cent were trade union members. The general ignorance of Soviet laws on the part of officials who were closely involved with village affairs and 'their inability to defend the interests of the poor and middle peasants against kulak domination,' as well as their 'attempt to approach the peasant merely through verbal agitation,' led, in Stalin's opinion, to a bad state of affairs in the countryside. To improve matters, Stalin said, was a task of primary importance for the party, and nothing should be overlooked which in one way or another offered 'important opportunities for agitation in the countryside.[68]

64 *Ibid.*, pp. 128–9.   65 *Ibid.*, p. 143.
66 Stalin's speech at the Second Congress of Soviets, *Pravda*, 30 January 1924, p. 6.
67 *KPSS v rezoliutsiiakh*, II, p. 49; *KPSS o profsoiuzakh*, p. 160.
68 Stalin, *Works*, VI, pp. 200–1, 217, 228, 318–19, 324–5.

The congress, in praising the leadership of the Agricultural and Forestry Workers' Union, called upon it to 'continue its work in accordance with the resolutions of the Twelfth Party Congress.'[69] But it noted that the work of the Agricultural and Forestry Workers' Union was in need of much improvement if it was to meet its organizational and recruiting tasks among the village proletariat. The reason for this was said to be primarily the wide dispersal of the batraks and their total 'isolation from the centres of culture.' The congress also noted many instances of lack of communication between trade union recruiters and individual batraks; condemned some 'harmful deviations' in the manner in which the trade unions attempted to protect batrak interests; and, as a way of improving the situation, recommended that the recruitment and organization of batraks be carried on henceforth by experienced cadres of paid trade union organizers. The resolutions further called for a special census of the batraks, the setting up of batrak trade union cells or committees of the countryside, a wide educational program for the batraks, and their speedy inclusion in the 'life of the society.'

Although the resolutions were mainly directed to the peasantry, other workers – those employed in the sovkhozes (state farms), experimental agricultural stations, and forestry – were also mentioned. For the first time since 1919 and the formation of the union, the party requested that greater attention be paid to the needs of agricultural specialists such as agronomists, land surveyors, and foresters. The resolutions conceded the impoverished financial position of the Agricultural and Forestry Workers' Union and pledged the party to provide aid both directly from party organs and indirectly through the Communist sections of the ACCTU. Other unions having a rural base of operations such as the construction workers were to help out with the tasks of recruiting and organizing the widely dispersed village proletariat. To provide organizational assistance in the countryside, the Communist section of the ACCTU was to see to it that a special co-ordinating commission was set up in the ACCTU, with one of the 'most authoritative comrades' at its head.

However, the party was not to rely entirely on the peasantry or the agricultural trade union in developing closer links between the workers and the peasants. The resolutions called for the establishment of so-called zemliachestva (native region fraternal societies) and other kinds of workers' groups which were to strive for the smychka (cultural unity) of town and village. As Stalin clearly indicated, leadership initiative was to be in the hands of the urban proletariat. In line with this idea the resolutions pointed out that the 'organizing of the village in many cases can be begun in the cities by those workers who have ties with the villages.' He was referring here to the

69 *KPSS o profsoiuzakh*, pp. 160–2.

practice of shefstvo (supervision), whereby individual factories in the cities acted as patrons of state farms, co-operatives, and other rural enterprises. How extensive the shefstvo movement became in 1923–5 was indicated by the fact that in Leningrad alone shefstvo associations had 375,000 members; in the country as a whole about one million persons took part in the movement.[70]

The most crucial resolution dealt with the problem of female labour in the countryside and in many respects it repeated the recommendations of the Eleventh Party Congress in calling for spreading the influence of the party among women peasants through 'political and cultural education,' recruiting them into the party and the trade unions, and releasing them from the routine drudgery by building kindergartens, restaurants, etc.[71] The resolution concluded that the participation of women in the work of the party, trade unions, and soviets was indispensable and called on the party and other soviet organs to correct this situation.[72]

In his book *The Peasant Question*, originally published in 1925, Stalin blamed the weakness of party work in the villages on the fact that it did not possess in the countryside a 'wide non-Party peasants' action group that could link the Party with the tens of millions of toiling peasants.'[73] It represented only a thin film on top of an ocean of non-party people; because of this it 'cannot stand the strain ... often breaks, and, instead of there being a connecting bridge, a blank wall sometimes rises between the Party and the non-Party masses in the countryside.' Failure to create such a linking aktiv (action group) of numerous and 'genuine' peasants would doom the party to 'chronic ailment in the countryside.' In order to ensure that the political activity of the peasantry did not become 'detached from the leadership of the workers,' the party was to channel it by drawing peasants into the work of governing the country. This action was necessary, Stalin said, because of the changes that were taking place in agriculture, leading to a 'differentiation among the peasantry' and the 'formation of two camps: the camp of the kulaks, who are

70 *Istoriia profdvizheniia v SSSR* (2nd ed.; Moscow: Profizdat, 1961), p. 232.
71 It was attached seemingly as an afterthought to the resolutions after the congress was over, although according to the explanation of the commission editing the stenographic reports this resolution was worked out by the Central Committee of the party on the explicit recommendation of the party congress. *KPSS o profsoiuzakh*, pp. 170, note 1, 171.
72 The problem of lack of women workers among the membership of the party and trade unions was discussed again at the January 1925 Plenum of the Central Committee, with a special reference to the conditions in the eastern regions of the USSR. The Fourteenth Party Conference (27–29 April 1925) reminded the party activists to do all they could to recruit female labourers into the party and trade unions. *KPSS o profsoiuzakh*, pp. 176, 184.
73 Stalin, *Works*, VI, pp. 318–19.

striving to capture the commanding positions in the countryside, and the camp of the poor peasants, who are seeking allies against the kulaks.' The party was to help in this struggle, but the precondition for success was that 'there must be no domineering, and an atmosphere of mutual confidence must be created between party and non-party people.'[74]

Primarily for these reasons, at the October 1925 Plenum the party's Central Committee called for less interference by the party in trade union work. The plenum disclosed that the party had supplanted the trade union organizations in many areas of activity, thus considerably weakening the 'normal methods of trade union work' and consequently 'lowering the authority of trade unions in the eyes of the wide toiling masses.' By calling for restraint in party control over trade unions the plenum did not recommend eliminating such control entirely; it simply pointed out that henceforth such control should be exercised more discreetly via Communist factions and groups within the trade unions.[75] Stalin recommended 'the utmost flexibility in relation to the present day peasantry – that is what is demanded of the Party now. To win the peasantry over to the side of the proletariat – that is now the Party's task.' The party should do everything in its power to make the 'alliance between the workers and peasants' successful, but it should not forget for one moment that 'the dictatorship of the proletariat signifies leadership of the peasantry by the proletariat.'[76]

In his report delievered to the Fourteenth Congress (18–31 December 1925) Stalin referred back to the April conference and the October plenum in defence of his policies in the countryside and especially the efforts to appeal to the middle peasants.[77] During the debate that flared up at the congress, largely instigated by the so-called 'Left Opposition,' Stalin was accused of having a 'pro-kulak' policy at the expense of the poor peasants. He denied the charge, stating that 'because we are Marxist, because we are Communists, we must lean on the poor peasants in the countryside,' and added that the representatives of the poor peasants were the party's 'agents in the countryside.'[78] But, he said, the poor peasantry was widely dispersed and efforts should be made to organize them properly

into an independent political force capable of serving as an organized bulwark of the proletariat in the countryside in the struggle against the kulaks, in the struggle to win over the middle peasants ... We should push the slogan that the poor peasants

---

74 *Ibid.*, pp. 324–5, 332–3; and *Works*, VII, pp. 124–5.
75 *KPSS o profsoiuzakh*, pp. 195–6.
76 Stalin, *Works*, VII, pp. 216–17.
77 A middle peasant was defined as one who neither hired labourers nor hired himself out.
78 Stalin, *Works*, VII, pp. 338–40.

at least stand on their own feet, that they must – with the aid of the Communist party and the state – organize themselves into groups; that ... in all the arenas of rural public life they must learn to fight the kulaks; but fight, however, not only by appealing to the GPU, but by a political struggle, by an organized struggle. Only in that way can the poor peasants become hardened, only in that way can the poor peasants be transformed from a dependent group into a bulwark of the proletariat in the countryside.[79]

The Fourteenth Congress further acknowledged the failures of the trade unions in the countryside. The resolutions noted that 'the first attempt to infiltrate the countryside through the unions ... did not produce the anticipated results,' even though a great deal of effort had been spent by the trade unions on this task. This failure was diagnosed by the congress as, on the one hand, a simple case of overextension, trying to do too much with almost no trained cadres and with too little experience. On the other hand, it was attributed to excessive meddling in the affairs of the countryside by the urban industrial trade unions, which resulted in a great deal of confusion in the villages and disrupted the work of the Agricultural and Forestry Workers' Union. Thus the line formerly taken by the party and ratified by the Thirteenth Party Congress that the workers in agriculture could be organized with the direct assistance of industrial trade unions had to be modified considerably. Henceforth, the resolution stated, the 'penetration of the village' should be accomplished through the union best suited to operate in the countryside – the Agricultural and Forestry Workers' Union; the unions which served a large number of seasonal labourers such as the construction workers, miners, etc.; those industrial trade unions which served workers whose places of employment were located in the countryside.

The Agricultural and Forestry Workers' Union was placed at the head of the unions interested in village labour. But this recognition did not mean that all was well with the work of the union. On the contrary, it was pointed out that its efforts were spread too thinly over too many tasks with the result that much that had been done was ineffectual, and unfortunately 'its successes and failures seem to be decisive for all of our work in the villages.'[80]

One remedy to improve the Agricultural and Forestry Workers' Union was to purge all undesirable elements. From now on it was to become an organization 'uniting in its ranks only the real proletarians and semi-proletarians of the villages, for *whom the sale of their own labour power is the basic means of subsistence.*'[81] The union was specifically warned not to accept as members

79 *Ibid.*, pp. 340–1.   80 *KPSS o profsoiuzakh*, p. 210.
81 *Ibid.* Italics in original.

those peasants who were away from their own farms only seasonally or temporarily, because to do so would be to run 'the risk of being swamped by petit-bourgeois elements.' In effect the leadership of the Agricultural and Forestry Workers' Union was called upon to focus its attention on strengthening its organizational set-up rather than to waste its efforts in recruiting new members, with the exception of women, who were to be recruited whenever possible.

A purge of petit-bourgeois elements and the establishment of the pure proletarian character of the union membership were only two preconditions for success. Others involved increasing members' participation in union affairs. To do this the union was called upon to build up its aktiv from among the agricultural labourers and to move in the direction of 'constructing all of its organs from the bottom up' on the 'foundations of normal electivity.'[82] In this task it was assured the support of the party, government, and ACCTU, which was to work out the measures required to assist not only the Agricultural and Forestry Workers' Union but other unions which also had a large number of seasonal labourers.

The relationship of the party to the union was to be one of vanguard to mass organization, and the party organs were warned, as they were in October 1925, not to supplant the trade unions but to guide them. An interesting indication of party concern with the work of the trade unions was the setting up of republic and oblast trade union councils. At the same time the Communist factions within the trade unions were told to exercise every precaution to prevent any possibility of the emergence of 'federalism' within the trade union movement.[83]

COLLECTIVIZATION

The Fifteenth Party Congress (2–19 December 1927), which discussed the 'socialist reconstruction' of the economy under the First Five Year Plan, also considered among other things the forthcoming collectivization of agriculture. Although its resolution was deliberately vague and said nothing about the degree and tempo of industrialization, it was obvious that the period of 'intensification of the class struggle in the countryside' was about to begin. In his report to the congress Stalin, who was now completely in charge of the party, boasted of the assistance rendered by the state to the

82 *Ibid.*, p. 211.
83 *Ibid.*, p. 214. This is an especially interesting development as there was a great deal of pressure from the non-Russian areas of the USSR for the application of a federalist system in the trade union structure.

'working peasantry in general and the poor peasants in particular' and called on the party 'to continue along the line of further improving the main mass of the peasantry, primarily of the poor peasants, to strengthen the alliance between the working class and the peasantry, to raise the prestige of the working class and of its party in the countryside.'[84] No wonder, then, that the party again deemed it necessary to stress the role of the Agricultural and Forestry Workers' Union.

Heavy emphasis was now placed on the protection of agricultural labour in kulak enterprises and on the strict enforcement of the appropriate provisions of the Labour Code. In addition the provisions of social insurance laws applicable to agricultural labour were to be strictly observed. Finally, the recruitment drive among batrak elements and the poorer peasantry was to be intensified considerably. The formula of the Fourteenth Party Congress that only hired labour had the right to trade union membership was fully retained. The Fifteenth Party Congress reiterated the importance of the shefstvo or patronage of industrial enterprises over given agricultural enterprises in the countryside, especially but not exclusively in the sphere of 'cultural work in the villages.'[85] The latter task was also emphasized in the circular of the party's Central Committee sent out in April[86] and again in the Central Committee decision of 21 May 1928 in which agricultural trade union functionaries were castigated for not taking sufficient measures to raise the cultural level of the members, and for ignoring the party's directives on the 'renewal of leading cadres' and failing to advance workers not only into 'positions of responsibility' but even into positions in the lower trade union organs. In fact, the trade union was not getting on with the purge to the satisfaction of the party.[87] The situation was especially unsatisfactory in the non-Russian republics, where, as the resolution phrased it, 'proletarian cadres are still small,' and where side by side with proletarians are still found well-to-do peasants

---

84 Stalin, *Works*, x, pp. 324–5. Throughout 1927 Stalin continued to speak at great length of the alliance between the workers and the peasantry. See 'K voprosu o raboche-krestianskom pravitel'stve: Pis'mo tov. Dmitrieva: Otvet tov. Stalina,' *Bol'shevik*, no 6 (15 March 1927), pp. 96–102; 'O trekh osnovnykh lozungakh partii po krestianskomu voprosu: Pis'mo tov. Ian-skogo i otvet tov. Stalina,' *Bol'shevik*, nos 7–8 (15 Aprill 1927), pp. 125–35; Stalin, *Works*, ix, pp. 185–92, 208–19; *Ibid.*, x, pp. 203–4; *Problems of Leninism* (4th ed.; Moscow 1928).
85 *KPSS o profsoiuzakh*, p. 266.
86 'Ob uluchshenii raboty sredi sezonnykh rabochikh,' *Spravochnik partiinogo rabotnika* (Moscow 1930), vii, no 1, p. 366.
87 'O sostave rukovoditelei proforganizatsii i merakh po ukrepleniiu profsoiuzov rabotnikami,' *Spravochnik partiinogo rabotnika*, pp. 387–9; *KPSS o profsoiuzakh*. p. 282.

or even 'an element very close to the kulaks' in positions of responsibility within both the trade unions and other Soviet organizations.[88]

Some improvement in the work of the Agricultural and Forestry Workers' Union did occur as a result of these exhortations by the party, but it was not enough to satisfy party leaders. In a major pronouncement on the Agricultural and Forestry Workers' Union issued by the Central Committee on 4 March 1929, the top party leadership concluded that the measures suggested by the Central Committee on previous occasions had been carried out 'only partially,' that this situation was intolerable, and that the party would have to make an effort to achieve a real 'breakthrough' to improve its work 'among the agricultural and forestry workers.'[89] The reason for the concern about party and trade union work in the countryside at this particular time was the 'sharpening of the class struggle' and the need to prepare batrak masses, in alliance with the poor and middle peasantry to carry the fight to the 'kulak elements.'[90]

By the end of 1929 Stalin openly called for the 'liquidation of the kulaks as a class' and condemned what he termed the 'bourgeois-liberal policy' of the 'right opportunists' who opposed the application of 'extraordinary measures' against the kulaks.[91] To pursue the fight against the kulaks the Communist faction within the Central Committee of the union was instructed to a / intensify recruitment activity among agricultural and forestry workers so that a majority would become members of the union (the conditions of membership, however, were not to be relaxed, and only those who worked as hired labourers could become trade union members); b / cultivate the aktiv primarily from among the poorer elements of the peasantry; c / work out methods for protecting the economic interests of batraks and shepherds, especially those employed on kulak-owned farms; d / make a sustained effort in advancing batraks and women workers to positions of responsibility within the union both at the local and higher levels; e / improve trade union work in all agricultural enterprises by involving even greater numbers of workers in the production conferences; and take necessary measures to improve living conditions of the workers at least in some of the largest sovkhozes; f / take care of the needs of the specialists; g / improve the content of the newspaper *Batrak* and of other newspapers serving the batraks, adapt trade union journals to the variety of groups and professions existing among the agricultural and forestry

88 Resolution of the party Central Committee plenum of 16–17 November 1928. *KPSS o profsoiuzakh*, p. 309.
89 'O rabote sredi s. kh. i lesnykh rabochikh i itogakh VI vsesoiuznogo s'ezda soiuza sel'khozrabochikh,' *Spravochnik partiinogo rabotnika*, p. 377.
90 *Ibid.*; *KPSS o profsoiuzakh*, p. 318.
91 *Pravda*, 29 December 1929; Stalin, *Works*, XII, p. 174.

workers, and intensify control over the rabkors (workers' correspondents) so that they would take up the questions and problems centring on the batraks and the peasantry.[92]

The Communist factions within the ACCTU and Central Executive Committee of the USSR, and the Commissariat of Labour, the Central Administration of Social Insurance, the Commissariat of Health, the state publishing houses, and party organs in general were instructed in great detail on how best to improve the work of the union and to serve the interests of its members. The ACCTU was told to work out a number of 'concrete measures' in order to make it possible for other unions to help the agricultural and forestry workers. The inter-trade union organs were to be instructed specifically to provide all possible help to the union, and especially to see to it that urban centres provided enough in the way of 'cultural services' to the rural areas.

The Central Executive Committee and its local organs were to take a greater interest in settling labour conflicts, in setting up the union centres known as 'Batrak Homes,' in educating the working masses of the countryside in the intricacies of current labour legislation, and in advancing individuals from among the village poor to positions of responsibility in the Soviet apparatus.

The Commissariat of Labour and its organs were to combat with all the means at their disposal unemployment among agricultural and forestry workers and violations by kulaks of the provisions of the Labour Code. The Social Insurance Administration was to oversee the appropriate application of the social insurance legislation. The Commissariat of Health was instructed to improve its services among the rural workers; the Commissariat of Education was required to eliminate illiteracy among the village poor; and the state publishing houses were to supply the villages with the necessary literature, making sure that such literature was provided in the many languages of the various peoples inhabiting the USSR. The Co-operative Movement was called upon to work out speedy measures for mass inclusion of batraks within its ranks. Likewise, batraks were to be given the right to be hired ahead of other unemployed categories of workers. Finally, the Work in the Village Section and the Organization Bureau of the party Central Committee were called upon to set up party and Komsomol organizations in the sovkhozes with the express purpose of working with the batraks. In addition, the Work in the Village Section was required to settle once and for all the relationship of the batraks with the 'groups of poor peasants,' KKOV, KNS, Koshchi, and other organizations. Henceforth the influx of party workers into the trade union was to

92 *KPSS o profsoiuzakh*, pp. 319–20.

increase, and transfers of experienced trade union workers to other trade unions were kept to a minimum.[93]

The Sixteenth Party Conference (23–29 April 1929) called for an all-out war against 'capitalist elements' in the countryside and announced that a purge would take place in the soviet and trade union apparatus.[94] A month later, on 27 May 1929, the party Central Committee issued another pronouncement on trade union tasks in the villages. This document is of interest among other reasons for its catalogue of deficiencies in trade union work in the countryside and for its suggestions on how best to improve the existing situation. Noting that the 'solution of the tasks of socialist reconstruction of the village' by way of a smychka with the 'poor and middle layers of the peasantry' under conditions of 'sharpened class struggle' required that the 'leadership of the working class in the village be strengthened' and 'ties with the proletarian city improved.' the party Central Committee called on all 'organs of the proletarian dictatorship' – and particularly trade unions – to face up to the new responsibilities and tasks of agriculture, to help in the collectivization drive, to support the organizations of batraks and the village poor, and to work for their 'unity with the middle peasantry' against the kulaks.[95]

The trade unions were considered by the party to be one of the more important control levers in the countryside, primarily because of their large membership. According to the Central Committee statement there were approximately four million members of various trade unions in addition to many seasonal labourers who could be utilized by the party in the 'socialist transformation' of the village. But although this large force was available, the Central Committee found that very little had been done to bring it into action. The trade unions not only had failed 'to utilize all the existing possibilities in strengthening proletarian influence' in the countryside, but even worse 'did not give this task sufficient attention.' In many cases, the declaration went on, 'the tasks were misunderstood' and sometimes 'totally ignored.' Individual officials had not received sufficient preparation to assume the responsibilities of 'leaders and organizers' in the movement, and the trade unions did not inject themselves in any influential way into the work of 'state organs' and 'co-operative societies' in order to 'repulse the counter-attack of kulak elements.' The Agricultural and Forestry Workers' Union had not received much support from other unions, which also had failed to develop powerful ties with the shefstvo associations. The Central Committee gloomily concluded that the directives of the

---

93 *Ibid.*, p. 322.   94 *Ibid.*, p. 346.

95 'Ob uchastii profsoiuzov v obshchestvennoi zhizni derevni,' *Spravochnik partiinogo rabotnika*, VII, 2, pp. 296–8; *KPSS o profsoiuzakh*, p. 369.

Fourteenth and Fifteenth Party Congresses on work in the countryside were being carried out in a 'highly unsatisfactory manner,' and that the situation would have to be rectified as soon as possible.

The remedies suggested by the Central Committee were not new and followed directly and logically from the ills uncovered. The first and most important objective in the hierarchy of priorities was to change the attitude of trade unions towards their obligations in rural areas and to direct their activities along the lines laid down by the November 1928 Plenum of the party Central Committee and by the Eighth Congress of Trade Unions: workers brigades should be sent from the cities into the villages with the purpose of invigorating the campaigns undertaken by the party. The second suggestion dealt with the shefskie obshchestva (patronage associations) and their joint activities in the villages with the trade unions. The Central Committee recommended again, as it had on previous occasions, the broadest possible participation of trade unions in the work of these associations. The latter, helped by the trade unions, were to make the links between the city and the village stronger and 'to assist trade unions in the organization of the batraks and the village poor.' The party factions within trade unions were called upon to direct and guide the work of these organizations. They were to pay very close attention to seeing that propaganda in favour of collectivization was properly and systematically disseminated, and that 'resistance to the kulaks' did not diminish.

Although this declaration of the party's Central Committee resembled previous pronouncements with respect to trade union work in the countryside, it was not simply a repetition of things said in the past. The trade union movement as a whole was called upon to make contributions to the 'socialist transformation of the rural areas,' but the party recognized that in order to avoid a great deal of confusion some co-ordinating authority would have to take charge of the situation. Naturally, the party assumed the task of providing overall control and direction to the movement. In trade union affairs, however, the Agricultural and Forestry Workers' Union was to act as the spearhead of the movement, while a Permanent Commission on the Work in the Village Section of the ACCTU was to be the co-ordinating centre. The Central Committee, therefore, called on all trade unions to support the work of the Agricultural and Forestry Workers' Union and to aid it 'in rallying to its ranks the batraks and other agricultural workers' and in raising their political and cultural level, liquidating illiteracy, and training trade union activists.[96]

The four unions called upon to help the Agricultural and Forestry Workers' Union were, quite logically, composed in large part of the village intelligentsia

96 KPSS o profsoiuzakh, pp. 369–73.

– teachers, physicians, etc.[97] The party said it relied on them to be in the fore-front of 'cultural activities,' but they were also to watch carefully for 'cases of the coalescence of separate parts of the state apparatus with kulak elements' and to expose them mercilessly.[98] The Asiatic regions of the USSR where, ac-cording to the party's Central Committee, the cultural level of the inhabitants was much lower than in the European parts of the country and where the 'pro-letarian stratum was especially weak' were to receive the lion's share of atten-tion outside of the so-called 'areas of complete collectivization.'

The November 1929 plenum of the Central Committee which ousted Bu-kharin from the Politburo reiterated the slogan that 'the collectivization of the countryside should take one of the more important places in the work of trade unions.' The guiding role of the working classes in the kolkhoz (collective farm) movement was to be fortified by a decisive promotion of workers into positions of organizers and leaders in the collectivization movement. This in-struction meant that the Agricultural and Forestry Workers' Union was re-quired to intensify its efforts to convince batraks to join the collective farms.[99] The union from now on was not only required to recruit its membership from among the rural labourers but was supposed to make sure that large numbers became members of the collective farms.[100]

At the same time the party began to put pressure on the trade unions in agriculture to restrict union membership only to 'reliable elements.' The order of the party's Central Committee of 5 December 1929 plainly stated the need 'to intensify regulation of the growth of the non-industrial trade unions' (con-struction workers, agricultural and forestry workers, sugar workers, etc.). On the party's recommendation the ACCTU was to work out measures to make it harder to become a trade union member, an objective achieved by extending the duration of the working period which qualified a person for trade union membership. Such a measure, it was felt, would make it more difficult for 'for-eign-class elements' of both the cities and villages to 'infiltrate industry' through these unions.[101]

Throughout 1929 and the beginning of 1930 still another form of control was exercised by sending into the countryside a large army of city workers called 'dvadtsiatipiatitisiachniki,' the 'group of 25,000.' These workers are credited in Soviet sources with having played an important role in the collec-

97 These were the following unions: 1 / Workers of Educational Institutions; 2 / Workers in Governmental Institutions; 3 / Communications Workers; 4 / Medical and Sanitation Workers.
98 *KPSS o profsoiuzakh*, p. 372.   99 *Ibid.*, pp. 397–8.
100 See chapter 3 of this study.   101 *KPSS o profsoiuzakh*, p. 406.

tivization of agriculture and in 'liquidating the kulaks as a class.' During 1930 the 'patronage movement,' whereby a factory in the city would take charge of some enterprise in a rural area, became widespread throughout the country.[102] In addition these efforts were probably designed to raise quickly the skills of the rural personnel.

The Sixteenth Party Congress (26 June–13 July 1930) met while a wide-spread purge was in progress. Tomsky, who had lost his position as the head of the trade unions the year before (June 1929), was now ejected from the Polit-buro as well, and 'the triumph of the apparatchiki was complete.'[103] Yet the Sixteenth Party Congress coincided with a slow down in the collectivization drive marked by Stalin's 2 March 1930 article, 'Dizziness from Success,' in which he blamed overzealous local Communists and administrators for ex-cesses in forcing collectivization. The congress was thus concerned with re-assessing the party's tactics in the countryside in order to pursue the course of collectivization to a victorious end. In his report to the congress Stalin declared that the 'Bolshevik offensive' must go on, and he described the offensive in terms of 'mobilizing the class vigilance and revolutionary activity of the masses against capitalist elements in the countryside,' 'organizing the reconstruction of the entire practical work of the trade unions, co-operatives, soviets and all other mass organizations to fit the requirements of the reconstruction period,' expelling from them 'alien and degenerate elements,' and 'mobilizing the Party itself for organizing the whole offensive.'[104] The role of the trade unions in this scheme remained important. They were to 'combat the bureaucratic perver-sions of the state and economic apparatus,' to educate 'new thousands and tens of thousands of proletarians' for their tasks as organizers of the 'socialist econ-omy,' and to explain to the widest possible number of workers that 'the quick tempo of industrialization and the socialist reconstruction of agriculture is the only correct path towards a radical improvement of the material situation of the working class and of all the toiling masses' of the country. All those among the trade union leaders who opposed the use of urban workers for the tasks of transforming agriculture, especially those who in any way criticized sending the 'group of 25,000' into the countryside, were accused of 'trade-unionistic' devi-ation and were roundly condemned. The party congress went on to approve the sending of urban workers into the villages and called upon the trade unions to select 'new thousands of proletarians' for work in the kolkhozes.

102 Cf. appendix VII, p. 216; Profsouiz rabochikh sel'skogo khoziaistva, p. 55; KPSS o profsoiuzakh, pp. 411–14, 415 ff.
103 M. Fainsod, How Russia is Ruled (rev. ed.; Cambridge: Harvard University Press, 1964), p. 190.
104 Stalin, Works, XII, pp. 320–1; Pravda, 29 June 1938.

The Agricultural and Forestry Workers' Union especially was to play an ever-growing role in the new situation. The workers in sovkhozes, the congress noted, were particularly helpful in the collectivization drive, and the party was told to extend systematic support to this group of agricultural workers, as well as to the batraks. At the same time the work of shefstvo, shock brigades, and shock workers was to continue at top speed. Finally, the congress approved the purge of the trade unions that had been conducted by the Central Control Commission and the Workers' and Peasants' Inspection as a measure needed to bring the trade unions into harmony with the party line, and in order that the tendency to remain 'apolitical,' which had manifested itself at the Eighth Congress of Trade Unions, be totally eliminated.[105]

Right after the congress was over the collectivization campaign was resumed. This time both terror and persuasion were used to get peasants to join the kolkhozes. At the same time efforts were made to keep the group of 25,000 reasonably well satisfied and operating. Party workers were instructed to help them in every way possible and to send those who showed themselves to be exceptional to the higher educational institutes for further training.[106]

Six months later, upon recommendation of the party, the Fifth ACCTU Plenum of January 1931 decided to enlarge the number of trade unions from twenty-three to forty-four. The credit for this move has been given to Stalin.[107] To supplement the group of 25,000 the party insisted on greater activity among the shefstvo brigades, which, already strong, were to be utilized in the countryside in whatever capacity the party wished. At the beginning of 1931 in Moscow oblast alone there were 480,000 sheftsvo brigade members, in Leningrad oblast 166,748, in Ivanovo oblast 400,000, while there were 300,000 in the North Caucasus and 55,000 in the Urals. In 1931 the industrial trade unions sent 20,273 brigades with 60,700 men to the spring sowing campaign, while 6,972 brigades with 26,200 men were sent in the grain harvesting campaign. In Western Siberia close to 4,000 union members were sent to the countryside, of whom about 1,200 remained there as permanent employees.[108]

In June 1933 the amalgamation of the Commissariat of Labour with the ACCTU meant that the trade unions were called upon to perform the administrative functions of the state apparatus. It was a further step in the decline of trade unions as organizations designed to protect the rights of the workers. And even then a further disintegration of the trade unions was contemplated.

The Seventeenth Party Congress (26 January–10 February 1934) celebrated

105 *KPSS o profsoiuzakh*, pp. 431–9.
106 *Ibid.*, pp. 441–2.
107 S. Bregman, 'Stalin i profsoiuzy,' *Trud*, 23 December 1939, p. 2.
108 *Istoriia profdvizheniia v SSSR*, pp. 298, 303.

the liquidation of the remnants of the 'anti-Leninist groups' and launched the Second Five Year Plan. It was also responsible for a decision of the 'reorganization of the Party and Soviet apparatus,' which led in turn to a thorough reorganization of the trade unions and complete confusion among their ranks.[109] Of the fourteen trade unions existing in agriculture at that time only one, the Union of Machine Tractor Station (MTS) Workers, revealed any sign of activity, or at least activity approved by the party.[110]

The period between the Seventeenth (1934) and Eighteenth (1939) Party Congresses was marked by an unparallelled campaign of repression and vengeance against former opposition. The ravages of the purge, which extended throughout the entire party and governmental apparatus and claimed hundreds of thousands of victims, also reached the Soviet trade unions. The decline of the Soviet trade unions in the 1930s was so notorious that it was even recognized in the Soviet press, especially during the so-called 'trade union crisis' of 1935–7.[111] As indicated above, the unions were invested with the authority of official organs of Soviet labour administration by a decree of 23 June 1933. Under these conditions, the steady decline of the trade unions was inevitable, and at the end of the 1930s the need for the very existence of trade unions was widely questioned.

Perhaps it was the war that saved the unions, for 'under wartime conditions ... food and housing, employment of women who had to care for their families, care for soldiers' dependents, war orphans and disabled veterans back from the war ... all required great efforts in the communities and even more so in plants. The unions, with some prewar experience in similar fields, were almost automatically drawn into this war work. This gave them a new lease on life.'[112] This new emphasis on social welfare activities, however paternalistic and however much combined with well-known sweatshop functions, continued to favour trade union development after the war and became noticeably stronger

109 *Profsoiuz rabochikh sel'skogo khoziaistva*, p. 68. See chapter 2 for a discussion of these changes.
110 *Ibid.*, p. 76.
111 N. Evreinov, *O svoeobraznom krizise profsoiuzov i ob ikh novykh zadachakh* (Moscow: Profizdat, 1936), especially pp. 15–16; Slutskii and Sydorenko, *Profsoiuzy Ukrainy posle pobedy velikogo Oktiabria*, pp. 121–4; *XVIII s'ezd VKP (b): Stenograficheskii otchet* (Moscow 1939), p. 158. It is possible to divide the early history of the Soviet trade unions into two distinct periods. During the first period which lasted from 1917 to 1929 the unions had at least some rights, and trade union members were able to elect their own candidates to posts of responsibility. In the second period, which began in 1929, not even this degree of independence was permitted, and the trade unions were totally subordinated to party control. F.S. Hayenko, *Trade Unions and Labor in the Soviet Union* (Munich 1965), p. 25.
112 Solomon M. Schwarz, 'Trade Unions in the Soviet State,' *Current History* (August 1959), p. 83; *Profsoiuz rabochikh sel'skogo khoziaistva*, p. 111.

after Stalin's death. The 'production theory' – the notion that the trade union's principal task is furthering production – has retained its undisputed hold in the USSR. Nevertheless, there has been a partial return to the 'defence theory' of the early 1920s, as is reflected in the party and government decrees of the late 1950s.

POST-STALIN PERIOD

The years 1953–63 were marked by significant internal changes in the USSR. Liberalization policies were evident in the reorganization of the legal system, in the sweeping changes in agriculture, and in the general revitalization of the economic system of the country. The trade unions were subject to these changes as well. However, the reforms within the unions did not attract a great deal of attention beyond the borders of the Soviet Union except for several articles in Western journals.[113]

Even less attention has been devoted to the organized workers in the agricultural branch of the economy. In fact, there does not seem to have ever been a single major article in English dealing with the trade unions in agriculture. Yet it was precisely in this area that the emphasis on the new trade union functions could first be noticed, preceding a similar effort in industry by at least four years. When, in the first half of 1957, the Soviet trade union press opened its pages to comments, criticisms, and suggestions with a view to subjecting all aspects of trade union structure and activities to close scrutiny, the major reorganization of unions in agriculture which began in the first part of 1953 had by then been largely completed. The reason for singling out the trade unions in agriculture for thorough reorganization ahead of the industrial unions was in all likelihood related to the fact that in 1953, for the first time since collectivization, Soviet policy-makers took stock of their agricultural resources, openly admitted their failures, and initiated a series of measures to rescue agriculture from the dead end in which Stalin had left it.[114] A not unimportant role in this

---

113 Paul Barton, 'The Current Status of the Soviet Worker,' *Problems of Communism*, IX (July–August 1960), pp. 18–27; *Ibid.*, IX (November–December 1960), pp. 38–47; Solomon M. Schwarz, 'Trade Unions in the Soviet State,' *Current History* (August 1959), pp. 79–84; E. Nash, 'Extension of Trade Union Functions in the Soviet Union,' *Monthly Labour Review*, LXXXI (December 1958), pp. 1391–2; Emily C. Brown, 'The Local Union in Soviet Industry: Its Relations with Members, Party and Management,' *Industrial and Labor Relations Review*, XIII (January 1960), pp. 192–215; Peter J. Potichnyj, 'The Recent Changes in Soviet Trade Unions' (unpublished master's thesis; Department of Public Law and Government, Columbia University, 1961).

114 The best studies of the twists and turns of the Soviet agricultural policy for the decade after 1953 are in Sidney I. Ploss, *Conflict and Decision Making in Soviet Russia: A Case Study of Agricultural Policy, 1953–1963* (Princeton: Princeton

reconstruction of agriculture was to be played by the trade unions. They were always regarded as transmission belts from the party to the masses. Now, in addition, they were delegated certain rights to direct social welfare and labour relations in order to make it easier for them to asume their function as shock absorbers, or buffers between the party and the government, on the one side, and the workers on the other.

At the September 1953 Plenum of the party Central Committee, N.S. Khrushchev delivered a special report which dealt with the crisis in agriculture in an unusually frank manner. The remedies he proposed were equally straight-forward. In addition to increased reliance on incentives to stimulate output and a substantial rise of capital investment in agriculture, Khrushchev called for an intensive effort to develop needed agricultural skills, to redirect agricultural specialists from office jobs to production assignments, and to bolster administrative and party controls in the countryside.[115]

The MTS, greatly strengthened both in skilled personnel and equipment, were to spearhead the initial effort in raising agricultural output. Tractor drivers who until then had been kolkhoz members temporarily assigned to the MTS for the period of field work became, by decision of the plenum, full-time employees of the MTS at a higher rate of pay than what they had previously earned as members of kolkhozes. The improvement in the position of tractor drivers was designed also to be an incentive for many former tractor and machine operators to return to agriculture from industry and other branches of the economy. At the same time the MTS directors and managers were warned by Khrushchev not to take revenge on these men for having earlier left agriculture for higher wages in industry.[116] This transfer involved large numbers of people: approximately 870,000 tractor operators; 187,000 brigade leaders; and 24,000 mechanics. In addition close to 50,000 machine operators returned to agriculture from industry.[117]

The resolutions of the plenum also called for greater controls over production and the conditions of everyday life in the countryside. To promote these objectives the party, on the recommendation of Khrushchev, committed a

University Press, 1965). See also Karl-Eugen Waedekin, *Privatproduzenten in der Sowjetischen Landwirtschaft* (Koeln: Wissensehaft und Politik, 1967), and his *Fuerungskraefte im Sowjetischen Dorf* (Berlin: Duncker & Humblot, 1969); Jerzy F. Karcz, ed., *Soviet and East European Agriculture* (Berkeley: University of California Press, 1967); Sigmund Diamond, ed., *The Soviet Union since Khrushchev: New Trends and Old Problems* (New York: Academy of Political Science, 1965).

115 *KPSS v rezoliutsiiakh*, III, pp. 610–53; *KPSS o profsoiuzakh*, pp. 577–618.
116 N.S. Khrushchev, *Stroitel'stvo kommunizma v SSSR i razvitie sel'skogo khoziaistva* (Moscow: Gospolitizdat, 1962), I, p. 55.
117 *Ibid.*, p. 229.

large number of Communists from the cities to the MTS and collective farms. Khrushchev proposed that 50,000[118] be sent, although as he himself admitted nearly a year and a half later no more than 30,000 Communists were actually sent.[119] This still represented a very substantial shift of personnel. By 1955 the MTS employed approximately two million workers, including combine operators, machine operators, drivers, and repair personnel, or over 200 per MTS.[120] Needless to say this large army of workers, most of them former kolkhozniks, flooded the ranks of the union. Almost overnight they had become members of the more privileged working class.

The September 1953 Plenum and the 1954 Plenum on the Virgin Lands were followed by the Thirteenth ACCTU Plenum in March 1954 and the First Congress of the Union of Workers and Employees in Agriculture and State Procurement in April of the same year. The latter two meetings were concerned primarily with the role of trade unions in the Virgin Lands campaign, and measures were taken to supply the large masses of sovkhoz and MTS workers with adequate trade union leadership in the new territories. The most important task was to provide the organizational framework needed to help settle the masses of migrating people and only then to see that they did not lack at least the minimum amenities of life. Yet even this assignment, it was felt, was too important to be left to trade unions alone, and the party moved speedily to assume control. In addition to thousands of Komsomol members, a large number of party members was dispatched to the newly tilled territories and placed in all positions of responsibility. From the beginning the leadership of the local trade union committees was in the hands of party members. In the initial stages of the campaign 420 Communists were sent to Kazakhstan alone to become chairmen of the rabochkoms (workers' committees) of the MTS and state farms.[121] At the same time as an effort was made to recruit people into the party in order to broaden its base in rural areas, the shefstvo movement of the more reliable industrial workers over enterprises in agriculture was revived and infused, as so often in the past, with the responsibility of providing the newly created sovkhozes and MTS with the proper techniques of tractor repair and maintenance, efficient use of electricity, etc.[122]

The greeting of the party's Central Committee to the Eleventh Congress of Trade Unions (June 1954) emphasized once again their important role in mobilizing the masses for further developing industry and agriculture, producing goods, and raising the cultural level of the toilers.[123] However, in addition

118 *Ibid.*, p. 75.   119 *Ibid.*, II, p. 24.   120 *Ibid.*, I, p. 425.
121 *Profsoiuz rabochikh sel'skogo khoziaistva*, p. 147.
122 *Istoriia profdvizhenniia v SSSR*, p. 445.
123 *XI s'ezd professional'nykh soiuzov SSSR: Stenograficheskii otchet* (Moscow: Profizdat, 1954), pp. 12–13.

to the above duties, the trade unions were instructed to display greater concern over what might be called the human element, one so important in the success or failure of any economic program or policy. The unions henceforth were to be vested with the power to check 'the revision of production norms and the setting up of tariffs,' as well as with the 'correct application in practice of the system of labour compensation, wage computations and the prompt payment of wages to workers and employes.'[124] These orders were reiterated in the decisions of the July 1955 Central Committee Plenum and were acted upon at the ACCTU Plenum, in the same month and at the Plenum of the Central Committee of the Union of Workers and Employees of Agriculture and State Procurement in October 1955.[125] At the ACCTU Plenum, but even more at the October meeting, those workers of the Central Committee of the union who were 'impassive observers' of the 'backward attitudes and practices' of economic leaders, especially in the areas of labour conditions and daily needs of the workers, were severely criticized.[126]

But the work of the union did not improve much. Khrushchev noted at the Twentieth Party Congress in February 1956 that the most important thing lacking in trade unions was a 'fighting spirit, a creative fire, sharpness, a sense of principle and initiative in raising the fundamental and vital problems whether in the sphere of production, of wages, of housing or in the sphere of satisfying the everyday needs of workers and employees.[127] The Second Congress of the Union of Workers and Employees in Agriculture and State Procurement, which was called soon afterwards (March 1956), acknowledged that the methods of work severely criticized by the party had still not been eliminated entirely. However, in the new statute adopted by the congress, more financial control was granted to local trade union committees by permitting a greater percentage of collected dues to remain in the hands of the union locals. This change did not, however, give the locals more power.

Although, generally speaking, the modifications in the organization instituted in the Union of Workers and Employees in Agriculture and State Procurement were completed in 1954, and although the functions of the trade union locals were broadened somewhat two years later, it was not until the decree of July 1958 that the rights and duties of the local committees were fully defined. The decree of the Presidium of the Supreme Soviet of the USSR

124 'Ustav sovetskikh profsoiuzov,' *Trud*, 19 June 1954, p. 1.
125 *Postanovleniia iiul'skogo plenuma TsK Kommunisticheskoi Partii Sovetskogo Soiuza 1955 goda* (Moscow: Gospolitizdat, 1955), pp. 17–18.
126 *Istoriia profdvizheniia v SSSR*, p. 451; *Profsoiuz rabochikh sel'skogo khoziaistva*, p. 157.
127 N.S. Khrushchev, *Otchetnyi doklad Tsentral'nogo Komiteta Kommunisticheskoi Partii Sovetskogo Soiuza XX s'ezdu* (Moscow: Gospolitizdat, 1959), p. 128.

came on the heels of a widespread discussion in the Soviet press, which sought to determine the proper place for trade unions in Soviet society.

The discussion was triggered by the February 1957 Plenum of the Central Committee, which dealt with problems of economic organization and laid the basis for the broad decentralizing reform announced at the May 1957 meeting of the Supreme Soviet. Within the framework of the public discussion of Khrushchev's 'theses,' a lengthy discussion on trade unions took place in the spring of 1957. In the Soviet trade union press a great deal of criticism was directed at both the organizational and the functional aspects of trade union work. Indeed, not since 1929 had there been a more conscious attempt on the part of leading as well as rank-and-file unionists to bring some efficiency into the work of trade unions and, if possible, to orient them towards 'proper trade union responsibilities,' meaning a much greater awareness of and concern with the social and industrial problems facing labour.

Some of the proposals which were made could certainly be classified as radical, and if adopted would have had far-reaching consequences for the future development of trade unions in the USSR. Two proposals were of special interest. One, which was outlined by Kh. Kerimov, chairman of the pipe factory in Azerbaidzhan, suggested a total amalgamation of the existing trade unions into one large trade union for the country as a whole; the second, on the contrary, envisaged a federal structure for the unions. According to the latter proposal, which was put forward by L. Illison, chairman of the Estonian Trade Union Council, and which found broad support in the non-Russian republics, each republic would have its own fully autonomous unions, the existing union central committees in Moscow would be abolished, and the ACCTU, appreciably weakened, would provide the only integrating link at the top of the trade union structure. The ACCTU would be composed of the delegates elected by the union-republican congresses who would be subject to recall by their constituencies.[128] Both of these suggestions were rejected by the party on the grounds that they disregarded the teachings of Lenin. It was also said that neither was acceptable because each 'failed to take into account the necessity of retaining the production principle and, given the new structure of administration, left unanswered various problems of production work and everyday needs, the solution of which should be carried out in a centralized manner.'[129]

After the proposals for a more radical reorganization of the trade union structure had been rejected by the party and by high-level trade union leaders, some other solution to trade union problems had to be found which not only

128 For a more detailed discussion of various proposals see Peter J. Potichnyj, 'The Recent Changes in Soviet Trade Unions,' pp. 11–67.
129 V.V. Grishin's address at the Sixth ACCTU Plenum, *Trud*, 12 June 1957, p. 2.

would fall in with traditional Soviet views but also would transform the trade unions into a more efficient instrument both with respect to the objectives of the state and the needs of the workers.

In this context agreement was reached in 1957 at the Sixth ACCTU Plenum to streamline the trade union structure by reducing the number of the unions from 47 to 23 and to redefine the rights and duties of trade union organs at all levels more clearly and completely than had been done until then.[130] The plenum also approved proposals which provided for shifting the centre of gravity of trade union leadership to the localities, giving the trade union councils in the republics wider powers and improving their work considerably. It should be mentioned that since 1958 each union republic has had its own trade union council, elected by the republican trade union congress.[131]

While the trade union councils in the union republics received greater powers to guide trade unions in the localities,[132] the role of the union central committees became somewhat narrower.[133] Let us consider, for example, the powers of the Central Committee of the Union of Workers and Employees in Agriculture and State Procurement. The Central Committee could no longer decide any question referring to agricultural workers on a nation-wide scale as it used to in the past, nor could it take part in drafting the economic plan for its branch of the economy on a national basis. Its function was to participate in working out comprehensive wage structures and unified standards of labour protection and safety and to take part in the work of the State Planning Committee, the Scientific and Technical Committee, and other all-union bodies. It was also responsible for maintaining international contacts and representing the union in international trade union organizations.[134]

Although as noted above some changes did take place at the higher levels of the trade union structure, the primary trade union organs received the greatest degree of attention in the discussion on how best to reorganize trade union work. But the changes themselves were not forthcoming until after the December 1957 plenum of the party's Central Committee.[135] Following the recom-

---

130 Verbatim reports of the Sixth ACCTU Plenum, *Trud*, 12–13 June 1957; *Istoriia profdvizheniia v SSSR*, p. 459; *Postanovleniia plenumov VTsSPS odinadtsatogo sozyva, 1954–1958* (Moscow: Profizdat, 1961), pp. 79–85.
131 Andrei Verbin, *Soviet Trade Unions* (London: Soviet News Booklet, 1958), p. 15.
132 Cf. *Ustav professional'nykh soiuzov SSSR* (Moscow: Profizdat, 1954) with *Ustav professional'nykh soiuzov SSSR* (Moscow: Profizdat, 1959), especially articles dealing with the powers of trade union councils.
133 Cf. article 29 of the 1954 Ustav with article 31 of the Ustav of 1959; V.I. Prokhorov, 'Profsoiuzy i voprosy truda,' *Voprosy truda* (Moscow: Gospolitizdat, 1958), pp. 140, 134–5, 153.
134 *Istoriia profdvizheniia v SSSR*, p. 459.
135 *KPSS v rezoliutsiiakh*, IV, pp. 300–13; *Materialy dekabr'skogo (1957 goda) plenuma TsK KPSS* (Moscow: Gospolitizdat, 1957), pp. 12–13.

mendations of the party plenum the Presidium of the Supreme Soviet in July 1958 decreed new regulations on the rights of local trade union committees.[136] Of course, many of the powers given legal form in 1958 were already in effect in many enterprises and state farms, but they lacked recognition and authority. Their formalization and extension brought a different feeling to the enterprises, producing a greater awareness of rights, a greater recognition by workers that their union had new powers and was able to do more for them, and – apparently – a greater respect by directors for the rights of the workers.

If the newly acquired rights of local committees are compared with those of 1925, in addition to other less significant features two important similarities can be discerned: the right of the committee to approve dismissals of workers, and the right to recommend dismissals of unsuitable supervisory personnel and the right to enforce workers' rights under the law.[137] This is not to equate the political, economic, and social situations in both periods; they were basically different. While the rights of local committees specified by the 1925 rules reflected the struggle of the trade union leadership to maintain trade unions as independent organizations free from total subordination to state and the Communist party, the 1958 extension of the local committees' rights did not mean freedom from the influence or direction of the Communist party. Professor Hazard emphasized clearly that 'creation of the permanent production committees to coordinate employment matters with the managers of the factories has increased trade-union prestige at that level, but soon after the Communist Party's organizations in the same places were given new powers to audit all managerial decisions so that the trade unions are held in their accustomed secondary place.'[138]

What explains the new official line on the functions of trade unions? Obviously there is no single cause. Edmund Nash suggests for instance, that the extension of trade union rights in the enterprises had purely economic roots and that 'the expanded trade union functions are almost exclusively directed toward promoting efficiency and the greater production which will be required if the ever increasing production goals are to be achieved.'[139] But this is only a partial explanation of why local trade union bodies have greater responsibilities. A more comprehensive answer is offered by Professor Hazard, who sees in the extension of trade union rights 'the Soviet answer to an ill formulated

136 *Spravochnik profsoiuznogo rabotnika* (Moscow: Profizdat, 1964), p. 192 ff.
137 ILO, *The Trade Union Movement in Soviet Russia*, pp. 283–87, and compare with the law of 15 July 1958 in *Spravochnik profsoiuznogo rabotnika*, p. 192 ff.
138 John N. Hazard, *The Soviet System of Government* (2nd rev. ed.; Chicago: University of Chicago Press, 1960), p. 61; *KPSS o profsoiuzakh, 1956–1962* (Moscow: Prozfidat, 1963), pp. 71–84; *XXII s'ezd Kommunisticheskoi Partii Sovetskogo Soiuza: Stenograficheskii otchet* (Moscow 1962), III, p. 355.
139 Nash, 'Extension of Trade Union Functions in the Soviet Union,' pp. 1391–2.

desire of Soviet workmen to obtain some measure of participation in the operating decisions in the plants in which they work, particularly those decisions
regarding dismissals for incompetence and unfitness, as well as holiday arrangements and pay.'[140]

In my opinion both economic imperatives and existing social pressures,
however diffuse they may be, are responsible for the profound changes that
have occurred in trade unions.[141] Perhaps the second element is becoming
stronger. As some events of the recent past tend to show, social pressure is
increasingly finding expression especially among the younger generation of
workers. Discussed elsewhere in this study are the open dissatisfaction of workers with living and labour conditions in the Virgin Lands and the strikes in
Nikolaev, Odessa, and Novocherkassk. The fight to retain some trade union
rights and privileges by the MTS workers seems to be a part of the same story.
Nor is it far-fetched to wonder whether the granting of old-age pensions and
of comprehensive social insurance to kolkhoz members was done simply out
of the party leaders' concern for the plight of needy people in the rural areas.[142]
It appears, as will be shown in the following chapters, that the changed status
of the trade unions was intended both to satisfy in some measure the everyday
needs of the workers and to serve as a safety valve for relieving excessive dissatisfaction with prevailing conditions of labour.

Certainly, the vague nature of the provisions pertaining to labour participation in enterprise management in the new regulations, and the failure of various
schemes in recent years to increase the worker's involvement in directing the
economy, point to the fact that the manager's authority has remained intact.
'One-man management' remains a binding principle in industrial and economic
relations in the USSR, and no one seriously contemplates a return to the famous
'triangle' theory of the past.[143] In this respect the position of union labour in
kolkhozes continues to be circumscribed by the Model Statute as it was limited
previously by the Kolkhoz Statute.[144]

The extent of trade union power can be measured only by union service
functions. And even in this sphere, as the trade union press indicates and as it
is suggested elsewhere in this study, the volume of cases of disregard of workers' rights remains disturbingly high, raising the question of whether the Soviet
system makes adequate provision for the protection of the limited rights it has
granted to the workers. However, it is safe to say that as long as the higher

---

140 Hazard, *The Soviet System of Government*, pp. 59–60.
141 This view is also shared by Solomon M. Schwarz. See his 'Why the Changes?' in
     Abraham Brumberg, ed., *Russia under Khrushchev: An Anthology from Problems
     of Communism* (New York: Praeger, 1963), pp. 591–5.
142 See 'Primernyi Ustav Kolkhoza,' *Pravda*, 30 November 1969, pp. 1–2.
143 *KPSS o profsoiuzakh, 1956–1962*, p. 510.
144 'Primernyi Ustav Kolkhoza,' *Pravda*, 30 November 1968, pp. 1–2.

party and government authorities genuinely intend to ensure the protection of the rights of workers – and the overwhelming evidence suggests that this now appears to be the policy of the party – there is little reason to expect that the workers and trade union organizations will not strive to make use of their rights, especially if, as is often the case, they are led by Communist party members. And the longer such a policy is in operation the harder it will be for the party to change it except in a dire situation of international or domestic unrest.

The reorganization of the MTS in 1958 and the shift of thousands of workers who were often party members to collective farms went hand in hand with the tightening of party control in the rural areas. For the first time since the revolution it was possible to organize regular party cells on most collective and state farms with a consequent greater opportunity to exercise control from within rather than without. This also meant that the newly organized trade union groups in kolkhozes (from 1962 called trade union committees) would be either in the hands of party members or under their close supervision.[145]

This shift of large numbers of workers from the payrolls of the MTS to the kolkhozes naturally evoked no positive response on the part of the transferees, in spite of assurances that wage rates and working conditions on the kolkhozes would be maintained at least on the MTS level and that no deterioration in living conditions would be permitted to take place.[146] In fact, as is demonstrated elsewhere in this study, the MTS workers approached the whole problem of change with a great deal of anxiety and loudly demanded protection of their rights and their level of earnings. Both sides to this conflict, the party and government, on the one hand, and the workers on the other, used the trade union as an argument for their own position. By insisting on trade union membership the workers were able to make their demands known to the party and to defend their interests, financial and otherwise, without making them the primary focus of attention. The party, by promising to retain trade union membership for these workers in effect bound itself to protect their interests in the collective farms, avoiding at the same time specific commitments which might prove embarrassing in the future.[147]

---

145 According to the party statute adopted by the Twelfth Party Congress, if there are at least three Communists in any trade union local or any elected trade union organ they are obliged to form a Communist group. *XXII s'ezd*, III, p. 355.

146 Khrushchev offered his reassurance from the beginning. He continued to do so periodically. The last time he spoke on the subject was at the party's Central Committee Plenum of December 1963 at which time he said that 'the cadres which were sent into kolkhozes should retain trade union membership with all rights that such membership confers, e.g., social insurance etc.' Khrushchev, *Stroitel'stvo*, VIII, pp. 348.

147 N.S. Khrushchev, 'O dal'neishem razvitii kolkhcznogo stroia i reorganizatsii M.T.S.,' *Trud*, 28 March 1958, pp. 2–5; *Trud*, 1 April 1958, p. 1.

In this way the agricultural trade union became a buffer that facilitated communication between both partners to the dispute but prevented a direct clash of interests. The party decided to satisfy the worker's claims yet at the same time made certain that the workers were kept well in hand. Thus only trade union 'groups' and not the full-fledged local committees were permitted on the collective farms.[148] When these finally were made over into local 'committees,' the members were cautioned to use their legal rights sparingly because labour-management relationships on the collective farms differed from those on the MTS and sovkhozes.[149]

But although the powers of the trade union locals on collective farms were severely circumscribed, the promise to maintain the wage levels of transferred workers was kept by the party leadership. Among a number of measures especially designed to help backward farms, long-term state loans were provided with the express purpose of paying for administrative personnel and machine operators at the state farm wage rates. In addition the party specifically directed the collective farms to ear-mark almost half of their money income for wages.[150] The right to oversee labour conditions in the kolkhozes and to seek improvements with the help of the farm management was also granted to kolkhoz trade union organizations. In December 1958 a special meeting of the Central Committee of the Union of Workers and Employees in Agriculture and State Procurement was called to discuss ways and methods of improving labour conditions and labour safety on the collective farms.[151] The powers of the trade union locals over social insurance continued unchanged.

As has already been implied, after 1958 the labour force of collective farms consisted of two categories of workers, one more privileged than the other. This situation contained within it the danger of more forceful claims for better treatment by the underprivileged but could equally be exploited by the party for its own ends. The inequality between kolkhozniks and hired labour created a great deal of friction on the collective farms and was probably viewed as a first step on the way to a 'proletarianization' of the countryside as a whole. During this period other measures that were taken by the party and government, such as the 'socialization' of a number of collective farms (i.e., conversion into state farms), introduction of money wages instead of wages in kind for kol-

148 According to the Trade Union Statute, the trade union group does not have the right of the Primary Trade Union Organization. It is simply a subordinate unit of the local trade union committee. See Ia. Skliarevskii, 'Profkom i prevelenie kolkhoza,' *Sovetskie profsoiuzy*, no 16 (August 1965), pp. 13–15.
149 'What Should Trade Unions Do on a Collective Farm?' *Trud*, 16 March 1965, p. 2 as translated by the *Current Digest of the Soviet Press*, XVII, no 12 (1965), pp. 18–20.
150 *Ekonomicheskaia Gazeta*, 20 June 1964, p. 33; *Ibid.*, 8 August 1964, p. 33.
151 *Profsoiuz rabochikh sel'skogo khoziaistva*, p. 174, 175.

khozniks in some collective farms, and the imposition of restrictions upon private plots, suggested that this, indeed, might have been the ultimate objective behind the creation of two strata of collective farmers.

The emphasis on production was much more pronounced after 1959 than in the early Khrushchev period. Fulfilment of the Seven Year Plan was placed before Soviet society as the single most important objective, and Soviet trade unions were called upon to help in achieving it. The following passage addressed to the Twelfth Congress of Trade Unions in 1959 by the party's Central Committee illustrates this point:

At present the most fundamental, the most essential task of Soviet trade unions lies in mobilizing the efforts of the great working masses in view of the struggle for carrying out the historic decision of the Twenty-first Congress of the Party, for timely fulfilment of the Seven Year Plan and the targets fixed for 1959, the first year of the plan.[152]

The statutes adopted by the Twelfth Congress of Trade Unions dutifully followed the party's instructions by defining the purpose of Soviet trade unionism in the following way:

The central task of the trade unions is the mobilization of the masses in view of the struggle for further great expansions in all branches of the national economy, for further strengthening the economic and defensive power of the Soviet state, for fulfilling and overfulfilling the economic plans for technical progress, for an uninterrupted rise in the productivity of labour, for stricter economy and parsimony in all sections of the national economy, for the maximum exploitation of all resources and possibilities with the aim of a rapid increase in industrial and agricultural production and an uninterrupted rise in the material well being and cultural standards of the workers.[153]

Improvement in material welfare and cultural standards of the workers was far down on the list of priorities. Only after the idea of the gradual conversion of collective to state farms was de-emphasized and after the disastrous harvest of 1963 did the party leadership begin to cast around for other posible incentives to raise agricultural output. Khrushchev toyed with this idea at the De-

---

152 *XII s'ezd professional'nykh soiuzov SSSR 23–27 Marta 1959: Stenograficheskii otchet* (Moscow: Profizdat, 1959), p. 13.

153 See the Preamble to the Statute of Trade Unions in *Spravochnik profsoiuznogo rabotnika* (Moscow: Prozdat, 1962), p. 135, and in *Spravochnik profsoiuznogo rabotnika* (Moscow: Profizdat, 1969), pp. 180–1.

cember 1963 Plenum of the Central Committee but not until his speech to the
February 1964 Plenum did he reveal that he thought this could be done by
establishing a pension system financed partly by the state, the size of individual
pensions being dependent upon the degree of each farmer's participation in
collective production.[154] Under such an arrangement, he stated, there would
be an incentive to work harder even if earnings were low in order to receive
a larger pension later.[155] The post-Khrushchevian leadership went even further
in this respect by permitting the Kolkhoz Union to be set up and by establishing comprehensive social security schemes for kolkhozniks which approximate
the existing coverage for the workers but continue to lag behind in some important respects.[156] This move was probably designed to offset the glaring inequality between the wage workers and collective farmers, while still leaving
friction enough to uncover shortcomings in the management of the collective
farms.

Periodic purges, close party supervision, and the domination of urban leadership have made certain in the past that the functions of agricultural trade
unions have not exceeded the limits defined by the 'transmission belt' theory
of Soviet trade unionism. Recently, however, a trend towards a more paternalistic notion of the role of agricultural trade unions – one not entirely foreign
to that of shop unions in other parts of the world – has been in evidence. To
some extent, it seems, the unions are beginning to function as channels through
which a certain amount of genuine pressure from below is exerted.

154 Khrushchev, *Stroitel'stvo*, VIII, p. 348.
155 *Ibid.*, pp. 435, 438–41.
156 See 'Plenum VTSSPS,' *Trud*, 29 January 1970, pp. 1–2; A. Nagaitsev, 'Truzheniki
sela iubileiu,' *Trud*, 20 January 1970, p. 2; A. Golaev and A. Nagaitsev, 'Neotlozhnye
zadachi sel'skikh profsoiuzov,' *Trud*, 20 June 1970, p. 3; L.I. Brezhnev, 'Ocherednye
zadachi partii v oblasti sel'skogo khoziaistva' (Plenum CCCPSU), *Pravda*, 3 July,
1970.

2
Organization and structure

One of the difficulties of the early Agricultural Workers' Union was simply that its organizational structure resembled that of an industrial rather than agricultural trade union. It was not strange that this should have been the case, for unlike certain unions in industry, this union did not develop from the grass roots up but rather came into being as a result of centrally directed action. In many cases its branches were artificially created and artificially nurtured, with almost no opportunity for experimentation with the best bureaucratic structures. In the early years its organization was based upon, and its very existence dependent on, the establishment of state farms and communes. Since these were few in number and far apart, the whole structure of the union was shaky. Moreover, for many industrial workers and trade union leaders the Vserabotzem represented a conglomeration of 'petit-bourgeois elements,' something unpure and unreliable, at best to be avoided, and definitely not to be trusted.[1]

---

1 S. Kovgan, 'V soiuze vserabotzemles,' *Trud*, 26 April 1922, p. 3. 'Batraks are already members of the union, but they are not the entire proletarian element and soon we will have to consider some form of filtration.' Report from Odessa gubernia in V. Block, 'Rost batrachestva i taktika vserabotzemlesa,' *Trud*, 19 October 1923, p. 3. This emphasis on purity continued to exist and was very much in evidence on the eve of the collectivization drive. It was also practised against other groups of workers, e.g., those transferred from other unions. 'Postanovlenie VTsSPS o deiatel'nosti TsK soiuza sel'sko-khoziaistvennykh i lesnykh rabochikh,' *Trud*, 2 September 1927, p. 4.

The organizational structure of the union included, descending from top bottom, the Central Committee, gubotdel (gubernia section), uezdotdel (uezd section), and the mestkom or rabochkom (local committee).[2] However, unlike the situation in industry, the local committees were thinly spread over the countryside and, after the amalgamation of the union with the forestry workers in 1920, in the forests.

With the introduction of NEP it soon became apparent that some changes in this structure were in order if control from the centre was to be realized. Emphasis was placed on the task of organizing and absorbing the village proletariat, the so-called batraks, into the union in order to create a countervailing power vis-à-vis the richer peasants.[3] But the question of what organizational forms this recruitment drive was to take had to be answered.[4] It was of extreme importance to decide whether the batraks were to be included in the rabochkoms then in existence in the sovkhozes or whether a new local organization had to be set up. The decision to organize this element into separate local cells was not surprising. Given the intention of using the batraks in the fight against the kulaks it was much handier to have them organized separately, and their mode of life and employment diverged enough from that of workers in state farms that a somewhat different approach was required. Nor would it have been logical to expect sovkhoz rabochkoms, which were weak themselves, to look after the needs of this group of workers. Thus, sel'koms (village committees) were organized especially for batraks and these were directly subordinated to the next highest territorial organ, the so-called volsekretariats (village district secretariats). The rabochkoms, on the other hand, were grouped together territorially into grupprabochkoms

2 In late 1919 there were in existence 28 gubernia sections, 64 uezd sections, and 472 local committees in sovkhozes, communes, etc. The number of uezd sections was smaller than the number of uezds. In some uezds trade union sections were abolished, allegedly because of financial difficulties, which could also mean that they were not permitted to exist because they were not Bolshevik led. VTsSPS. *Otchet za 1919 god* (Moscow: Izdatel'stvo VTsSPS, 1920), p. 391.

3 'Batrachestvo na Ukraine,' *Trud*, 26 September 1923, p. 4.

4 The Fourth Congress of the union which was held in December 1922 turned to the question of how best to organize the work of trade unions under NEP conditions. It recommended first improvement in the financial status of the union, requested that membership dues be paid regularly and warned that less reliance should be placed on financial help from above. Between December 1922 and June 1923 when the Second Plenum of the Central Committee was held a valiant attempt was made to live up to these policies but without much success. At that time 37 gubotdels of the union were still totally dependent on financial help from the Central Committee. 'Plenum TsK vserabotzemlesa,' *Trud*, 1 June 1923, p. 2.

(district organization of workers' committees), which were organizationally on the same level as volsekretariats but completely separate from them.[5]

The difference was significant, for the grupprabochkoms were territorial organizations of this particular union, while the volsekretariats were the lowest inter-trade union organs in existence. The important task of organizing the village poor was not to be left in the hands of the Agricultural and Forestry Workers' Union itself, but rather was to be a joint effort of all trade unions existing in the locality, led by the more reliable and trustworthy industrial proletariat. This was never clearly stated in writing, but the underlying assumptions of this action were obvious to all concerned, and enough evidence exists to suggest that it was thoroughly disliked by the leadership of the Agricultural and Forestry Workers' Union.[6] Manipulation of the organization perpetuated divisions among the workers in the village but failed to solve the problem of centralized direction and control. Only the uezdotdels were now able to coordinate the work of the two branches, but the uezdotdels and uprofbiuro (uezd trade union bureau) were far removed from the localities and not always staffed with experienced people, much less good trade union leaders.

The desire to split the batraks from other categories of agricultural workers created special difficulties in the non-Russian areas of the Soviet Union, and particularly in Central Asia, where local attempts were made to attach the batraks directly to the Agricultural and Forestry Workers' Union rather than to keep them isolated as in other areas.[7] The reason for this was quite obvious: the batraks had to be isolated from the influence of native leaders who, because of unique circumstances were powerful and unlikely to submit willingly to central party control.

Central Asia was predominantly an agricultural region with only poorly developed industry. The gross production of agriculture in 1923–4 was 396

---

5 A. Kazakov, 'Batrachestvo i novye organizatsionnye zadachi vserabotzemlesa,' *Trud*, 2 December 1923, p. 1.

6 A.I. Grafov, 'Neobkhodim vykhod, o rabote soiuzov v derevne,' *Trud*, 14 December 1923, p. 1; 'V soiuze vserabotzemles,' *Trud*, 26 April 1922, p. 3. On the other hand, see those arguing in favour of an inter-union approach; 'Na pomoshch vserabotzemlesu,' *Trud*, 19 May 1922, p. 1.; A.I. Trufanova, 'O rabote na sele,' *Trud*, 8 March 1924, p. 3. The situation was so bad that this question was discussed at the plenum of the Central Committee of vserabotzemles, which was held in June 1923. See I. Chernov, 'Voprosy plenuma,' *Trud*, 1 June 1923, p. 2; 'Plenum TsK vserabotzemlesa,' *Trud*, 5 June 1923, p. 3.

7 In addition, the competition among the existing trade unions for members often spelled disaster for the Agricultural and Forestry Workers' Union. A. Nizhegorodtvsev, 'Voporsy razmezhevaniia v soiuze vserabotzemlesa v Turkestane,' *Trud*, 14 November 1923, p. 4.

million rubles, or 85 per cent of total production, as opposed to 69 million roubles for industry, or 15 per cent, mostly in cotton textiles. The main feature of the economy, which defined the general working conditions of the agricultural trade union in Central Asia, was this subordination of industry to a dominant agriculture. No less important was the very structure of industry in Central Asia. Of the total number of industrial enterprises, state factories make up 2 per cent, co-operatives 0.3 per cent, and private small artisan enterprises the remaining 97.7 per cent. As a result of these conditions there was at best a very weak trade union aktiv. Trade unions operated at a deficit, and proportionately there was a large bureaucratic apparatus in relation to the number of members. Thus, the political work of the trade unions in Central Asia was dependent on the peculiarities of the region, its economics, and the character of production relationships.[8]

According to the report of the Central Asian Bureau of the ACCTU, the 'trade unions of Central Asia emphasized recruitment into trade unions of hired workers from the native population, raising their cultural and political level, their class consciousness, and defending their economic and trade union interests.' Yet the report admits that the trade unions in fact tended to work primarily among the Europeans and to look down on natives. This was branded as 'misunderstanding of the general tasks of the working class,' and attempts were made to rectify the situation.

All these difficulties were compounded in endeavours to organize the village proletariat. Until the Fourth Turkestan Conference of Trade Unions in 1924 the Agricultural and Forestry Workers' Union did not carry on any work among the village proeltariat, who had been organized by the Koshchi (Union of Small Landowners), which had sections for batraks.[9] Soon, however, it was realized that if the batraks were to play an important role in the struggle against rich peasants they had to be placed under more reliable leadership. In Central Asia the one organization to which the party could turn was the Agricultural and Forestry Workers' Union, which was more trustworthy than the native organizations headed primarily by local nationals.

Thus in 1924 the Turkbiuro of the ACCTU, which was responsible for all trade union work in Turkestan, called a Conference of representatives of the party, Koshchi, and the Agricultural and Forestry Workers' Union, at which it was decided to give control of the Koshchi batrak sections to the agricultural union. This was done in a rather mechanical way by which the chairman of each batrak section was to be an ex officio representative of the union and

8 VTsSPS, Sredne-Aziatskoe Biuro, *Professional'nye soiuzy v Srednei Azii, 1924–1925: Otchet sredne Aziatskogo Biuro VTsSPS k pervoi sredne-Aziatskoi konferentsii profsoiuzov* (Tashkent 1925), p. 4.
9 *Ibid.*, p. 12.

was to have the decisive voice in Koshchi whenever a question related to the batraks arose.

However, this makeshift solution did not work, and conflict between Koshchi and the Agricultural and Forestry Workers' Union intensified. As a result the Turkbiuro of the ACCTU recommended to the Central Committee of the union that it replace its special agents sent from Moscow with a full-fledged bureau in Turkestan and also requested that much-needed personnel and materiel be sent to Turkestan for use in organizing the village proletariat. The Central Committee of the Agricultural and Forestry Workers' Union readily agreed to organize such a bureau, especially because the Turkbiuro released it from the obligation of contributing 10 per cent of its budget to inter-trade union funds. In addition, the Turkbiuro delegated several trade union activists from other unions to help the union in its organizational efforts.

Koshchi, however, bitterly resisted these encroachments on its authority. To put an end to Koshchi opposition a rather ingenious scheme was resorted to, which was designed to accomplish gradually what could not be done at once. As a first step, in regions where there were no Agricultural and Forestry Workers' Union organizations, batraks were made members of the union without forfeiting their membership in Koshchi, but henceforth they were to pay their membership dues to the union only. In regions where union organizations existed the batrak sections within Koshchi were to be liquidated and their membership transferred to the union. At the beginning, there were no union organizations to speak of in Turkestan, so the effect of this decision was simply that most of the batraks organized within Koshchi were officially still members of the latter organization under direct supervision of the union. As could be foreseen, relationships between the union and Koshchi rapidly deteriorated, especially when the former demanded that the latter 'cut all ties with the batraks.'

In an attempt to clarify the situation, the Central Asian Bureau of the ACCTU forced the following provisions, which were designed to regulate affairs at the local level, through the republican inter-trade union congresses held at that time (January–June 1924):

The Agricultural and Forestry Workers' Union which unites hired workers in agriculture should harmonize its work of protecting the trade union and economic interests of batraks with the general tasks of raising and developing 'dekhan' economy. Dual membership of batrak in the union and 'Koshchi' should not lead, in the future, to undesirable friction and competition for the batrak, which until now has existed in the relations between these organizations.[10]

10 *Ibid.*

TABLE 2–1

Growth in membership of the Agricultural and Forestry
Workers' Union drawn from native groups in Central Asia,
January to October 1924

January	April	July	October
481 (100%)	1579 (328.2%)	2986 (620.7%)	9051 (1881.7%)

SOURCE: Vsesoiuznyi Tsentral'nyi Sovet Profsoiuzov, SredneAziatskoe Biuro,
Professional'nye soiuzy v Srednei Azli, 1924–1925 (Tashkent 1925), pp. 16–17.

Since both organizations in their relation to the batraks had strictly prescribed
and well-defined tasks, there should have been no reason for these difficulties.
Anyway the ambivalent situation was not permitted to exist for long. At the
end of 1924 and during 1925 a tremendous effort was made to place the structure of the Agricultural and Forestry Workers' Union on a firm foundation and
thereby to create conditions for the fulfilment of the second part of the resolution: total absorption of the batraks by the union. The results, clearly indicated
in tables 2–1 and 2–2 suggest the magnitude of growth of the union.

During the early 1920s, and especially after the administrative reorganization following the creation of the USSR in 1923, various changes were effected
in the structure of the Agricultural and Forestry Workers' Union. The transi-
tional period extended in some areas well into 1928 with both old and new
trade union organs existing side by side. This was true even of the Moscow
region where the volsekretariats existed until 1928. The new vertical organization of the union consisted of the Central Committee, republican committee,
oblast committee, okruzhotdel (county section), and local committee. The
rabochkoms (workers' committees) and sel'koms (village committees) – or, as
they were called in some areas, batrachkoms (batrak committees) – were still
separated from each other and subordinated to the next higher trade union
organ, the okruzhotdel, which replaced the former uezdotdel. Thus was perpetuated the lack of co-ordination of trade union work in the villages. Nor was
this gap filled by the existing inter-trade union organs, the so-called raisovprofs
(district trade union councils), at the raion (district) level. It was understand-
able, therefore, that some trade union leaders would press for the creation of
a union organ on the raion level which would be charged with the task of
co-ordinating trade union work at that level.[11] These demands were partially
successful, and at least in some areas the raikoms (district committee) were
created, sometimes in the face of bitter opposition from the centre, which was
beginning to worry about the extreme growth at all levels of the trade union
bureaucracy. In the Ukraine raion, raiprofbiuro (trade union bureaus) and

TABLE 2-2

Membership of the Agricultural and
Forestry Workers' Union drawn from
native groups of Central Asia as a
per cent of total Central Asian
membership, January to October 1924

January	April	July	October
13.1	30.2	31.2	54.9

SOURCE: Vsesoiuznyi Tsentral'nyi Sovet Profsoiuzov, SredneAziatskoe Biuro, *Professional'nye soiuzy v Srednei Azii, 1924–1925* (Tashkent
1925), p. 16.

raiotdels (raion sections) were established after the Sixth All-Union Congress
of Trade Unions in 1924. In Siberia raisekretariats (district secretariats) were
established. The result was hardly a reduction in the size of trade union
organs. In Siberia, for example, the number of paid trade union officials increased 13 per cent.[12]

Since 1918 there also had existed the horizontal organizations of the unions,
the inter-trade union councils, headed in Moscow by the supreme inter-trade
union executive body. The All-Russian (now All-Union) Central Council of
Trade Unions had been in existence since July 1917, and had maintained
bureaus for all important regions of the country. These territorial bureaus were
responsible for laying the organizational foundations of the Agricultural and
Forestry Workers' Union. The actual work was done through authorized agents
of the Central Committee of the union, who were attached to the ACCTU territorial bureaus or, in some cases, as in the Ukraine, through a bureau of the
Central Committee of the union established within the existing ACCTU territorial bureau (in the case of the Ukraine, the All-Ukraine Council of Trade
Unions). These arrangements are indicated in table 2–3.

Central Asia is again of interest, for as late as January 1924 there was no
separate organ of the Agricultural and Forestry Workers' Union. The bureau
of the Central Committee of the union did exist but only as a section in the
Central Asian Bureau of the ACCTU. On the republic level there existed within
the trade union councils of both the Uzbek SSR and the Turkmen SSR only the
so-called Tsentral'nye Pravleniia Vserabotzemlesa (Central Administrations

11 Kazakov, 'Batrachestvo,' p. 1.
12 VTsSPS, *Otchet VTsSPS k VII sezdu profsoiuzov* (Moscow: Izdatel'stvo VTsSPS,
1926), pp. 46–8.

TABLE 2-3

Higher organs of the union, 1921-4

1921		1922-3		1924	
Inter-trade union area organ	Existing organ of Agricultural and Forestry Workers' Union	Inter-trade union area organ	Existing organ of Agricultural and Forestry Workers' Union	Inter-trade union area organ	Existing organ of Agricultural and Forestry Workers' Union
Iuzhbiuro	Bureau	Ukrbiuro	Bureau	VUSPS	Republic committee
Uralbiuro	None	Uralbiuro	Authorized agent	Uralsovprof	None
Sibbiuro	Authorized agent	Sibbiuro	Authorized agent	Sibsovprof	None
Iugvostbiuro	Authorized agent	Iugvostbiuro	Authorized agent	Iugvostbiuro (liquidated)	None
Kavbiuro	Authorized agent	Zakavbiuro	Authorized agent	Zakavsovprof	Republic committee
Turkbiuro	Authorized agent	Turkbiuro	Authorized agent	Sredne-Aziatskoe Biuro	Bureau
Sev-Zapadbiuro	None	Sev-Zapadbiuro	Authorized agent	Sevzapsovprof	None
Kirgizbiuro	Authorized agent	Kirgizbiuro	Authorized agent	Kirgizsovprof	Republic committee
		Dal'vostbiuro	Authorized agent	Dal'vostsovprof	None

*SOURCE: For 1921, "Organizatsionnaia deiatel'nost' VTsSPS za 1921 god," *Trud*, 1 January 1922, p. 2; for 1922–4, VTsSPS, *Profsoiuzy SSSR 1922–4: Otchet VTsSPS K VI S'ezdu professional'nykh soiuzov* (Moscow 1924), p. 4.

of the Agricultural and Forestry Workers' Union).[13] Later, these pravlenia (administrations) were reorganized into the republican committees of the union.

At the beginning of 1926, with the Seventh Congress of Trade Unions, the situation in all trade unions was considerably stabilized and the trade union structure took on more or less the character that it now possesses. From that time one can speak of the Agricultural and Forestry Workers' Union as a firmly established entity. But important changes were in the offing, and they did not bypass this union. In preparation for the coming revolution in agriculture the union was ordered to strengthen its local cells, and for this purpose a great number of workers were transferred from other unions. These workers were to be organized separately if their numbers warranted it rather than being included within the existing rabochkoms or selrabochkoms. The union was ordered to organize cells in as many localities as possible and to forbid the amalgamation of members of several villages into one local committee. From then on each village was entitled to have a local committee of the union. In addition, more attention was to be given to agricultural specialists, who were to be registered and organized in their own branches. They were also to be assigned a greater role in trade union work, and the sections and subsections of the union were to be placed under their guidance.[14] Growth in the membership of local cells of the union continued, reaching 23,000 in June 1929.[15]

But even by 1929 the union had failed in many respects to fulfil the tasks assigned to it by the party. Other trade unions were instructed to provide assistance, but although both the party and the Eighth Trade Union Congress called for such help to the union in 1928, it was slow in coming. Unity between the party and the trade union was again emphasized in the editorial in *Trud* of 9 June 1929: 'in the relationship between the Party and the trade unions not for a minute can there be tolerated any crack or split which would disturb the current work of the transmission belt from the Party to the proletarian masses. This would pose a serious threat to the whole system of the dictatorship of the proletariat ...'[16]

---

13 VTsSPS, Sredne Aziatskoe Biuro, *Professional'nye souizy v srednei Azii*, p. 47.
14 'Postanovlenie prezidiuma VTsSPS o deiatel'nosti TsK soiuza sel'khoz. I lesnykh rabochikh SSSR,' *Trud*, 2 September 1927, p. 4.
15 M. Vsevolodov, 'Rabota ot sluchaia k sluchaiu,' *Trud*, 5 June 1929, p. 4. At least one source gives the following numbers for local organizations: for 1 January 1925 – 13,000; for 1 January 1927 – 27,879. 'Rabota sredi sel'khozlesrabochikh,' *Trud*, 3 July 1927, p. 1.
16 'Protiv opportunizma za leninskuiu vyderzhannost' v profsoiuzakh,' *Trud*, 9 June 1929, p. 1.

THE CHANGES OF 1929

On 28 June 1929 the Presidium of the ACCTU announced that a special commission had been organized whose task would be to supervise trade union work in the countryside. Shvernik was appointed chairman of this commission which was composed of the chairmen of the Agricultural and Forestry Workers' Union, Union of Education Workers, Medical and Sanitation Workers' Union, and others whose work was in some way connected with the countryside.[17] Two days later the Central Committee of the Communist party called for a strengthening of the old sovkhozes and ordered all workers employed in the subsidiary industrial enterprises of the sovkhozes to amalgamate with the Agricultural and Forestry Workers' Union. Seasonal workers employed as builders, if they numbered over a hundred in a sovkhoz, were also to become members of the union.[18]

Rapid alterations in the trade union membership appear to have greatly disrupted the work of the Agricultural and Forestry Workers' Union. At the Plenary Meeting of the Central Committee of the union, held in January 1930, voices were heard urging a 'speedy completion of the changes being instituted so that they would not interfere with the spring sowing campaign.'[19] But these moves were followed in 1930 by the complete destruction of the Union of Sugar Workers and the transfer of its members into the Agricultural and Forestry Workers' Union. Opposition to the regime had developed among the sugar workers, and the simplest remedy was to legislate it out of existence.[20] At the same time it was suggested that new provisions should be made for the forestry workers, who were organized in three separate groups: the lumberjacks, who were members of the Agricultural and Forestry Workers' Union; the forest transport workers, who were members of the Transport Workers' Union; and the woodworkers, who were members of the Woodworkers' Union. It was now proposed that a single union of forestry workers be set up, 'because the trade union of agricultural workers has enough to do in agricultural and as a result the work in forestry might suffer.'[21] Words were soon followed by

17 'Profsoiuzy na pomoshch derevne,' Trud, 28 June 1929, p. 4.
18 'Ob ukreplenii starykh sovkhozov, iz postanovleniia TsK VKP(b),' Trud, 30 June 1929, p. 4.
19 'Plenum TsK sel'khozlesrabochikh,' Trud, 21 January 1930, p. 4.
20 'Plenum TsK sakharnikov za sliianie s soiuzom sel'khozlesrabochikh,' Trud, 20 July 1930, p. 2; 'TsK soiuza sel'khozlesrabochikh za sliianie s sakharnikami,' Trud, 11 August 1930, p. 3.
21 'Trem soiuzam v lesu tesno,' Trud, 7 August 1930, p. 3.

deeds, and the Forestry Workers' Union was established by the ACCTU decree of 6 September 1930.[22]

Changes in the Agricultural and Forestry Workers' Union, now the Agricultural Workers' Union, coincided with a reorganization of the ACCTU itself, which in turn reflected to a great extent the modifications made in the party's Central Committee Secretariat in the 1930s.[23] The ACCTU was reorganized into ten sections and a bureau for physical culture. One of the sections, the Section for Work in the Villages, was responsible as its name implies for co-ordinating the work of trade unions in the countryside. Specifically, it was made responsible for a / questions of workers' sheftsvo and the socialist reconstruction of the village; b / recruiting and dispatching trade union personnel into kolkhozes, sovkhozes, and agricultural economic organizations; c / carrying out basic agricultural campaigns; and d / strengthening and assisting the Agricultural Workers' Union.[24]

Throughout 1930 all the trade unions were under constant pressure to reorganize. In July the okrugs as well as the okrug committees of the unions were abolished, and in their place inter-trade union organs were created on the raion level. In all rural raions where there were five or more local committees of various trade unions it was proposed that raisekretariats be set up; authorized agents of oblast trade union councils were to be sent to co-ordinate work in other rural raions. The Agricultural Workers' Union, as well as the Union of Education Workers and the Union of Soviet Trade Workers, received special permission to set up the raipravlenia if there were 250 or more members of the particular trade union in a given raion. The raisekretariats as well as raipravlenia were to be elected for one year only. To strengthen these organs no less than 90 per cent of the trade union personnel of former okrug committees were to be transferred into raions, and the unused financial resources of the former okrug committees were to be given to the new raion organs.[25]

This structure was elaborated by Zhdanov, head of the Organization Section of the ACCTU, and then widely discussed in the press. In general there was agreement on the need to reorganize, but some felt that Zhdanov had not paid enough attention to the raion organs. Certainly this was the feeling of the Stalingrad Okrug Trade Union Council which, after self-liquidation, had set

22 'Sozdaetsia edinyi soiuz rabochikh lesnoi promyshlennosti,' *Trud*, 29 September 1930, p. 4.
23 M. Fainsod, *How Russia is Ruled* (rev. ed.; Cambridge, Mass., 1964), pp. 191–3.
24 'Po voprosu o strukture i metodakh raboty VTsSPS: Postanovlenie prezidiuma VTsSPS ot 8 Ianvaria 1930 goda,' *Trud*, 25 January 1930, p. 3.
25 'Kakoi dolzhna byt' struktura profapparata posle likvidatsii okruzhnykh zvenev,' *Trud*, 18 July 1930, p. 3.

up a Raion Trade Union Bureau instead of a sekretariat with the intention of providing better supervision of single members not attached to any trade union cell. The bureau proposed creating a raikom in each raion where there were some cells of the Agricultural Workers' Union with no limitations on the total number of members required. The tasks of a raikom in the new bureau's view consisted of supervising 'weak trade union committees in kolkhozes, rabochkoms in sovkhozes and mestkoms (local committees) in raion experimental stations.' Although not much different from Zhdanov's, the bureau's proposal nevertheless did include several important points. Moreover, it revealed the highly significant fact that there already were trade union committees in kolkhozes.[26] They were, however, liquidated when collectivization was completed. The Moscow Oblast Trade Union Council came out most strongly in support of creating a trade union council at the raion level, stressing that only in this way would it be possible for the party properly to 'guide' the work of the trade unions.[27] This strong support was the best indication of future developments.

Only a few days later (8 August 1930) raisovprof (raion trade union councils) in rural areas, and gorsovprofs (city trade union councils) in towns were set up. An article in *Trud* on 24 September 1930 outlined what the functions of the raisovprofs should be.[28] The *Trud* article was followed by a detailed resolution of the ACCTU, instructing leaders of the newly created raisovprofs not to set up elaborate 'sections' but to conduct work with the help of 'organizers' responsible for separate branches of work.[29] The raisovprof was to have five such organizers responsible respectively for 1 / organizing of mass campaigns; 2 / questions of production and labour in sovkhozes, lumber, factories, and kolkhozes; 3 / questions of wages; 4 / culture and everyday needs; and 5 / the elimination of illiteracy. The size of raion staffs was strictly regulated, beginning with one paid worker for up to 3,000 trade union members and rising to seven paid workers if there were more than 100,000 trade union members in the raion.

The lower organizational structure of the Agricultural Workers' Union was as follows:
1 Raikom, to be organized if within a given raion there were 250 or more members of the union, grouped in no less than five local cells.
2 In the sovkhozes there would be a / rabochkom (workers' committee),

26 'Ukrepim politicheskoe i khoziaistvennoe znachenie raiona,' *Trud*, 18 July 1930, p. 3.
27 'Moskovskie profsoiuzy vyskazyvaiutsia za raiprofsovety,' *Trud*, 21 July 1930, p. 2.
28 V. Popov, 'Raisovprof organizator perestroiki derevni,' *Trud*, 24 September 1930, p. 3.
29 'Postanovlenie prezidiuma VTsSPS o meropriiatiiakh v sviazi s likvidatsiei okrugov ot 8 avgusta,' *Trud*, 26 September 1930, p. 4.

b / uchastkom (division committee), c / tselevoi profsoiuznyi upolnomo-chenyi (trade union representative for special purposes), d / grupporg (group organizer) in production groups of tractor operators, mechanics, animal breeders, gardeners, etc. In large sovkhozes, which spread over wide areas, raikoms and rabochkoms were to be set up.

3 In MTS and kolkhozes rabochkoms were to be set up if there were no less than fifteen members working as hired labourers. If there were less than that number, upolnomochenyi (authorized agent) of the union would carry on the leadership functions.

4 A sel'rabochkom (village committee) was to be established if there were fifteen members or more within the area of the village soviet; otherwise an upolnomochenyi would supervise union affairs.

It was further stipulated that all raikoms and lower trade union organs should be led by 'volunteers' rather than paid workers. However, if the raikom united more than five hundred workers it was to have one paid trade union worker. But here again the lower organs of the Agricultural Workers' Union could be exempted from this regulation, special circumstances warranting and with permission from the Central Committee of the union.

The regulations for conferring union membership were also altered for trade unions in agriculture. In industry the factory committee had the right to accept applications for trade union membership and could pass on them. But in the non-industrial trade unions, including the Agricultural Workers' Union, this right was taken away from their local committees and transferred to raikoms and raimestkoms. Here one could see another indication of the tightening of controls that went along with the collectivization drive.

The resolution also accorded greater recognition to specialists, who were not only permitted, but urged, to organize into special ITS (Engineering and Technical Sections) at the local level. In addition, if there were no less than ten such local sections within a raion, and if such sections were distributed among three or more unions, an MBIT (Inter-trade Union Bureau of Engineers and Technicians) was to be created within the Raion Trade Union Council, with one paid worker for 500 ITS members, two for 10,000 or more, and three if the ITS membership stood at over 100,000. If there were 75 ITS members within the Agricultural Workers' Union in a given raion, and if the obkom of the union gave its consent, an ITS bureau could be organized within the union raikom.[30] If there were fewer than 75, an authorized agent was to be attached to the raikom. However, neither bureau nor agent would be paid for this work, which was to be done strictly on a voluntary basis.

30 *Ibid.* In addition to the agricultural trade union, only the builders' and miners' unions were given this privilege.

THE REORGANIZATION OF 1931

The structure established by the resolution was swept away by another reorganization of trade unions that began in 1931. In January the Sixth Plenum of the ACCTU met and, under express orders from the Central Committee of the party, agreed to reorganize thoroughly the existing trade unions. As we have already seen, for about two years prior to this plenum constant changes occurred in the number of trade unions, but the tendency was to amalgamate rather than to subdivide. Now, however, the ACCTU was ordered to split the existing unions. As a result, forty-four new unions were created out of twenty-three old ones.[31] This time the trade unions in agriculture were not spared.

The Agricultural Workers' Union was split into four new unions: the Trade Union for Workers of Agricultural Sovkhozes; the Trade Union for Workers of Animal-breeding Sovkhozes; the Trade Union of MTS Workers and Batraks; and the Trade Union for Workers of the Sugar Industry.[32] The reorganization also affected the trade union structure at the local level. The sel'koms, which had united the batraks, were abolished; the raikoms were liquidated. At the same time rabochkoms in the sovkhozes and MTS were subordinated directly to krai and oblast committees.[33] Shortly after, on 20 February 1931, the ACCTU decreed that a middle link should be established in all Soviet trade unions. This step was probably taken to avoid the chaos and confusion which resulted from collectivization. Table 2–4 shows the new oblast trade union structure. With the exception of the Ukraine, oblast links were not set up in the union republics (some of which were not subdivided into oblasts).

In this rather arbitrary manner the structure of non-industrial trade unions was largely forced into accord with the structure of industrial trade unions. The raiprofsovets (inter-trade union councils on the raion level) were, however, retained. These organs together with the party raikom and the party political sections in individual enterprises were charged with supervising the 'transformation of agriculture' and thus exerted a somewhat greater degree of

31 The plenum noted that the Sixteenth Party Congress had assigned to the new executive of the ACCTU the task of giving effect to the policy summed up in the words 'carry on with production.' The ACCTU considered that the existing organization of the trade unions made it difficult for them to play a part in the management of industry. The number of economic bodies with which they had to deal was constantly increasing and, at the same time, there had been a considerable growth in the number of trade union members. In view of these facts it was decided to subdivide certain unions.

32 This union was the oldest one of all, having been in existence since before the revolution. It is therefore somewhat misleading to trace its beginning only to January 1931, as has been done by Soviet sources. *Profsoiuz rabochikh sel'skogo khziaistva*, p. 61. See also appendix I.

33 *Ibid.*, p. 62.

TABLE 2–4

Oblast structure of three agricultural trade unions, February 1931

Region	Trade Union for Workers of Agricultural Sovkhozes	Trade Union for Workers of Animal-Breeding Sovkhozes	Trade Union of MTS Workers and Batraks
Moscow Oblast	Committee	Oblast committee	Oblast committee
Leningrad Oblast	Committee	Oblast committee	Oblast committee
All-Ukrainian	Committee	Republic committee*	Republic committee
Ural Oblast	Committee	Oblast committee	Oblast committee
Nizhegorod Krai	Committee	Krai committee	Krai committee
Ivanovo-Voznesen'sk Oblast	Committee	Oblast committee	Oblast committee
Central Blackearth Region	Committee	None	Oblast committee
Lower Volga Krai	Committee	Krai committee	Krai committee
Middle Volga Krai	Committee	Krai committee	Krai committee
Western Siberia Krai	Committee	Krai committee	Krai committee
Eastern Siberia Krai	Committee	Krai committee	Krai committee
Western Oblast	Committee	Oblast committee	Oblast committee
North Caucasus Krai	Committee	Krai committee	Krai committee
Far East Krai	Committee	Krai committee	Krai committee
Northern Krai	subordinated to Krai Committee of Animal Breeders	Krai committee	Severnyi Krai subordinated to Krai Committee of Animal Breeders
Tartar Republic	Central administration	Central administration	Central adminstitration
Belorussia	Central administration	Central administration	Central administration
Kazakh Krai	Committee	Krai committee	Krai committee
Crimea Oblast	Committee	Raion committee	Oblast committee
Bashkir Oblast	Committee	Oblast committee	Oblast committee
Dagestan Oblast	Committee	Oblast committee	Oblast committee
Azerbaidzhan	Central administration	None	Central administration
Georgia	Central administration	None	Central administration
Armenia	Central administration	None	Central administration
Uzbekistan	Central administration	None	Central administration
Central Asian Krai	Committee	Krai committee	Krai committee
Trans-Caucasus Krai	Committee	Krai committee	None
Turkmenistan	None	None	Central administration
Tadzhikistan	None	None	Central administration
Karelian Oblast	Committee (in charge also of Animal Breeders and MTS and Batraki	None	None
Iakutia Oblast	None	None	Oblast committee (in charge also of Animal Breeders and Agricultural Workers)

*Ukrainian obkoms are not given.
SOURCE: *Trud*, 24 February 1931, p. 4.

horizontal control over union members than that present in industry, where vertical ties between local cells and higher trade union organs were firmer.

The central organs of the new agricultural unions were created by proclamation of the ACCTU. 'Organizing bureaus' for each union were announced along with the names of the chairmen and other bureau members, and they were authorized to perform the functions of the future presidiums of the union central committees. The bureaus were selected between 8 and 28 March 1931.[34] The ACCTU in its decree of 12 March 1931 also ordered the newly created unions to hold their congresses as soon as possible and published specific dates in May when this was to be done.[35] Certain signs of friction suggested that this orchestration of 'elections' in the agricultural trade unions reflected resistance to the party's assault on the rural labouring population.[36]

What resulted from this reshuffling was that the Union of MTS Workers and Batrak emerged as the privileged one among the three unions in agriculture. The only one of the agricultural unions permitted to do so, it organized itself into sections, including the Wages and Norm Setting Section; the Mass-production Section; the Labour Protection Section; the Workers' Supply Section; the Culture and Technical Progress Section; the Organization and Control Section; and the Financial Section.[37] It was the first time that any trade union in agriculture had received such a grant of organizational power, giving the Union greater potential to respond to and supervise its lower organs, and to exert influence with party and state authorities, while at the same time being a more efficient bureaucratic instrument to control agricultural labour.

However, a great deal of confusion remained, and it appears that in the absence of clearly defined tasks, agricultural trade union organs did little at this time. In order to alleviate the situation somewhat the ACCTU, acting on the basis of recommendations proposed by the Ninth Congress of Trade Unions, decided in August 1932 on two courses of action. First, it ordered still another reorganization of all trade union organs, from the ACCTU down. Second, it assigned definite functions to each of them.[38] The ACCTU itself was reorganized

34 The following men were placed in charge: Maksimov – for Union of MTS workers and Batraks, *Trud*, 8 March 1931, p. 3; Grigorev – for Union of Workers of Animal-breeding Sovkhozes, *Trud*, 25 March 1931, p. 1; S.I. Ovchinnikov – Union of Workers of Agricultural Sovkhozes, *Trud*, 28 March 1931, p. 1.

35 'Sroki sozyva vsesoiuznykh s'ezdov professional'nykh soiuzov: Postanovlenie VTsSPS,' *Trud*, 12 March 1931, p. 6.

36 Cf. 'Na s'ezdakh rabochikh MTS i batrakov,' *Trud*, 17 May 1931, p. 1; 'Otkrylsia s'ezd rabochikh zemledel'cheskikh sovkhozov,' *Trud*, 29 May 1931, p. 1.

37 *Profsoiuz rabochikh sel'skogo khoziaistva*, pp 61–2.

38 'O razgranichenii funktsii proizvodstvennykh soiuzov i mezhsoiuznykh organov: Postanovlenie VTsSPS,' *Trud*, 2 August 1931, p. 1; 'Tipovaia struktura soiuznykh

into a number of sections, each consisting of several subsections: the Commission for Foreign Relations; the Administration Secretariat; the Trade Union Publishing House (Profizdat); All-Union Inter-Union Bureau of Engineers and Technicians (VMBIT); and a Bureau for Work Among Foreign Workers and Specialists. There was also a Central Bureau of Student Sections; a Bureau for Physical Culture; and a section for the newspaper *Trud*.

Even more important was the decision to strengthen the central committees of all unions, which had been expected after the reorganization of the Union of MTS Workers and Batraks. All central committees were required to set up the following sections and bureaus: a Wages and Norms Section; a Production and Labour Protection Section; a Workers' Supply and Everyday Needs Section; a Culture and Technical Propaganda Section; an Organization and Verification of the Execution of Orders Section; a Financial Section; a Bureau of Statistics; a Bureau of Physical Culture; a Bureau of Student Organizations; a Bureau of Production; and a Central Bureau for Engineers and Technicians. The central committee of each trade union was also required to direct the work of the union, while inter-trade union organs simply advised and co-ordinated work in the localities. This shift in the centre of gravity of effective control over local branches of unions was an example of the greater reliance on vertical bureaucratic chains of command characteristic of the fully developed Stalinist system of economic administration achieved in 1932 and early 1933.

The structure of the newly established raisovprofs was modified accordingly. Each raisovprof would have 1 / an organizer responsible for organization and verification of the execution of orders; 2 / an organizer for workers' supply and everyday needs; 3 / an organizer for cultural and mass work; 4 / a bureau of physical culture; 5 / an inter-trade union bureau for engineers and technicians; and 6 / in large raisovprofs, with the permission of a higher trade union council and of the ACCTU, an organizer for wages and production work could be appointed.[39]

Finally, the local committees (FZMK) were also reorganized. For this purpose an organizational model was published in *Trud* and the unions were directed to follow it in modifying existing structures.[40] The model provided that the structure of trade union bodies must vary according to the number of union members in an enterprise. Enterprises in which the number of trade

organov na predpriiatii: Postanovlenie prezidiuma VTsSPS,' *Trud*, 28 August 1932, p 1; 'Struktura gorodskikh i raionnykh sovetov professional'nykh soiuzov,' *Trud*, 28 August 1932, p. 1; 'Postanovlenie prezidiuma VTsSPS o strukture apparata VTsSPS,' *Trud*, 2 August 1932, p. 1.
39 'Ukrepim profsovety sel'skikh raionov,' *Trud*, 5 January 1933, p. 3.
40 *Trud*, 28 August 1933.

unionists did not exceed five hundred would have two trade union bodies: a rabochkom and a profgruppa. The rabochkom would have four organizers: one dealing with wages, technical methods, and representation of the workers in the body for settling disputes, the RKK (Rates and Conflict Commission); another with questions of production, safety, and production conferences; another with the food supply and living conditions of the workers; and the last with educational activities and technical propaganda. The profgruppa, run by a single individual on a voluntary basis, was assigned responsibility for trade union affairs at the very lowest level in the various sectors of production units. These measures brought about a degree of uniformity and order but did not raise the trade unions from the low status into which they fallen by 1933.

The trade unions were not spared the purge that was sweeping the Soviet Union. The ACCTU ordered new elections to be held in rabochkoms, designating the period between 15 January and 15 February 1933 for agricultural unions.[41] Not only the rabochkoms, where 'fluidity of trade union workers' was admitted, but the newly created raisovprofs were also purged.[42] And in 1932 the beginning was seen in some rural areas of the great famine which assumed catastrophic proportions in 1933.[43] The famine was not due to natural causes but to a conscious effort to eradicate 'anti-Soviet' elements. As a result some six million peasants died. The purge in the countryside conducted off and on since 1928 was intensified after the January 1933 Plenary Meeting of the party, at which politotdels (political departments) were established in the MTS and sovkhozes.[44] One of the most important tasks of these politotdels was to conduct the purge of the MTS and sovkhozes in order to cleanse them of all 'enemy elements.'[45] Under the circumstances, it is hardly surprising that from 1933

41 'O perevyborakh fabzavmestkomov: postanovlenie prezidiuma VTsSPS o srokakh perevybornoi kompanii FZMK po soiuzam,' *Trud*, 23 November 1932, p. 1.
42 'Pochemu eti raisovprofy ne avtoritetny?' *Trud*, 5 December 1932, p. 2. It charges that they are inactive, that there is too much 'fluidity of trade union cadres,' that they pay no attention to the work of local organizations, etc.
43 Fedor Belov, *The History of a Soviet Collective Farm* (New York: Praeger, 1955).
44 Especially in the period from the fall of 1930 to the middle of 1931, the purge was carried on in the kolkhozes, during which about 30 per cent of them were purged. *Kolkhozy vesnoi 1931 goda: Statisticheskaia rozrabotka otchetov kolkhozov ob itogakh vesennogo seva 1931 goda* (Moscow-Leningrad 1932), p. 104.
45 'Tseli i zadachi politicheskikh otdelov MTS i sovkhozov: Rezoliutsiia obedinennogo plenuma TsK VKP(b) po dokladu tov. Kaganovicha priniataia 11 ianvaria 1933 goda,' *Trud*, 14 January 1933, pp. 2–3; see also 'Klassovoi vrag u sovkhoznoi molotilki,' *Trud*, 9 January 1933, p. 3; 'Uroki rabochkoma Luchanskogo sovkhoza,' *Trud*, 4 February 1933, p. 4; 'Blazhennoi son u podnozhzhia Surama,' *Trud*, 22 March 1933, p. 3; 'V MTS i MTM Odesskoi oblasti zaseli kulaki, pianitsy, vory,' *Trud*, 1 November 1933, p. 1; *Materialy ob rabote politotdelov MTS za 1933 god* (Moscow-Leningrad 1934), pp. 40–4. The purge was also reflected in the fluidity of raboch-

on the politotdels and not the trade unions began to play the major role in mobilizing and directing labour in agriculture.[46]

THE REORGANIZATION OF 1934

In April 1934 there were clear indications that the structure of the trade unions might once again be subjected to radical changes. At this time the reorganization of the People's Commissariat of State Farms was decreed, and the central as well as local organs of the commissariat were drastically reorganized.[47] On 4 April 1934 the Central Committee of the Communist party and the Council of Peoples' Commissars issued a resolution relating to the reorganization of the Commissariat of Agriculture.[48] This resolution was aimed at abolishing the so-called 'functional principle' and strengthening the principle of unity in management. It seemed to establish a closer connection between control from Moscow and the actual work of production. Departments of the commissariat were to correspond to the branches of production, and each was to deal with all questions affecting a particular crop. Thus, there were to be thirteen departments concerned with the following crops: cereals and oil yielding plants, sugar beets, cotton, flax and hemp, livestock, horses, veterinary services, subtropical crops, forestry, tobacco, silk, technical and higher agriculture schools, and political control. In addition, there were sections for the internal administration of the commissariat dealing with finance, staffing, supervision, statistics, etc. In order to make control of cereals and stock-raising more effective, the different provinces of the USSR were divided into four groups, the inspection of which was entrusted to assistant chiefs of the departments concerned who were to be appointed especially for that purpose. The commissariats of agricul-

---

kom chairmen. For example, in the Ural oblast in seven months in one sovkhoz twenty-two chairmen of the rabochkom were changed; in some sovkhozes they were changed at the rate of five to seven times in six months. 'Uralobkom soiuza zem-sovkhozov ne vozglavil bor'bu za bol'shevitskuiu uborku urozhaia,' *Trud*, 24 August 1933, p. 3; 'Resheniia IX sezda eshche ne doshli do rabochkomov zernosovkhozov,' *Trud*, 23 September 1932, p. 2; 'Kto rukovodit rabochkomami zernosovkhozov v ikh borbe za khleb?' *Trud*, 4 January 1933; 'Ten' predrabochkoma v Kolyshleiskoi MTS,' *Trud*, 25 March 1933, p. 2; 'Konveier predrabochkomov,' *Trud*, 17 May 1933, p. 2; 'MTS nuzhny krepkie predrabochkomy,' *Trud*, 16 September 1933, p. 2; Iu.S. Borisov, *Podgotovka proizvodstvennykh kadrov sel'skogo khoziaistva SSR v rekonstruktivnyi period* (Moscow 1960), p. 129.
46 'Opyt massovoi raboty politotdelov vsem rabochkomam MTS i sovkhozam,' *Trud*, 26 April 1933, p. 3.
47 'O reorganizatsii Narkomsovkhozov SSR i ego mestnykh organov,' *Trud*, 24 April 1934, p. 1.
48 *Trud*, 4 April 1934, p. 1.

ture of the union republics were also reorganized. The jurisdiction of krai and oblast sections of the Union Commissariat of Agriculture was extended to include collective farms not yet served by the MTS and the non-collectivized sector.

On 22 April 1934 the Commissariat of State Farms was similarly reorganized.[49] Four major departments were to deal with particular branches of production: the Department for Agricultural Sovkhozes; the Department for Dairy-farming Sovkhozes; the Department for Pig-raising Sovkhozes; and the Department for Sheep-raising Sovkhozes. There were also departments for Educational Establishments and Political Affairs; the functional sections were to be abolished. (Prior to the reorganization there had been twenty-one departments, of which only six dealt with production.) Local inspection was entrusted to the assistant chiefs of the major departments. The commissariat was to appoint delegates to the governments of the various republics, but delegates to the autonomous republics and regions were eliminated. The administrative structure of the state farms and trusts was modified too.[50]

The apparatus of the central committees of trade unions was expanded to include a social insurance fund; a wages section; inspectors, who were to be attached to the local union branches; a factory inspection service; a section for propaganda; a section for the organization of workers' clubs; a section for sports; a section for work among students; a section for work among engineers and technicians; a statistics section; an accounting service; and a general administrative office. The Fourth Plenum of September 1934 stressed the need to liquidate the middle organs in some unions, to strengthen the instructor apparatus, to shift to volunteer work in place of work performed by paid bureaucrats (these were to be reduced by 35 per cent), and to create special sections for the leading professions. Each of these sections (e.g., the section for engineers and technical workers) was to have its own bureau in the central committee.[51] More than ever before, technicians and specialists were to be segregated from the membership of the unions.

Finally, the reorganization meant a further redefinition of the functions of inter-trade union councils. They lost the right to administer social insurance, a function they had until then possessed, but were given the right to supervise the preparation of estimates and the expenditure of social insurance funds by various unions. The councils were forbidden to meddle with the administrative departments of any union. Their purpose was not to lead, but to supervise.[52]

49 *Trud*, 22 April 1934, p. 1.
50 *Industrial and Labour Information*, L (April 1934), p. 400.
51 'Za dal'neishuiu perestroiku professional'nykh soiuzov,' *Trud*, 5 September 1934, p. 1; see also the speech by Maksimov, *Trud*, 8 September 1934, p. 3; 'O perestroike profsoiuzov,' *Trud*, 6 September 1934, p. 1.
52 'Za dal'neishuiu perestroiku professional'nykh soiuzov,' *Trud*, 5 September 1934, p. 1.

Any criticism that this reorganization signified an abandonment of the 'production principle' and was a direct attack on the existing trade unions was simply attributed to thwarted careerism, or worse:[53]

Already at the present time individual comrades in the localities are beginning to mumble among themselves that the reconstruction of trade unions is a frontal attack on the trade unions and an attempt to erase their possibilities, etc. ... When we began to investigate where the root of these attitudes lies, we discovered rather quickly that the reduction in staff and in the paid apparatus is the cause of this dissatisfaction.[54]

Although the party's intention of reducing the size of the union bureaucracy clearly did not strike the fancy of trade union officials, the latter were apparently no less concerned with the headlong decline of trade union authority and power.

The reorganization that took place in 1934 resulted in one hundred and fifty-four new unions as compared with the forty-seven resulting from the reorganization in 1931. In agriculture fourteen new trade unions were created out of the three unions in existence at that moment (not counting the Sugar Workers).[55] The Trade Union for Workers of Agricultural Sovkhozes was split into four unions: the Union of Workers of Grain-growing Sovkhozes (headquarters in Moscow); the Union of Workers of Vegetable-growing Sovkhozes (headquarters in Moscow); the Union of Workers of Garden and Vineyard Sovkhozes (headquarters in Rostov-on-Don); the Union of Workers of Cotton-growing Sovkhozes and MTS (headquarters in Tashkent).

The Trade Union for Workers of Animal-breeding Sovkhozes was split into seven unions: the Union of Workers of Pig-raising Sovkhozes (headquarters in Moscow); the Union of Workers of Sheep-raising Sovkhozes (headquarters in Rostov-on-Don); the Union of Workers of Horse-breeding Sovkhozes (headquarters in Rostov-on-Don); the Union of Workers of Feather and Poultry Sovkhozes (headquarters in Moscow); the Union of Workers of Dairy and Meat Sovkhozes of the South and Centre (headquarters in Moscow); the Union of Workers of Dairy and Meat Sovkhozes of the Urals and Siberia (headquarters in Novosibirsk); and the Union of Workers of Dairy and Meat Sovkhozes of Kazakhstan and Central Asia (headquarters in Tashkent).

The Trade Union of MTS Workers and Batraks was split into three new

53 'Krupneishii etap,' *Trud*, 6 September 1934, p. 1. See also N. Shvernik's speech to the Fourth Plenum of ACCTU, *Trud*, 9 September 1934, p. 1.
54 'Uporno borot'sia za usvoenie novykh metodov rukovodstva,' *Trud*, 10 September 1934, p. 2.
55 'O perestroike profsoiuzov: Postanovlenie IV Plenuma VTsSPS,' *Trud*, 9 September 1934, p. 2. See appendix I.

unions: the Union of MTS Workers of the South and Centre (headquarters in Kharkov); the Union of MTS Workers of the East (headquarters in Novosibirsk); and the Union of Workers in Land Organs (Agricultural institutions) (headquarters in Moscow).

As can be seen, the reorganization was carried out on the basis of two principles: by type of production and by region. The Union for Workers of Agricultural Sovkhozes was reorganized according to the production principle, which led to a great deal of fragmentation. This was also the case for some of the animal-breeding sovkhoz unions. However, the last three on the list above were reorganized according to the territorial principle with two of them located outside of Moscow. The Union of MTS Workers and Batraks was also reorganized on the territorial principle, or at least, that part of it which did not include white-collar personnel in zemel'ny organy (land organs) with central committees outside of Moscow.

It is striking that while the unions in state farms were split, and hence visibly weakened, the strongest union of all, the MTS union, was deliberately strengthened. Also of interest is the fact that the process of singling out employees – white-collar personnel – and separating them from the workers continued, as is evident in the creation of the separate union of employees in land organizations.

A desire to control the trade unions more closely seems to have been the basic explanation for the changes. Shvernik in his speech to the Eighteenth Party Congress in 1939 was quite explicit in this respect, quoting Stalin to the effect that 'the Party concluded that dividing up the trade union organizations and reducing their dimensions was the best means to make it easier for Party organs to lead these organizations and to make the process of leadership more concrete, alive and operative.'[56] In short, the splitting of trade unions was designed to facilitate control by the party.[57]

To be sure, other explanations for the new reorganization were offered as well. The excessive size of the unions was one such reason. Large trade unions were said to have experienced difficulties in 'registering the needs and peculiarities of the numerous varieties of production and professions, and of organizing the servicing of them in a differentiated manner.'[58] Still another argument was that only by splitting the unions and transferring some of the central committees away from Moscow and into the areas of main concentration of the

---

56 Shvernik's speech, *Trud*, 15 March 1939, p. 4.
57 This motive is disputed by both Armstrong and Hajenko, who argue that it was done in order to take over the international labour movement. John A. Armstrong, *Ideology, Politics, and Government in the Soviet Union: An Introduction* (New York: Praeger, 1962, p. 59; F. Hajenko, 'The Soviet Trade Union Movement,' *Bulletin* (Institute for the Study of the USSR) v (January 1958), p. 40.
58 'Za dal'neishuiu perestroiku professional'nykh soiuzov,' *Trud*, 5 September 1934, p. 1.

trade union organizations would they be able to do a satisfactory job of guiding trade union work.[59] There may have been a degree of truth in these assertions. Nevertheless, the effect of the reorganization was to dissipate whatever degree of autonomous power the agricultural trade unions had formerly possessed.

The Fourth Plenum of the ACCTU was convened in September 1934 in order to adjust the structure of the trade unions to the newly organized state administration. Commencing in the spring of 1935 the new unions in agriculture were considered to be ready to cope with their responsibilities. What happened, however, was entirely the opposite. As a result of the reorganization, a majority of the unions became so weak that for all practical purposes they ceased to function. The shift of trade union officials from one place to another, the ongoing purge, disaffection created by staff reductions and the absence of regulations indicating which group of workers belonged to which union had a generally demoralizing influence both on trade union functionaries and on the workers themselves, many of whom had been deprived in practice of their social security and other benefits.[60]

In November 1934 the Central Committee of the Communist party resolved to strengthen further the party's position in the countryside. The result was a change in the status of the politotdels which had been set up in the MTS in January 1934. These sections were now amalgamated with the local regular party cells, increasing the leverage of ordinary party committees. In addition, agricultural departments were attached to the local committees, and another secretary was nominated for each committee in the principal agicultural areas. In each MTS a zampolit (deputy chairman for political affairs) was appointed, who was responsible to the local party committee for political activities. The secretaries of the local committees and the zampolits of the MTS were named by the Central Committee of the party and could be removed only with its consent. The officials of the disbanded MTS politotdels were transferred to the local committees of the party or appointed zampolits of the MTS. This reorganization was to have been completed in the southern part of the Soviet Union by February 1935 and in other parts of the country by March 1. The politotdels in the sovkhozes were, however, retained.[61]

In November 1935 the reorganization of the Commissariat for Grain and Livestock-farming Sovkhozes was announced.[62] Objectives of the reorganiza-

59 *Ibid.*; see also '154 professional'nykh soiuza,' *Trud*, 8 September 1934, p. 3; 'O perestroike profsoiuzov,' *Trud*, 6 September 1934, p. 1. Out of 154 trade unions, the central committees of 65 unions were located outside Moscow. See also Speech by Maksimov, *Trud*, 8 September 1934, p. 3.
60 'V kakom zhe, nakonets, my profsoiuze?' *Trud*, 12 June 1935, p. 3.
61 *Pravda*, 29 November 1934.
62 'O reorganizatsii narodnogo kommissariata zernovykh i zhivotnovodcheskikh sovkhozov,' *Trud*, 29 November 1935, p. 3.

tion were to establish closer contact between the commissariat and the sov-khozes through the abolition of intermediary links, and to extend the powers of managers in such farms. The order provided that all the regional groups or trusts of sovkhozes were to be abolished, with the exception of those in certain remote areas, and that in the future the commissariat itself would assume direct control of such farms. It may be recalled that the major departments of the commissariat had already undergone alterations in 1934. These depart-ments were now to be reorganized taking into account both the territorial dis-tribution of the sovkhozes and the nature of their type of product. The follow-ing major departments were thus established: the Department of Grain Sovkhozes (with five regional departments); the Department of Meat and Dairy Sovkhozes (with nine regional departments); the Department of Pig Sovkhozes (with six regional departments); the Department of Sheep Sov-khozes (with three regional departments); and a special Department for Karakul Sheep Sovkhozes. The major departments for Educational Establish-ments and Political Affairs established in 1934 were maintained without change. As a consequence of the reorganization, which was to be completed by 15 January 1936, the number of officials of the Central Administration of Sovkhozes was reduced from 6,203 to 2,300. Most of the officials of the abolished trusts were sent to work in the sovkhozes.[63]

This general crackdown on bureaucrats was also extended to the trade unions.[64] As has been pointed out above, attempts had been made to eliminate personnel in the past but were usually unsuccessful. One escape for the threat-ened bureaucrat was simply to get transferred upstairs, and this was done by officials of the Union of Workers of Grain-growing Sovkhozes. When its twelve obkoms were liquidated the personnel there were supposedly to be transferred to the local committees, yet the staff of the Central Committee leapt from thirty-three to forty-four.[65] Other efforts at cutting back staffs were unsuccess-ful as well, for the strength of officials in resisting transfer to the backwoods was impressive. The bureaucracy possessed phoenix-like qualities of continuous resurrection and growth. In the Central Committee staff of the Union of Work-ers of Feather and Poultry Sovkhozes in 1935–6 there were twenty-six persons. In 1940 there were forty-three, of whom twenty were accountants and other technical personnel or, put another way, there was one technical worker for each responsible worker.[66] This growth in the number of paid trade union

63 *Ibid.*; see also *Pravda* and *Izvestiia*, 29 November 1935. For an interesting view on the Soviet bureaucracy see Gur Ofer, 'The Service Section in the Soviet Union' (unpublished PH D. thesis; Harvard University, 1968).
64 'V tsentral'nykh komitetakh soiuzov,' *Voprosy profdvizheniia*, no. 12 (1 November 1937), pp. 59–61.
65 S. Smuglyi, 'Neiasnye roziasneniia,' *Trud*, 16 January 1937, p.3.
66 N. Kozhanov, 'Uporiadochit' shtaty TsK profsoiuzov,' *Trud*, 26 January 1940, p. 3.

officials in the period from 1937 to 1940 was also admitted in *Trud* and in Shvernik's speech at the Tenth Plenum of the ACCTU in August 1940.[67]

In 1940 the number of paid trade union officials was reduced. The impetus for this change was the reorganization of trade union finances, which until this time had been derived from the members' contributions and from funds placed at the disposal of local trade union committees by the management of enterprises, establishments, etc. The financial contributions from the enterprises were now abolished, forcing the trade unions to cover their expenses exclusively out of membership dues. Out of the total of 650 million roubles collected by the trade unions, only 260 million, or 40 per cent, were to be spent on administrative expenses and the remuneration of personnel. The new regulations divided all of the existing trade union central committees into four groups and fixed the maximum proportion of contributions which could be allocated to administrative expenses and remuneration of staff by each. The first group, which comprised thirty-two central committees, could not spend over 25 per cent; the second group, comprising thirty-four central committees not over 30 per cent; the third group, comprising sixty-five central committees not over 40 per cent; and the fourth group, comprising thirty-two central committees 50 per cent. The agricultural trade unions were placed in the last group, emphasizing once more their weak constitution and the great number of officials needed to run them.

The reorganization of finances and the reduction of paid officials were not presented as ends in themselves. The main objective was to transform the system of union management by making the unpaid trade union worker the central figure in the leadership of trade union organizations.[68] The unions were to see to it that not only the local committees but even some raion and higher committees should be run by unpaid trade union members, with the treasurer being the only paid official. This mode of management was not, however, to infringe on the duties of trade unions as administrators of social insurance or to affect the moneys received by them for the protection of labour, cultural activities, etc.

To add to the unions' growing difficulties, the inter-trade union councils were abolished at the Sixth Plenum of the ACCTU in April 1937. As a result of this constant manipulation conducted in an atmosphere of growing terror, trade union work came almost to a standstill.[69] The press increasingly frequently

67 I. Baikalov, 'Sviaz' s massami osnovnoe uslovie uspekha v rabote profsoiuznykh organizatsii,' *Trud*, 15 September 1940, p. 1; Shvernik's speech, *Trud*, 27 August 1940, p. 1.
68 N. Evreinov, 'O sokrashchenii platnogo apparata profsoiuzov,' *Trud*, 15 January 1937, pp. 3–4.
69 Slutsky and Sydorenko, *Profsoiuzy Ukrainy*, p. 121; I. Vilianskii, 'Profsoiuznaia zavad,' *Trud*, 4 April 1937, p. 2; *Profsoiuz rabochikh sel'skogo khoziaistva*, pp. 70–21.

reported cases of embezzlement of trade union funds. Whether or not such cases were real or contrived, the situation, especially in some trade unions in agriculture, appeared to be so bad that the ACCTU had to take action to remedy it. In some areas violation of labour laws became an everyday occurrence, wages were held up, pensions and insurance premiums were not paid, and sick benefits were not distributed to ill workers.[70]

'Trade union democracy' was totally absent. 'Elections' were replaced by appointment from above where local trade unions were concerned, and higher offices were co-opted. The presidiums of many union central committees were completely inactive, and in most cases trade union congresses were simply not convened. Agricultural trade unions were particularly affected. For example, out of the sixty-three oblast committees which existed prior to the 1934 re-organization in the Trade Union of Workers in Land Organs, the membership of thirty-four was appointed by the Organizing Bureau of the unions Central Committee rather than 'elected' at oblast union conferences. The Central Committee of the Union of Workers of Feather and Poultry Sovkhozes did not once report on its work during the whole period. And the 'elections' in the Union for Workers of Animal-breeding Sovkhozes were held for the last time in 1932.[71]

It is true that the Sixth Plenum of the ACCTU held in 1937 instructed that congresses and elections be held in all trade unions during that year. The order was generally obeyed and the trade unions in agriculture held their congresses in the winter of 1937–8. But the 'elections' which took place were of a peculiar nature, for the purges which raged across the country in 1936-7 did not bypass the trade unions. According to Shvernik's speech at the Seventh ACCTU Plenum on 5 September 1938 the elections held in the unions throughout the winter of 1937–8 brought about great changes in the composition of trade union organs. The local committees of all trade unions were renewed by 70 to 80 per cent while 65 per cent of their chairmen were replaced. Oblast and krai committees were renewed by 92 per cent, central committees by 96 per cent, and presidiums of central committees by 87 per cent.[72]

The data for trade unions in agriculture are incomplete, but those which are available indicate that great changes also took place within these organizations. In the Union of Workers in Land Organs 45 per cent of the members of local committees were newly elected. In the Union of Workers of Poultry-breeding Sovkhozes almost 50 per cent of all members of local committees were recently elected. The same was true for the Union of Workers of Meat

70 'Postanovlenie prezidiuma VTsSPS ot 25 marta 1935 goda po dokladu TsK soiuza miaso-molochnykh sovkhozov Urala i Zapadnoi Sibiri,' *Trud*, 3 April 1935, p. 1.
71 *Profsoiuz rabochikh sel'skogo khoziaistva*, p. 79.
72 Shvernik's speech, *Trud*, 5 September 1938, p. 1.

and Dairy Sovkhozes of the South and Centre.[73] The dimensions of the purge are also revealed by the figures for the reduction of paid officials in the agriculture unions. In two of the unions for dairy and meat sovkhoz workers the reduction of the paid apparatus averaged 80 per cent; the Union of Workers of Dairy and Meat Sovkhozes of Kazakhstan and Central Asia's local committees reduced their apparatus by 75 per cent (obkoms by 90 per cent). In 1937 the Central Committee of the union underwent a turnover of 100 per cent; the republican committees, kraikoms, and obkoms of 87 per cent.[74] The fluidity in other agricultural unions was over 50 per cent.[75]

The lack of replacements became so serious that a call was issued to train the newly elected cadres as rapidly as possible. Otherwise, it was pointed out, the work of the trade unions would be brought to a standstill. Some trade union organs, as was the case of Ordzhonikidze kraikom, had even been left with no chairman.[76] In order to speed up the training of new cadres funds were provided for that purpose by the ACCTU, and those central committees which did not spend it for that purpose were heavily criticized.[77]

To compound the confusion even further, the process of splitting unions, which had been started in 1931, continued. As already noted, out of the twenty-three existing trade unions in 1931, forty-four new ones had been created. And this number grew further to forty-seven on the eve of the 1934 organization. At that time, the existing trade unions were again subdivided and out of them 154 new unions were created. In March 1939 the number stood at 168, and in December 1939 this number had grown to 193 trade unions.[78] Between 1934 and 1939 some thirty-nine new trade unions had thus come into existence.[79] This process of organizational fission occurred in agriculture, although to a somewhat lesser extent. Thus, for example, by a resolution of the presidium of the ACCTU of 5 February 1939 the Union of MTS workers of the Centre and South was split into two new trade unions.[80] (Their organizing congresses were held in November 1939.)[81]

73 *Profsoiuz rabochikh sel'skogo khoziaistva*, p. 80.
74 Raisov's speech, *Trud*, 8 May 1939, pp. 2–3.
75 *Profsoiuz rabochikh sel'skogo khoziaistva*, p. 80.
76 V. Logvinov, 'Kraikom profsoiuza bez predsedatelia,' *Trud*, 23 March 1940, p. 4.
77 R. Shlaen, 'Politicheskaia ucheba profsoiuznykh kadrov,' *Trud*, 28 August 1938, p. 2; I. Baikalov, 'Sviaz' s massami osnovnoe uslovie uspekha v rabote profsoiuznykh organizatsii,' *Trud*, 15 September 1940, p. 1.
78 Shvernik's speech at the Eighteenth Party Congress, *Trud*, 15 March 1939, p. 4; *Bol'shaia sovetskaia entsiklopediia* (2nd ed.; Moscow 1955), xxxv, p. 162; *Ibid.*, USSR, *1947*, p. 1754.
79 S. Bergman, 'Stalin i profsoiuzy,' *Trud*, 23 December 1939, p. 2.
80 'Zasedanie Prezidiuma VTsSPS,' *Trud*, 6 February 1939, p. 3.
81 'Pervyi s'ezd profsoiuza MTS Tsentra,' *Trud*, 29 November 1939, pp. 3–4; 'Pervyi s'ezd profsoiuza MTS iuga,' *Ibid.*

There were some bold voices which called for a measure of consolidation and pointed to the complete disorganization prevalent among trade unions in the provinces. At the Seventh Plenum of the ACCTU help in September 1938, for instance, the chairman of the Central Committee of the Union of Workers of Sheep-breeding Sovkhozes tried to call the attention of the plenum to the plight of unions in the localities. To offset the existing fragmentation of unions, he proposed the creation of republican trade unions of animal-breeding sov-khozes. These, he felt, should unite workers in all animal-breeding farms. His suggestion was silently ignored at the plenum, although his position was sum-marized in *Trud*.[82]

A similar proposal was presented at the Eighth Plenum of the ACCTU held in the spring of 1939. In his speech to the plenum, Murashkin, the chairman of the Central Committee of the Union of Workers of Dairy and Meat Sovkhozes of the Urals and Siberia, suggested that in order to improve trade union work in the localities some degree of amalgamation was necessary. In his opinion, the following trade unions ought to have been reamalgamated: the Union of Workers of Dairy and Meat Sovkhozes, the Union of Workers of Horse-breed-ing Sovkhozes, the Union of Workers of Sheep-raising Sovkhozes, and the Union of Workers of Pig-raising Sovkhozes. Reamalgamation, he felt, would not violate the 'production principle' but rather would have a beneficial effect on the unions by strengthening the middle trade union organs.[83] This proposal differed from the one made at the Seventh Plenum in that it looked towards national rather than republican unions. For some time it was as completely ignored as the former. However, other demands were voiced at the Eighth Plenum of the ACCTU, and some changes did take place. With a great deal of satisfaction the chairman of the Central Committee of the Union of MTS Work-ers of the Centre and the South, Petrovskii, noted that the Section for Wages of the ACCTU had finally managed to organize a special office responsible for wages in agriculture. Nonetheless, he criticized the fact that the ACCTU Organization Section had only three instructors responsible for work in agri-culture. He suggested that an Agricultural Section should be set up within the ACCTU.[84] This proposal also met with silence.

However, the Eighth Plenum did not completely ignore the situation in agricultural trade unions, and in its resolutions of 28 April 1939 the ACCTU did call on the unions both in industry and in agriculture to schedule elections in the primary organizations.[85] As a result of these instructions new rounds of

82 *Trud*, 8 September 1938, p. 7.
83 *Trud*, 8 May 1939, p. 3.
84 Petrovskii's speech at the Eighth VTsSPS Plenum, *Trud*, 26 April 1939, p. 3.
85 'Postanovlenie VIII plenum a VTsSPS ot 28 aprelia 1939,' *Trud*, 18 May 1939, p. 1.

elections were held at all levels from the local committees up to the central committees of the unions. In agricultural trade unions national congresses were held in the fall and winter of 1939.

This effort was designed to improve trade union work and organization. It failed. The Tenth Plenum of the ACCTU held in August 1940 provides the best evidence of this failure. There it was again admitted that the trade unions suffered from 'too much formalism and bureaucratic methods of work.' There were 'too many paid trade union officials,' and hence trade union work was 'divorced from the masses.' The trade union structure needed 'some improvement.'[86] Lines of reform were, of course, suggested. The first and the most important matter that was taken up was the question of trade union 'bureaucrats.' In his speech Shvernik made the inevitable complaint that individual trade union leaders were to blame for the existing state of affairs, as they failed to appreciate that the quality of trade union work did not necessarily depend on the number of paid trade union officials available. This wrong notion of what would aid in increasing the effectiveness of the unions produced a situation in which the numbers of paid workers not only did not diminish, but on the contrary appreciably increased. Shvernik thus admitted failure in dealing with the size of the union bureaucracy and also exploded the myth that the former subdivision of trade unions was designed at least partly to reduce the number of paid officials.

As in the past the Tenth Plenum resolved to reduce the number of paid officials several-fold.[87] The funds saved in this way were to be put to use in providing culture and satisfying the everyday needs of the workers. Trade union organs at all levels were forbidden to pay officials' salaries out of enterprise funds, an illegal practice widely in use, and the resolutions established a new table regulating the number of paid officials.[88] In general, as compared with the similar regulations of August 1930, the provisions represented a marked concession to the trade union bureaucracy, who numbered almost twice what they had before.[89] Of course, by now the new trade union hierarchy

86 Shvernik's speech, *Trud*, 27 August 1940, p. 1.
87 'Ob ustranenii nekotorykh nedostatkov v profsoiuznom apparate i uluchshenii raboty profsoiuznykh organov,' *Trud*, 27 August 1940, p. 1.
88 This ratio of paid officials to workers was as follows: one for 500–2000; 2/2000–3000; 3/3000–5000; 4/5000–10000; 5/10000–15000; 6/15000–25000; 7/25000–35000; 8/35000 or over. The tsekh (shop) or otdelencheskii (division) committee which had more than 1500 workers was to have one paid official. 'Ob ustranenii nekotorykh nedostatkov v profsoiuznom apparate i uluchshenii raboty profsoiuznykh organov,' *Trud*, 27 August 1940, p. 1.
89 See 'Postanovlenie prezidiuma VTsSPS o meropriiatiiakh v sviazi s likvidatsiei okrugov,' *Trud*, 26 September 1930, p. 4.

had been thoroughly 're-educated' and there was no need to thin it out as drastically as before.

Henceforth volunteers were to carry on the heaviest load of trade union work both in the higher trade union organs and in the local committees. They were to be of special importance in the latter, where they were to help within the existing standing temporary commissions. In addition, the mass work of trade unions was to be transferred to the tsekh (shop committees in industry) and otdelencheskii (subdivision committees in agriculture). To ensure that these bodies remained active they were to hold meetings at least once every month and a half. The existing profgrupps were to be reorganized in such a way that each one would consist of twenty members. This, it was said, would aid in providing better services for the workers.

In the higher trade union organs from raikoms up to and including obkoms the existing presidiums were abolished and the sections which had been set up within them liquidated. In their place the following commissions were set up: Organization and Mass Work; Labour Protection; Wages; Social Insurance; Culture and Mass Work; and Living and Everyday Needs.[90] It was further provided that all trade union committees from the obkom to the raion level were to meet every week. The role that the party members were to play within the trade unions was again heavily stressed by quoting from Zhdanov's speech at the Eighteenth Party Congress (1939) in which he said that 'the direct task of Communists who work in trade unions is to carry on educational work in trade union organizations in such a way that as a consequence of such work the upper strata of the trade union aktiv will approach the level of partiinost.'[91]

Contrary to what some have written, the Tenth Plenum of the ACCTU did not consider the question of the forthcoming trade union reorganization.[92] But there was a hint that some new changes might be in the offing when the plenum decided to amalgamate into larger units the existing voluntary sporting associations in order to improve their functioning.[93] It was therefore possible to imagine that changes in the same direction might be forthcoming within the unions as well. But these changes did not come about until early in 1941.

Meanwhile, moves were made to consolidate control over the trade unions of the newly annexed areas of the Baltic States, Western Ukraine, Western

90 The following standing commissions are mentioned: wages, labour protection, culture, living and everyday needs, social insurance councils, and in addition temporary commissions were to be created when needed. *Trud*, 27 August 1940, p. 1.
91 I. Baikalov, 'Sviaz' s massami osnovnoe uslovie uspekha v rabote profsoiuznykh organizatsii,' *Trud*, 15 September 1940, p. 1.
92 It is stated by some that it did. *Profsoiuz rabochikh sel'skogo khoziaistva*, p. 87.
93 Baikalov, 'Sviaz s massami,' p. 1.

Belorussia, and Bessarabia. The methods applied bore close resemblance to those used in taking over the trade union organizations after the October revolution. At first the trade unions were amalgamated and reorganized according to the 'production principle.' However, no attempt was made to create local sections of all the existing Soviet trade unions. Thus in Latvia, for example, in place of the former fifty-two trade unions twenty-seven new Soviet unions were set up.[94] Also, in Latvia, unlike in the rest of the USSR, one agricultural trade union was created uniting both workers and employees. This arrangement survived the second world war and lasted until one trade union for agricultural workers in the whole of the USSR was finally set up. The reason for this special treatment of Latvian agricultural labour is completely obscure.

THE REORGANIZATION OF 1941

Although nothing was said about reorganization at the Tenth Plenum of the ACCTU, a reshuffle of the existing structure of trade unions was begun early in 1941. This new change was based on an amalgamation into larger groups of some of the trade unions (including the agricultural ones) and a further subdivision into smaller units of others. In agriculture, as a result of these changes ten new trade unions were created out of the existing fifteen unions.

The first changes, announced in February 1941, concerned the reorganization of the Union of Workers in Land Organs and the Unions of MTS Workers. The announcement of the ACCTU Presidium of 1 February 1941 stated that the 'further existence of independent separate trade unions uniting workers in the MTS and in the Land Organs was not expedient,' and that these unions would form a base on which five territorial trade unions of MTS and Land Organ Workers would be set up.[95] The result of this reorganization was the establishment of the following trade unions: the Union of Workers of MTS and Land Organs of the Centre (headquarters in Moscow); the Union of Workers of MTS and Land Organs of the South (headquarters in Rostov-on-Don); the Union of Workers of MTS and Land Organs of the East (headquarters in Novosibirsk); the Union of Workers of MTS and Land Organs of Ukraine and Moldavia (headquarters in Kiev); and the Union of Workers of MTS and Land Organs of Kazakhstan and Central Asia (headquarters in Alma Alta).[96] Thus, out of three territorial unions and two production-based unions, five territorial unions were created. Three of them had, of course, existed before: those of the

---

94 'Reorganizatsiia profsoiuzov Latvii,' *Trud*, 24 November 1940, p. 1.
95 'Obedinenie profsoiuzov rabochikh MTS s profsoiuzom rabochikh zemel'nykh organov,' *Trud*, 2 February 1941, p. 1. See appendix I.
96 *Ibid.*; *Profsoiuz rabochikh sel'skogo khoziaistva*, p. 87.

Centre, the South, and the East. The trade union for Kazakhstan and Central Asia was created by amalgamating those workers who were employed by MTS but had been members of the Union of Workers of Cotton-growing Sovkhozes with the employees in land organs. The Ukrainian and Moldavian unions came into being after the areas formerly under the jurisdiction of the trade union of the South (including Bessarabia) were geographically separated. This reorganization was done very quickly; only twenty-one days after the first order to reorganize went out from the ACCTU the existing central committees were liquidated and new ones set up.[97]

Out of the eleven existing sovkhoz trade unions five new territorial unions were set up.[98] They included the Union of Sovkhoz Workers of the Centre (headquarters in Moscow); the Union of Sovkhoz Workers of the South (headquarters in Rostov-on-Don); the Union of Sovkhoz Workers of the East (headquarters in Novosibirsk); the Union of Sovkhoz Workers of Ukraine and Moldavia (headquarters in Kiev); and the Union of Sovkhoz Workers of Kazakhstan and Central Asia (headquarters in Alma Alta).[99] This reorganization, it seems, did not meet with unanimous approval. From 16 May until it was interrupted by the German invasion, a discussion raged in the press as to how best to improve the work of the trade unions in the countryside.[100]

97 The Central Committee of the MTS South was liquidated first. *Trud*, 22 February 1941, p. 4; The Central Committee of the Union of Workers of Land Organs was officially liquidated on 1 March 1941. *Trud*, 1 March 1941, p. 4.
98 The ACCTU in announcing this reorganization failed to mention two unions, the Union of Workers of Garden and Vineyard Sovkhozes and the Union of Workers of Cotton-growing Sovkhozes and MTS, and listed only the remaining nine trade unions in sovkhozes. See 'Organizatsiia territorial'nykh profsoiuzov rabochikh sovkhozov,' *Trud*, 28 March 1941, p. 1. It appears, however, that these two trade unions did remain in existence throughout the war period. See 'V borbe za vysokie urozhai: na s'ezdakh profsoiuza rabochikh sel'skogo khoziaistva,' *Trud*, 7 January 1948, p. 2. See appendix I.
99 *Ibid.*; *Profsoiuz rabochikh sel'skogo khoziaistva*, p. 87. In May workers in sugar-beet sozkhozes were united with the sugar workers. See 'Obedinenie soiuzov sakharnoi promyshlennosti i rabochikh sveklosovkhozov: Postanovlenie prezidiuma VTsSPS ot 8 maia,' *Trud*, 11 May 1941, p. 1. Its Central Committee was to be liquidated on 5 June 1941, and the unified Central Committee was to be located in Kharkov.
100 I Bortnikov, 'O profsoiuznoi rabote na sele,' *Trud*, 16 May 1941, p. 3; F. Baksheev, 'Fakty i mysli,' *Trud*, 20 May 1941, p. 3; I Pivikova, 'Prisoediniaius' k mneniiu tov. Bortnikova,' *Trud*, 20 May 1941, p. 3; S. Kriuchin, 'Ob'edinit' sily i sredstva,' *Trud*, 22 May 1941, p. 3; A. Goriachev, 'Nazrevshii vopros,' *Trud*, 22 May 1941, p. 3; I. Cheremisinov, 'Moi vozrazheniia tov. Bortnikovu,' *Trud*, 24 May 1941, p. 3; A. Gorshkov, 'Ob'edinit' profsoiuznye organizatsii sela,' *Trud*, 24 May 1941, p. 3; I Shatov, 'Vopros zasluzhivaiushchii bol'shego vnimaniia,' *Trud*, 24 May 1941, p. 3; M. Ryss, 'Sozdat' edinu bazu kul'turno-massovoi raboty,' *Trud*, 29 May 1941,

If the assertion by some experts on Soviet trade unions that Stalin intended eventually to do away with the unions is true, then a possibility does exist that the discussions might have been an initial step in this direction.[101] One article suggested the amalgamation of all trade unions in the countryside, with the exception of the teachers' union, into 'one Union of Village Workers' (rabotnikov sela).[102] The teachers were to be permitted to have their own separate union. Had the purpose of this article been to lay the groundwork for a further amalgamation and complete liquidation of the trade unions (and this is hardly self-evident), it came to nothing, perhaps only because of the outbreak of war.[103]

The congresses of the new trade unions scheduled to be held in 1941 were postponed because of the war, and in fact met only in 1947. For eight years the level of activity of the agricultural trade unions was low, and no national congresses were held. There can be little doubt that for the duration of the war the industrial unions were accorded strictly preferential treatment, which reflected the 'imperatives of Soviet wartime economic mobilization.' The unions in agriculture continued to exist and to function but on a much smaller scale than those in industry. One indication of this was the fact that all of them were headed by organizing bureaus rather than central committees, as was the case for trade unions in industry.[104] On 11 July 1945 a meeting of the organizational sections of all the central committees of agricultural trade unions was held for the purpose of discussing necessary improvements in trade union affairs. Organizational work was the primary topic of discussion, and a special commission was created and charged with the task of improving trade union

p. 3; F. Potapenko, "Skontsentrirovat' vse sredstva,' *Trud*, 29 May 1941, p. 3; T. Koval, 'Mnenie aulnogo vracha,' *Trud*, 29 May 1941, p. 3; N. Sumchenko, 'Svoevremenno podniatyi vopros,' *Trud*, 11 June 1941, p. 3; L. Amdur, 'Nuzhny li mezhsoiuznye komitety?' *Trud*, 11 June 1941, p. 3; S. Zudin, 'Finansovye neuraditsy,' *Trud*, 11 June 1941, p. 3; E. Vasil'eva, 'Sredstva mestkomov nado kooperirovat',' *Trud*, 11 June 1941, p. 3; A. Veiman, 'Protiv raspylennosti,' *Trud*, 21 June 1941, p. 3; P. Sabo, 'Bumazhnoe rukovodstvo,' *Trud*, 21 June 1941, p. 3; V. Studenikin, 'Nuzhen mezhsoiuznyi klub,' *Trud*, 21 June 1941, p. 3; A. Zakharov, 'Laboratoriia v gostinnitse,' *Trud*, 21 June 1941, p. 3.

101 See Schwarz, 'Trade Unions in the Soviet State,' p. 83.

102 A. Gorshkov, 'Obedinit' profsoiuznye organizatsii sela,' *Trud*, 21 May 1941, p. 3.

103 Elsewhere it has been argued that it was the war which saved and eventually strengthened the trade union movement in the USSR. For example, as soon as October 1941 the first articles appeared in *Trud* indicating that the Soviet leadership had decided to utilize the existing trade union organizations in helping with the war effort. 'Zavodskii profaktiv v dni voiny,' *Trud*, 3 October 1941, p. 3; 'Pervostepennaia zadacha profsoiuznykh organizatsii,' *Trud*, 3 October, 1941, p. 1.

104 P. Kazakov, 'Vyshe uroven' organizatsionno-massovoi raboty: k itogam soveshchaniia zaveduiushchikh orgotdelami TsK profsoiuzov,' *Trud*, 31 July 1945, p. 3.

structure in the villages.[105] Simultaneously a press campaign stressed the need to mobilize the trade union masses and to instil in them an enthusiasm for the cause of postwar reconstruction. The press was full of hints of possible important changes in the organizational structure of trade unions. In the period 1945–7 agricultural trade unions received the lion's share of attention, a sign of changing economic priorities and a recognition of the critical state of Soviet agriculture.[106] Almost two years after the end of the war, it was decided that elections should be held in the trade unions, and an order to that effect with detailed instructions on how to proceed was issued at the beginning of February 1947.[107]

The trade unions were directed to convene their congresses, commencing in May 1947, with conferences at the oblast and krai levels to be called one month prior to the national congress of the particular union. The Sixteenth Plenum of the ACCTU, convened in April 1947, followed directly on the heels of the local elections in the unions and the February Plenum of the Central Committee of the Communist party which dealt with agriculture.[108] At the Sixteenth Plenum of the ACCTU in contrast with the Fifteenth Plenum (end of 1946) trade unions in agriculture received a fair amount of attention. The leadership of these unions was criticized severely for failing to accomplish their organizational and production tasks, and the usual promises were extracted from them to correct their work in the future.

The national congresses of the trade unions began on 20 May 1947 and continued until the end of the year.[109] The results of the congresses were generally regarded as satisfactory, and the work at only six union central committees out of one hundred and thirty-nine was declared unsatisfactory. Out of

105 'Soveshchanie po organizatsionno-massovoi rabote profsoiuzov,' *Trud*, 12 July 1945, p. 1; 'Na soveshcheniakh po org-massovoi rabote profsoiuzov,' *Trud*, 13 July 1945, p. 1.
106 'Usilit' raboty profsoiuzov na zagotovkakh,' *Trud*, 14 August 1945, p. 1; 'V VTsSPS: Profsoiuznye organizatsii v borbe za vysokii urozhai,' *Trud*, 1 April 1945, p. 1.
107 'V VTsSPS: O poriadke provedeniia oblastnykh, kraevykh, respublikanskikh, dorozhnykh, basseinovykh konferentsii i s'ezdov profsoiuzov,' *Trud*, 11 February 1947, p. 1; 'Instruktsiia o provedenii vyborov profsoiuznykh organov,' *Trud*, 8 February 1947, p. 2.
108 'XVI plenum,' *Trud*, 19, 20 April 1947. See also 'Postanovleniia XVI plenuma,' *Trud*, 11 May 1947, p. 2.
109 'Nachalis' s'ezdy profsoiuzov,' *Trud*, 21 May 1947, p. 3; For the report of the first congress of the Union of Workers of MTS and Land Organs of the South see 'Na s'ezdakh profsoiuzov,' *Trud*, 25 November 1947, p. 2; First Congress of the Union of Sovkhoz Workers of the South see 'Na s'ezdakh profsoiuzov,' *Trud*, 28 November 1947, p. 1; 'Na s'ezdakh profsoiuzov,' *Trud*, 19 December 1947, p. 1; First Congress of the Union of Workers of MTS and Land Organs of Ukraine and Moldavia see 'Na s'ezdakh profsoiuzov,' *Trud*, 9 December 1947, p. 2; 'XVII plenum VTsSPS,' *Trud*, 27 December 1947, p. 2.

these six unions, two happened to be in agriculture: the Union of Sovkhoz Workers of Kazakhstan and Central Asia, and the Union of MTS and Land Organs Workers of the East.[110]

But the work of the unions did not seem to improve appreciably after the congresses. Lack of activists and the outmoded trade union structure which led to bureaucratic paper-shuffling were cited as the primary causes. It was, therefore, more than a hint that new changes were in the offing when on 22 September 1948 *Trud* printed an article by the authorized agent of the ACCTU in the Tatar ASSR dealing with the poor condition of trade union activists in the villages and the generally deplorable state of trade union work in the countryside.[111] The main points of the article were that a / trade unions in rural areas were spread too thinly; b / raikoms in general were poorly staffed and even lacked commissions responsible for conducting daily trade union work and where such commissions existed, they performed their tasks poorly; c / many chairmen of raikoms and rabochkoms had no conception of what trade union work was all about, and some of them were not even trade union members; and d / obkoms were not familiar with what was going on at the local level. In fact, one rabochkom chairman had been in jail for a year, but the obkom did not know anything about it.[112]

THE REORGANIZATION OF 1948

In order to improve the effectiveness of trade unions in agriculture, the presidium of the ACCTU in its decree of 29 October 1948 ordered still another amalgamation of the existing unions.[113] Shortly thereafter, on 15 November, unified plenums of the unions were held which approved the suggested reorganizations.[114] The astonishing result of these meetings was that the eleven existing unions in agriculture were divided into two unions: the Union of Sovkhoz Workers of the USSR, and the Union of MTS and Land Organs Workers of the USSR.[115]

110 'Profsoiuzy posle s'ezdov,' *Trud*, 8 January 1948, p. 1; N.V. Popova, 'O rabote s profsoiuznym aktivom,' *Trud*, 20 January 1948, pp. 2–3; 'V borbe za vysokie urozhai: Na sezdakh profsoiuzov rabotnikov sel'skogo khoziaistva,' *Trud*, 7 January 1948, p. 2.

111 A. Dolotkazin, 'O sel'skikh profsoiuznykh aktivistakh,' *Trud*, 22 September 1948, p. 2.

112 *Ibid.* Others hoped that the trade union councils in the republics could do something about the deplorable condition of the trade union staff. M. Babaev, 'Nakanune mezhsoiuznoi konferentsii,' *Trud*, 22 October 1948, p. 2.

113 *Profsoiuz rabochikh sel'skogo khoziaistva*, p. 124.

114 'Na plenumakh TsK profsoiuzov,' *Trud*, 17 November 1948, p. 1.

115 The admission has been made in at least one Soviet source that the six unions of sovkhoz workers had been united in one union of sovkhoz workers during the

The Union of Sovkhoz Workers united the five former unions of sovkhoz workers and replaced several central committees with one located in Moscow. The Union of MTS and Land Organs Workers united the five regional unions; its new Central Committee was also to be located in Moscow. No special elections were to be held to approve the new central committees, which subsequently were formed simply by joining together former central committees and their staffs. The 'control commissions' of both unions came into being in exactly the same manner. The central committee plenums of both unions did decide, however, to hold national congresses of their respective unions as soon as possible. The Union of Sovkhoz Workers decided to hold its First Congress in February 1949. The Union of MTS and Land Organs Workers scheduled its congress for March of that year.[116]

The official explanation for the new reorganization of the unions is only half true. It was said at the time, and has since even been repeated, that the splitting of the unions after 1931 was necessary in order to bring them closer to production units, thus making them more effective. After 1948 division of the unions was no longer necessary because they had managed to develop a sufficient number of qualified cadres to make close central supervision no longer necessary.[117] This explanation obscures the fact that the process of fragmentation did not produce the effect described above but rather had a weakening effect on the trade unions.[118] Nor is it true to say that the trade union cadres were of sufficient number and quality, because as can be observed from the discussion in the press prior to the amalgamation, the staffs of agricultural trade unions were small, inexperienced, and inactive. It is probably much closer to the truth to say that the amalgamations occurred as a result of the February Plenum of the Central Committee of the CPSU, which called for further 'sacrifices' and reorganizations to make the Five Year Plan a success. Just as the desire to facilitate political control prompted the division of unions in the 1930s, so the objective of economy now motivated their amalgamation.

The first congresses of both trade unions were held in March 1949 – in the Ukrainian city of Kharkov, not Moscow.[119] It appears that the date for the Congress of the Union of Sovkhoz Workers, scheduled for February, was post-

war. This step was attributed to economic and efficiency factors, namely the small number of trade union members. *Istoriia profdvizheniia v SSSR*, p. 367. See appendix I.

116 'Na plenumakh TsK profsoiuzov,' *Trud*, 17 November 1948, p. 1. The unions of garden and vineyard workers as well as that of the tea and subtropical sovkhozes continued to exist separately.

117 *Profsoiuz rabochikh sel'skogo khoziaistva, op. cit.*, p. 125.

118 Slutsky and Sydorenko, *Profsoiuzy Ukrainy*, p. 121.

119 'S'ezd rabochikh i sluzhashchikh MTS i zemorganov,' *Trud*, 6 March 1949, p. 2; 'Bol'she vnimaniia koldogovoram v MTS,' *Trud*, 24 March 1949, p. 2. For the report

poned a month. No explanations were offered for either of these curious pheno-
mena. Perhaps they were connected in some way with the so-called 'Leningrad
case' which was then underway. Local elections and reorganizations began in
November 1948 but were interrupted and not completed until after the first
national congresses of both unions in March 1949.

In April 1949, after an interval of seventeen years, the Tenth Congress of
Soviet Trade Unions was held in Moscow. This event was, in a way, an indication that the trade unions had received a new lease on life.[120] At this congress
the representatives of both agricultural trade unions demanded that more attention be paid to their unions than hitherto, including more coverage of their
activities in the newspaper *Trud*. Specific demands for favourable action were
also voiced. For example, M.E. Iotko, the chairman of the Union of MTS and
Land Organs Workers, requested a speedy decision on the question of whether
or not to create obkoms for his union in Belorussia which had over six hundred trade union organizations to supervise.[121]

Both agricultural trade unions held their second congress in March 1951:
the Union of Sovkhoz Workers in Kharkov, and the Union of MTS and Land
Organs Workers in Saratov.[122] Neither of these congresses introduced any
organizational changes. In September 1951, however, acting in accordance
with an August joint resolution of the party's Central Committee and the
Council of Ministers dealing with socialist competition, and in accordance with
directives on the same subject of the Sixth Plenum of the ACCTU held in August,
plenums of the central committees of both unions met and introduced organizational changes. Both plenums were attended by central committee members
and by the chairmen of obkoms, repkoms, and by a large number of activists.
As a result of these discussions, the production and mass section was set up
within the central committee of each, with corresponding sections at the
republican, krai, and oblast levels. At the same time the primary trade union
organizations were told to organize production and mass commissions.[123]

THE REORGANIZATION OF 1953

Further reorganization was in store for the agricultural trade unions following
Stalin's death. On 18 April 1953 the Presidium of the ACCTU decreed another

on the First Congress of Sovkhoz Workers see 'Mnozhit' riady stakhanovskikh
    sovkhozov,' *Trud*, 26 March 1949, p. 2.
120 See 'X-yi s'ezd profsoiuzov SSSR,' *Trud*, 19–29 April 1949.
121 M.E. Iotko's speech, *Trud*, 24 April 1949, p. 2.
122 *Profsoiuz rabochikh sel'skogo khoziaistva*, p. 129; 'U rabotnikov sela,' *Trud*,
    18 March 1951, p. 1.
123 *Profsoiuz rabochikh sel'skogo khoziaistva*, p. 131.

amalgamation of the trade unions in the countryside.[124] The Union of Workers and Employees in Agriculture and State Procurement that was now organized grouped together the two existing trade unions in agriculture and, in addition, an organization which until then had always been separate, the Union of Workers in Flour Mills and Grain Elevators. Again the reorganization was explained as an attempt to improve and strengthen trade union work in agriculture and to reduce the number of paid officials. It is much more plausible to assume, however, that the reorganization was an attempt to bring the trade union structure into line with the changes in the structure of the Soviet ministries. Indeed, one article openly stated that this reorganization was only one link in the changes that occurred in the USSR in 1953 in anticipation of the highly significant September 1953 Plenum of the Central Committee of the CPSU, which was concerned with the problems of agriculture.[125]

The decree of the ACCTU was immediately obeyed. On 18 April 1953 the first meeting of the central committee of the new union was held and a presidium elected. The speed with which this was done suggests that it was primarily an attempt to facilitate a further extension of party control in agriculture. In September the Plenum of the Central Committee of the CPSU addressed itself to the tasks of improving agricultural production. Following this plenum, the Union of Workers and Employees in Agriculture and State Procurement became extremely active. Throughout October and November meetings of oblast, krai, and republican committees of the union were held, leading up to the Second Plenum of the newly created union in December 1953.[126] In December a consultative conference was also convened in Moscow attended by the chairmen of the MTS and sovkhoz committees of the union. The purpose of this conference was to indicate the tasks of trade unions in improving conditions in agriculture. Soon after these events, the February 1954 Plenum of the Central Committee of the CPSU announced the Virgin Lands campaign, in which the Union of Workers and Employees in Agriculture and State Procurement was to play a significant part.[127] The party plenum was followed by the Thirteenth Plenum of the ACCTU, which discussed in greater detail the question of the role of the trade unions in this campaign.[128]

124 'Plenum TsK profsoiuza rabochikh i sluzhashchikh sel'skogo khoziaistva i zagotovok,' *Trud*, 19 April 1953, p. 1; *Profsoiuz rabochikh sel'skogo khoziaistva*, p. 134.
125 'Plenum TsK profsoiuza rabochikh i sluzhaschikh sel'skogo khoziaistva i zagotovok,' *Trud*, 19 April 1953, p. 1.
126 *Profsoiuz rabochikh sel'skogo khoziaistva*, p. 144.
127 N.S. Khrushchev, 'O dal'neishem uvelichenii proizvodstva zerna v strane i ob usvoenii tselinnykh i zalezhnykh zemel',' *Pravda*, 24 February 1954, pp. 1–3.
128 *Profsoiuz rabochikh sl'skogo khoziaistva*, p. 149; 'Uchastie profsoiuzov v rabote po pod'emu sel'skogo khoziaistva,' *Trud*, 18 April 1954, p. 1.

In an atmosphere of change and expectation generated by the Virgin Lands program the First Congress of the Union of Workers and Employees in Agriculture and State Procurement took place in early April 1954.[129] Although at the congress itself no extensive criticisms of existing conditions were voiced, soon afterwards it was pointed out that if trade union tasks were to be fulfilled, the number of paid officials had to be increased at the local level. Shortly afterwards the ACCTU agreed to increase the number of paid chairmen of local trade uinon committees. But the selection of paid workers proceeded very slowly. For example, by 17 April twenty-five such men were to be designated of whom twenty were to be selected by the ACCTU while five were to be chosen by the Saratov oblast sovprof, but by 20 May only one man had been selected by the sovprof and none of the twenty from Moscow had arrived.[130]

At the congress some suggested setting up either village trade union councils (if more than one trade union had local committees in the given locality) or at least raion trade union councils, whose task would be to co-ordinate the work of trade unions in rural areas.[131] Reminiscent of the raion trade union councils of the early 1930s and the volsekretariats of the 1920s, the proposal was not adopted and nothing more was heard of it for some time.[132]

The Second Congress of the union, held after the Twentieth Party Congress in March 1956, adopted regulations and a statute.[133] At the congress there was

129 The congress opened on 5 April. 'Vyshe uroven' raboty na sele,' *Trud*, 6 April 1954, p. 2; 'Vchera na s'ezdakh: u rabotnikov sela,' *Trud*, 7 April 1954, p. 2; 'Privedem v deistvie use rezervy: pervyi s'ezd rabochikh i sluzhaschikh sel'skogo khoziaistva i zagotovok,' *Trud*, 8 April 1954, p. 2; 'Na plenumakh TsK profsoiuzov,' *Trud*, 10 April 1954, p. 2.
130 K. Voinov, 'V nadezhde na rozshirenie shtatov: pochemu ne nalazhivaetsia profrabota v novykh sovkhozakh,' *Trud*, 20 May 1954, p. 2.
131 N. Perov-Terent'ev, 'Na sele nuzhny mezhsoiuznye proforgany,' *Trud*, 26 May 1954, p. 2; F. Potashnikov, 'Zhilishchno-bytovaia rabota profsoiuznogo komiteta,' *Trud*,
132 There were pobably some voices to that effect at the Eleventh Congress of Trade Unions, which was held in June 1954. For example, S.V. Egurazdov criticized the existing structure of the obkoms by saying that there were too many functional sections within them whose work was not properly co-ordinated. He also was critical of the practice of setting up 'sections on production and mass work.' According to him, 'the questions of socialist competition cannot be decided separately from those of organization of labour norms and wages.' He proposed the amalgamation of the commissions. *Trud*, 9 June 1954, p. 4. For this he was later severely reprimanded by M.G. Gatullina-Urazova, who states that the amalgamation of commissions would be an error and that 'permanent commissions in local committees were created in 1937–38 on the initiative of the Party and that they fully justified themselves.' *Trud*, 15 June 1954, p. 3.
133 *Profsoiuz rabochikh sel'skogo khoziaistva*, p. 159. A heated discussion raged in the USSR in the spring and summer of 1957 over the trade unions and their functions.

a great deal of talk about collective leadership, democracy, and criticism and self-criticism as the best tools for achieving mass mobilization and a rise in production. But no organizational changes were advanced until late 1957, when the December Plenum of the Central Committee of the CPSU devoted its attention specifically to the work of the trade unions.[134] As a result of destalinization and the party's new attitude towards the trade unions, a greater degree of freedom of action was given to the local union committees.[135]

THE 1958 DEBATE

Of much greater immediate importance for the future of the agricultural trade union was the decision of the CPSU Plenum of February 1958 to reorganize the MTS.[136] The Third Congress of the union, held in April 1958, addressed itself to some of the problems raised by this forthcoming reorganization.[137] But although a great deal was said about the tasks of the union in the new situation, such as 'participating actively in setting up the RTS (Repair Tractor Stations) and staffing them with qualified cadres,' very little is known about what was then being said about the fate of MTS workers and their status as trade union members. Changes were introduced into the union's statute, but in the absence of a copy of the statute it is impossible to say with precision what particular changes beyond the change of name and liquidation of local committees in the MTS were instituted.[138] It is highly probable that the statute regulated the setting up of trade union committees in the newly created RTS.

Almost certainly, however, the question of kolkhoz trade union organizations was completely ignored.[139] Nor is it possible to determine with full cer-

---

But this only indirectly affected the Union of Workers and Employees in Agriculture and State Procurement. During this period many trade unions were amalgamated (their number again stood at forty-seven). For a more detailed discussion see Peter J. Potichnyj, 'The Recent Changes in Soviet Trade Unions' (unpublished master's thesis; Department of Public Law and Government, Columbia University, 1961).

134 *Profsoiuz rabochikh sel'skogo khoziaistva*, p. 163.

135 'O pravakh fabrichnogo, zavodskogo, mestnogo komiteta professional'nogo soiuza,' *Pravda*, 16 July 1958, p. 1.

136 'O dal'neishem razvitii kolkhoznogo stroia i reorganizatsii mashinno-traktornykh stantsii,' *Trud*, 18 April 1958.

137 *Profsoiuz rabochikh sel'skogo khoziaistva*, p. 165.

138 N. Nikitushkin and N. Beliaev, 'Uverennym shagom: s'ezd profsoiuza rabochikh i sluzhashchikh sel'skogo khoziaistva i zagotovok,' *Trud*, 10 April 1958, p. 2. 'V obstanovke bol'shego podema: na s'ezde profsoiuza rabochikh i sluzhashchikh sel'skogo khoziaistva i zagotovok,' *Trud*, 8 April 1958, p. 1; 10 April 1958, p. 2.

139 An article written during the Fourth Congress of the Union in 1960 complained that

tainty whether this question was raised at the congress at all, although it is quite difficult to see how it could have been overlooked, especially as discussion of this point had become quite heated and was extensively reported in the press since permission to discuss the issue was given in a special decree issued by the presidium of the ACCTU.[140] Because of its importance as an indicator of the changes that have occurred in the USSR in recent years, it is worthwhile to consider this discussion in more detail.

Elsewhere in this study, the question of trade union membership will be considered. Here an attempt will be made to reconstruct only that part of the discussion which dealt with organizational questions. The first of these was the problem of which organizational form would best encompass former MTS trade union members who were now kolkhoz employees. Eliminating for discussion purposes those who flatly opposed the setting up of trade union organizations in kolkhozes there remain the protagonists of two distinct schemes. One group argued that the best way to solve the whole problem would be to set up rabochkoms uniting all trade union members within any given kolkhoz. The most outspoken supporter of this idea was S.V. Egurazdov, the chairman of the Union of Workers and Employees in Agriculture and State Procurement, who stated that, 'to do otherwise would be to go counter to the interest of the production principle.' He was especially opposed to the idea that only trade union groups should be set within kolkhozes and that they should be placed under the direct control of RTS rabochkoms, because 'all basic questions of kolkhoz growth after the reorganization will be decided by the management of the kolkhoz and not by the RTS.' Therefore, he argued, 'in these conditions dual subordination of trade union organs is inconceivable ... a primary trade union committee should therefore be located in the kolkhoz' and should 'carry on its work jointly with the kolkhoz managements.'[141]

Egurazdov was supported in this proposal by, among others, the chairman of the Krasnodar Trade Union Council, M. Gladkov, who would not have limited trade union membership to former MTS employees but would have

nothing had been done to help former trade union members now in kolkhozes.
I. Paramonov and F. Rasporkin, "Govoriat khoziaeva zemli,' *Trud*, 1 April 1960, p. 2.
140 See 'Ob uchastii profsoiuznykh organizatsii v obsuzhdenii tezisov doklada N.S. Khrushcheva "O dal'neishem razvitii kolkhoznogo stroia i reorganizatsii MTS": Postanovlenies prezidiuma VTsSPS,' *Trud*, 11 March 1958, p. 1. The very first article that appeared in this discussion was in *Trud*. F. Breus, 'Kurs vernyi, za nami delo ne stanet: reportazh s sobraniia mekhanizatorov MTS,' *Trud*, 11 March 1958, p. 2; International Labour Organization, *The Trade Union Situation in the USSR* (Geneva 1960), p. 92.
141 S.V. Egurazdov, 'O profsoiuznykh organizatsiikh na sele,' *Trud*, 26 March 1958, p. 2.

given union membership to those kolkhozniks who wished it: 'Further development of the kolkhoz system not only does not stand in contradiction to the inclusion of kolknozniks among the trade union membership, but demands it.'[142] Egurazdov's view did not prevail, but he continued to press it at the Twelfth Trade Union Congress in March 1959.[143]

A much more numerous group of supporters of trade union organizations in kolkhozes took the view that at the present time it was possible to set up trade union groups only and not full-fledged independent local committees. One of the most important voices in support of this view was that of M. Kabanov, a senior scientific assistant of the Institute of Marxism-Leninism of the Central Committee of the CPSU. He supported the idea of trade union membership for former MTS employees, offering the appropriate quotations from Lenin and Khrushchev, but he stopped short of assigning the trade union rights of local committees to the trade union bodies of kolkhozes. 'I think,' he said, 'it would be correct to create at first trade union groups of machine operators and workers in electrical stations and subsidiary enterprises; then in animal husbandry farms; and finally in the field brigades.' These trade union groups, he felt, should be closely tied to the local trade union committees in the RTS. But although opposed to giving trade union groups in kolkhozes status independent of the local committees, he did not exlude such a possibility for the future: 'At a given period, there will arise a need for the trade union of the entire kolkhoz.'[144] Other supporters of this view (e.g., N. Abdullaev, chairman of the Uzbek Republic Committee of the Union of Workers and Employees in Agriculture and State Procurement, and A. Mikhailov, a kolkhoz agronomist) also thought that the first step should be groups and that only in the future should trade union locals be organized in kolkhozes.[145] This view prevailed and received the sanction of the higher trade union organs.[146]

142 M. Gladkov, 'Davaite podumaem i ob etom,' *Trud*, 27 March 1958, p. 2.
143 S.V. Egurazdov's speech, *Trud*, 26 March 1959, p. 3. By now, he argued, it was foolish not to transform trade union groups into independent local committees free from the RTS rabochkoms because a / RTS had a very small number of employees and workers, on the average 30–40, and no paid trade union workers; b / kolkhoz trade union groups united on the average from 25–150 members each and thus were larger and could act independently; and c / raikoms should be created to co-ordinate the work of all local committees.
144 M. Kabanov, 'Podderzhivaiu predlozhenie mekhanizatorov Eubekshi-Kazakhskoi MTS,' *Trud*, 8 March 1958, p. 1.
145 N. Abdullaev, 'Mozhet li profsoiuz ob'edinat' kolkhoznykh mekhanizatorov?' *Trud*, 20 March 1958, p. 2; A. Mikhailov, 'Slovo kolkhoznogo agronoma,' *Trud*, 22 March 1958, p. 2.
146 See 'O zadachakh profsoiuznykh organizatsii v sviazi s postanovleniem TsK KPSS i

Thus, a discussion that lasted close to four months ended in a victory for the former MTS workers, whereby they retained their trade union rights and privileges. They were not permitted to set up local committees, but they were allowed trade union groups subordinated to the local committees in the RTS. This decision was widely acclaimed in the press, and throughout 1958 and the beginning of 1959 the newspapers featured accounts of how trade union groups were enthusiastically organized by former MTS workers.[147] At the same time there were also reports that some kolkhoz chairmen were opposed to the idea of setting up trade union groups and tried to place all kinds of obstacles in their path.[148]

Soon, however, it was realized that the rabochkoms of RTS were not capable of directing, guiding, and co-ordinating the work of kolkhoz trade union groups. The main reason was that they themselves had no paid apparatus and were quite small in comparison to the trade union groups. Sometimes an RTS had to serve an entire raion where in the past there had been five or even six MTS.[149] Hence there was more and more agitation in favour of allowing some trade union body at the raion level to guide and co-ordinate trade union work.[150] This proposal gained added weight in those areas in which the obkoms charged with this responsibility were also weak, or in areas such as the Kirgiz republic, where obkoms had been abolished altogether and all local trade unions subordinated directly to the Republican Committee.[151] It should be added, of course, that the inactivity of local trade unions was not only a result of lack of proper co-ordination from higher trade union organs, but also – and perhaps to an even greater extent – to past habits of passivity. Even though

Soveta Ministrov SSSR (O dal'neishem razvitii kolkhoznogo stroia i reorganizatsii mashinno traktornykh stantsii),' *Trud*, 8 June 1958, p. 1.
147 D. Marakov, 'Profsoiuznye gruppy v kolkhozakh,' *Trud*, 18 June 1958; 'Pered bol'shoi zhatvoi,' *Trud*, 18 June 1958, p. 1; 'Profsoiuznye gruppy v kolkhozakh,' *Trud*, 1 July 1958, p. 1; I. Pikorevich, 'V dni zhatvy,' *Trud*, 8 July 1958, p. 1; 'Bol'shaia zhatva,' *Trud*, 11 July 1958, p. 1.
148 F. Rasporkin, 'Kak eto nachalos,' *Trud*, 25 July 1958, p. 2; 'Goriachie dni,' *Trud*, 29 July 1958, p. 2.
149 M. Gladkov, 'Novoe v zhizni sel'skikh profsoiuzov,' *Trud*, 3 August 1958, p. 2; K. Zhukov, 'Neustanno rastit' i vospityvat' profsoiuznye kadry,' *Trud*, 10 October 1958, p. 2.
150 'Profsoiuznye gruppy v kolkhozakh,' *Trud*, 27 August 1958, p. 1; K. Zhukov, 'Neustanno rastit' i vospityvat' profsoiuznye kadry,' *Trud*, 10 October 1958, p. 2. During the reorganization discussions in 1957 the creating of raion sovprofs was rejected. A. Gorshkov, 'Polozhit konets razobshchennosti,' *Trud*, 19 April 1957, p. 2; K. Zen'ko and L.L. Semenova, 'Rabotu profsoiuzov na uroven' novykh zadach,' *Trud*, 11 June 1957, p. 2; 'Trudiashchyiesia sovetuiut,' *Trud*, 20 April 1957, p. 2; A. Akopian, 'Na uroven' novykh zadach,' *Trud*, 7 May 1957, p. 3.
151 A Tiumenbaev, 'Bez lishnikh zvenev,' *Trud*, 21 October 1958, p. 2.

the trade union locals did receive greater rights and responsibilities in July 1958, these rights were far from fully exercised.[152]

The local committees of the Union of Workers and Employees in Agriculture and State Procurement were especially inactive and in some localities not even properly organized. This unfortunate state of affairs was disclosed at the Third Plenum of the ACCTU, which met in Moscow in January 1960 and severely criticized trade union work in the Ukraine, Kazakhstan, and the Stavropol and Novosibirsk oblasts, the primary grain-producing regions of the country. In addition, the performance of the Central Committee of the union was discussed and severely criticized, especially for bureaucratic and formalistic methods of work in the Ukraine and Kazakhstan.[153]

The Fourth Congress of the union, held in March and April 1960, echoed these criticisms.[154] One speaker was bold enough to declare that 'even now the question of the trade union organization in kolkhozes has not yet been solved.'[155] The Fourth Congress 'demanded that the rabochkoms of sovkhozes, RTS and other agricultural enterprises fully utilize their rights given to them by the Party and government, and fight decisively all attempts to minimize the role of the mass public organization.'[156] This verbal prodding did not help a great deal. Moreover, the RTSs themselves proved a failure and were replaced by a new organization, the Vsesoiuzsel khoztekhnika (All-Union Farm Machinery Association), which was formed in early 1961 to procure machinery for both collective and state farms and to service it through its own country machinery associations.[157] This change undermined one argument against the establishment of trade union committees in kolkhozes.

THE CHANGES OF 1962

In 1962 the Ministry of Agriculture was replaced by an agency called the All-Union Committee for Agriculture, which was charged with the duty of coordinating agricultural plans and of assuring fulfilment of party and state directives. The chain of command of the new All-Union Committee for Agri-

---

152 'Polozhenie o pravakh fabrichnogo, zavodskogo, mestnogo komiteta professional'-
    nogo soiuza,' *Spravochnik profsoiuznogo rabotnika* (Moscow: Profizdat, 1952),
    pp. 155–9.
153 *Profsoiuz rabochikh sel'skogo khoziaistva*, p. 193.
154 'S'ezd profsoiuza rabochikh i sluzhashchikh sel'skogo khoziaistva i zagotovok,' *Trud*,
    29 March 1960, p. 2.
155 K. Poromonov and F. Rasporkin, 'Govoriat khoziaeva zemli,' *Trud*, 1 April 1960,
    p. 2.
156 *Profsoiuz rabochikh sel'skogo khoziaistva*, p. 194.
157 Hazard, *The Soviet System of Government*, p. 132.

culture ran through committees at the republic and oblast levels to the local level, where inter-raion production administrations were established. These administrations, vested with broad authority in agricultural management at the local level, were to supervise state and collective farms. At the November 1962 Plenum of the Central Committee these changes were extended with the party apparatus also being organized into two parts – one concerned with industry and the other with agriculture – according to the production principle. The first point of co-ordination for these separate hierarchies was located at the republic level, where there was to be a single Central Committee and Presidium.[158]

The 1962 reforms in agricultural administration and party structure necessitated changes also in the organization of the trade unions. The Eleventh Plenum of the ACCTU, which met in late 1962, resolved that 'the structure of the trade union should be subordinated to further growth of the national economy.'[159] The territorial principle on which the inter-trade union councils were based was found especially wanting in its capacity to direct equal attention to the problems of industry and agriculture. As a result it was resolved that the inter-trade union councils at the krai and oblast level would be split into two independent councils: one co-ordinating the functions of unions operating in industry, construction, transportation, and municipal services; the other concerned with trade unions in agriculture and those serving the rural population.[160] In addition, the republican inter-trade union councils and the inter-trade union councils of the autonomous oblasts each received a bureau responsible for the trade unions in industry and a bureau for agriculture.[161] Similar bureaus were also established in the ACCTU.[162] The structure of inter-trade union organs is illustrated in figure 1.

In those krais and oblasts in which two inter-trade union councils were to be set up, the following unions were also to have two oblast or krai committees: Workers of State Trade and Consumer Co-operatives, Workers of State Institutions, Workers of Culture, Workers of Education, Workers of Higher Schools and Scientific Institutions, and Workers of the Rural Construction and Building Materials Industries. In those areas where the situation warranted it committees of the inter-trade union councils were also to be established in the kolkhoz-sovkhoz production administrations. Committees of the

158 Fainsod, *How Russia is Ruled*, p. 203.
159 'Boevaia programma v deistvii,' *Sovetskie profsoiuzy*, no 2 (January 1963), p. 3. These changes were embodied in the Trade Union Statute adopted by the Thirteenth Trade Union Congress, November 1963, *Trud*, 13 November 1963, pp. 2–3.
160 *Ustav professional'nykh soiuzov SSSR* (Moscow: Profizdat, 1963), article 15.
161 *Ibid.*, article 39.
162 *Ibid.*, article 30.

FIGURE 1

Structure of inter-trade union organs, 1962–4

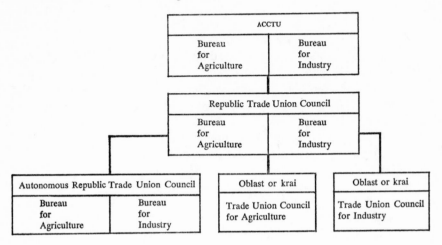

Union of Workers and Employees in Agriculture and State Procurement were to be established within each sovkhoz-kolkhoz production administration in order to co-ordinate the activities of union committees in kolkhozes and sovkhozes and other rural enterprises.[163] Figure 2 illustrates the new structure.

This division closely parallelled the new structure of the party apparatus. In both, the republic was the level at which the two halves of the organization met. It seemed that there was a much greater degree of centralized supervision than before, when control had been exercised through the MTS. Now both the state and collective farms were treated equally in this respect. (It could be that this move was to facilitate the inclusion of the collectivized sector within the state sector in the near future.) With the removal of Khrushchev in 1964 all of the above changes were cancelled and the structure reverted to that which had existed in the period prior to 1962. This brought about the re-establishment of the Ministry of Agriculture and consequent reorganization of trade union structure to fit the new situation.

SOVKHOZ TRADE UNION ORGANIZATIONS

Turning to the sovkhoz trade union committees, it may be said that their present structure and function are in most instances dictated by the particular

163 *Ibid.*

FIGURE 2

Structure of the Union of Workers and Employees in Agriculture and State Procurement, 1962–4

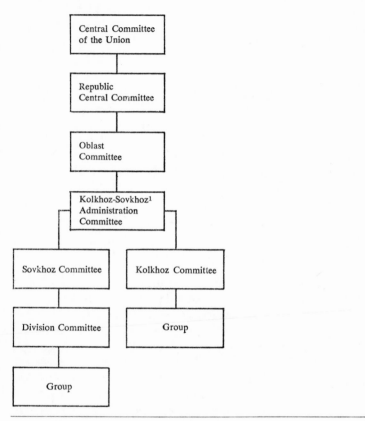

1   In 1965 the Kolkhoz-Sovkhoz Administration Committee was replaced by the Raion (District) Committee of the Union.

nature of the work their members are doing.[164] This assertion is particularly true of agriculture, where the work is of a seasonal character and where each individual is called upon to perform many tasks requiring varied lengths of time and performed at different times of the day.

164 For example, the local trade union committees in sheep-breeding farms are nomadic. N. Ogolev, 'Sviaz' s massami eto osnovnoe,' *Trud*, 21 February 1936, p. 3; 'Prof-gruppa v stepi,' *Trud*, 26 March 1940, p. 3.

TRADE UNION CONFERENCES

In an agricultural environment, unlike in the factory, it is often quite impossible to call a general meeting of all the workers of an enterprise. It was found that it would be necessary for many people to travel inconveniently long distances, and that because of this important work in the field or elsewhere on the farm would be left undone. It was also realized that each job was done by a given group of people and that it was comparatively easy to get these people together for a meeting. As a result, it was decided to hold 'conferences' rather than general meetings in the sovkhozes.[165] These conferences are called by the rabochkoms periodically and are attended by delegates elected by the members of each trade union group. The conference is formally valid when no less than two-thirds of the delegates are present. Meetings are also occasionally held which include only people in particular lines of work, such as mechanics, millers, workers in the poultry farm, or shepherds. On the other hand, meetings of the trade union and management aktiv are called quite frequently.[166]

ELECTIONS

The rabochkom is elected either by a general meeting of the trade union members of a sovkhoz or by a 'conference.' The rabochkom as well as the revizionnaia kommissiia (auditing commission) are elected for a period of one year. The rabochkom usually varies in size from five to eleven members, but in very large sovkhozes, especially those set up in the Virgin Lands, it may be even larger, rising to twenty or more members. Voting at elections is supposed to be secret. Nominations can be made either by a list presented to the electoral meeting or from the floor. Each candidate can be criticized and removed from the list if objections are raised against him. To be elected, a person has to receive a majority of votes in comparison with other candidates and the votes of no less than 50 per cent of the trade union members or delegates present at the electoral meeting. Votes are counted by an auditing commission elected for this purpose at the meeting by an open vote. The statute also permits emergency or non-periodic elections, which can be held if at least one-third of the trade union membership of the sovkhoz so desires, or if the higher trade union organ so orders.[167]

165 M. Mel'nikov, *Delegatskie sobraniia v sovkhozakh na plantatsiiakh i v selakh* (Moscow: Knigoizdatel'stvo VTsSPS, 1928).
166 V. Kon'kov and V. Liutikov, *Kak organizovat' rabotu profsoiuznogo komiteta v sovkhoze* (Moscow: Profizdat, 1962), p. 9.
167 *Ibid.*, p. 10.

The Fifth Congress of the Union of Workers and Employees in Agriculture and State Procurement, held in March 1962, introduced into its statute those provisions of the new party program which required that at least one-half of each executive committee of any public organization not be re-elected and that the leading workers of mass organizations not be elected for more than two terms.[168] But these innovations were dropped after the Twenty-third Party Congress decided to reverse these provisions in the party statutes. And in 1965 the raion committees replaced the Committee of Kolkhoz-Sovkhoz Administrations.[169]

COMMISSIONS

The work of the rabochkom is carried on either by permanent or temporary commissions. Since 1957 the number and need for such commissions has been decided by each rabochkom independently. Until then these questions were within the jurisdiction of the higher trade union organs.[170]

The chairmen of the commissions are chosen by open vote at the first meeting of the rabochkom when the chairman, vice-chairman, and treasurer, of the rabochkom are elected. Usually those designated are requested to fill out their commissions by the next meeting of the rabochkom.[171] The following permanent commissions are ordinarily organized: Wages; Production and Mass Work; Invention and Rationalization; Labour Protection; Social Insurance; Living and Everyday Needs; Control over Trade Enterprises and Public Dining; Pensions; Mass Culture; and Work among the Children. The commissions thereby mirror the basic duties of the trade unions.

Since the objective of having the commissions is not only to fulfil specific tasks but also to elicit participation in public activities by as many people as possible, the commissions themselves are frequently subdivided into smaller groups. For example, the Mass-Production Commission of the rabochkom of the Shuiskii Sovkhoz, Ivanovo oblast, is subdivided into two groups, one for 'socialist competition,' the other for economic analysis of the performance of the sovkhoz. Often, the Commission for Living and Everyday Needs has subgroups for control over repair jobs in individual homes or sovkhoz pro-

---

168 *Programma Kommunisticheskoi Partii Sovetskogo Soiuza priniataia XXII sezdom KPSS* (Moscow: *Pravda*, 1961), pp. 102–3.
169 At that time about 2,500 Raikoms were organized: 'Profsoiuzy-aktivnye uchastniki vsenarodnoi bor'by za dal'neishii pod-em sel'skogo khoziaistva,' *Sovetskie profsoiuzy*, no 24 (December 1966), p. 32.
170 Kon'kov, *Kak organizovat'rabotu*, p. 11; He probably had in mind the December plenum and the law on factory committees of 1958.
171 *Ibid.*, p. 16.

perty and for stimulating individual efforts in the building of housing.[172] Of special interest is the establishment of the Commission on Workers' Gardens, which represents an attempt to run the work of individual plots collectively.[173]

In addition to permanent commissions there are also temporary or ad hoc commissions, which are organized from time to time. Their job is one of spot-checking and determining what has been left undone, or should be done; in short, one of investigation.[174] In small trade union organizations temporary commissions frequently take the place of permanent ones. Quite often the number of trade union members does not permit the creation even of temporary commissions, and in such cases the work is performed by individual members of the rabochkom.

DIVISION COMMITTEES

The rabochkom relies on its activities, not only on the various commissions, but also on otdelencheskie komitety (division committees). These are the sovkhoz equivalent of 'shop committees' in industry, and are organized to carry on trade union work in particular divisions of the sovkhoz. In certain matters (e.g., the admission of new members) they are vested with a degree of autonomous authority, although they are ultimately subordinate to the rabochkom of the sovkhoz; 'in some cases these committees are permitted to deal directly with the management of enterprises.'[175]

TRADE UNION GROUPS

There are also trade union groups organized in various brigades – the field-tractor brigade, livestock-tending brigade, garage, etc. – subordinate either to a division committee or directly to the rabochkom.[176] The groups are led by a trade union group organizer elected for a period of one year by the group in an open vote at its general meeting. To help him carry on the job, a number of individuals are elected and designated as social insurance delegates, mass-production organizers, cultural work organizers, labour inspectors, sports organizers, etc. The number of these activists, who are also elected for a period

172 *Ibid.*, p. 22.   173 *Ibid.*, pp. 22–3.
174 *Ibid.*, p. 23.
175 Otdeleniia or otdelencheskie komitety are mentioned first in *Trud* (30 December 1939) as being in existence in state grain sovkhozes, while the Second Congress of the Union of Workers of Grain-growing Sovkhozes mentions these subdivisions as existing within the local organizations: rabochkom, otdelenie, tsekhom (uchast-kom), and profgruppa. 'Posle s'ezda profsoiuza,' *Trud*, 30 December 1939, p. 3.
176 Kon'kov, *Kak organizovat' rabotu*, p. 34.

of one year by an open vote, depends entirely on the local trade union committee.[177]

KOLKHOZ TRADE UNION ORGANIZATIONS

The existence of trade union groups in kolkhozes has already been mentioned. These have been led by trade union group organizers since 1962. However, groups with not less than fifteen members have been transformed into regular rabochkoms, thereby partially satisfying demands expressed since 1958. In 1966 there were over 36,000 trade union committees in the kolkhozes, or slightly less than half of the total of 76,000 trade unions locals in the country. These in turn were subdivided into 200,000 trade union groups. Trade unions committees in kolkhozes can be larger than sovkhoz committees, and there are cases in which kolkhoz rabochkoms have over two hundred members, whereas those in sovkhozes never have more than twenty-five to fifty members.

The procedure of setting up permanent and ad hoc commissions within kolkhoz rabochkoms follows the same pattern as that of the sovkhozes. However, in contrast to the situation in sovkhoz rabochkoms, the activities of some commissioners were discouraged as being in violation of the Collective Farm Statute and of the Model Statute of the Collective Farm.[178] And in this respect there is a great deal of difference between rabochkoms in kolkhozes and those on state farms.

177 *Ibid.*, p. 35.
178 This matter is discussed in detail in following chapters. 'Profkom kolkhoza, chem emu zanimatsia,' *Trud*, 16 March 1965, p. 2; Ia. Skliarevskii, 'Profkom i pravlenie kolkhoza,' *Sovetskie profsoiuzy*, no 16 (August 1965), pp. 13–15; 'Profsoiuzy-aktivnye uchastniki vsenardnoi bor'by za dal'neishii pod'em sel'skogo khoziaistva,' *Sovetskie profsoiuzy*, no 24 (December 1966), p. 31.

3

Agricultural trade union membership

According to the 'Model Statute of an All-Russian Industrial Trade Union' approved by the All-Russian Central Council of Trade Unions in 1919, 'all wage earners and salaried employees regularly employed in agriculture who take part in the processes of production, or who contribute directly thereto,' could become members of the given trade union.[1] The second Labour Code of the RSFSR, adopted in November 1922, contained a special chapter dealing with trade unions of workers and salaried employees. As subsequently amended and supplemented, it still is one of the basic legislative sources on trade unions in the USSR. This code refers only to workers and employees and therefore does not determine the rights of other citizens to join trade unions, but article 151 implies that persons 'employed for remuneration' may be members of trade unions: 'The trade unions in which citizens employed for remuneration in state, public and private undertakings, institutions and businesses are organized shall be entitled to appear before the various authorities in the name of persons employed for remuneration as parties to collective contracts and to represent them in all matters relating to work and conditions of life.'[2]

When the code was drafted wage earners could be employed in state-owned and public and private undertakings and institutions. Later provisions in trade

---

1 'Model Constitution of an All-Russian Industrial Trade Union,' in International Labour Office, *The Trade Union Movement in Soviet Russia* (Geneva 1927), 273 ff.
2 Kodeks Zakonov o trude RSFSR, *Sobranie Uzakonenii RSFSR*, no 70 (November 1922).

union statutes specifically restricted eligibility for trade union membership. But the code itself ensured that all agricultural wage workers were eligible for membership in a union. In 1919, before an attempt was made to organize the batraks and privately employed individuals, the following categories of workers had the right to membership in the Vserabotzem (All-Russian Union of Agricultural Workers): workers and employees of state farms, state orchards, state cattle breeding farms, state dairies and experimental stations; labourers as well as specialists delegated to work in sovkhozes as representatives of central and local agricultural institutions; workers and employees in auxiliary trades serving state farms, such as mill workers, blacksmiths, saddlers, carpenters, joiners, machinists, tilers, coopers, shoemakers and tailors, were eligible for membership.[3] Workers and employees of the forest industry were organized in a separate Union of Forestry Workers, which as already noted was amalgamated with the Union of Agricultural Workers at the end of 1920[4] to form the Vserabotzemles (Agricultural and Forestry Workers' Union).

Before we turn to a statistical analysis of the Agricultural and Forestry Workers' Union membership, it should be pointed out that it is extremely difficult to arrive at any precise numerical description of the union, since the mass of its members were located in rural areas and in sovkhozes, which kept only rudimentary statistical records.[5] According to various sources the membership of the Agricultural Workers' Union was very small in the beginning. One study made in 1927 by a non-Soviet organization estimated that the union's membership was 577 in 1917, 2,462 in 1918, and reached 18,557 in 1919.[6] The same source gives the following data for membership in the Union of Forestry Workers: 1,968 in 1918, and 15,037 in 1919 on the eve of amalgamation with the Agricultural Workers' Union. This estimate is probably accurate enough. It corresponds closely with a Soviet source, which indicates that the Agricultural Workers' Union had over 4,000 members in the first half of 1918 and about 34,000 a year later in 1919.[7] If we combine the number of trade union members of both the Agricultural Workers and the Forestry Workers given separately by the ILO study we arrive at approximately the same number.[8]

3 *Trade Unions in Soviet Russia* (London: Independent Labour Party, 1920), p. 80. See also Appendix III.

4 *Profsoiuz rabochikh sel'skogo khoziaistva*, pp. 8, 16.

5 See appendix II for total membership figures in agricultural trade unions, 1917–70.

6 ILO, *The Trade Union Movement*, p. 67.

7 Lev Magaziner, *Chislennost' i sostav professional'nykh soiuzov SSSR* (Moscow: VTsSPS, 1926), p. 11.

8 At least two other sources place the total membership of the union in 1919 at 48,000; *Trade Unions in Soviet Russia*, p. 79; *Profsoiuz rabochikh sel'skogo khoziaistva*, p. 6.

In 1920 there was a rapid growth in the size of the agricultural trade union. In the middle of the year membership stood at 140,000, reaching 659,000 in July 1921.[9] From that moment on agricultural trade union membership began to decline to the low of 249,000 at the beginning of 1923, or by 61.5 per cent.[10]

Although the above figures cannot be accepted with complete confidence, it does appear that the years 1917 to 1921 were notable for a continued increase in union membership, and there are several reasons why this was so. The harsh living conditions of war communism and the civil war forced many to accept trade union membership as the only way either to retain or to obtain property, living quarters, clothing, and food. This was also the closed-shop period of obligatory membership in a union if the general assembly of workers in a given enterprise approved union affiliation – and such approval was always forthcoming.[11] Finally, the constant extension of Soviet power over new territories also helped in the general growth of trade union membership, including that of the Agricultural and Forestry Workers' Union.[12]

The cessation of hostilities which occurred on all fronts during 1920 enabled the Bolsheviks to take steps to put into operation the policy they announced at the beginning of 1921 that postulated a return to peaceful labour and economic reconstruction. The New Economic Policy, which emerged suddenly during the spring of 1921, had a decided effect on trade union membership. The drive to reregister trade union members and the general purge of 'undesirable elements' from trade unions already noted in chapter 1, as well as a partial return to voluntary membership, had a disastrous effect on the numerical strength of the unions, and particularly on the Agricultural and Forestry Workers' Union.[13] Other factors, such as the restriction of official services, the reduction in the number of employed women, and the closing of numerous enterprises, such as sovkhozes which took place during 1921–2 resulted in a further reduction in trade union membership,[14]

Commenting on this drop in trade union membership in one of his speeches, M.P. Tomsky admitted that the NEP had forced the trade unions to reorganize

9 ILO, *The Trade Union Movement*, p. 85; Lev Magaziner, *Chislennost'*, pp. 8, 11.
10 *Soviet Union Yearbook* (New York: B.W. Huebsch, 1926), p. 437. 'An article in *Trud* states that there were in existence only 48 gubotdels and not 92 as reported. 'Na pomoshch Vserabotzemlesu,' *Trud*, 19 May 1922, p. 1.
11 See 'Model Constitution' art 8, ILO, *The Trade Union Movement*, p. 325.
12 *Profsoiuz rabochikh sel'skogo khoziaistva*, p. 8.
13 Lev Magaziner, *Chislennost'*, pp. 7–8.
14 The number of women was reduced by 38.4 per cent. *Ibid.*, p. 33. In Samara gubernia the number of sovkhozes was reduced from 64 to 19, with an appreciable reduction in the number of workers employed. 'Samarskii gubotdel: rabota za 1921 god,' *Trud*, 9 March 1922, p. 3.

their ranks and to exclude from membership semi-proletarian elements. 'This,' he continued, 'did lower trade union membership, but raised the ideological strength and fighting capacity of the unions.'[15]

THE NEP AND RECRUITMENT OF BATRAKS

During 1923 a general upturn in the membership of the Agricultural and Forestry Workers' Union was visible. Aside from seasonal fluctuations, membership was influenced by two important factors. The first of these, which brought about a reduction in membership, the elimination of some existing sovkhozes and a number of forestry stations or a reduction in their personnel. This was more than offset, however, by the increase in membership resulting from the recruitment of batraks that began in earnest only in 1923.[16] In addition, during 1923 the Agricultural and Forestry Workers' Union extended its organization to many workers in the pripisnye (the so-called attached sovkhozes), who until then had been affiliated with industrial and other unions; workers in agricultural co-operatives were also transferred to the union by 1923. The most important addition to trade union membership, however, came as a result of the recruitment of batraks. For example, the number of batraks in the union rose from approximately 29,000 on 1 October 1923 to 83,000 on 1 October 1924, an increase of roughly 200 per cent.[17] Table 3–1 shows the territorial distribution of the batraks and the speed with which they were organized. For the same period, the relationship between the total membership of the Agricultural and Forestry Workers' Union and the number of batraks within the union can be seen from table 3–2.

15 *Trud*, 19 December 1922, p. 2. There are few examples of 'pure proletarian' trade unions; in Olonetskaia oblast (Petrozavodskaia gubernia) there were 1,227 members of the union, of whom 108 were forestry workers, 200 sovkhoz workers, and 919 employees of the Commissariat of Agriculture. 'V Petrozavodskom gubotdele Vserabotzemlesa,' *Trud*, 15 February 1922, p. 3; in Samara gubernia out of 127 existing local committees of the union 52 were committees of employees of the Commissariat of Agriculture. 'Samarskii gubotdel,' *Trud*, 9 March 1922, p. 3.

16 P. Lezhnev-Fin'kovskii, 'Rabota v derevne i rol' vserabotzemlesa,' *Trud*, 14 February 1924, p. 1.

17 However, as the figures for 1923 released at the plenum in February 1924 show the Agricultural and Forestry Workers' Union had 298,339 members, of whom 27,447 were batraks. Batraks were organized too slowly it is said, with only about 2.75 per cent of them in the union. 'Plenum TsK vserabotzemlesa,' *Trud*, 24 February 1924, p. 3. In February 1923 in the nine gubernias served by the Iuzhbiuro (Ukraine) there were 14,000 batrak members and 330 volsekretariats. 'Rabota sredi batrakov na Ukraine: beseda s predsedatelem Iuzhbiuro Vserabotzemlesa t. Keder,' *Trud*, 10 February 1923, p. 3.

TABLE 3–1

Territorial distribution and unionization of batraks in selected areas, October 1923 to October 1924

Area	October 1923	January 1924	April 1924	July 1924	October 1924
Ukrainian Republic	18,000	14,000	15,000	19,000	26,000
South-East	1,000	2,000	4,000	6,000	16,000
Urals Region	1,000	1,000	2,000	5,000	9,000
Caucasus	2,000	2,000	6,000	6,000	8,000
Kirgiz Republic	1,000	1,000	4,000	5,000	6,000
Siberia	1,000	1,000	1,000	2,000	6,000
Turkestan	no data	no data	no data	4,000	4,000
Volga Region	1,000	no data	2,000	4,000	4,000
Central Agricultural Region	2,000	2,000	1,000	3,000	4,000
Other Regions	2,000				

SOURCE: Lev Magaziner, *Chislennost' i sostav professional'nykh soiuzov SSSR* (Moscow: VTsSPS, 1926), p. 13.

TABLE 3–2

Distribution of total membership of Agricultural and Forestry Workers' Union and of batrak members by selected areas, October 1924

Area	Total membership	Batraks	Batraks as per cent
North Caucasus and Dagestan	21,000	8,000	38
Caucasus	12,000	8,000	66
Ukrainian Republic	30,000	26,000	86
Urals Region	14,000	9,000	64
Turkestan	9,000	4,000	44
South-East	21,000	16,000	76
Kirgiz Republic	no data	8,000	
Siberia	no data	6,000	

SOURCE: Lev Magaziner, *Chislennost' i sostav professional'nykh soiuzov SSSR* (Moscow: VTsSPS, 1926), p. 13.

It may be noted that on 1 August 1923 there were 37,614 batraks registered in the Ukraine, of whom 12,072 were members of the union, while there was a total of 61,808 agricultural workers in the union organized within 1,258 rabochkoms and 440 village committees; there were also 402 raion (volost) secretariats.[18]

18 A. Keder, 'Vserabotzemles na Ukraine,' *Trud*, 26 September 1923, p. 2. S. Linin ('Batrak Ukrainy,' *Trud*, 5 July 1927) points to the growth of the union. In the Ukraine on 1 April 1923 there were 53,000 members and on 1 April 1927 there were

TABLE 3–3

Distribution of total membership of Agricultural
and Forestry Workers' Union and batrak members
in Central Asian region, January to October 1924

Date	Total membership	Batraks	Batraks as percentage
1 January	3,676	481	13
1 April	5,236	1,579	30
1 July	9,565	2,986	31
1 October	16,520	9,051	54

SOURCE: Vsesoiuznyi Tsentral'nyi Sovet Professional'nykh
Soiuzov, Sredne – Aziatskoe Biuro, *Professional'nye soiuzy v
Srednei Azii 1924 – 1925 god*: *Otchet Sredne – Aziatskogo
Biuro V.Ts. S.P.S. k I – oi Sredne – Aziatskoi Konferentsii
Profsoiuzov* (Tashkent 1925), p. 13.

This drive to organize batraks as rapidly as possible is also well illustrated
by the data for Central Asia presented in table 3–3 which clearly show the
growing influence of batraks within the union. In only eight months this element rose in the Central Asian branch of the Agricultural and Forestry
Workers' Union from about 13.1 per cent to about 54.9 per cent of the total
membership.

However, batraks constituted a much smaller fraction of the total membership in the Soviet Union as a whole. Table 3–4 indicates changes within the
categories of workers comprising the union, represented in percentages for
January and July 1924. From these data it is evident that the increase in
membership was primarily a result of the organizing of batraks, whose share
and influence within the union steadily grew. Their numbers in the union
continued to increase but at a slower pace, and in 1928 they constituted 17.5
per cent of the total membership, while sovkhoz workers made up 28.5 per
cent of the total, or the same share as in January of 1924.[19]

Throughout 1924 and the beginning of 1925, further growth occurred in
the union, which reached a total membership of 497,636 in April 1925. The
regional distribution of agricultural trade union members is seen in table 3–5,
which lists political subdivisions of the country and gives the total number
of members for each.

During 1925 the Soviet Union experienced intensive industrial and economic growth, reflected in the recruitment of labour and the increase in trade

232,000, while the total number of workers in agriculture was 464,000. Thus, only
about 50 per cent were organized within the union.

19 *Profsoiuz rabochikh sel'skogo khoziaistva*, p. 47.

TABLE 3–4

Percentage distribution of membership in
the Agricultural and Forestry Workers'
Union by type of enterprise and selected
other categories, January and July 1924

	January 1924	July 1924
State farms	28.5	23.2
Forestry	29.4	24.8
Agricultural and forestry enterprises	19.4	18.8
Small enterprises		2.8
Communes	0.2	0.2
Other enterprises	0.6	1.4
Batraks	8.2	15.9
Students	4.5	4.8
Unemployed	9.2	8.1
TOTAL	100.0	100.0

SOURCE: Lev Magaziner, *Chislennost' i sostav professional'nykh soiuzov SSSR* (Moscow: VTsSPS 1926),
p. 13.

union membership. By April 1926 the Agricultural and Forestry Workers'
Union had a total membership of 922,300, this growth resulting not only from
continued efforts to recruit batraks, shepherds, and other categories of
workers from among the village proletariat, but also from transfers stemming
from the new trade union demarcation.[20] The Second ACCTU Plenum, held
in 1925, decided to shift lumberjacks from the Union of Woodworkers to the
Agricultural and Forestry Workers' Union; the same plenum also transferred
workers on sugar plantations and workers on tobacco plantations into the
union.[21] The Third ACCTU Plenum (February 1926) decreed that the small
groups of industrial workers in the villages should also fall within the jurisdiction of the union.[22] In some areas of the country these transfers accounted
for most of the union's growth.[23]

20 In twenty-two months from January 1924 to October 1925, the number of farm
   workers in the union increased from 23,000 to 261,000. *Biulleten VTsSPS*, 12 June
   1926.
21 VTsSPS, *Otchet VTsSPS k VII s'ezdu professional'nykh soiuzov* (Moscow: VTsSPS,
   1926), p. 21.
22 Only groups of five members or less were to be transferred in this manner. This
   number was later raised to fifty members and, with the agreement of the central
   committee of the given union, an even larger number. Those enterprises which had
   twenty-five men or more and which were located in raion centres, as well as smaller
   groups in the vicinity, were to remain within their trade unions. The same rule also

The union was also responsible for the organization of seasonal labourers who belonged to various other trade unions but lived in areas where these unions had no organization of their own. In 1926–7 these included: construction workers, 32,000; miners, 24,311; woodworkers, 729; metallurgical workers, 564; food workers, 252; and sugar workers, 300. This arrangement, however, did not last long and each trade union made a special effort to keep in touch with their membership at all times.[24] Also during this period a new attempt was made to eliminate some of the confusion of the situation by demarcating trade union spheres of influence.[25]

The rapid growth of membership in the Agricultural and Forestry Workers' Union continued up to early 1930, when once again membership began to decline. But let us first consider the extent to which the union was in fact able to organize the agricultural workers: the percentage of agricultural labourers who actually did become trade union members. Data on this question are presented in tables 3–6 and 3–7. The tables clearly show that the rapid increase in union membership after 1923 did not appreciably raise the percentage of trade unionists among agricultural workers. In fact, the opposite seems to be the case. The only union showing a constant tendency towards a decrease in the percentage of members versus non-members is the Agricultural and Forestry Workers' Union. In July 1923 90.9 per cent of the workers in agriculture were unionists, while in January 1924 the percentage fell to 86.6 per cent, and then to 69.5 per cent in April 1926, to 57.1 per cent in April 1928, and to the low of 40.4 per cent in October 1931.

This discrepancy between the growth of the union's membership and the decline in the number of organized workers in the union in relationship to

applied to enterprises of fifteen men or more located at railroad stations. *Ibid.*, pp. 33–4. See also VTsSPS, *Otchet VTsSPS k VIII s'ezdu professional'nykh soiuzov* (Moscow: VTsSPS, 1928), p. 26.

23 In 1926 in the Caucasus area alone the growth was the result of large transfers from the unions of builders, narpit (food workers), and gruzchiki (loaders). A. Slavinkov, 'V pote litsa,' *Trud*, 5 July 1927, p. 3. For the Soviet Union as a whole in the period between July 1926 and July 1928, the increase in membership amounted to 363,000 new members, or 63.3 per cent. VTsSPS, *Otchet VTsSPS k VIII s'ezdu*, p. 27.

24 Seasonal labour was able to enter trade unions almost at will, which created great problems. So the ACCTU, following instructions of the Eighth Congress of Trade Unions, worked out a scheme according to which all hired hands could become trade union members if they worked two months continuously; all other seasonal workers could become trade union members if they worked as hired labour throughout the season each year, accumulating a given number of seasonal days. Each union had the right to determine the number of such seasonal days as a condition for entering the trade union. However, seasonal workers who worked as foremen in kolkhozes or artel's could not become trade union members. *Ibid.*, pp. 91–2, 96.

25 See appendix IV.

TABLE 3–5

Distribution of membership in Agricultural and Forestry
Workers' Union by republics and oblasts, 1 April 1925

SOVIET UNION (USSR)	497,636	AUTONOMOUS OBLASTS-RSFSR	
		Votskaia	1,480
RUSSIAN FEDERATION (RSFSR)	331,188	Zyrianskaia	751
		Kalmytskaia	502
EUROPEAN PART-RSFSR		Kara-Kirgizskaia	1,448
Arkhangelsk	1,128	Mariiskaia	1,155
Astrakhan	1,478	Chuvashskaia	1,030
Briansk	4,500		
Gomel	3,314	AUTOMOUS REPUBLICS-RSFSR	
Iaroslavl'	4,058	Bashkir	6,738
Ivanovo-Voznesensk	2,715	Buriat-Mongol	2,817
Kaluga	4,122	Dagestan	997
Kostroma	2,689	Karelian	996
Kursk	5,363	Kirgiz	24,895
Leningrad	11,863	Crimean	7,960
Moscow	23,868	Volga-German	1,215
Murmansk	71	Tatar	6,341
Nizhegorod	10,063		
Novgorod	4,100		
Orel	4,302	RSFSR-REGIONS	
Penza	4,116	Central Industrial	44,920
Pskov	5,152	Central Black-earth	44,258
Riazan	4,863	Volga	47,011
Samara	6,031	Northern Oblast	31,187
Saratov	9,243		
Severo Dvinsk	1,120	UKRAINIAN REPUBLIC	94,319
Smolensk	7,416		
Stalingrad	6,130	Volyn	5,827
Tambov	5,470	Donetsk	7,701
Tver	5,239	Ekaterinoslav	10,063
Tula	5,508	Kiev	14,016
Ulianovsk	3,550	Odessa	77,088
Ural	28,880	Podolia	10,145
Vladimir	6,357	Poltava	11,358
Vologda	3,044	Kharkov	10,252
Voronezh	6,014	Chernigov	5,030
Viatka	4,362	Moldavian	1,939
Severo-Kavkazkii Raion	40,394		
		BELORUSSIAN REPUBLIC	14,889
SIBERIA-RSFSR			
Altai	5,880	TRANSCAUCASIAN REPUBLICS	36,382
Eniseisk	6,677	Azerbaidzhan	22,737
Irkutsk	3,667	Armenia	9,622
N. Nikolaevsk	4,275	Georgia	4,023
Omsk	4,849		
Tomsk	2,824	UZBEK REPUBLIC	19,421
FAR EAST-RSFSR		TURKMEN REPUBLIC	1,437
Amur	2,053		
Zabaikalsk	460		
Primorskaia	2,422		

SOURCE: Lev Magaziner, *Chislennost' i sostav professional'nykh soiuzov SSSR* (Moscow: VTsSPS, 1926).

TABLE 3-6

Trade union membership as a
percentage of total eligible agricultural
labour force, 1 January 1923 to
1 January 1936

Date	Trade union membership
1 January 1923	95.9
1 July 1923	90.9
1 January 1924	86.6
1 July 1924	74.0
1 October 1924	78.5
1 January 1925	75.4
1 April 1925	74.6
1 October 1925	70.7
1 April 1925	69.1
1 April 1926	69.5
1 October 1926	47.4
1 October 1927	44.1
1 April 1928	57.1
1 October 1928	47.0
1 October 1931	40.4
1 January 1932	57.1
1 January 1935	66.8
1 January 1936	74.7

SOURCES: Vsesoiuznyi Tsentral'nyi Sovet Profsoiuzov, *Otchet k VI s'ezdu*, p. 13; Vsesoiuznyi
Tsentral'nyi Sovet Profsoiuzov, *Otchet k VII
s'ezdu*, pp. 22–4; Vsesoiuznyi Tsentral'nyi Sovet
Profsoiuzov, *Otchet k VIII s'ezdu*, p. 29; *Statistika Truda*, no 1 (1929); *Industrial and Labor
Information*, vol 30, p. 277; Vsesoiuznyi Tsentral'
nyi Sovet Profsoiuzov, *Materialy k otchetu IX
s'ezdu*, p. 193; and *Industrial and Labor Information*, vol 60, pp. 249–50.

TABLE 3-7

Trade union membership as a percentage of eligible labour force on
state farms and Machine Tractor Stations, 20 April 1932 and
September 1934

	State farms		MTS	
Trade unions	20 April 1932[a]	September 1934[b]	20 April 1932	September 1934[b]
Union of Workers of Agricultural Sovkhozes	39.0	49.0		
Union of Workers of Animal-Breeding Sovkhozes				
Union of MTS Workers and Batraks				73.0

[a]*Trud*, 20 April 1932, p. 2.
[b]M. Shvernik, speech at the Sixth ACCTU Plenum, September 1934.

the total labour force in agriculture is, indeed, rather puzzling. But it can probably be explained by the increase of the total labour force in the country, the availability of better statistical information, the reduced necessity of becoming a trade union member because of the greater availability of employment, and the possibility of voluntary individual membership in the union and voluntary payment of trade union dues.[26]

In the period between 1927 and 1931, in addition to the above factors the purges also had a detrimental effect on the percentage of workers in the agricultural trade union. In July 1927 *Trud* declared:

The local organizations, which are still weak in many cases, could not safeguard proper recruitment of workers into trade union membership, continued to interpret directives of the Central Committee in relation to these matters very broadly and accepted into membership peasants and artisans who only worked temporarily as hired hands.[27]

The same article called for recruiting primarily the proletarian element which was still 'to a great extent ... outside the union.' This purge was to leave all batraks in the union, 'even those who are being paid in kind.' Additional effort was to be made to promote proletarians to leadership positions, and in fact a great deal was done, so that out of 100,000 elected trade union officials, 65 per cent came from among the workers. The majority of these, however, did not occupy the full-time, paid trade union positions.[28]

As a result of the 1927 purge, the percentage of organized agricultural labourers declined significantly. Soon, however, the policy of including proletarian elements only was reversed as a result of the Fifteenth Party Congress (December 1927) and the decision to collectivize agriculture, and again emphasis was placed on carrying on organizational work among all the poorer elements of the village.[29] This policy was reiterated in the circular of June 1928 addressed to all members of the party and the proletariat which contained guiding instructions for party organizations, trade unions, and soviet

26 One Soviet source indicates that the lower percentage of organized workers was due to better statistics on lumberjacks, who had no right to trade union membership, and to the employment of larger numbers of workers in agriculture. VTsSPS, *Otchet VTsSPS k VIII s'ezdu*, p. 30.
27 'Rabota scredi sel'khozrabochikh,' *Trud*, 31 July 1927, p. 1.
28 'Ukreplenie soiuza sel'khozlesrabochikh,' *Trud*, 2 September 1927, p. 1.
29 *KPSS o profsoiuzakh*, p. 266. Beginning in 1928 a number of huge new state farms were organized on free land in the Southeastern, Eastern, and Southern regions of the USSR. But they proved to be failures and were subdivided later. Fainsod, *How Russia is Ruled*, p. 529.

officials.[30] One of the unions' tasks was 'to absorb into the trade unions the more backward classes of workers and to devote special attention to the material, cultural and political uplift of these workers (particularly agricultural workers, unskilled labourers, women and young persons).'[31]

The Sixth Congress of the Agricultural and Forestry Workers' Union, which met in Moscow from 27 November to 8 December 1928, turned its attention to the question of trade union membership. It was stated at the congress that the flow of new members into the union had slackened, and that union organizations were finding some difficulty in recruiting members.[32] This circumstance, it was said, was largely a result of the tactics of employers and especially rich kulaks, who preferred to engage non-union men. But apart from acts of intimidation, the great obstacle to the enrolment of new members was the ignorance of the workers, who were often unaware of the very existence of the union, or who failed to understand the advantages to be gained from joining it. There were even cases of a number of workers voluntarily leaving the unions. In Kiev oblast, for example, the number of trade union members steadily diminished, especially among the batraks, whose number within the union shrank by 23 per cent between 1927 and 1928.[33] In Novosibirsk approximately one-half of the batraks organized within the union left it voluntarily because, so they claimed, it did not offer them protection from the kulaks.[34] Wage earners in sovkhozes, it was revealed at the congress, also saw no reason to become trade union members, because they could be dismissed from work for a simple error or for being slightly critical of the management. The trade unions neglected these people or sometimes even showed a certain hostility towards them. Although the wage earners were considered privileged persons by the party and the government, in fact their condition was generally no better, and often worse, than that of workers employed by the peasants. The result was that the percentage of organized workers slowly declined.[35] This situation within the union, as revealed by the Sixth Congress,

30 'Obrashchenie TsK VKP(b) o samokritike,' *Spravochnik partiinogo rabotnika*, pp. 305–7.
31 *Ibid.*; *Pravda*, 3 June 1928, p. 2.
32 'Soiuz i novye kadry rabochikh,' *Trud*, 28 November 1928, p. 3; 'VI vsesoiuznyi s'ezd sel'khozlesrabochikh,' *Trud*, 28 November 1928, p. 1; *Trud*, 8 December 1928.
33 'Sokrashchenie chisla chlenov soiuza sel'skokhoziaistvennykh rabochikh,' *Trud*, 11 August 1928, p. 3.
34 P.V-ov, 'Batraki govoriat: Iz kraevoi konferentsii batrachestva i bednoty,' *Trud*, 6 February 1929, p. 2.
35 Although agricultural trade union membership rose to 1,362,000 in July 1928, an increase of 59 per cent from 1926, only about 25 to 30 per cent of all eligible proletarians were trade union members. 'VI vsesoiuznyi s'ezd sel'khozles rabochikh,' *Trud*, 30 November 1928, p. 1. For example, attempts to organize batraks continued at a

evoked a rapid response by the Central Committee of the Communist party, which issued a special directive in March 1929 aimed at increasing the recruitment of workers by the Agricultural and Forestry Workers' Union.[36]

ON THE EVE OF COLLECTIVIZATION

At the Plenum of the Central Committee of the Agricultural and Forestry Workers' Union, held in Moscow at the beginning of June 1929, it was admitted that in the period from 1928 to 1929, recruitment of members had slackened significantly, and that in some areas, such as the Ukraine, there had even been a decline of 5 per cent in the union's membership.[37] The plenum further revealed that out of 716,000 forestry workers, only 83,000, or 11.6 per cent, were members of the union, while out of 547,000 workers in the sovkhozes only 162,000, or 29 per cent, could be considered union members. To remedy the situation the plenum recommended that the organization drive should be intensified among the village poor, even going so far as to permit recruitment of people in the past excluded from trade union membership, such as owners of one horse and batraks who worked for an individual farmer as a hired labourer but who received wages in kind rather than in money. The plenum also decided that all workers and promyshlenno-podsobnykh (employees of industrial enterprises) located on sovkhoz territory and processing its produce were henceforth to be members of the Agricultural and Forestry Workers' Union. And if their number exceeded one hundred men within the territory of a sovkhoz, seasonal construction workers were also to be members of the union.[38]

But these were only the beginnings of the tremendous changes which the union was to experience as a consequence of the defeat and expulsion of Tomsky in 1929 and of the decision to accelerate the collectivization drive. The first event signalled the end of the trade unions as organizations designed to protect the worker and made them into state organs designed to control the

slow pace in Kazakhstan because of their nomadic or semi-nomadic mode of life. Thus, out of 130,000 batraks, only 40,000 were members of the union. The same situation existed in Turkmenistan and Uzbekistan. 'VI vsesoiuznyi s'ezd sel-khozles rabochikh,' *Trud*, 1 December 1928. 'VI vsesoiuznyi s'ezd sel'khozles rabochikh,' *Trud*, 28 November 1928, p. 1.

36 'Postanovlenie TsK VPK(b) ot 4 marta 1929 g: O rabote sredi sel'sko-khoziaistvennykh i lesnykh rabochikh i itogakh VI vsesoiuznogo s'ezda soiuza sel'khozrabochikh,' *Spravochnik profsoiuznogo rabotnika*, pp. 377–380; *KPSS o profsoiuzakh*, pp. 318–23.

37 'Pochemu zamedlilsia rost soiuza?' *Trud*, 4 June 1929, p. 1.

38 'Ob ukreplenii starykh sovkhozov: Iz postanovleniia TsK VKP(b),' *Trud*, 30 June 1929, p. 4.

TABLE 3–8

Workers and employees in sovkhozes, 1928 to 1931

Date	Workers				Salaried employees	Total
	Permanent	Seasonal	Temporary	Total		
July 1928	71,000	71,100	428,600	570,700	28,300	559,000
July 1929	90,600	99,800	429,900	620,300	31,800	652,100
August 1929	90,600	125,500	415,100	631,100	31,800	663,000
August 1930	249,400	348,400	441,300	1,039,100	63,200	1,102,300
August 1931	645,000	660,000	696,000	2,000,000	150,000	2,150,000

SOURCES: VTsSPS, *Materialy k otchetu IX s'ezdu, op. cit.*, p. 134; data for the year 1931 are from preliminary figures of Gosplan.

TABLE 3–9

Workers and employees in agricultural sovkhozes, August 1930 to August 1931

Date	Workers				Salaried employees	Total
	Permanent	Seasonal	Temporary	Total		
August 1930	145,200	129,500	146,000	420,700	36,400	457,100
August 1931	417,200	303,200	232,500	953,600	70,600	1,024,200

SOURCE: VTsSPS, *Materialy k otchetu IX s'ezdu*, p. 134.

working masses and stimulate them to fulfil higher production goals. The second caused tremendous upheavals in the union's membership because of the large influx of labour into sovkhozes and MTS. As table 3–8 illustrates, in July 1928 there were 559,000 workers and salaried employees in sovkhozes, in August 1930 this number reached 1,102,300, and in August 1931 it had climbed to over two million. The number of permanent workers rose by almost ten times in three years, while the number of salaried employees rose about six-fold. An even more rapid growth in the number of permanent workers occurred in agricultural sovkhozes alone, as is seen in table 3–9. With the increase in the number of MTS from 385 in 1930 to 1,574 in 1931, the number of workers employed by them also grew steadily, reaching 126,822 in the fourth quarter of 1931.[39]

The Agricultural and Forestry Workers' Union grew correspondingly during this period. From 1,632,500 members in 1929, its membership increased to

39 VTsSPS, *Materialy k otchetu VTsSPS IX s'ezdu profsoiuzov* (Moscow: Profizdat, 1932), p. 229; VTsSPS, *Kratkii otchet VTsSPS IX s'ezdu* (Moscow: Profizdat, 1932), p. 42.

1,829,000 in August 1930, reaching a high of 2,049,600 in 1931.[40] This growth resulted from greater efforts to organize batraks and also from transfers from other unions, especially the Sugar Workers' Union, which was amalgamated with the Agricultural Workers' Union in 1930.

Recruiting activities were greatly intensified in 1929 and at the beginning of 1930 among the batraks, who were not only to be organized within the union but also convinced to enrol in the kolkhozes as well. These instructions of the November 1929 plenum of the party's Central Committee were echoed by the Third Plenum of the Central Committee of the Agricultural and Forestry Workers' Union in February 1930 in a decree emphasizing this new function of the union.[41] The task was performed speedily: in 1930 batraks employed by individual farmers made up about 30 per cent of the membership of the Agricultural and Forestry Workers' Union, while in January 1932 they constituted only 9 per cent of the total union membership.[42] By August 1930 Shvernik, in his speech to the Sixth Congress of the Profintern, pointed out that around 700,000 batraks had been enrolled in kolkhozes.[43] He implied that the batraks were members both of the trade union and of the kolkhoz, which was in fact the case. In one of its information releases the Central Committee of the union explicitly stated that batraks enrolled in the kolkhozes retained trade union membership and paid trade union membership dues of ten kopecks per month.[44] The Central Committee of the union also instructed all of its lower organs (republic, krai, and oblast) to create special funds to be used in helping the batraks, who were entering kolkhozes. These funds were to be further supplemented from unemployment reserves, voluntary contributions, etc., and the organs of Sotsstrakh (social insurance) were ordered to pay unemployment compensation to the batraks, at least until the 1930 harvest was in. These decisions had two purposes. First, in outlining trade union functions in the collectivization drive, they were a warning to those who advocated abolishing the Agricultural and Forestry Workers' Union altogether, and an

40 VTsSPS, *Kratkii otchet VTsSPS IX s'ezdu*, p. 42; VTsSPS, *Materialy kotchetu IX s'ezdu*, p. 28.
41 *KPSS o profsoiuzakh*, p. 369 ff; *Profsoiuz rabochikh sel'skogo khoziaistva*, p. 51.
42 *Ibid.*, p. 63.
43 N.M. Shvernik, 'Rol' professional'nykh soiuzov v sotsialisticheskom stroitel'stve,' *Trud*, 27 August 1930, p. 2.
44 'Batrakov v kolkhozy,' *Trud*, 26 January 1930, p. 3. A.I. Pravdin, 'Profsoiuzy Belorussii raboty s batrachestvom i bednotoi ne vedut,' *Trud*, 20 February 1930, p. 4; G., 'TsK sel'khozlesrabochikh zabyl o batratsko-bedniatskikh gruppakh,' *Trud*, 20 February 1930, p. 4; I. Sheingan, 'Rabochie brigady: Organizatory batratsko-bedniatskoi aktivnosti,' *Trud*, 20 February 1930, p. 4; V. Bulgakov, 'Na Shipke ne spokoino,' *Trud*, 20 February 1930, p. 4.

indication that this union should even be strengthened.[45] Second, by giving trade union membership and all its rights to a particular group of kolkhoz members, the leadership created a privileged group set apart from the rest of the kolkhozniks which, at least in the beginning stages of the collectivization campaign, could be used as a watchdog in the kolkhozes.

The union's membership was also affected by the shifting of workers from kolkhozes into sovkhozes and vice versa, and discussion at the plenum of the Central Committee of the union, held in January and February 1930, revolved around this problem. In her speech at the plenum, Iachmennikova, a member of the Central Committee of the union, confirmed that 'the Agricultural and Forestry Workers' Union in the face of the total collectivization of agriculture is gradually becoming the union of sovkhoz and lespromkhoz workers.' She further called for a transfer of batraks who were union members into 'permanent jobs in the sovkhozes' and from sovkhozes into collective farms those 'workers who are connected with peasant farms.' It is impossible to determine who she meant by this category of workers. It may be that she had in mind those semi-proletarians who owned some livestock and agricultural implements and who had joined the union in 1928 and 1929 and had then been placed in the sovkhozes. Iachmennikova also pointed out that the batrak masses should be transferred into 'the MTS and the forestry industry,' and complained that the union was not able to deal with this problem properly and that failure to do so could hurt the spring sowing campaign.[46] But the privileged position of batraks in kolkhozes slowly diminished, and many of them were gradually turned into ordinary kolkhozniks.

The Agricultural and Forestry Workers' Union also grew during collectivization as a result of an influx from other trade unions, particularly from urban and industrial unions. This army of disciplined workers, known as the group of 25,000 was sent into the villages by decision of the November 1929 Party Plenum.[47] Approximately 71 per cent of them were sent into the

45 There are several indications in the Soviet press for this period that a sizable group existed within the party and trade unions which advocated liquidating the Agricultural and Forestry Workers' Union. One reason could have been that they could not reconcile membership in kolkhozes with that in trade unions. That these voices were strong is seen in the fact that they required rebuttal in the form of the statement of the Central Committee of the union on this matter. 'Batrakov v kolkhozy,' *Trud*, 26 January 26 1930, p. 3.
46 'Dat' sovkhozam postoiannye proletarskie kadry,' *Trud*, 21 January 1930, p. 4.
47 The exact number is given as 27,519 workers. Among others, it comprised 9,000 metallurgical workers, 4,000 textile workers, 4,500 railroad workers, 1,500 construction workers. *Profsoiuz rabochikh sel'skogo khoziaistva*, pp. 54–5. For regional distribution, age, party membership, see appendix VII where the breakdown of

kolkhozes.[48] At the same time, however, there was a considerable outflow of membership because of the separation of the forestry workers from the union and the amalgamation of these workers in October 1930 with the Union of Woodworkers into a separate Union of Forestry and Woodworking Industry Workers.[49]

As indicated in chapter two of this study, throughout the latter part of 1930 the entire trade union press was full of comments on how best to reorganize the existing union structure. The actual reorganization came in January 1931, when the Agricultural Workers' Union was split into four separate unions. A result of this reorganization and the later delineation of jurisdiction among different trade unions is that we are certain who were trade union members at this time and to what occupations they belonged.[50] The statistics on changes in trade union membership for the period are given in table 3–10. The most significant change, apart from the subdivision itself, was the separation already noted of the sugar workers into their own union of Sugar Industry Workers, encompassing workers both in sugar mills and sugar plantations. The second important development was the fact that the Union of MTS Workers and Batraks emerged as the strongest union in agriculture, numbering some 891,800 members, while in the two unions of sovkhoz workers the combined membership was 834,800. The MTS Workers and Batraks remained the most important union even after experiencing a decline of some 8.6 per cent in its membership in 1932, or approximately 76,500 members, probably because of

this group is given according to sex, age, party membership, etc. The data encompass only 23,409 members but are useful in determining the composition of this group. Shvernik's speech at the Fifth Congress of the Red International of Labour Unions in *Piatyi kongress Profinterna 15–30 augusta 1930: Stenograficheskii otchet* (Moscow: Izdatel'stvo Profinterna, 1930), p. 527.

48 M. Shvernik, 'Zadachi profsoiuzov v rekonstruktivnyi period,' *Trud*, 14 July 1930, p. 3; 'Plenum TsK sakharnikov za sliianie s soiuzom sel'khozrabochikh,' *Trud*, 20 July 1930, p. 2; 'TsK soiuza sel'khozlesrabochikh za sliianie s sakharnikami,' *Trud*, 11 August 1930, p. 2. There are no precise statistics which would help to determine the number of workers thus transferred. The total number of sugar workers in 1931 was 149,000 and these were separated from the Agricultural and Forestry Workers' Union. In 1934 their total was 172,000, of whom industrial workers made up 102,000 and sovkhoz workers 70,000. Thus, according to this estimate close to 90,000 joined the union.

49 'Trem soiuzam v lesu tesno,' *Trud*, 7 August 1930, p. 3; 'Sozdaetsia edinyi soiuz rabochikh lesnoi i lesoobrabatyvaiushchei promyshlennosti: postanovlenie prezidiuma VTsSPS ot 16 sentiabria,' *Trud*, 29 September 1930, p. 4.

50 See appendix v; for the distribution of new members of selected trade unions by nationality in the 1920s and 1930s see appendices viii and ix. For the categories of workers in agriculture who were eligible to become members of trade unions in 1931 see appendix v.

TABLE 3-10

Distribution of workers and trade union members among agricultural trade unions from October 1931 to January 1932

Name of trade union	Total number of workers (trade union and non-trade union)		Members of trade unions (employed)		Employed membership of trade unions as a portion of all workers		Total number of trade union members (employed and unemployed)		Percentage changes from 1 October 1931 to 1 January 1932, all workers and all trade union members	
	October	January	October	January	October	January	October	January	Workers	Trade union members
Workers of Agricultural Sovkhozes	1,088,500	737,900	425,000	459,100	39,000	62,200	457,400	518,700	−32.2	+13.4
Workers of Animal-Breeding Sovkhozes	828,500	814,700	344,700	428,200	41,600	52,600	377,400	475,500	−1.7	+26.0
MTS Workers and Batraks							891,800	815,300		−8.6
Total for agriculture without MTS Workers Batraks	1,917,000	1,552,600	769,700	887,300	40,400	57,100	834,800	994,200	−19.0	+19.1
Total for agriculture with MTS Workers and Batraks							1,726,600	1,809,500		+9.25
Sugar Industry Workers	295,800	245,100	135,000	136,000	45,600	55,600	149,900	149,800	−17.1	−0.1

SOURCES: VTsSPS, *Materialy k otchetu IX s'ezdu*, pp. 168–9; D. Rodionovich, "Rabota profsoiuzov v derevne," *Trud*, 20 April 1932, p. 2.

the purge which struck the MTS and other enterprises whose workers were united in the union.[51]

Both sovkhoz unions together increased their membership by 19.1 per cent in relation to the total number of sovkhoz workers in the same period, or by 159,400 members over the last quarter of 1931. This result was obtained because of greater organizational efforts and also a decrease in the total number of workers employed in sovkhozes from 1,970,000 to 1,552,600.

THE POST-COLLECTIVIZATION CHANGES

Membership in agriculture trade unions reached a high point during 1931 and 1932. From then on there was a visible decline in trade union membership in the countryside, while the percentage of organized workers in the total labour force seemed to be rising slightly.[52] Looking at individual unions we see that 49 per cent of all eligible workers in agricultural sovkhozes were trade union members, 54 per cent in animal-breeding sovkhozes, and 73 per cent in enterprises served by the Union of MTS Workers and Batraks.[53] The reasons for the decline in union membership were probably the continuance of the purge, famine conditions in some areas of the country, and the new wave of reorganization that swept the trade unions as a result of the Seventeenth Party Congress held in January and February 1934.[54]

Table 3–11 indicates the changes that occurred as a result of the new reorganization. Both sets of data (1932 and 1934) are combined in table 3–12. When these two tables are examined, it emerges that although there was a slight rise in trade union membership in agricultural and animal-breeding sovkhozes, there was an almost three-fold reduction in the membership of the Union of MTS Workers. This decline indicates, first, that the purge was carried out thoroughly in the MTS. But the other explanation for the drop is implied in the changed name of this particular union between 1932 and 1934, whereby the 'and Batraks' was simply dropped. After the 'liquidation of the kulaks as a class,' it would have been strange, indeed, to admit that there still were batraks in existence. Yet what did happen to the batraks? The answer is that probably

51 Iu.S. Borisov, *Podgotovka proizvodstvennykh kadrov sel'skogo khoziaistva v rekonstruktivnyi period* (Moscow: Akademiia nauk, 1960), p. 127 ff.
52 See Nancy Nimitz, *Farm Employment in the Soviet Union, 1928–1963* (Santa Monica: Rand Corporation, 1965); also her 'Farm Employment in the Soviet Union, 1928–1963,' in J.F. Karcz, ed., *Soviet and East European Agriculture*, pp. 178–9, 186–7, 189, 197.
53 Speech by Shvernik at the Fourth Plenum of VTsSPS in September 1934, *Trud*, 9 September 1934, p. 1.
54 For a detailed discussion of these changes, see chapter 2 of this study.

TABLE 3–11

Membership in agricultural trade unions, 1932 and 1934

January 1932		April 1934	
Trade Union	Number of members	Trade union	Number of members
Workers of Agricultural Sovkhozes	518,700	Workers of Grain-growing Sovkhozes	246,000
		Workers of Vegetable-growing Sovkhozes	136,000
		Workers of Garden and Vineyard Sovkhozes	68,000
		Workers of Cotton-growing State Sovkhozes and MTS	115,000
		TOTAL	565,000
Workers of Animal-Breeding Sovkhozes	475,500	Workers of Pig-raising Sovkhozes	171,000
		Workers of Horse-breeding Sovkhozes	21,000
		Workers of Sheep-breeding Sovkhozes	50,000
		Workers of Feather and Poultry-breeding Sovkhozes	24,000
		Workers of Dairy and Meat Sovkhozes of the Centre and the South	154,000
		Workers of Dairy and Meat Sovkhozes of the Urals and Siberia	76,000
		Workers of Dairy and Meat Sovkhozes of Kazakhstan and Central Asia	42,000
		TOTAL	540,000
MTS Workers and Batraks	815,300	MTS Workers of the Centre and the South	202,000
		MTS Workers of the East	65,000
		TOTAL	267,000
Workers in Land Organs	n.d.	Workers in Land Organs	182,000
		TOTAL	182,000
TOTAL	1,809,500	TOTAL	1,554,000

NOTE: The number of Workers in Land Organs is unknown, although estimates indicate there may have been as many as 240,000 members. The two sugar workers' unions existing in 1934 had a total membership of 172,000 members.
SOURCES: VTsSPS, *Materialy k otchetu IX s'ezdu*, pp. 168–9; *Trud*, 9 September 1934, p. 2.

TABLE 3–12

Changes in the membership of agricultural trade unions, January
1932 to April 1934

Union	January 1932	April 1934	Changes	
			Absolute	Per cent
Workers of Agricultural Sovkhozes	518,700	565,000	+ 46,300	8.9
Workers of Animal-Breeding Sovkhozes	475,500	540,400	+ 64,500	13.6
MTS Workers	815,300	267,000	− 548,300	− 67.3
Workers in Land Organs		182,000		

most of those who survived the purge were made over into ordinary kolkhozniks, in contrast to some of their former comrades who, by virtue of remaining in the MTS, were turned into the vanguard of the village proletariat. Others
were transferred into sovkhozes and became trade union members there.

During 1935 and 1936, when there was an increase of 4.4 per cent in the
total number of trade unionists in the country, a further drop occurred in the
total number of trade union members in agriculture. The total of 1,455,000
agricultural trade unionists represented a decrease of 1.3 per cent between
1 January 1935 and 1 January 1936. On the other hand, the percentage of
eligible workers belonging to unions rose among agricultural workers from
66.8 per cent in January 1934 to 74.4 per cent in January 1936. This rise was
again directly related to a decline in the number of agricultural workers.
Tractor drivers were an exception; their number rose from 226,100 in January
1935 to 406,300 a year later. The workers of grain-growing sovkhozes, on
the other hand, experienced a sharp decline in membership, falling from
341,400 in January 1935 to approximately 221,000 in January 1936.[55] The
situation in individual unions was poorer than the average figures indicate.
The Union of Workers of Garden and Vineyard Sovkhozes had an especially
low percentage of organized membership. In Voronezh oblast, for example,
only 57 per cent of all eligible workers and salaried employees were members
of the union in 1935, and only 39 per cent of the members paid their membership dues.[56] In the sheep-breeding sovkhozes only 70 per cent of all eligible
employees were enrolled in the union in 1936.[57]

From 1936 on it is almost impossible to determine the dynamics of agricultural trade union membership, as no comprehensive data were made available.

55 *Voprosy profdvizheniia*, no 8 (1936), p. 129.
56 T. Varvarin, 'Metodom ... okrika,' *Trud*, 22 June 1935, p. 3.
57 N. Ogolev, 'Sviaz' s massami ... eto osnovnoe,' *Trud*, 21 February 1936, p. 3.

The bits and pieces that are spread over the pages of newspapers and journals do not provide sufficient information to permit a student to reach any positive conclusions. It would seem, however, that exhaustive statistical data were not published because they were unavailable to the Soviet authorities as well. It is now quite openly admitted that in the period between 1932 and 1937 trade union activities reached their lowest point, and several trade unions did not report on their activities at all. Those which are specifically mentioned as being almost totally inactive included the Union of Workers in Land Organs, the Union of Workers of Vegetable-growing Sovkhozes, the Union of Workers of Feather and Poultry Sovkhozes, and the Union of Workers of Animal-breeding Sovkhozes.[58] At the local level, no elections were held in agricultural trade unions between 1933 and 1937.[59] It was typical of the situation in these unions that even as late as 1949, M.E. Iodko, the chairman of the then existing Union of MTS and Land Organ Workers failed to mention the size of the membership in his union in his speech to the Tenth Congress of Trade Unions.[60]

Some random examples throw a bit of light on the question of trade union membership. The Union of Workers of Cotton-growing Sovkhozes and MTS in 1937 managed to organize only 65 per cent of eligible workers in the Soviet Union as a whole, while in Uzbekistan, the country's main cotton-producing region, only 60 per cent of the eligible workers were found to be trade union members.[61] The Trade Union of Land Organ Employees in 1938 failed to organize 93,524 eligible employees of the enterprises served by this union; the number of those in the union was not given.[62] In 1947 the Union Workers of MTS and Land Organs of the South reported at its First Congress that over 30,000 workers and specialists were outside of the union.[63] The Union of Workers of Sheep-breeding Sovkhozes in 1939 enlisted 62,000 members, or 76.3 per cent of a potential 82,000.[64] In the same year the Union of Workers of Grain-growing Sovkhozes had 71.8 per cent of the eligible workers in its ranks.[65] The chairman of the Union of MTS Workers of the East, Katorgin, boasted at the Eighteenth Party Congress in March 1939 that his union was

58 *Profsoiuz rabochikh sel'skogo khoziaistva*, p. 79.
59 Slutsky and Syderenko, *Profsoiuzy Ukrainy*, p. 121.
60 *X s'ezd professional'nykh soiuzov SSSR: Stenograficheskii otchet* (Moscow: Profizdat, 1949), pp. 107–13.
61 I. Vilenskii, 'Pristanishche dlia temnykh elementov,' *Trud*, 24 March 1937, p. 3. The number of workers is not given.
62 'Preniia po otchetu TsK soiuza,' *Trud*, 17 January 1938, p. 2.
63 'Na s'ezdakh profsoiuzov,' *Trud*, 25 November 1947, p. 2.
64 'Vtoroi s'ezd profsoiuza rabochikh ovtsevodcheskikh sovkhozov,' *Trud*, 15 November 1939, p. 3.
65 'Vtoroi s'ezd profsoiuza rabochikh zernovykh sovkhozov,' *Trud*, 24 November 1939, p. 4.

serving 150,000 people, but he did not say how many of those were trade union members.[66] He did admit two months later at the Eighteenth Plenum of the ACCTU, however, that over 30,000 workers and employees were outside the trade union organization.[67] The highest percentage of trade union members was to be found among the workers of horse-breeding farms, whose union served approximately 40,000 workers, of whom 32,000, or roughly 82.5 per cent, were members.[68] In 1947, it was reported that 84 per cent of the workers and employees in industry, construction, transport, and agriculture were trade union members.[69] The data for the trade unions in agriculture alone were not given, but the percentage for that sector would have been significantly smaller.

Workers in the sovkhozes

The total agricultural labour force by categories is known, of course, but it is incorrect to decide that corresponding percentages of it are enrolled in the trade unions.[70] The reason is that in both sovkhozes and in the MTS a sizable number of toilers did not have the right to trade union membership.[71] Sovkhoz personnel were sharply divided into two groups: the managerial staff and workers. The managerial staff, which consisted of the director, senior specialists, senior mechanic, senior zoo technician, senior veterinarian, agronomist-economist, the chief bookkeeper, and the ancillary administrative personnel, chief mechanic, and chief of the supplies department, had the right to trade union membership. The workers in sovkhozes were generally grouped into three basic types of brigades: tractor brigades, livestock brigades, and agricultural brigades. All of them could be divided into three groups: a / peredoviks (leading workers) composed of repair-shop mechanics, brigadiers, combine operators, etc.; b / mechanical staff and technical staff such as shop workers, truck drivers, tractor operators, and hitchmen as well as auxiliary agro-technical workers and office personnel; and c / general workers, who could be

---

66 I. Katorgin, 'Zhilishchno-bytovoe stroitel'stvo v MTS,' *Trud*, 1 March 1939, p. 2.

67 Katorgin's speech, *Trud*, 8 May 1939, p. 3.

68 'Vtoroi s'ezd profsoiuza rabochikh konevodcheskikh sovkhozov,' *Trud*, 12 November 1939.

69 'Zakliuchenie kollektivnykh dogovorov na predpriiatiiakh,' *Trud*, 10 April 1947, p. 2. L.N. Solov'ev, 'O provedenii otchetov i vyborov oblasnykh, kraevykh, respublikanskikh, dorozhnykh, basseinovykh i tsentral'nykh komitetov profsoiuzov,' *Trud*, 25 April 1947, p. 2.

70 US Congress, Joint Economic Committee, *Dimensions of Soviet Economic Power* (Washington, DC 1962); Naum Jasny, *The Socialized Agriculture of the USSR: Plans and Performance* (Stanford: Standford University Press, 1949).

71 Alexander Vucinic, *Soviet Economic Institutions: The Social Structure of Production Units* (Stanford: Stanford University Press, 1952), p. 99 ff.

subdivided into classified general workers and unskilled workers. The former have acquired professional status; the unskilled workers who work in the fields or in service institutions such as restaurants, have no professional status. The 'general workers' group includes large numbers of temporary workers, that is, seasonally employed kolkhozniks. Usually these unskilled workers are denied trade union membership in the sovkhoz, but at least since the 1947 February Plenum of the Central Committee of the CPSU a conscious attempt has been made to consolidate them into a permanent staff, with all kinds of concessions and inducements.[72] This group is also exposed to special propaganda activities conducted by the sovkhoz trade union organization with a view to impressing upon them the advantages of permanent sovkhoz employment, in order to try to curtail excessive seasonal fluidity of sovkhoz manpower.[73]

Workers in the MTS

Unlike the sovkhoz, the MTS did not rely exclusively on its own permanent staff but depended heavily on temporary workers drawn from the ranks of kolkhozniks.[74] These temporary employees were not paid for their labour from MTS funds or exclusively from the resources of their own kolkhozes; rather they were paid by the kolkhozes in which they worked.

The permanent employees of the MTS could be subdivided into the two main groups of management and workers. Management itself formed two distinct categories: the top-level group embraced the director, deputy director for political work, senior engineer-mechanic, senior agronomist, and chief book-keeper. The lower-level group included sectional mechanics and agronomists, chief of the MTM, the mechanic for complex farm machinery, and the MTS secretary in charge of technical-administrative work.[75] In addition to the managerial staff, the permanent MTS staff also included a differentiated group of workers classified as industrial labourers, encompassing operators of complex machinery, roving mechanics, repair workers, and various other skilled workers engaged in auxiliary branches of MTS work such as electricians,

---

72 Such as 1.25 acres of land and loans for building houses. *Vazhneishie resheniia po sel'skomu khoziaistvu za 1938–1946gg* (Moscow 1948), p. 118.
73 M. Dmitruk, 'Profsoiuzy i podv'em sel'skogo khoziaistva,' *Professional'nye soiuzy*, no 8 (August 1949), pp. 7–11.
74 Vucinic, *Soviet Economic Institutions*, p. 113 ff; Roy D. Laird, *The Rise and Fall of the MTS as an Instrument of Soviet Rule* (Lawrence, Kansas: Governmental Research Center, the University of Kansas, 1960), pp. 63 ff.
75 *Vazhneishie resheniia*, p. 245; D.M. Genkin and A.A. Ruskol, *Kolkhoznoe pravo* (Moscow 1947), p. 367; B. Kikin, 'O metodakh upravleniia proizvodstvom v MTS,' *Sotsialisticheskoe sel'skoe khoziaistvo*, no 3 (March 1947), p. 42.

communication workers, etc. Of the same status were the MTS white-collar employees (auxiliary administrative staff) and dispatchers, who provided liaison between the MTS headquarters and individual tractor brigades.

The third MTS group, temporary workers, was composed mainly of peasants who manned the tractor brigades and tractor aggregates. These temporary labourers, who continued to maintain membership in their respective kolk-hozes and in contrast with the permanent staff were considered members of the peasant class, made up over 50 per cent of the entire MTS personnel. In turn the kolkhozniks working for the MTS were classified into three groups. The top group consisted of brigade leaders, assistant brigade leaders, and auxiliary inspectors, a position established in 1942, primarily to keep a record of work accomplished by individual tractor operators and the brigade as a whole and also to control the use of fuel. The middle group consisted of tractor operators, divided into senior tractor operators, junior operators, and the hitchmen or operators of various agricultural implements pulled by the tractors. The lowest kolkoznik group included servicing squads engaged in hauling water, fuel, and other supplies.

Of the three main groups composing the MTS personnel only the first two, i.e., the management and permanent working force, had the right to trade union membership. In the early years they were served by the Union of MTS Workers and Batraks, the MTS Workers' unions, and the Union of MTS and Land Organs Workers. After the 1934 reorganization of the unions it appeared that MTS personnel were organized into two unions: management in the Land Organs union, and workers in the MTS Workers' unions.[76] If this actually was the case, then management's position was strengthened even more, because in addition to other privileges this special treatment would have further enhanced its officially bestowed high social status.

The third group, the peasants, did not have the right to be union members.[77]

76 Slutsky claims that the Union of Workers of Land Organs united workers in the MTS and sovkhozes. It is possible that it did encompass the management group. The rest were served by the existing sovkhoz unions and the MTS workers' unions. Slutsky and Sydorenko, *Profsoiuzy Ukrainy*, p. 119.
77 The following exchange is characteristic. Question: 'In our raion some workers and employees (cleaning women, night watchmen) are employed as hired labour by schools and hospitals, but at the same time are members of the kolkhoz and are employed there as well. Can these workers become trade union members?' Answer: 'Trade unions unite all toilers who work as hired labour. If the workers and employees mentioned by you are engaged in the village institution permanently and as hired labour, and are receiving wages, then they can become trade union members. The fact that they work in the kolkhoz in addition to their permanent jobs should not serve as an obstacle to their becoming trade union members.' 'V pomoshch nizovomu profaktivu,' *Trud*, 8 January 1936, p. 2.

Even tractor operators, who were considered an advanced group of kolkhozniks, could not qualify for trade union membership until after the September 1953 Central Committee Resolution on Agriculture when they became
full-time MTS employees compensated at higher rates than they had previously
received as kolkhozniks. The hitchmen and servicing squads were not, however, included in this change.[78]

Nevertheless it is difficult to state with any degree of assurance that the
production principle ensured that all workers and employees in the MTS and
sovkhozes belonged to any one trade union serving their enterprises. We have
noted above that the Union of Workers in Land Organs, during its independent
existence, in addition to officials of the Ministry of Agriculture and its organs
also united higher echelon workers of the MTS and sovkhozes. This was a clear
violation of the production principle of trade union structure that demanded
adherence to the formula, 'one enterprise – one union.' There are other
indications throughout the late 1930s of the failure to apply this principle
consistently. For example, when motor transport columns were organized in
the MTS in 1938 the drivers were made members of the Union of Chauffeurs,
causing loud protests by the MTS Workers' unions. The attempted transfer in
the same year of MTS repairmen (MTM workers) to the Medium Machine-
building Workers' Union was bitterly and successfully resisted.[79]

The jurisdictional confusion was perpetuated by the failure of the ACCTU
to come out with a completely new trade union map.[80] Because of this, no one
clearly knew to which unions various groups of workers belonged. The reorganization of the trade union structure initiated by the Tenth Plenum of the
ACCTU in 1940 was designed to bring some order into this confusion, but it
was not fully completed when the war intervened.

There are no statistics on trade union membership for the immediate prewar period. We may assume, however, that because of organizational efforts
and the inclusion of the newly acquired territories of the Baltic States,
Western Belorussia, the Western Ukraine, and Northern Bukovina, agricul-

78 *KPSS o profsoiuzakh*, pp. 604–5; G. Kotov, 'MTS reshaiushchaia sila v dal'neishem
   pod'eme sel'skogo khoziaistva,' *Trud*, 5 June 1954, p. 2. At the beginning of 1938
   there were 1,402,949 persons in the kolkhoz villages engaged in the basic mechanical work of the MTSS and MTMS. Of this number 943,000 were tractor operators,
   120,000 brigadiers, 247,000 combine operators and 215,000 truck and automobile
   drivers. A. Kuropatkin, 'O prevrashchenii sel'skokhoziaistvennogo truda v
   raznovidnost' truda industrial'nogo,' *Bolshevik*, xxvi, no 5 (15 March 1949), pp.
   42–55.
79 Speech of P.Ia. Malokhat'ko at the Seventh ACCTU Plenum in September 1938.
   Trud, 14 September 1938, p. 2.
80 Novorizhkin's speech, *Trud*, 8 September 1938, p. 3.

tural trade union membership was on the rise. It may further be assumed that this rise in membership was checked by the start of the war and was probably quite low at the cessation of hostilities. There was certainly a tremendous change in the composition of trade union membership during this period, reflecting the influx of women. But again, in the absence of precise statistical evidence, it is extremely difficult to say how large this influx was, although it must have been significant. It is known that in 1944 women made up 26.3 per cent of the total trade union membership in the Soviet Union, and that in 1947 their share rose to 35.4 per cent.[81] This percentage was probably even higher in agriculture.

THE POSTWAR CHANGES

The reorganization of October 1948 decreed by the Presidium of the ACCTU combined the eleven existing trade unions of agricultural workers into two unions, thus strengthening their membership considerably. At that time, over one million workers were employed by the sovkhozes.[82] Yet as late as 1951 over 150,000 eligible sovkhoz workers were still reported to be outside of the union.[83]

The situation was no better in the Union of MTS and Land Organs Workers. As N.V. Popova admitted at the Seventeenth ACCTU Plenum on 29 December 1947, 'many oblast and especially local organizations of the Union work poorly and need to be strengthened.'[84] In 1951 this union was reported as having 1,600,000 members in 20,000 organizations, led by 408,000 activists.[85] Although the organization was large, its rate of growth was not satisfactory: from 1950 to 1951, for example, its total membership grew by only 1.3 per cent. Individual oblast branches of the union fared worse. For example, in Tambov oblast from 1949 to 1950 organized workers made up only 80 per cent of the total eligible number of labourers in enterprises served by the union. In the period from June 1950 to June 1951 this number declined by 5.8 per cent. In Krasnodar krai there was no growth in membership during the same period.[86]

In 1953, as noted in chapter 2, a further growth and consolidation took place in the unions serving agricultural workers. The decision of the ACCTU

81 N.V. Popova, 'O rabote s profsoiuznym aktivom,' Trud, 29 January 1948, pp. 2–3.
82 Profsoiuz rabochikh sel'skogo khoziaistva, p. 125.
83 'Na konferentsiiakh i s'ezdakh profsoiuzov,' Trud, 29 March 1951, p. 1.
84 Popova, Trud, 29 January 1948, pp. 2–3.
85 Profsoiuz rabochikh sel'skogo khoziaistva, p. 129.
86 V. Andreev, 'V nadezhde na tsirkular: tysiachi rabochikh sela eshche ne vovlecheny v profsoiuz,' Trud, 5 June 1951, p. 2.

Secretariat on 18 April 1953 to amalgamate the sovkhoz workers' unions with the Union of MTS and Land Organs Workers and with the Union of Workers in Flour Mills and Grain Elevators not only resulted in a single Union of Workers and Employees in Agriculture and State Procurement but also in a strengthening of the union membership.[87] Also during 1953, and especially in October of that year, a large number of workers joined the MTS, 'many of them from industry.'[88] Most of them probably became trade union members.

Finally, in 1953 and the beginning of 1954 the union received a tremendous boost in membership thanks to a change in the status of the hitherto temporary MTS workers who, with the exception of the hitchmen and servicing squads and as a result of the party decision to improve agricultural output, were made full-time MTS workers and as such acquired the right to trade union membership. Out of 1,250,000 of these new MTS workers, approximately 600,000, or 50 per cent, became trade union members right away.[89] In 1954 the total number of agricultural union members equalled 4,800,000, with 870,000 of them considered trade union activists.[90] The union served in addition to its own members approximately six million workers and employees in 1954.[91] Two years later, at its Second Congress held in March 1956, the overall numerical strength of the union had reached 5,159,000 persons.[92] The total number served by the union was well over six million, of whom approximately 2,039,000 were on state farms.[93] Yet according to S.V. Egurazdov, chairman of the Central Committee of the union, about one million eligible workers in rural areas were outside trade unions.[94] In April 1958 at the time of the Third

---

87 There are no statistics available on the strength of the Workers in Flour Mills and Grain Elevators. In 1934, the last date such statistics were available, this union numbered 168,000 members, organized in 23 oblast committees. Its Central Committee had 176 officials. 'O perestroike profsoiuzov,' *Trud,* 9 September 1934, p. 3.

88 V. Volchikhin, 'Sel'skie mekhanizatory rabotaiut kruglyi god,' *Trud,* 29 March 1956, p. 2.

89 *Profsoiuz rabochikh sel'skogo khoziaistva,* p. 150. See also *Itogi vsesoiuznoi perepisi naseleniia 1959 goda: SSSR, svodnyi tom* (Moscow: Gosstatizdat, 1962), pp. 159–60.

90 *Ibid.,* p. 150.

91 These figures were given at the newly created union in April 1954.

92 *Profsoiuz rabochikh sel'skogo khoziaistva,* p. 158. See also 'Postanovlenie IV Plenuma VTsSPS ob itogakh XX s'ezda KPSS i zadachakh profsoiuzov,' *Trud,* 31 March 1956, pp. 1–2.

93 *Profsoiuz rabochikh sel'skogo khoziaistva,* p. 158; *The Soviet Union in Facts and Figures* (London: Soviet News, 1956), p. 22.

94 S. Egurazdov, 'O profsoiuznykh organizatsiiakh na sele,' *Trud,* 26 March 1956, p. 2. In Kazakhstan there were 600,000 trade union members. S. Taktamysov, 'Sovershenstvovat' profsoiuznuiu rabotu,' *Trud,* 27 March 1958, p. 2.

Congress of the union, its membership had risen to over six million and it served over 6,500,000 workers and employees, with trade union activists alone reaching the imposing figure of 1,400,000 persons.[95] In the MTS at the end of their existence there were 186,000 specialists and 1,500,000 machine operators, most of whom must have been union members.[96]

LIQUIDATION OF THE MTS AND UNION MEMBERSHIP IN KOLKHOZES

The Third Congress of the union, which was held shortly after the February Plenum of the Central Committee of the Communist party and the First Session of the Fifth Convocation of the Supreme Soviet of the USSR in March 1958, had to face the question of trade union membership as a result of the reorganization of the MTS. The congress limited itself only to a resolution that the branches of the union 'would actively participate in the setting up of the RTS, providing them with cadres,' and would see to it that the 'organization of labour and wages' would be improved and strengthened.[97] Nothing was mentioned at the congress about the discussion of trade union membership in the kolkhozes, although it is hard to see that such an important and hotly contested subject could have been ignored. It is therefore worth taking a closer look at the changes resulting from the MTS reorganization.

On 22 January 1958 Khrushchev in a speech to agricultural officials in Minsk officially proposed the dissolution of the MTS and the sale of their machines to the kolkhozes. Reorganization of the MTS was the main item on the agenda of the Plenum of the Central Committee and the CPSU 25 and 26 February 1958, and Khrushchev explained his proposal in detail at this meeting. After these steps, a public discussion of the MTS reorganization took place. At the end of March the discussion came to a close at a meeting of the Supreme Soviet at which Khrushchev made a further long speech about the reorganization of the MTS.[98] Khrushchev's proposals were embodied in the law passed by the Supreme Soviet on 31 March 1958.[99]

95 *Profsoiuz rabochikh sel'skogo khoziaistva*, p. 164.
96 Egurazdov, 'O profsoiuznykh organizatsiiakh na sele,' *Trud*, 26 March 1958, p. 2.
97 *Profsoiuz rabochikh sel'skogo khoziaistva*, pp. 164–5.
98 N.S. Khrushchev, 'O dal'neishem razvitii kolkhoznogo stroitel'stva i reorganizatsii MTS: Doklad na sessii Verkhovnogo Soveta SSSR, 27 marta, 1958,' *Trud*, 28 March 1958, pp. 2–5.
99 Article 7 of the law provided that 'the Council of Ministers of the USSR should secure correct utilization of machine operators and specialists being transferred to work in the kolkhozes and to take proper care of their material security.' 'Zakon o dal'neishem razvitii kolkhoznogo stroia i reorganizatsii mashinno traktornykh stantsii,' *Trud*, 1 April 1958, p. 1.

The discussion about the status of the transferred workers, however, lasted much longer, ending only on 8 June 1958, three months after it was begun by a resolution of the VTsSPS on 11 March 1958.[100] But in actuality it had already been in full swing, having started with an article in *Trud* on 4 March 1958.[101] It is worthwhile considering this article in greater detail because it summarized thoroughly all the arguments raised at an MTS meeting in favour of safeguarding the trade union rights and benefits of workers being transferred into kolkhozes.

At least one of the discussants voiced strong disapproval of the plans to transfer MTS workers into the kolkhozes, because 'we are people with qualifications, we have technical experience. Why should I, for example, go into a kolkhoz and be put on the same level with the rest of them there?'[102] He openly expressed an attitude towards the kolkhozniks prevalent among MTS workers that they were unable to adapt to mechanical processes, were clumsy in carrying out work assignments, and lacked a capacity for organized endeavour. Others who seemed to agree with this view asserted that 'we are valuable people ... because of our technical knowledge and experience,' yet warned against 'extolling our own values.' But they also pointed out that their knowledge and experience was genuinely valued by the party and by Khrushchev, evidenced by the fact that his 'theses' specified that MTS cadres who were being transferred into kolkhozes should be 'utilized properly,' placed in 'the key positions of the production process,' and that machine operators should be 'guaranteed a minimum wage.' In short, this argument ran, the will of the party should not be resisted. The party knew what it was doing, and the interest of former MTS personnel would be safeguarded. As one of the discussants stated, the opposition to being transferred into kolkhozes was silly, for after all 'did not most of us come from them in the first place?' This was a reference to the September 1953 decision of the party to give the 'mechanizers' the status of permanent workers in the MTS.

100 It should be pointed out that there were some workers in the kolkhozes who were also trade union members. These were specialists, workers, and employees who were sent to work in kolkhozes for various purposes. 'O profsoiuznom chlenstve rabochikh i sluzhashchikh i spetsialistov komandirovanykh na rukovodstvennuiu rabotu v kolkhozy: Postanovlenie VTsSPS ot 23 maia, 1955g,' *Spravochnik profsoiuznogo rabotnika* (Moscow: Profizdat, 1962), p. 170; 'Ob uchastii profsoiuznykh organizatsii v obsuzhdenii tezisov doklada N.S. Khrushcheva "O dal'neishem razvitii kolkhoznogo stroia i reorganizatsii MTS": Postanovlenie VTsSPS,' *Trud*, 11 March 1958, p. 1.
101 F. Breus, 'Kurs vernyi za namo delo ne stanet: reportazh s sobraniia mekhanizatorov MTS,' *Trud*, 4 March 1958, p. 2. See also International Labour Office, *The Trade Union Situation in the U.S.S.R.: Report of a Mission from the International Labour Office* (Geneva 1960), p. 92.
102 Breus, *Trud*, 4 March 1958, p. 2.

There was no division among this group on the necessity of retaining trade union membership or of establishing trade union organizations in the kolkhozes. As one of them stated, 'the use of machinery requires safety regulations, proper conditions of work, labour protection, etc. ...' It was the trade union's function to exercise proper control over these matters, as it was its function as well to see that 'paid vacations are granted,' that 'absence due to temporary incapacity is paid,' and that 'medical care is available.' 'We are used to this service,' it was argued, and the 'trade union organization should go to kolkhoz with us.' It was also argued that labour disputes could be arbitrated only by a union, and that 'mass cultural work' would suffer if there were no trade union.

The argument that whether or not trade union organizations would be permitted in the kolkhoz should depend entirely on the will of the kolkhoz members themselves was also raised. But the party dismissed it by saying that 'the fate of the Kolkhoz Statute' itself was uncertain, that great changes were taking place in the collectivized sector of the economy, that further changes would inevitably follow, leading eventually to a period in which the kolkhozes themselves would be raised to the level of the socialized sector (e.g., state owned), and that these changes would transform the labour of the kolkhozniks, bringing them ever closer to the status of industrial workers. The implication was that trade unions would hardly be out of place in the kolkhozes.

As far as the individual kolkhozniks themselves were concerned, it was argued that they not only did not oppose the trade union, but in fact would like to join it. As one of the discussants said 'each time work begins in the fields, the trailer hands come to me and to the trade union organizer and say, let us join your trade union. I say to them, you are members of a kolkhoz and you have no trade union organization. They answer, we and your tractor drivers work on the same unit, we do the same job, we eat out of the same pots and we want to have the same rights in the ordinary affairs of the brigade as the machine-tractor staff.' This attitude, the speaker contended, revealed that the establishment of trade unions in kolkhozes would also be supported by the ordinary kolkhozniks.

The form as well as the content of the article suggested that it had probably been ordered by the party to calm the fears of the machine operators and also to guide the discussion into proper channels. This suspicion is reinforced by the fact that two days later another article appeared in *Trud*, written by M. Kabanov, an associate of the Institute of Marxism-Leninism, which referred directly to the article above.[103] In it the question of trade union membership

103 M. Kabanov, 'Podderzhivaiu predlozhenie mekhanizatorov Enbekshi-Kazakhskoi MTS,' *Trud*, 8 March 1958, p. 1.

for former MTS workers was again raised. The demands of the transferred workers, so the author felt, were timely and in no way an obstacle to progress. In his opinion, Lenin would have approved of trade unions in kolkhozes, for the thought that in the future trade unions would gradually extend their activities to the 'toiling masses of the village' ran through 'many of his speeches, articles, and pamphlets which deal with trade union problems.'[104] Kabanov, however, would have temporarily limited trade union membership to the machine operators who were being sent into kolkhozes. They were to be the nucleus around which trade union organizations within kolkhozes could be built. In addition he would give trade union membership to 'workers in animal husbandry farms, where labour is to a large extent mechanized,' and to 'operators of kolkhoz electrical stations.' Nowhere did he mention that the legal status of kolkhozniks as part owners of their enterprise could be an obstacle to their acquiring trade union membership. Since it cannot be assumed that Kabanov was not familiar with the provisions of the Labour Code and the Trade Union Statute, most likely he anticipated that the status of the kolkhozniks was to be changed in the near future through the transformation of kolkhozes into sovkhozes and of kolkhozniks into hired workers.

Others who raised their voices in favour of kolkhoz trade unions were also not bothered by the legal status of the kolkhozniks. The chairman of the Krasnodar kraisovprof, M. Gladkov, proposed for example that all kolkhozniks be given trade union membership because 'this will strengthen educational work among them,' and would draw them into 'management of production.' He argued that to include kolkhozniks within unions not only 'does not contradict further development of the kolkhoz system' but would on the contrary contribute to this process.[105]

Those who opposed continued trade union membership for transferred MTS workers raised the legitimate point that the real question involved was not trade union membership per se but the rights and privileges that union membership can offer, such as vacations, sick leave, pensions, etc. These, they felt, could be made secure in some other way and with much less risk. In the opinion of K. Kovtun, the chairman of the Odessa obkom of the union, to permit such trade union organizations would be to run the risk of stimulating contention in the kolkhozes: 'I do not agree with those comrades who think a trade union organization ought to be set up in the kolkhoz to unite machine operators, i.e., a relatively small group from among the members of the kolkhoz ... This would

104 *Ibid.* He is especially fond of Lenin's speech at the first Congress of the Petrograd Gubernia Agricultural and Forestry Workers' Union and of the resolution for the Ninth Party Congress also written by Lenin.
105 M. Gladkov, 'Davaite podumaem i ob etom,' *Trud*, 27 March 1958, p. 2.

be harmful because the people in a kolkhoz would be divided into members of the trade union and members of the kolkhoz. Such a division would destroy the unity of the collective.'[106] This line of reasoning was implicit in the proposals of all who opposed trade union membership for any special category of kolkhoz workers.[107]

The discussion came to an end at the beginning of June with the publication of the resolutions of the ACCTU on 8 June 1958.[108] According to the resolutions, all machine operators and specialists who were transferred from the MTS into kolkhozes would retain their trade union membership, and all workers in kolkhozes employed as hired labourers, such as carpenters, would be granted the right to become trade union members.[109] The 1958 MTS reorganization and the retention of trade union membership by the ex-MTS workers transferred into kolkhozes is, perhaps, one of the clearest examples of organized pressure and its influence on the party in recent years. Paradoxically, the very medium through which the pressure was exerted – the trade union – was an organization designed above all else to perform the function of political control. This development revealed that the trade union is potentially not only a channel of direction and control from above but also a conduit for communication and pressure from below. Further, the MTS reorganization shows that the party leadership is not immune to such pressure, especially if it does not overstep the bounds of order and force repressive measures, but on the other hand the exertion of pressure is potentially dangerous in just this respect.

Admittedly, there are several points that are unclear. For example, we do not know why the party leadership permitted the widespread discussion to take place. One explanation could be that a decision was taken by the party leadership prior to the discussion and then a guided debate was permitted so as to support the decision. Another explanation could be that the stresses and strains of the transformation were used by the party both to get necessary in-

---

106 K. Kovtun, 'Ia ne soglasen s Bogorodskimi mekhanizatorami,' *Trud*, 18 March 1958, p. 2.
107 V. Karavaev, 'Ob okhrane truda v kolkhozakh,' *Trud*, 19 March 1958, p. 2; M. Annenko 'Pervye shagi raboty po novomu,' *Trud*, 9 March 1958, p. 1; M. Makhnov, 'K priemu mekhanizatorov gotovy,' *Trud*, 6 March 1958, p. 1. For a more recent case of pressure on the collective farm to meet the needs of its members on the basis of equality with the unionized workers see A. Khomiakov, 'Profkompravleniiu pomoshchnik,' *Sovetskie profsoiuzy*, no 10 (May 1968), pp. 20–1.
108 'O zadachakh profsoiuznykh organizatsii v sviazi s postanovleniem TsK KPSS i Soveta Ministrov SSSR "O dal'neishem razvitii kolkhoznogo stroia i reorganizatsii MTS",' *Trud*, 8 June 1958, p. 1.
109 'Profsoiuznye gruppy v kolkhozakh,' *Trud*, 1 July 1958, p. 1.

formation on the state of the economy and at the same time to permit the alleviation of pent-up emotions. But a third explanation may be – and there is some evidence to suggest this (for example, the discussion started even before official sanction was given by the ACCTU) – that the disaffection among the workers was great enough to make itself felt to the extent that the party decided to go along with it and by doing so to try to modify some of their ideas and to turn the situation to its own advantage. Certainly the solution smacks of compromise. The party did not take away trade union membership from the transferred workers, but at the same time it did not permit at that time the setting up of full-fledged trade union organizations in kolkhozes. Only trade union groups were established which were subordinated to the local committees of trade unions in the RTSs and in many significant respects had no right to interfere in the activities of kolkhoz managements. The party did not overlook the possibilities for control in the kolkhozes presented by the influx of ex-MTS workers. While the existence of two classes of kolkhozniks carried with it the danger of inflaming the desire of the mass of the peasantry for a better life, it also created friction which could be manipulated by the party for its own ends. It should be added here that the question of trade union membership for ordinary collective farmers continues to animate discussions in the Soviet press to this day. The debate over thie question became quite extensive during 1969 just prior to the Third Congress of the Collective Farmers, and the Eighth Congress of the union had addressed itself to this question in January 1968.[110]

The decision to include all hired labour in the kolkhozes within the union became one source of membership growth in the post-1958 period. Still another source of trade union membership expansion was, at least until late 1964, the growth in number of state farms at the expense of the kolkhozes, pushing agricultural trade union membership to seven million in March 1960 and to approximately eleven million in February 1963. In 1967 the union

110 I. Shkuratov, 'Sotsial'noe strakhovanie kolkhoznikov,' *Ekonomicheskaia Gazeta,* no 23 (June 1970), p. 23; 'O zadachakh profsoiuzykh organizatsii v sviazi s resheniiami Tret'ego Vsesoiuznogo S'ezda Kolkhoznikov,' *Trud,* 11 January 1970, p. 2; I. Shkuratov 'Vysokii dolg profsoiuzov sela,' *Sovetskie profsoiuzy,* no 12 (June 1966), pp. 1–3; N. Glukhov, 'Profkom pomoshchnik pravleniia,' *Sovetskie profsoiuzy,* no 13 (July 1969), pp. 22–3; I. Pavlov, 'Novyi etap razvitiia kolkhoznogo stroia,' *Sovetskie profsoiuzy,* no 18 (September 1969), pp. 16–17; N. Popov, 'Za dostoinyi uklad v piatiletku,' *Sel'skaia zhizn,* 19 January 1968, pp. 1–3; N. Popov, 'Mnozhit' uspekhi v trude,' *Sel'skaia zhizn,* 20 January 1968, p. 2; Dmitri Polianski's speech at the Third Congress of Collective Farmers, *Pravda,* 26–9 November 1969. It should be added here that Polianskii's scheduled closing speech at the congress was not delivered. The significance of this event is still unclear. *Sel'skaia zhizn',* 25 September 1965.

membership rose to 13,864,000[111] and in 1970 to over fifteen million[112] In kolkhozes alone there were 37,000 trade union committees with a membership of some 2,600,000 workers in 1968. And in 1970 in kolkhozes there were over three million mechanizers who were trade union members.

From the preceding discussion it may be concluded that it is very likely that Lenin's principle of limiting membership in agricultural unions to persons who were, to some extent at least, engaged as hired workers still retains its validity in the minds of Soviet officialdom. This would explain the fact that no significant changes have appeared in the language of article 1 of the Trade Union Statute or in the section dealing with primary trade union organizations.[113] And since no change has been made in article 151 of the Labour Code,[114] the legal provisions relating to hired workers, in combination with the Trade Union Statute, provide grounds for doubting whether as matters now stand there is room in the existing trade union structure for non-employed categories of kolkhozniks. The debate is not yet over. It is possible that as inequalities in wages and social insurance between kolkhozniks and higher labour are eliminated the pressure for trade union membership by collective farmers will diminish.

However, as part of the drive to raise productivity in agriculture, and owing to the need to retain labour against the competing attractions of industrial

---

111 K. Paramonov, F. Rasporkin, 'Govoriat khoziaeva zemli,' *Trud*, 1 April 1960, p. 2; 'Organizatory sorevnovaniia na sele,' *Trud*, 19 February 1963, p. 1; *Spravochnoia kniga o profsoiuzakh* (2nd ed.; Moscow: Profizdat 1968), p. 348.

112 'Novye rubezhi sela,' *Sovietskie profsoiuzy*, no 5 (March 1970), pp. 11–12.

113 Prior to 1959 the statute provided that members of producers' co-operatives (artel's) were not eligible for trade union membership. *Ustav professional'nykh soiuzov SSR utverzhden XI s'ezdom profsoiuzov SSSR 15 iiunia 1954g* (Moscow: Profizdat, 1955), article 10. This prohibition was deleted when the statute was amended in 1959. However, collective farms and producers' co-operatives were still not specifically mentioned in article 1. *Ustav professional'nykh soiuzov SSSR utverzhden XII s'ezdom profsoiuzov SSSR 27 marta 1959g* (Moscow: Profizdat, 1959), articles 1 and 10. This is still the case in the newest statute, although further change in the language is in evidence. Article 1 specifically mentions only sovkhozes and refers to others simply as 'enterprises and institutions.' The same is true of articles 45 and 46 describing membership and functions of the primary trade union organizations. *Ustav professional'nykh soiuzov SSSR utverzhden XIII s'ezdom profsoiuzov SSSR 1 noiabria 1963g* (Moscow: Profizdat, 1963); *Ustav professional'nykh soiuzov SSSR utverzhden XIII s'ezdom profsoiuzov SSSR*, as amended by the Fourteenth Congress of Trade Unions of 4 March 1968 in *Materialy XIV, s'ezda professional'nykh soiuzov SSSR* (Moscow: Profizdat, 1968), pp. 115–48. The amended statute does mention the trade union organization in the collective farm in the section dealing with the primary trade union organizations.

114 See above p. 96

employment, a trend can be discerned towards replacing the traditional method of payment in kind by payment in money on a fixed and periodic basis. This concept of 'guaranteed monetary labour payment' is based on a system of norms and piece rates and is regarded as 'the logical culmination of all progressive changes that have occurred in recent years in the distribution of kolkhoz income.'[115] Remuneration on this basis is in fact expected to lead to an obliteration of the distinction between working class and peasant forms of income distribution.[116] When this happens the membership of agricultural trade unions will again grow tremendously. But even before this ideal situation is achieved there is nothing to prevent the Soviet Communist party from sweeping away this bit of legal myth that makes kolkhozniks part owners of an enterprise, if the party feels the price involved is worth paying. It would thereby open the way for the peasant to become a trade union member, entitling him to basic rights and privileges long denied him. Such a turn of affairs, however, is unlikely in the near future. As the recent decision to extend social insurance to kolkhizniks shows, this will be a long and slow process.

115 T. Zaslavskaia, 'Garantiinaia denezhnaia oplata truda v kolkhozakh,' *Voprosy Ekonomiki*, no 2 (February 1959), pp. 115, 116.
116 *Ibid.*, p. 88.

4
Finances

The financial situation of the trade union in agriculture reflects its strengths and weaknesses more clearly than does either its organizational structure or its membership. In the early years of its existence at least it reveals the degree of union dependence on outside sources. Unfortunately, the absence of the necessary statistical data makes impossible anything more than a general sketch of the problem. In order to understand the financial situation of the agricultural trade union better it is necessary to relate it to the financial practices characteristic of all unions, the most important of which is the centralized method of administering trade union funds.

The proposal to have a central trade union fund was originally made at the First Congress of Trade Unions and was subsequently approved by the Second Congress, which proceeded to take measures to bring the scheme into operation. According to the provisions adopted, executives of the local unions were requested to transfer all membership contributions to the corresponding trade union subsection, and these bodies had, in turn, to forward these moneys to the gubernia sections after deduction of the sum earmarked in the budget for their administrative expenses. Of the total sum received from the subsection, the gubernia sections were to transmit 30 per cent to their central committee and 10 per cent to the gubernia inter-trade union council. The remaining 60 per cent was retained by the sections and was considered as an advance on their budgetary estimates.[1] Finally, the central committees were requested to pay to the ACCTU 10 per cent of all moneys received by them.

---

1 These arrangements continued to exist until the liquidation of inter-trade union

The Second Congress of Trade Unions also adopted an important resolution which stated that the entire revenue from contributions belonged to the central committees of the unions, and that the sums left at the disposal of subordinate trade union bodies should be considered short-term loans. The congress also defined the notion of a single trade union fund:

In view of the character of the Russian trade union movement, all special funds, such as strike funds, reserve funds, etc. controlled by the local organizations must be wound up and transferred to a fund common to the whole trade union movement. The ACCTU will also form a special relief fund for foreign organizations, which fund wil be supported by gifts and special credits.

In the early days of the revolution there was no fixed rate for contributions. In some unions contributions were a certain proportion of the wages earned, but in others no definite rule existed. In 1919, however, it was felt 'that in view of the constant depreciation of the rouble it is best to adopt a percentage of wages system,' whereby membership dues would be set at a fixed fraction of any worker's wage. This percentage at first was fixed at one per cent and was later increased to 2 per cent. This remained the procedure until 1926 when the Seventh Congress of Trade Unions decided to switch to membership dues based on a sliding scale.[2]

Up to 1919 there was no legislation of any kind permitting the deduction of contributions from a worker's wages, but a resolution adopted in 1920 by the Third Congress of Trade Unions stated that 'with the permission of the local trade union authorities the management of an enterprise or institution may deduct trade union contributions from the worker's wages. Further ... all sums thus collected are to be sent by the management to the trade union organization concerned, accompanied by a list of workers showing the amount deducted from each person mentioned.'[3]

This method of financing proved to be of great benefit to the Bolshevik leaders. In the first place it led to the introduction of compulsory membership in the unions. Secondly, giving complete financial control to the central organ of the union placed it in a strong position in relation to the local organizations. This power was increased by a resolution adopted by the Second Congress of Trade Unions according to which 'trade unions may receive special grants from a state commissariat to cover work of general utility (education, protec-

councils was an accomplished fact. 'IV vsesoiuznyi s'ezd sel'khozlesrabochikh,' *Trud*, 1 December 1928, p. 2.
2 VTsSPS, *Otchet VTsSPS k VII s'ezdu profsoiuzov* (Moscow 1926), p. 136.
3 International Labour Office, *The Trade Union Movement in Soviet Russia* (Geneva 1927), p. 70.

tion of labour, etc.).' At the same time the primary organs, the factory committees, were not included in these arrangements. Their administrative expenses were borne entirely by the enterprise concerned.

While this system, which was intended to provide ample financial resources for the union, was in the process of being established a number of measures were also adopted to meet urgent requirements. These included extensive government subsidies to the unions. During 1918, for instance, the ACCTU received only 280,000 roubles in contributions but 1,680,000 roubles in grants from the government authorities and the Communist party.[4] The situation did not improve in 1919. The financial report of the ACCTU to the Third Congress of Trade Unions stressed the fact that, while the contributions paid during the year amounted to four million roubles, expenditures exceeded six million roubles. The financial position of the oblast inter-trade union councils was especially poor, and in 1919 the ACCTU had to subsidize them to the amount of 1,500,000.[5] Moreover, the proportion of the contributions due the ACCTU was paid with great irregularity. Only two unions made their payments promptly, and many others paid contributions without furnishing any details concerning their membership.

Trade union financial affairs went from bad to worse during the following year and a half (January 1920 to May 1921). No figures for separate unions are available, but the balance sheet of the ACCTU submitted to the Fourth Congress contained the following items:

REVENUE
Contributions   16,725,295
Subsidies from the Committee of Labour Expenditures   205,000,000
Subsidies to the Central Committee and inter-trade union organs   69,841,629

Thus, it can be seen that in 1920, in spite of all the measures described above, the ACCTU could no longer depend on contributions by the unions. On the contrary, the ACCTU was obliged to finance the unions to enable them to accomplish the many new and difficult tasks they had undertaken. The unions in this way had become to a large extent financially dependent on the state. They continued to expect contributions from their members without the members being entirely aware of the fact, since all contributions had taken the form of a simple deduction from wages. But the sum received in contributions, which fluctuated greatly on account of the fluidity of wage rates, represented only a small item in the budget of the unions. In order to keep the immense bureaucratic union machine working and to allow the unions to perform their duties, it had become necessary to resort to state subsidies on a large scale.

4 *Ibid.*   5 *Ibid.*, p. 71.

There are no statistical data to indicate that the Agricultural and Forestry Workers' Union was in a relatively better condition. Indeed, one can assume that because of its type of membership financial problems were even more acute than in other unions.

THE NEW ECONOMIC POLICY

The NEP led to a complete change in the party's attitude towards the trade unions. After February 1922 the ACCTU decided that the trade unions should be relieved of all responsibility for state services and that in the future they should be dependent solely on members' contributions. The ACCTU, however, did in fact continue to receive government subsidies. The ACCTU also reserved the right to finance organizations falling into debt and in this way softened the effect of the decision that unions should rely on membership dues. As we shall see later this particular policy was especially beneficial to the Agricultural Workers' Union, which was continually in debt.[6]

The principles of trade union finance approved by the Trade Union Congress were confirmed by the ACCTU. The affiliation fee for each member was fixed at half a day's wages and the monthly contribution at 2 per cent of total monthly wages. The sums thus obtained were distributed in the following manner. The gubernia section that collected contributions paid 10 per cent of the total to the gubernia trade union council and 5 to 25 per cent to the central committee of the union. The latter paid 10 per cent of the sum it received to the ACCTU.[7]

In view of the conditions in the country, it is obvious that even a partial suppression of state subsidies to trade unions was bound to create great difficulties. This was especially true in view of the fact that now the system of paying individual dues had to be restored. During the period of close dependence on state subsidies most of the trade unions had engaged a large staff (and the Agricultural and Forestry Workers' Union was no exception) to meet the needs of administration, vocational education, the distribution of supplies, social insurance, etc. A reduction of this staff now had be be effected.

The financial situation of the unions that resulted from this reform was disturbing. The hardest hit were Agricultural and Forestry Workers' Union, the Builders' Union, and others which employed seasonal labourers or village proletariat, which were hard to keep organized, let alone to solicit for membership dues. This problem did not become acute until 1922, as all workers were simply registered in a trade union and in effect felt no pecuniary obligations, since the enterprise employing them was responsible for paying contributions. The Agricultural and Forestry Workers' Union was confronted with

6 *Ibid.*, p. 81.   7 *Ibid.*, pp. 81–2.

one additional problem when the decision was taken to organize the batraks, most of whom were employed by individual farmers or more well-to-do peasants, for it proved almost impossible to collect membership dues from this group of workers. Because it was also this union more than any other that was subject to periodic purges in order that it might retain its proletarian character, the goal of financial independence was never fully achieved. Furthermore, at this period the irregularity with which the wages were paid, combined with a sudden fall in the purchasing power of the rouble, resulted in the worker receiving on payday only a mere fraction of the money due him, and this did not encourage him to pay his contributions.[8] Finally, the collectors of membership dues were not yet at all efficient in performing their task. The problem was so serious that it was necessary to stimulate their zeal by giving them a certain percentage of the contributions collected.[9] (This tax-farming procedure was finally condemned by the Sixth Congress of Trade Unions in 1924.)[10]

As a result of all these difficulties the payment of contributions was seriously in arrears in Soviet trade unions. In 1923, despite some improvement, the sums paid never exceeded 80 or 90 per cent of those due; in most cases the proportion was even lower. In Siberia in the spring of 1923 the figure was 80 per cent; in Belorussia it was 60 to 70 per cent. In Transcaucasia, 45 per cent of the members supposed to pay individually did not pay; and in Baku, after the adoption of the system of individual payment, trade union receipts fell by 20 and even 40 per cent. There are no separate statistics for the Agricultural and Forestry Workers' Union for this period, but the tone of discussions of the union's financial position and the collection of dues at its Fourth Congress in December 1922 seemed to indicate that the situation was serious.[11]

Expenditure practices were no less unsatisfactory than collection practices. Once contributions were collected by a gubernia section of a union they were used by the latter to meet its own expenses, and only a reduced portion was transmitted to the gubernia trade union council or to the central committee of the union. But even the gubernia departments were receiving on an average only three-quarters of the proportion of contributions due them. The same was true, of course, of the payments of the central committees of the trade unions to the ACCTU. In April 1923 three central committees, among them that of the Agricultural and Forestry Workers' Union, made no payments. In fact the

8 VTsSPS, *Otchet VTsSPS k VI s'ezdu professional'nykh soiuzov* (Moscow: VTsSPS, 1924), p. 112, mentions the territorial distribution of the union and the low wages of individual workers as the reason for failure to pay contributions.

9 ILO, *The Trade Union Movement*, p. 91.

10 VTsSPS, *Shestoi s'ezd profsoiuzov: stenograficheskii otchet* (Moscow: Izdatel'stvo VTsSPS, 1925), p. 137.

11 'Vserossiiskii s'ezd rabotnikov zemli i lesa,' *Trud*, 21 December 1922, p. 5.

Central Committee of the union closed the first half of 1923 with an 80 per cent deficit. In the third quarter of 1923 financial circumstances worsened – the central committee of the union alone had an income of 3,721 roubles and expenditures of 8,261 roubles – and they did not improve in January or February of 1924.[12] The deficit was not so large for the union's gubernia sections, which were allowed to spend about 75 per cent of their receipts. If they were short they merely limited their payments to the higher organizations. The union's Central Committee, on the other hand, spent about five times as much as it received in contributions.[13]

One method of meeting these large deficits was to draw on subsidies from higher organizations. Thus the ACCTU from January to March 1923 received three and a half million roubles from the government, almost all of which were distributed among the local organizations. A good share of this subsidy went to support the Agricultural and Forestry Workers' Union. Another method consisted of borrowing from economic trust, commercial unions, etc. Still another was the illegal use of funds which were to be reserved for educational purposes, unemployment relief, etc., or the withholding of money paid by the management of enterprises for the maintenance of rabochkoms (2 per cent of total wages). A further method was to squeeze illegal donations out of management to the sum of up to 10 per cent of total wages.

The reasons for such high deficits were to be found not only in bad financial management and the embezzlement of funds but also in extremely high administrative expenses at all levels of the trade union structure.[14] In 1921 there was an average of one paid official for every one hundred members. In 1922, following the first staff reductions, there were only six officials for every one thousand members. Henceforth, however, the process of reduction slowed down, and in the Agricultural and Forestry Workers' Union the number of officials even increased because of efforts to organize the batraks, with a consequent rise in expenditures.[15] In April 1923 the Plenum of the ACCTU decided that the number of trade union officials should be reduced to the ratio of one official for every five hundred members and that their salaries should not absorb more than 50 per cent of receipts. This decision was ignored almost totally. Salaries and administrative expenses together constituted 80 to 90 per cent of total trade union expenditures. The Agricultural and Forestry Workers' Union spent more than other unions for these purposes.[16]

12 VTsSPS, *Otchet VTsSPS k VI s'ezdu*, pp. 111–12.
13 *Ibid.*, p. 117.
14 *Ibid.*, p. 113.
15 VTsSPS, *Otchet VTsSPS k VII s'ezdu*, p. 158.
16 VTsSPS, *Otchet VTsSPS k VI s'ezdu*, p. 113.

A Plenum of the Central Committee of the union held in February 1924 voiced concern over its financial situation.[17] The report of the Auditing Commission showed that a large number of lower trade union organizations failed to discharge their financial responsibilities before the Central Committee of the union. But in order to ease the lot of the ordinary worker the plenum decided that social security rates were too high and should be reviewed.[18] Improvement was noted towards the end of 1924, when the payment of dues became more or less stabilized. Even then, however, there were arrears, estimated in the better organized branches of the union to be about 8 to 12 per cent, rising to 30 to 60 per cent in other branches.[19] In 1925 the payment of dues again became very irregular, and it was quite common in some branches to find two-thirds of the members neglecting to pay at all, while a rate of 50 per cent non-paying members was considered normal for the period.[20]

One of the main causes of these dues irregularities was widespread abuse by union bosses of so-called voluntary contributions. By means of resolutions passed by local trade union committees, or by central committee plenary meetings, workers were compelled to become members of various public organizations, such as MOPR (International Organization for Aid to Fighters for Revolution), ODVF (Society of Friends of the Air Fleet), etc., which often had nothing in common with the idea of trade unionism but managed to absorb between 10 and 12 per cent of the wages of the workers. The Sixth Trade Union Congress which met in November 1924 finally decided that the total amount of contributions payable must not exceed 4 per cent of the wages earned and that it was up to the workers to join or to remain outside these so-called free associations.[21]

Corrupt trade union officials continued to be exposed in 1925, and it appears that the number of cases of embezzlement, illegal advances, etc., had become more frequent. For example, the Nizhegorod section of the Agricultural and Forestry Worker's Union spent 976 roubles out of the cultural fund, 300 roubles out of the rabochkom fund, and 494 roubles out of the batrachkom fund in order to pay its staff.[22]

Mismanagement of trade union funds, the lack of understanding displayed by the trade union with regard to the wishes and requirements of the workers, the authoritarian and uncompromising attitude of the trade union leaders, together with the arbitrary manner in which the trade union affairs were con-

17 'Plenum TsK vserabotzemlesa,' *Trud*, 24 February 1924, p. 3.
18 'Plenum TsK vserabotzemlesa,' *Trud*, 29 February 1924, p. 5
19 *Trud*, 18 October 1924.
20 VTsSPS, *Otchet VTsSPS k VII s'ezdu*, pp. 138–9.
21 ILO, *The Trade Union Movement*, p. 93.
22 ACCTU Circular, *Trud*, 18 July 1925; VTsSPS, *Otchet VTsSPS k VII s'ezdu*, pp. 140–2.

ducted led to the workers entirely losing interest in their occupational organizations. Collection methods did not improve in 1925, with the result that a large percentage of dues was never received: in Armenia 45 per cent of the members failed to pay membership dues; in the Ukraine 50 per cent; in Georgia 31 per cent; and in Azerbaidzhan 22 to 35 per cent.[23] In July 1925 a complete conversion to voluntary payment of membership dues took place, following directives of the Second ACCTU Plenum held in May 1925.[24] Expenditures for administration and personnel also grew. Thus, the Agricultural and Forestry Workers' Union in 1924 spent 80.7 per cent of its revenues for administration and staff. In 1925 this expenditure grew to 98.2 per cent of revenues.[25]

In his report to the Fourteenth Congress of the Communist party Tomsky, having admitted the existence of serious mismanagement of trade union funds, called for a reorganization of the accounting system of trade unions and for an increase in the powers of supervision of auditing committees[26] His recommendations were echoed at the Sixth Congress of the Agricultural and Forestry Workers' Union, which was held in Moscow from 18–30 January 1926.[27]

The Third ACCTU Plenum, which took place in Moscow from 6 to 11 February 1926, directed part of its attention to 'economizing and improving the handling of trade union funds.' The plenum also decided that the possibility should be considered of reducing the number of trade union officials in order to be in a position to increase subsidies to clubs and to the unemployed.[28] But it was stipulated that the reduction did not apply to the Agricultural and Forestry Workers' Union, whose membership was rapidly expanding.[29]

The report to the Eighth Congress of Trade Unions, held in Moscow from 10 to 23 December 1928, gave a revealing picture of the financial condition of the unions and especially of the Agricultural and Forestry Workers' Union.[30] The greatest single influence on the trade union financial picture was held to be the slowdown in the growth of trade union membership; the slow increase in workers' wages in the two years since the Seventh Congress in 1926 was also cited. Inevitably the revenues and spending, especially of industrial unions, were reduced. The growth in membership of the Agricultural and Forestry Workers' Union was, of course, rather rapid – 24.4 per cent between 1926 and 1928 – but a great deal of confusion still existed over this union's finances. The practice of siphoning money into special funds was especially

23 *Ibid.*, pp. 138–9.
24 *Ibid.*, p. 133.
25 *Ibid.*, p. 158.
26 *Trud*, 21 November 1925, pp. 1–2.
27 *Trud*, 19–31 January 1926.
28 *Trud*, 7–12 February 1926.
29 *Trud*, 19–31 January 1926.
30 'VIII Vsesoiuznyi s'ezd profsoiuzov,' *Trud* and *Pravda*, 11–25 December 1928.

condemned because, the report stated, it created shortages in administrative funds, and in order to cover the deficit the money was then illegally withdrawn from special funds. Thus, for example, forty gubernia sections of the Agricultural and Forestry Workers' Union showed a deficit in January 1927 of 73,000 roubles from special funds.[31]

Expenditures by Soviet trade unions for personnel and administrative needs, after experiencing a sharp decline between 1924 and 1925, began to increase. The recommendations of the ACCTU Presidium of March 1927 to reduce staff, which were repeated again in the ACCTU circular of December 1927 and again supported by the Third ACCTU Plenum in February 1928, did not have much influence, least of all in the Agricultural and Forestry Workers' Union. The expenditures of the union for administrative and personnel needs in percentages of total income were 97.2 per cent in 1924; 72.1 per cent in 1925; 77.4 per cent in 1926; and 79.2 per cent in 1927.[32] It is clear that expenditures for personnel and administration needs were again showing a tendency to increase in the late 1920s because of the drive to increase the recruitment of batraks. Appropriations into special funds for the same period as percentages of total income were as follows: 1924, 0.6 per cent; 1925, 2.9 per cent; 1926, 3.0 per cent; 1927; 5.2 per cent.[33] A clearer picture of the union's expenditures in 1927 is provided by table 4-1.

Available data provide the following information on the income of the Agricultural and Forestry Workers' Union during the mid-1920s. In 1926 the sum of total organizational resources plus special funds of the local branches amounted to 647,000 roubles. In 1927 this amount rose to 941,000 roubles, a growth of 45.5 per cent; of these funds the local organizations paid 403,000 roubles to the Central Committee of the union. The financial status of the Central Committee of the union was as follows: its administrative and operative expenditures as a percentage of total income amounted to 63.7 per cent in 1924; 86.5 per cent in 1925; 77.5 per cent in 1926; and 78.5 per cent in 1927. At the same time the Central Committee paid into special funds the following percentages of total income: in 1924, 1.2 per cent; 1925, 1.3 per cent; 1926, 4.5 per cent; 1927, 4.2 per cent. The sum of total organizational resources plus special funds of the Central Committee of the union amounted in 1926 to 61,000 roubles, and in 1927 to 119,000 roubles, which represented a growth of 95.1 per cent. For the union as a whole the sum of total financial resources plus special funds amounted in January 1927 to 708,000 roubles, or an average of 0.64 roubles per member, and in January 1928 to 1,060,000

31 VTsSPS, *Otchet VTsSPS k VIII s'ezdu*, p. 151.
32 *Ibid.*
33 *Ibid.*, p. 160.

TABLE 4–1

Expenditures by Agricultural and Forestry Workers' Union per member, 1927

Average membership	Average expenditure per member in roubles	Expenditure as percentage of total		
		Administrative needs	Payments to inter-trade union councils and ACCTU	Payments into special funds
1,188,000	4.90	85.8	8.0	5.5

SOURCE: VTsSPS, *Otchet VIII s'ezdu profsoiuzov* (Moscow 1928), p. 161.

roubles, or an average of 0.83 roubles per member, representing a growth of 29.7 per cent.[34]

In the management of its financial affairs, the Agricultural and Forestry Workers' Union led all other unions in the amount of money wasted, embezzled, or misappropriated. Of course, it was also the largest union insofar as the number of primary trade union organizations was concerned, uniting 18,300 primary organizations, and the absence of qualified personnel and the constant shakeups of the union perhaps had something to do with the number of thefts and illegal uses of union funds.[35] But attitudes prevalent towards embezzling and embezzlers were also relevant. Sometimes a responsible official who had embezzled money was appointed to another post just as important as the first one because of his proletarian origin. There was a tendency to view embezzlement not as a disgrace or a crime but as a misfortune. Thefts took place everywhere from the local trade union committees to the Central Committee, and according to Tomsky there was even an accounting category entitled 'unknown,' meaning that there had been a theft somewhere, but no one knew where. The chairmen of local trade union committees headed the list of malefactors. Embezzlers were divided about equally between Communists and non-party people. Young persons were especially prone; they composed not over 9 per cent of the union's entire membership but furnished 12.2 per cent of the thieves.[36]

The percentage of expenditure devoted to the immediate needs of union members (benefits, education, physical culture, etc) varied widely among Soviet trade unions in the 1920s. The Agricultural and Forestry Workers' Union used only 5 per cent of its outlays on these ends in 1927–8, whereas the corresponding figure for the Union of Metal Workers was from 50 to 55

34 *Ibid.*, pp. 163–73.   35 *Ibid.*, p. 184.
36 Tomsky's speech to the Eighth Trade Union Congress, *Trud*, 13–15 December 1928.

per cent.[37] But attempts were being made to increase benefits to members of the agricultural union. The Eight Trade Union Congress in 1928 restated in its resolutions that a reduction in administrative expenses ought to be undertaken and asked the union to see that at least 50 per cent of dues were effectively used for the immediate benefit of trade unionists.[38] It resolved to cut down contributions to local inter-trade union councils by 10 to 18 per cent and urged more frequent and thorough auditing of trade union accounts, stressing that there should be no hesitation in bringing guilty parties to justice.

In the years between the congress and the Ninth Trade Union Congress in 1932 tremendous changes took place in Soviet trade unions not only organizationally but also in their financial policy. At the Fifth Plenum of the ACCTU it was decided to introduce drastic changes in trade union finances in addition to reorganizing the trade union structure. One centralized budget was established, giving unchallenged power to the ACCTU to control all the trade union budgets. Henceforth trade union finances were, to a great extent, out of the reach of individual union central committees, not to mention local branches, and expenditures were not in any way related to the size of trade union membership or the volume of dues collected. This arbitrariness was reflected in the favouritism shown industrial trade unions during this period. The Central Committee of the Miners' Union, for example, sent 3,165 roubles to the ACCTU in 1927–8, received back from the VTsSPS 6,017 roubles, or 2,852 roubles more than it contributed.[39] There are no data on how much money was given to the Agricultural and Forestry Workers' Union or later on to the various agricultural unions. There can be no question, however, that a proportionately smaller amount of money was available to agricultural trade unions than to their more fortunate urban brothers. But paradoxically enough, the centralization of the budget assured a much steadier income for the agricultural trade unions than they had enjoyed in the past when they were dependent primarily on membership dues and irregular subsidies from the government.

THE CHANGES OF 1933

At the end of 1933 further changes in trade union finances were decreed. By virtue of an order issued on 16 August 1933 by the Council of People's Commissars, the Central Committee of the Communist party, and the ACCTU, the level of trade union dues, hitherto permitted to rise up to 2 per cent of the monthly wage, was reduced to no more than one per cent as of 1 September

37 'VIII Vsesoiuznyi s'ezd profsoiuzov,' *Trud*, 13 December 1928.
38 'V pomoshch tsekhovomu profrabotniku,'*Trud*, 6 January 1928.
39 VTsSPS, *Materialy k otchetu VTsSPS IV s'ezdu*, p. 213.

TABLE 4–2

Scale of trade union membership dues,
1933–61

Monthly wages (in old roubles)	Monthly membership dues
100 – 500	0.50 per month per 100 roubles
501 – 600	4.00 roubles
601 – 700	5.00 roubles
700 and over	1 per cent

TABLE 4–3

Scale of trade union membership dues,
1961–70

Monthly wages (in new roubles)	Monthly membership dues
10 – 50	0.05 per month per each 10 roubles
51 – 60	0.40 roubles
61 – 70	0.50 roubles
70 and over	1 per cent

1933[40] The dues were collected under a system common to all unions and were calculated on the basis of the scale reproduced in table 4–2. Membership dues for non-working pensioners and for students receiving no grants were set at fifty kopecks per month. On joining a union, a new member paid an admission fee equivalent to one per cent of his monthly wages.

This system of membership dues is still in force, as article 53 of the 1968 Trade Union Statute clearly indicates. However, as a result of the 1961 currency reform both wages and dues were reduced by a factor of ten. Current monthly dues are indicated in table 4–3. For pensioners, students receiving no grants, and women who leave work temporarily to take care of children, monthly dues are set at five kopecks.[41] The admission fee for joining a union remains at one per cent of the monthly wage or, in the case of students, one

40 *KPSS o profsoiuzakh* (Moscow 1957), p. 484; 'Postanovlenie Prezidiuma VTsSPS o svodnom godovom finansovom otchete proforganizatsii za 1932g., biudzhete profsoiuzov na 1933 g., i vypolnenii plana sbora chlenskikh vznosov za I-oe polugodie 1933 g.,' *Trud*, 15 August 1933, p. 3; 'O sokrashchenii otchislenii ot zarabotnoi platy rabochikh i sluzhashchikh,' *Izvestiia*, 17 August 1933, p. 2.
41 ILO, *The Trade Union Situation in the USSR* (Geneva 1960), p. 80; *Ustav professional'nykh soiuzov (1963)*, article 52; *Ustav professional'nykh soiuzov (1968)*, article 53.

per cent of the scholarship or grant. For students who have no grants, the admission fee is set at five kopecks. Trade union members in collective farms are subject to similar provisions concerning membership and admission dues.[42]

Supplementary provisions were contained in instructions issued on 31 August 1933 by the ACCTU, under which the system of dues payment by means of stamps was retained.[43] The order also restricted optional contributions by declaring that workers and salaried employees were not to pay contributions to more than two voluntary societies, although they were permitted to become members of more than two such societies if they wished. In addition, the managements of enterprises were forbidden to deduct optional contributions from wages. Supplementary contributions by the workers for such purposes as the construction of pigsties, rabbit hutches, etc., were also forbidden.

The central committees of the various trade unions, including those in agriculture, were instructed to reduce by 30 per cent their administrative personnel whose salaries were paid out of trade union dues. They were also required to review the staffing of lower executive organs of the trade unions with a view to a corresponding reduction. In the inter-trade union councils, the reductions imposed amounted to 35 per cent, and the same percentage was fixed for the staff of the ACCTU, all of which were to be effected before 15 September 1933. As on previous occasions these demands were never met.

More important changes in the financial affairs of the trade union came about as a result of the abolition of the Commissariat of Labour in 1933 and the transfer of its functions to the ACCTU. By a degree promulgated on 10 September 1933 and supplemented by a resolution of the ACCTU on 11 September, the ACCTU and the central committees of the different unions took possession on 15 September of the funds of the social insurance system and of all its sanatoria, rest homes, research institutes, etc., and also of the funds of the Commissariat of Labour and its local organs.[44] Funds required by the trade unions to fulfil their new tasks were taken until the end of 1933 from the budgets of the Commissariat of Labour and the Central Department of Social Insurance. From 1934 the ACCTU was required to draw up and submit for the government's approval a consolidated trade union budget for social insurance and labour protection.

The Presidium of the ACCTU decided on 16 December 1936 to attempt once again to reduce the number of paid trade union officials and to reorganize the

---

42 *Ustav 1968*, article 53. See also *Spravochnik profsoiuzogo rabotnika* (Moscow 1969), pp. 564–6.
43 *Trud*, 1 September 1933.
44 'O poriakke sliianiia Narkomtruda SSSR s VTsSPS: Postanovlenie Sovnarkoma SSSR i VTsSPS ot 10go sentiabria 1933g.,' *Trud*, 11 September 1933.

finances of the unions.[45] The funds of local branches of the trade unions had hitherto been derived from members' contributions and from funds placed at the disposal of the workers' committees and local trade union committees by the management of enterprises. The decree abolished financial contributions from the enterprises. Henceforth, the trade unions had to cover their expenses almost entirely out of membership dues.

This financial reorganization involved not only a reduction in the number of paid officials, amounting to as much as 50 per cent in the case of cultural institutions such as clubs, 'red corners,' athletic fields, etc., but also a reduction in the funds allocated to central and regional committees and joint organizations. From 1 January 1937 such allocations were limited to 3 per cent of the members' contributions, as compared with 8 per cent before the reorganization; the sums transferred to the ACCTU by the union central committees were reduced by half.

The decree also divided all the trade union central committees into four groups and fixed the maximum proportion of dues which could be allocated for administrative expenses and remuneration of staff in each. The first group, composed of thirty-two central committees, including those with the largest funds (metal workers, workers in engineering undertakings, electrical power workers, etc.), was prohibited from spending more than 25 per cent of total dues for these items; the second group, composed of thirty-four central committees (miners, workers in the petroleum industry, etc.), could allocate 30 per cent; the third group, consisting of sixty-five central committees, could allocate 40 per cent; and the fourth group of thirty-two committees could allocate 50 per cent. The fourth group included all trade unions in agriculture. Thus the unions which were least able to do so were spending most of their money for administrative purposes.

Unfortunately, there is no complete information on the financial status of agricultural trade unions in the 1930s, but available data point to financial difficulties within some of the unions. For example, the Central Committee of the Trade Union of MTS Workers of the East reported at its congress in 1937 that only 84 per cent of the members' dues were received for the year 1930.[46] In September 1938 K.A. Tikhonov, a member of the Presidium of the Central Committee of the same union, speaking at the Seventh Plenum of the ACCTU admitted that the distribution of trade union funds among local and higher trade union organs defied comprehension and requested that a new trade union statute clarify matters.[47] There were also complaints at the plenum that the

45 *Voprosy profdvizheniia*, no 1 (January 1937), p. 17.
46 'Otchet-TsK soiuza,' *Trud*, 27 November 1937, p. 3.
47 K.A. Tikhonov's speech, *Trud*, 20 September 1938, p. 2.

ACCTU and Shvernik personally paid no attention to the agricultural trade unions. M.T. Maksimov, who made this accusation, also pointed out that not only did these trade unions lack financial support from the ACCTU but very often their property was taken away from them without remuneration or replacement.[48]

Individual agricultural unions continued to spend more money for administrative needs than they were allowed. For example, the Sixth Plenum of the Central Committee of the Union of Workers of Cotton Farms and MTS was told that the union executive spent 2,657,000 roubles for the wages of its 810 paid trade union workers, or 159 per cent of the membership dues collected, and it was claimed that 60,000 roubles were stolen outright.[49] The same situation existed within the Union of Workers in Land Organs where large sums of money were said to be spent by trade union officials for banquets and other entertainment. Failure to collect membership dues in the Union of Workers of Grain-growing Sovkhozes for eleven months of 1937 led to a deficit of 1,257,000 roubles.[50]

The unions, nevertheless, continued to receive specified funds from the state to enable them to perform the functions of a government nature with which they were entrusted, such as the administration of social insurance, protection of labour, improvement of living conditions, and cultural activities.[51] The money, however, was to be kept separate from the trade union funds proper and was not to be used for payment of trade union officials. Separate accounts had to be kept, and trade unions had to report regularly on utilization of these funds to the state authorities and to their members. In practice, they often failed to do so, and funds were quite regularly misused.

The collection of membership dues also lagged. The Presidium of the ACCTU in its decree of 7 March 1938 pointed out that several trade unions were retrograde in recruiting new members and that they did not collect their members' dues on time. As a result, it was only possible to assemble 85.5 per cent of the trade union budget for 1937, outstanding dues for that year amounting to ninety-six million roubles.[52] There are no detailed statistics for arrears of dues in the agricultural trade unions, but they must have been large

48 Speech by Maksimov, *Trud*, 8 May 1937, p. 3; speech by Malokhat'ko, *Trud*, 14 September 1938, p. 2.
49 I. Vilenskii, 'Pristanishche dlia temnykh elementov,' *Trud*, 24 March 1937, p. 3.
50 B.O. Kolod'ko, 'Krugovaia poruka,' *Trud*, 8 January 1938, p. 2; 'Preniia po otchetu TsK soiuza,' *Trud*, 17 January 1938, pp. 2–3.
51 N. Evreinov, 'O sokrashchenii platnogo apparata profsoiuzov,' *Trud*, 15 January 1937, pp. 3–4.
52 'O svodnom profbiudzhete professional'nykh soiuzov na 1938 god,' *Trud*, 9 April 1938, p. 2.

because they were the least well organized unions, had the smallest percentage of membership in relation to the number of eligible workers, and the largest administrative staff.

In addition to dues, a small part of union funds were derived from the proceeds of the sale of tickets and from collections made by cultural, educational, and sports institutions under the control of trade unions. This source of union funds was again probably very small for agricultural trade unions because such activities in them were almost non-existent after 1934. Apparently improvements have occurred since 1949, and especially since 1953, when one trade union in agriculture was set up. There are no statistics, however, to prove or disprove these assumptions. Since 1959 an additional payment, equivalent to 0.15 per cent of the factory wage fund, has been paid by enterprises as a contribution to union funds. Drawn not from the wage fund itself but from other sources, this contribution is devoted only to cultural and sports activities.[53]

1958 TO THE PRESENT

Some changes in the distribution of trade union funds were instituted in 1958 when, as a result of the transfer of a number of responsibilities of trade union bodies from the central to regional organizations, supervision of financial work was also decentralized. Decisions on certain financial questions are now the responsibility of inter-trade union councils and local trade union committees. Budgetary expenditure is now discussed and planned at all levels. At the local level the draft budget is prepared by the primary trade union committee and submitted to the general meeting of members for approval. As far as expenditure is concerned, a higher trade union body has the right to limit the amount to be spent by a lower body on administrative costs but apparently has no right to restrict the amount that may be spent on cultural activities.[54] In 1970 the amount of money which went to primary trade union committees was approximately 70 per cent, whereas in 1954 it amounted to 52 per cent of the total budget. Since 1970 the union has also been responsible for administering the centralized pension and social security funds for collective farms.[55]

Expenditure at the local level is verified and controlled by auditing commissions elected in enterprises at the same time as the committees of primary trade union organizations. These commissions keep a continuous watch over income and expenditure, and their recommendations are binding on the com-

53 ILO, *The Trade Union Situation*, p. 80.
54 *Ustav professional'nykh soiuzov (1968)*, article 55
55 B. Lewytzkyj, *Die Gewerkschaften in der Sowjetunion* (Frankfurt am Main: Europaeische Verlagsanstalt, 1970, p. 23.

mittees unless they are contrary to decisions of a higher trade union body. Auditing commissions are generally composed of members who work in the finance department of an enterprise. The financial activities of entire trade unions are examined by the Auditing Commission of the ACCTU, which reports to the national congress of trade unions.[56]

56 *Ustav professional'nykh soiuzov (1968)*, articles 59, 26, and 32.

5
Conditions of labour

In the opinion of the Communist party, the Soviet regime could not afford to neglect the interests of the agricultural labourers, who formed – or were supposed to form – the link between the proletariat and the peasantry. Until 1921, therefore, the Soviet government expressly forbade the hiring of agricultural labour.[1] The situation changed with the introduction of the NEP, by which all previous agrarian legislation was annulled and the status of agricultural workers defined.[2] Articles 39–41 of the new Agricultural Code recognized the right of peasants cultivating their own land to hire labour, provided that the provisions of the legislation on agricultural labour were not violated. This legislation, however, was not strictly enforced or at least less strictly than for the case of industrial workers, especially with regards to working hours.[3]

The Agricultural and Forestry Workers' Union was singularly unable to get for agricultural labourers what the industrial Labour Code offered to indus-

---

1 Decree on the Land in *Istoriia sovetskoi konstitutsii v dokumentakh, 1917–1956* (Moscow: Gosiurizdat, 1957), p. 49.
2 Zemel'nyi kodeks RSFSR, *Sobranie uzakonenii i rasporiazhenii rabochego i krestianskogo pravitel'stva RSFSR* (15 November 1922), articles 39–41. From now on referred to as *Sobranie uzakonenii*.
3 V. L'vov, 'Zarabotnaia plata rabochikh sovkhozov,' *Trud*, 24 August 1923, p. 2; M. Kekhn, 'Kollektivnye dogovory soiuza rabzemlesa,' *Trud*, 25 August 1923, p. 2; V. L'vov, 'Rabochii den' selsko-khoziaistvennykh rabochikh,' *Trud*, 6 September 1923, p. 2.

trial workers, namely an eight-hour day with time-and-a-half for overtime not exceeding a total of 120 hours of overtime per year. In actual fact, the duration of the working day in sovkhozes varied according to season, district, and the age and sex of the worker, as can be seen from table 5–1 which is based on observations of 400 adult and 100 juvenile workers. Table 5–2 shows that the length of the working day varied to a greater extent in private farms, and it appears that the working day was generally longer on private than on state-owned farms, particularly in the summer months. Workers had to work longer on private farms precisely in those areas the trade union was unable to penetrate.[4]

In 1925 the Soviet government passed new legislation (Provisional Rules) concerning the employment of paid workers in agriculture in an attempt to complete the Agricultural Code and to regulate its interpretation.[5] Until then, the Agricultural Code contained no concrete provisions covering the real conditions of employment of paid workers and could be interpreted in the most arbitrary fashion. According to the Provisional Rules, agricultural enterprises were divided into two groups: a / those of an industrial type having the right to employ paid labour in accordance with the general provisions of the Labour Code and general industrial legislation; b / farms which required auxiliary labour and had the right to employ such labour. The Provisional Rules further specified that the contract of service was to be made in writing, that such contract could not be made more than one year in advance, nor for longer than a year, that it must be registered with the local soviet, and that it must fix conditions of labour at least equal to those fixed by the Provisional Rules.

Surprisingly, the Agricultural and Forestry Workers' Union was excluded from the formalities of drawing up the contract. The Provisional Rules simply stated that it was not necessary for the union to assist. Although this should not have prevented the union from seeing to it that proper conditions of labour were adhered to, the unfortunate situation was that the union for all practical purposes was unable to improve working conditions. The ineffectiveness of the union in agriculture was revealed in the speech by Tomsky at the Fourteenth

4 M. Voroshilin, 'Dogovornaia praktika v soiuze vserabotzemles,' *Trud*, 31 January 1923, p. 2; 'Profrabota na sele,' *Trud*, 8 February 1923, p. 3; Kekhn, p. 2; L'vov, 'Rabochii den',' p. 2; A. Rapoport, 'Byt batraka,' *Trud*, 1 September 1923, p. 2.
5 *Ekonomicheskaia zhizn'* (23 April 1925); 'Vremennye pravila ob usloviiakh primeneniia podsobnogo naemnogo truda v krestianskikh khoziaistvakh,' *Sobranie zakonov i rasporiazhenii raboche-krestianskogo pravitel'stva Soiuza Sovetskikh Sotsialisticheskikh Respublik*, no. 26 (29 April 1925), article 183 (from now on referred to as *Sobranie Zakonov*); 'Instruksiia k Vremennym Pravilam ob usloviiakh primeneniia naemnogo truda v krestianskikh khoziaistvakh,' *Sobranie uzakonenii*, no 54 (September 1925), article 411; *Ibid.*, no 103 (10 November 1927), article 693.

TABLE 5–1

Average length of working day in selected sovkhozes, 1923, in hours and minutes

Region	Spring	Summer	Autumn	Winter
MOSCOW				
Men	9:07	9:10	8:57	8:51
Women	8:41	8:34	8:28	8:14
Children	6:26	6:28	6:21	5:58
SARATOV				
Men	10:33	10:35	9:44	8:36
Women	10:50	11	10:18	8:08
Children	9:55	10	9:24	7:23
POLTAVA				
Men	9:07	9:09	8:50	8:13
Women	10	11	9:40	8:40
Children	8:36	8:04	8	11

SOURCE: *Trud*, 6 September 1923.

TABLE 5–2

Average length of working day in selected private agricultural enterprises, 1923, in hours and minutes

Region	Spring		Summer		Autumn	Winter
	During spring sowing	Normal period	Normal period	During harvest	Normal period	Normal period
POLTAVA						
Men		9	13		9	
Women		9:30	12:21		8:54	7:28
MINSK						
Men		9:49	15:21		9	
Women		9:40	15:50		9:20	
DON AREA						
Men	12:17		12:12	15:02	11:50	8:51
Women	10:36		12:34	14:24	11:20	10:58

SOURCE: *Trud*, 6 September 1923.

Party Congress in 1925.[6] And the chairman of the union, Antselovich, admitted as much at the Fifth Congress of the union held in Moscow in January 1926.[7] According to him, errors were more numerous than successes 'in the work of the Central Committee and the other organizations of the Union.'[8] At

6 See chapter 1.   7 *Trud*, 19–31 January 1926.   8 *Trud*, 21 January 1926.

the same time the rank-and-file workers complained bitterly in the press about the lack of interest taken in them by representatives of the union. Among other things, they stated that the extent to which employers observed labour agreements was hardly controlled, if at all, by the trade unions; that the responsible officials of the trade unions were often persons completely unacquainted with agricultural and forestry work and therefore were unable to form any proper judgment on the conditions of labour of the members, their requirements, or complaints; and that the difficulties were exacerbated by the fact that the village soviets were largely composed of peasants who employed paid workers, were distrustful of the union, and tried, often successfully, to hinder its work.

It was repeatedly pointed out at the congress of the union that labour conditions in agriculture in general left much to be desired and that the non-observance of the terms of collective agreements by employers who were subject to little or no control was a source of great hardship to the workers. Agricultural labourers for whom a prolongation of the working day beyond eight hours was allowed by law, complained that employers abused their rights and compelled them to work from twelve to fourteen hours a day and in some cases longer.[9] In addition, large numbers of workers had no weekly day off, and the indemnity for annual holidays not taken was never paid, although it was provided by law. Moreover, many agricultural workers were afraid to become trade union members or, if they were members, to complain about conditions of labour for fear of being discharged by their employers. Such dismal conditions were not limited to private farms. The position of workers on sovkhozes was not much better, and their housing conditions were especially intolerable. The workers were forced to accept the accommodations offered to them even when, in spite of the law, they were practically uninhabitable.

Kaplun, chief of the Labour Protection Department of the Commissariat of Labour, speaking at the ACCTU Plenum in June 1926, admitted the unfortunate labour conditions.[10] He emphasized the infringement of legislation affecting agriculture and the fact that the fault appeared to lie mainly with the Labour Inspectorate and the Agricultural and Forestry Workers' Union who were lax in carrying out their duties in this respect. Neglect of the rights of labourers, it should be added, was not unusual. As the speech of Tomsky and the debates at the Fifteenth Party Congress (1926) indicated, the unions generally were passive in their role of labour protector and on the whole refused to help the workers. When, for example, irregularities were brought to their notice, and even when the claims of the workers were absolutely well founded, they

9 'Okhrana truda v derevne,' *Trud*, 5 February 1924, p. 4.
10 *Trud*, 10 June 1926.

avoided involvement and remained neutral.[11] Nor did this situation change significantly in the two years between the Fifteenth Party Congress and the Eighth Congress of Trade Unions in 1928.[12]

Some illegal practices were disclosed by *Trud* in 1927.[13] It seems that state enterprises, in order to avoid the obligations of social insurance, annual holidays, and other expenditures prescribed by labour legislation for regular agricultural workers began to employ temporary workers. This meant that the management of enterprises would discharge a number of workers and immediately afterwards re-engage them only to repeat the process after an interval.

At the end of May 1927, the Plenum of the Agricultural and Forestry Workers' Union met in Moscow in order to consider a number of questions affecting labour in agriculture.[14] Having observed that conditions of labour for agricultural workers were very different both from a practical and a legislative standpoint from those of industrial workers, the plenum went on to catalogue a number of grievances voiced by agricultural labour. Many cases of the wholesale violation of the Provisional Rules of 1925 were noted. The obligation to conclude written contracts was not strictly observed, and in some areas, for example the Urals, about 37.9 per cent of the paid workers on small farmsteads and 81.2 per cent in large state enterprises were engaged by verbal agreements only. The registration of contracts by the oblast soviets was carried out with great irregularity and often with considerable delay. The duration of these contracts was often excessively short. In the Urals region the largest number of agreements fell within the three- to six-month category, and in Moscow oblast only one per cent of the total number of agreements were of one year's duration. The number of hours of work was another grievance, and many irregularities were uncovered. Again in the Urals region approximately 90 per cent of all agricultural workers laboured more than ten hours a day, while in Moscow oblast the work day varied from 13.9 hours for shepherds' assistants to 12.2 hours for domestics.[15] The number of days worked per

11 *Trud*, 22, 30, 31 October and 1, 2 November 1926.
12 See report on the Eighth Congress of Trade Unions, *Trud*, 11–25 December 1928; *Pravda*, 11–25 December 1928.
13 *Trud*, 22 March 1927.
14 *Trud*, 22–3 May 1927; see also D. Elisev, 'Nekotorye itogi primeneniia zakona o naemnon trude v krestianskom khoziaistve,' *Voprosy truda*, no 2 (February 1927), pp. 28–36; K. Varshavskii, 'Otvestvennost' nanimaiushchikhsia za prichinenyi vred,' *Voprosy truda*, nos 2–3 (February–March 1927), pp. 69–80; 46–55; 'Professional'noe dvizhenie,' *Pravda*, 4 June 1924, p. 7.
15 N.V. Batratskii trud v krestianskikh khoziaistvakh na Urale,' *Voprosy truda*, no 3 (March 1937), pp. 92–7.

month varied from 27.4 days for field workers to 30.9 days for shepherds' assistants. In short, although the labour agreements provided for weekly rest periods and the observance of official holidays, these provisions were not properly adhered to.[16]

Supervision of the enforcement of regulations governing the employment of paid labour in agriculture was entrusted to a body of agricultural labour inspectors. This body was founded in 1925 but in 1927 was still very small and included only 175 inspectors for the whole of the USSR.[17] On account of their numerical weakness, the inspectors were quite unable to exercise close supervision of conditions of labour or even of the terms of contracts of service.[18]

At the Eighth Congress of Trade Unions (1928) Dogadov, secretary of the ACCTU, in his co-report dealing with the status of all of the unions, pointed out that the system of concluding agreements, which gave rise to excessive delay, had been somewhat improved, and that the process was not as slow as before.[19] He further noted that 93.6 per cent of all unionists were covered by collective agreements. However, instances of breach of contract were still very frequent, giving rise to great discontent among the workers. The unions not only did not keep a close watch on the enforcement of agreements but quite frequently failed to carry out the obligations they had assumed in signing the agreement.

In the discussion that followed the question of defending workers' interests was raised. Such problems as the lack of proper food and housing, length of the work day, the lack of hygiene in working establishments, and the illegal use of pregnant or nursing women in heavy jobs were all raised at the congress. From the discussion it appears that agricultural labour lagged behind the industrial working class with respect to conditions of labour and protection of their rights. For this and other obvious reasons the congress decided that unions should send their most active members to private enterprises in the countryside.[20]

It was not until 20 February 1929 that a decree was promulgated by the Central Executive Committee and the Council of Peoples' Commissars of the USSR which defined the application of labour legislation to agricultural workers.[21] First, the decree reaffirmed the key notion of the earlier Provisional

16 S. Linin, 'Batrak Ukrainy,' Trud, 5 July 1927, p. 3.
17 Industrial and Labour Information, 23 (October 1927), p. 290.
18 'VI vsesoiuznyi s'ezd sel'khozlesrabochikh: okrana truda i strakhovanie batrakov,' Trud, 2 December 1928, p. 1.
19 'Doklad tov. Dogadova,' Trud, 13 December 1928, pp. 3–5.
20 'Rezoliutsii VIII s'ezda profsoiuzov,' Trud, 6 January 1929, pp. 3–4; Trud, 12, 18, 20 December 1928; 'Pochemu slaba zashchita naemnogo truda v derevne,' Trud 4 December 1928, p. 2; I. Ede, 'Soiuz na sele,' Trud, 28 December 1928, p. 5.
21 Sobranie zakonov, no 14 (1929), article 117.

Rules that the Labour Code applied without modification to paid workers employed in agricultural enterprises of an industrial type such as large private fruit and vegetable farms and plantations and large agricultural enterprises owned and managed by the state. The decree left unchanged the regulations of the Provisional Rules relating to conditions of work of paid agricultural workers on small and medium-sized peasants' farms. As has been stated above, the Provisional Rules gave several privileges to employers by modifying or suspending parts of the Labour Code. The only change introduced by the decree affected the position of the kulaks. First, the kulak was required to draw up a contract in writing with each of his employees, and his option of making oral contracts was revoked. Henceforth the employee had to be represented in the transaction by his union, although in cases in which a collective agreement existed between the employer and the Agricultural and Forestry Workers' Union, the requirement to draw up a written contract for each worker was waived and the worker was merely to be provided with a wages book. The contract had to be submitted for approval to the village soviet, which was to refuse to approve provisions in the contract involving conditions of work less favourable than those laid down by law or which interfered with the social and political liberty of the worker. Any employer who did not comply with the instructions of the village soviet to alter provisions in labour contracts contrary to existing legislation was liable to prosecution.

The work day continued as a rule to be limited to eight hours. But during the sowing, harvesting, and hay-making seasons it was permissible to extend them to ten, or eight for persons between fourteen and seventeen years of age (who usually were limited to six hours per day). Remuneration for the extra hours was to be at a rate not less than time-and-a-third, and in cases where agreement was not reached on the question of overtime pay, the extra hours had to be paid for in accordance with the provisions of the Labour Code, which called for an increase of 50 per cent for the first two hours and 100 per cent for any additional hours. No work was permitted on Sundays and holidays unless it was of an urgent nature and then only with the consent of the workers, and all such work had to be paid for at double rates or, as an alternative, a compensatory rest had to be granted.

Housing was to be supplied. A worker who was temporarily unable to carry on his work had the right to retain his accommodation for a period of two months from the time his regular work was interrupted, and a worker who was dismissed before his contract had expired, if he had no other accommodation, could occupy his dwelling for fifteen days from the date of his dismissal. The employer was further required to transport any worker who became ill to the nearest hospital or to call in a physician for examination and treatment of the patient.

If any disputes between employers and workers arose these were to be submitted to the conciliation committee of the local soviet if both parties agreed. Otherwise, disputes were to be settled by the nearest ordinary court. There was also a detailed provision for the payment of wages and social insurance for agricultural labour which is discussed elsewhere in this study.

The legislation appeared to be directed primarily against the kulaks. But there was no clear definition of who was to be regarded as a kulak until such a definition was supplied by a decree of 21 May 1929 which enumerated the peasant farms to which the decree of 20 February 1929 was to apply.[22] The decree defined a kulak as a / any person who systematically employed hired labour in agricultural work or in handicrafts, insofar as the employment of such labour deprived him of the right to vote; b / any person who owned a mill, a butter factory, or any other industrial or semi-industrial establishment in which power-driven machinery was used; c / any person who regularly rented engines and agricultural machinery to peasants; d / any person who rented dwellings or work places during the agricultural season; e / any agriculturist who engaged in commercial or financial operations or who was the agent or servant of a religious body.

But even here rather important exceptions were made in the application of the Labour Code and the provisions of the decree of 20 February 1929 to kulaks. It was further provided that the decree did not apply to peasant undertakings unless their gross receipts amounted to at least 1,500 roubles a year and 300 roubles for each adult member of the family.[23] Thus the provisions

---

22 *Ibid.*, no 34 (1929).

23 In 1926 an enquiry carried out by the Central Statistical Bureau grouped the farms employing agricultural labour into three categories in accordance with the area of cultivation. In the first category, farms cultivating less than two desiatins (1 desiatin = 2.7 acres) made up 25 per cent of the total number of farms, and employed 7.6 per cent of the total workers on contract, 21.6 per cent of the day workers, and 29.2 per cent of the total jobbers. The second category was composed of farms cultivating 2.1 to 10 desiatins, which made up 69.8 per cent of the total number of farms. They employed 65.6 per cent of the total number of workers on contract, 69.3 per cent of the total day workers, and 68.5 per cent of the total number of jobbers. The third category of farms cultivated more than 10 desiatins, and they made up 5.2 per cent of the total number of farms. These farms employed 26.8 per cent of the total number of workers on contract, 9.1 per cent of the day workers, and 2.3 per cent of the jobbers. Thus approximately two-thirds of the paid workers in agriculture were employed in this period on the farms in the second category which were generally considered as average-sized holdings, although it should also be noted that the farms in the third category did play an important part in the employment of workers on contract. These farms were the only ones to engage workers by the year. On them the workers were employed almost exclusively in the fields, while on the other types more than half of the paid hands helped with the domestic work. *Industrial and Labour Information*, 23 (October 1927), pp. 283–4.

of the decree applied to probably no more than one-fourth of the workers on contract in agriculture. But then it was just a beginning.

Later in the year a new decree was issued laying down regulations for the employment of hired labourers by 'working peasants.'[24] The new decree, unlike the decree of February 1929, superseded the regulations embodied in the Provisional Rules. It expressly stipulated that its provisions applied only to peasant farms on which hired workers were employed merely to assist the owner and his family, who did most of the work themselves. But in many respects it resembled the decree of February 1929. The requirement for a contract, the terms of the contract, and the need to register it with the local soviet were similar. The employment of children under twelve years of age was strictly forbidden, and persons between the age of twelve and seventeen years and pregnant women were not to be employed except at light work. The ordinary work day was to be eight hours and not to exceed ten hours during seasons of special activity. The amount of wages had to be no less than the minimum rate laid down by the state and not more than 50 per cent of the wage could be paid in kind. The food provided for the worker had to be of the same quality as that consumed by the employer, and rent could not be an item of wages. The private employer was not required to pay contributions to social insurance for the workers employed by him, but when an uninsured worker was maimed or killed in his service, the employer was liable to the worker or his family for a sum equal to that which would be paid in the same circumstances by the social insurance fund.

According to the decree the employer was required to allow the worker the time off needed to take part in elections or village and trade union meetings without any deduction of wages. If a worker was nominated to attend a Communist party or trade union congress, the employer was obligated to grant him the necessary leave, although without obligation to pay wages during this period. Workers under eighteen years of age were to be allowed to attend academic courses during the periods of urgent work. Any disputes which arose were to be settled by the committees of the local soviet or by the ordinary courts of first instance.

The role of the union in protecting agricultural labour in private establishments was of minimal significance. The union could represent the worker in the initial stages of drawing up a contract, if he desired, and supposedly could see to it that the conditions of contract were fulfilled, and, if they were not, could advise the worker what possible course of action was open to him.[25] But there can be no doubt that, however limited, the provisions of the decree

24 Decree of 11 July 1929, *Izvestiia NKT*, nos 34–5, (July 1929).
25 *Ibid.* See also 'Zashchita interesov sel'khozrabochikh,' *Trud*, 29 May 1929, p. 4; 'Iskrivlenie klassovoi linii,' *Trud*, 1 June 1929, p. 3.

did prove restrictive of the freedom of action of the employer peasant, and in this way it was in harmony with the general policy of the 'socialist offensive' against all elements of the individualist economy that had been enunciated at the Fifteenth Party Congress in December 1926 and the Fifth Congress of Soviets in May 1929. This policy was carried a step further when on 6 January 1930 the Central Committee of the party called for the 'liquidation of the kulaks as a class.' The Central Executive Committee in its decree of 1 February 1930 provided for the confiscation of all kulak property and for the expulsion of kulaks from their native districts. As a consequence, in these areas of total collectivization the employment of wage labour in agriculture and the leasing of land were forbidden.[26]

POST-COLLECTIVIZATION PERIOD

Then on 23 June 1933 the Central Executive Committee of the USSR abolished the Commissariat of Labour and invested the trade unions, and specifically the ACCTU, with the duties and powers of the abolished commissariat.[27] According to Shvernik, the development of economic life necessitated essential changes in the tasks of the Commissariat of Labour, which had not been in a position to fulfil them by reason of its 'isolation from the masses' and its lack of 'direct contact with production.' The new policy of emphasizing the close relationship between social insurance and the 'maximization of production' were said to have bewildered the Commissariat of Labour. Therefore, it was best to transfer its functions to the trade unions, which were better suited to improving the productivity of labour. Wages and insurance were henceforth to be linked to labour productivity. Labour discipline was to be made stricter, but at the same time the trade union primary organizations were to be vested with rights of inspection of labour protection measures and hygiene.[28]

An attempt to improve the living conditions of the worker was made in 1936. On 19 April, the Central Executive Committe and the Council of Peoples' Commissars issued a decree providing for the consolidation of the

26 'Dobit' nepmana – v gorode, kulaka – v derevne,' *Trud*, 1 June 1929, p. 3; R.S., 'Rukovoditeli bez klassovogo chut'ia,' *Trud*, 4 January 1930, p. 2; V. Mazharov, 'Vedushchaia rol' sovkhozov v peredelke s. kh. trebuet perestroiki raboty proforganizatsii,' *Trud*, 29 October 1931, p. 3.
27 By government decree issued on 10 September 1933 and supplemented by an order of ACCTU of 11 September 1933, the new functions of the trade unions were laid down. 'O poriadke sliianiia Narkomtruda SSSR s VTsSPS,' *Trud*, 11 September 1933, p. 1.
28 'Reshitel'no uluchshit' bytovye usloviia rabochikh sovkhozov,' *Trud*, 16 May 1933, p. 3.

different regulations relating to funds set up for the payment of bonuses and for the improvement of the living conditions of workers. Out of a single fund, the so-called manager's fund, would come the needed financial resources. At least half of the manager's fund was to be allotted to the construction of dwellings for the workers, engineers, and salaried employees of the enterprise. The fund was also to be used for improving the 'material and cultural conditions' of the workers by establishing nurseries, kindergartens, clubs, etc. The plan for the use of the fund was to be drawn up by the manager in agreement with the local trade union committee. No other funds for these same purposes were to be established in enterprises. Enterprises for which the plan did not provide for any profit in 1936 were authorized to pay into the manager's fund 3 per cent of the savings achieved through planned reduction in costs of production and 50 per cent of all savings achieved in excess of the plan.

At the same time the party decided to establish a procedure for taking care of workers' complaints. The Commission of Soviet Control at its Third Plenum (May 1936) adopted a decree laying down guidelines to be observed in dealing with workers' complaints.[29] The decree provided that workers were not to be dismissed or refused employment for reasons such as social origin, previous convictions, etc. Further, it proposed revision of penalties imposed on employees of soviet administrative departments as the result of past purges because, it said, such penalties had in most cases lost their significance. It also forbade any fresh penalties of this sort without the special permission of the Commission of Soviet Control. The decree also required all organizations and establishments to register every complaint, to see that all complaints were dealt with, and to supervise the execution of the decision taken. A time limit had to be fixed for the consideration of each complaint, and the complainant had to be informed by the establishment concerned in every case that his complaint entailed protracted investigation. The Office of Complaints of each enterprise, together with the agents of the Commission of Soviet Control, had the obligation to see that all complaints were dealt with by administrative departments, enterprises, and trade unions.

A month later, on 11 June 1936, the Presidium of the Central Executive Committee of the USSR approved the draft of a new constitution, which was published for discussion by the whole population. The constitution introduced the final prohibition on employment of labour in individually owned enterprises or farms.[30]

---

29 'O rassmotrenii zhalob trudiashchikhsia,' *Izvestiia*, 30 May 1936, p. 1.
30 *Konstitutsiia (Osnovnoi zakon) Soiuza Sovetskikh Sotsialisticheskikh Respublik* (Moscow: Gosiurizdat, 1958), article 4.

General conditions of labour, however, did not improve, a fact confirmed by the Seventh ACCTU Plenum of September 1938. At the plenum Shvernik stated candidly that workers' working, living and educational conditions were not substantially better than they were when discussed at the Sixth Plenum. In fact, he pointed out, contrary to the decisions of the Sixth ACCTU Plenum trade unions and economic organizations had not renewed the practice of concluding collective agreements. Shvernik admitted as well that the trade unions had not yet completed the tasks entrusted to them with respect to workers' protection and safety. In his opinion the trade unions were responsible for the fact that certain enterprises sometimes demanded excessive overtime.

That safety rules were frequently violated is not surprising in view of the fact that there were only 5,124 labour inspectors in the entire Soviet Union in January 1938. No data on labour inspectors for agriculture alone are available for this date. The accident rate in agriculture is, however, known to have been very high because, among other reasons, of a lack of safety devices and improper working conditions. An attempt was made to improve the situation in 1938 and 1939 when a campaign was conducted to improve labour conditions, but although some progress was registered, most of it was concentrated in industry and not in agriculture.[31]

SECOND WORLD WAR TO THE PRESENT

There is no need to emphasize that whatever progress had been made by agricultural unions in bettering working conditions largely disappeared during the war. The labour situation in agriculture became critical during the period of general mobilization. Not only qualified workers but also a majority of trained trade union officials were sent to the front.[32] The large influx of women workers into labouring jobs in industry and agriculture which began in early 1939 continued as the war went on. In agriculture an attempt was made beginning in 1939 to train at least 100,000 women tractor drivers as rapidly as possible.[33] The Komsomol, the trade unions, and the managers of MTS were requested to support the movement, bonuses were given to tractor drivers, mechanics, etc., who taught women to drive tractors, and a special committee was set up to oversee the movement.[34]

---

31 At the same period (1 January 1938) there were in the country as a whole 458,000 voluntary trade union inspectors. This number rose to 600,000 in January, 1941. *Istoriia profdvizheniia v SSSR*, pp. 347–8.

32 *Istoriia profdvizheniia v SSSR* (2nd ed.; Moscow 1961), p. 366.

33 'Molodye patriotki uchites' upravliat' traktorom,' *Pravda*, 1 April 1939, p. 1.

34 'Postanovlenie TsK VLKSM, Narkomzema SSSR: Narkomata Sovkhozov SSSR: O podgotovke bez otryva ot proizvodstva 100 tisiach zhenshchin-traktoristok,' *Komsomol'skaia Pravda*, 2 April 1939, p. 1.

The war itself, however, helped to revive the trade union movement in the USSR and not least with respect to union concern for labour protection and conditions of labour. Granted, the emphasis was primarily on helping the ever-increasing number of war invalids who in many cases required special conditions in order to be productive. With this in mind special commissions were set up at the end of 1942 in both industrial and agricultural enterprises charged with the task of overseeing the application of labour legislation regarding war invalids.[35] And, although not to the extent claimed by the Soviets, one ought to assume that the influx of women did have some influence on conditions of labour. Nurseries had to be provided for their children, and medical care, safety precautions, and industrial hygiene were emphasized much more than in the past.[36] This was especially so in the 1950s.

However, not until 1947 was the practice of signing collective agreements revived. The twelve-year period (1935–47) during which no collective agreements were concluded could be regarded as least progressive from the point of view of the conditions of labour, safety, and accident prevention. This situation changed when, acting upon the instructions of the CPSU Central Committee, the Sixteenth ACCTU Plenum of April 1947 required that all trade unions and economic organizations make an effort to conclude collective agreements.[37] It is, of course, correct to say that the trade union leadership was not motivated in this instance primarily by a desire to improve conditions of labour. However, the existence of this form of agreement could in the long run serve the needs of the workers and in fact did. The collective agreements provided the unions with a certain leverage in insisting on the maintenance of minimum safety and labour standards, and in this way signified the wartime and postwar evolution in the fortunes of Soviet trade unions.

Further advances in this field were made in 1949 when the Tenth Congress of Trade Unions (April 1949) decided that it was time to begin talking about everyday needs of the workers, living conditions, the introduction of the normal eight-hour working day, production hygiene, rest and vacation periods, etc. As a result of the congress decisions, labour safety and production hygiene became acceptable topics for discussion on the local level, and the number of production accidents at the end of the decade underwent a three-fold decrease as compared with the year 1929.[38]

But the greatest changes in the whole approach to problems of conditions

---

35 'O rabote profsoiuznykh organizatsii po rabochemu snabzheniiu i bytovomu obscluzhivaniiu rabochikh i sluzhashchikh,' *Istoriia profdvizheniia v SSR*, p. 379.

36 N.T. Dodge, *Women in the Soviet Economy: Their Role in Economic, Scientific and Technical Development* (Baltimore: Johns Hopkins, 1966).

37 *Postanovleniia plenumov VTsSPS deviatogo sozyva* (Moscow: Profizdat, 1949), p. 315.

38 *Istoriia profdvizheniia v SSSR*, p. 430.

of labour and the satisfaction of everyday needs of the workers came in the 1950s. In this respect the transfer of the large number of tractor drivers from kolkhozes to the MTS was particularly significant. The abrupt transformation that occurred in their status, from kolkohzniks into a privileged class of workers with the right to trade union membership and most of the rights and privileges connected therewith, must have had a profound effect on the thinking of these people. When the MTS were abolished in 1958, most of them were again transferred to collective farms. But it proved impossible to take the trade union membership away from them or to reduce their pensions, their sick leave, their vacations. On the contrary, the government had to extend at least some of the privileges, as the pension laws of 1964, 1967, and 1970 indicate, to the ordinary kolkhozniks.

The Virgin Lands campaign started by Khrushchev's speech of 23 February 1954 had a tremendous and lasting impact on the growth and powers of the trade unions in agriculture. More than 150,000 workers and technicians were initially mobilized to settle in the new lands. Tens of thousands of students from all over the Soviet Union were also sent to help with the cultivation of the Virgin Lands, and it is claimed some 350,000 Komsomols were dispatched to the Virgin Lands from Leningrad oblast alone.[39] Harsh living conditions and lack of accommodation and amenities created tremendous pressure on the government and the party to meet the everyday needs of the new settlers. In many instances the government was unable to respond to the demands of these workers, and many of them left the area. The fluctuation of settlers can be seen from this account in *Pravda*: 'In 1960 and 1961, 103,650 tractor drivers were trained (in Kazakhstan) and 53,744 equipment operators arrived from other parts of the country to take up permanent jobs. During the same period, more than 100,000 equipment operators left the state and collective farms.'[40] But what was even worse from the point of view of the party and government as far as conditions in the Virgin Lands were concerned was that many of the younger workers were not to be pacified by promises. They wanted things done to improve their conditions of life and either left for home or were willing to fight for positive action.[41] Work stoppages occurred in several industrial complexes in Kazakhstan, and the government took speedy measures to alleviate the situation.

39 *Profsoiuz rabochikh sel'skogo khoziaistva* (Moscow 1961), p. 146.
40 'V Kazakhstane plokbo gotoviat kadry mekhanizatorov,' *Pravda*, 15 July 1962, p. 4.
41 There were several reports of bad living conditions in Kazakhstan in the Soviet newspapers of that period. *Komsomol'skaia Pravda*, 19 March 1959; *Kazakhstanskaia Pravda*, 28 October 1959; speech of D.A. Kunaev at the Tenth Kazakh Party Congress, as reported in *New York Times* by Harry Schwartz (15 October 1959; 8 December 1959; 6 January 1960); S. Dovhal, 'Rebellion of Young People in Temir-Tau,' *Problems of the Peoples of the USSR*, no 6 (1960), pp. 31–6.

Agricultural trade unions were called upon to play an important role in this campaign from the beginning. In April 1954 the various existing trade unions in agriculture were amalgamated into one Union of Workers and Employees in Agriculture and State Procurement. And it was primarily this union that, with the support of the ACCTU and other trade unions, was assigned responsibility for looking after workers' needs in the new territories. In 1954 it sent 625 trade union officials into the sovkhozes and MTS of the Virgin Lands, while later on some sixty brigades composed of leading trade union officials were sent into the new territories with the purpose of organizing a more civilized life. As a result of these efforts, approximately 1,500 MTS and some 445 sovkhozes received permanent libraries and librarians.[42] The trade union was also asked to prod the responsible ministries in order that the housing of Virgin Lands workers as well as their other needs be properly satisfied.[43] But the Twentieth Party Congress (February 1956) criticized the work of trade unions in general and that of the agricultural trade union in particular for continuing to work in a bureaucratic fashion and not paying sufficient attention to either workers' needs or production processes. Henceforth the trade unions were to get rid of the 'cult of personality,' put their organizations on a more 'democratic' basis, 'respect criticism,' and raise the 'political consciousness and production output of the workers.'[44]

Of great importance for the unions was the plenum of the party Central Committee of December 1957. As on previous occasions the plenum called on the unions to raise the productivity of the working masses, to contribute to the growth of agriculture and to the material and cultural security of the workers.[45] The plenum recommended that the 'production conferences' organized in enterprises be made permanent, and in July 1958 a decree of the Council of Ministers and the ACCTU turned this recommendation into law.[46]

Meanwhile, in April 1956 a decree had been promulgated which discontinued prosecution of workers absenting themselves from work without valid

<hr />

42 *Profsoiuz rabochikh sel'skogo khoziaistva*, p. 149.

43 *Ibid.*, p. 152.

44 *KPSS o profsoiuzakh*, pp. 666–73.

45 *KPSS o profsoiuzakh, 1956–1962* (Moscow 1963), p. 71; *Materialy dekabr'skogo 1957 goda plenuma TsK KPSS* (Moscow: Gospolitizdat, 1957), pp. 12–13.

46 *Ibid.* In Belorussia 445 sovkhozes had permanent production conferences with 25,000 members. In Kazakhstan there were 1,130 of these organizations with a total of 41,000 members. *Profsoiuz rabochikh sel'skogo khoziaistva*, p. 191. For the 20 oblasts in 1961 these production conferences united 118,000 workers. *Ibid.*, p. 191. Some speculate that this move was made primarily under pressure from the workers and under the influence of the Polish and Yugoslav experience. Some like Paul Barton disagree with this view. See Abraham Brumberg, pp. 263–79; *Russia under Khrushchev* (New York 1963), *Spravochnik partiinogo rabotnika* (Moscow: Gospolitizdat, 1959), p. 700.

reason, repealed the penalties for unauthorized changes of employment, and withdrew from the union the authority to effect compulsory transfers of workers from plant to plant. And although, as one authority on Soviet labour law has indicated, the 1956 decree did not put an end to the use of coercion in maintaining labour discipline, it initiated the most significant change in the Soviet worker's status since the death of Stalin.[47]

In the period since 1953 more attention has also been directed towards providing workers with adequate living quarters.[48] The Soviet source claims that the RTS and sovkhozes in the period between 1953 and 1959 received from the government twelve billion rubles, which were spent on the construction of thirteen billion square metres of housing space. At the same time workers and employees were able to build nine billion square metres of living space on their own. In Kazakhstan alone about three million square metres of living space were built, in addition to 237 schools, 183 kindergartens, 125 clubs, 132 red corners, and 47 hospitals.[49] However, in the absence of a meaningful basis of comparison it is difficult to appraise the significance of these data.

Participation of the unions was further strengthened by the extension in July 1958 of the rights and duties of the local committees in matters of working conditions, labour disputes, and job security.[50] The local committee was empowered to participate, together with the management, in any discharge, in the establishment or change of any production standard, in defining details of the wage system and hours schedule; in approving or denying authority to engage in overtime work; in setting up the classification of work and workers by labour grades; in the distribution of premiums and of awards and honours in socialist competitions; in the distribution of the living space under the control of the enterprise; and in the expenditure of the enterprise fund. The changes of 1958 approved the position of the trade union with regard to labour disputes and questions affecting the job security of workers.[51] In particular, the requirement that management could not dismiss employees without trade union approval was a real gain for the local trade union committee.

Beginning with the war, and continuing to today, a trend can be observed in the direction of greater attention to workers' needs, especially with respect

47 Jerzy Gliksman, 'Recent Trends in Soviet Labor Policy,' *Problems of Communism*, V, no 4 (July–August 1956), p. 2.
48 *Profsoiuz rabochikh sel'skogo khoziaistva*, p. 174.
49 *Ibid.*, pp. 212, 213.
50 'O pravakh fabrichnogo, zavodskogo, mestnogo komiteta professional'nogo soiuza,' *Pravda*, 16 July 1958.
51 V. Prokhorov, 'Profsoiuzy na novom etape,' *Sovetskie profsoiuzy*, VI, no 18 (December 1958), p. 9.

to labour relations. The Model Statute adopted in 1949 by the Tenth Trade Union Congress claimed the right of trade unions to 'speak on behalf of workers and employees before state and public organs in questions relating to their work and needs.'[52] This point was further strengthened by the Eleventh Trade Union Congress of 1954 which specifically empowered the trade union locals to check 'the revision of production norms and setting up of tariffs' as well as 'the correct application in practice of the system of labour compensation, the correctness of wage computations, and the prompt payment of wages to workers and employees.'[53] The Twelfth Trade Union Congress, held in April 1959, went even further in this respect and declared in the new statute that the trade union locals 'represent the workers and employees before the management of the plant, institution or organization in all questions of labour, daily life and culture.'[54]

Since 1958 the trade unions have begun to exercise greater influence over labour protection. The Inspection Section of the ACCTU was charged with responsibility for working out the safety and sanitation and industrial hygiene regulations and with overseeing the implementation of these regulations in individual factories and enterprises through the inspectors attached to subordinate trade union organs. These rules and regulations applied equally to industry and to agriculture. But in agriculture the trade union inspectors, who to this day are not the best qualified individuals, have additional problems. For example, as is correctly stated by B. Lewytzkyj, if a collective farm after a long wait is delivered a tractor which is clearly unsafe the chairman of the kolkhoz as well as the trade union and individual kolkhozniks are presented with a dilemma. Should they return this tractor to the factory and wait perhaps another year on the grounds that it may be unsafe or shift the responsibility for an accident to an individual tractor driver?[55]

Progress has been achieved over time in obtaining trade union rights in general and the rights of the primary organizations in particular. A comparison of the present rights of the local committee with those embodied in the regulations published in 1925 leaves the impression that the basic rights and functions of the primary trade union organization are now more or less the same as they were in 1925 before they were gradually whittled away.[56] However, there is one exception where trade unions in agriculture are concerned, and it

52 *Ustav professional'nykh soiuzov SSSR (1949)*; *Trud*, 11 May 1949.
53 'Zabota o cheloveke zakon nashego obshchestva,' *Trud*, 19 June 1954, p. 1.
54 *Ustav professional'nykh soiuzov SSSR (1959)*; *Trud*, 2 April 1959, pp. 2–3.
55 B. Lewytzkyj, *Die Gewerkschaften in der Sowjetunion* (Frankfurt am Main: Europaeische Verlagsanstalt, 1970), p. 95.
56 International Labour Office, *The Trade Union Movement* (Geneva 1927), pp. 283–5.

relates to the kolkhoz trade union committee, whose function is important enough to merit separate analysis.

First, it should be noted that in principle the Trade Union Statute and all other laws generally applicable to trade unions apply to trade unions in collective farms as well. However, there seems in practice to be one essential difference between the local trade union organization in a kolkhoz and, for example, the local organization in the sovkhoz. The workers on state farms are considered hired labourers and the legal relations between the manager and the worker are regulated by the existing labour laws. On a collective farm work is done by full members of the farm, who are considered part owners and because of this their legal rights are regulated by the Collective Farm Statute, and since 1969 by the Model Statute adopted by the Third Congress of Collective Farmers.[57] The difference in status between members of the same agricultural union was discussed in an article in *Trud* which raised a number of questions.[58]

Under the Collective Farm Statute, the article pointed out, the power of hiring and firing belongs only to the general meeting of the kolkhoz. Because of this allocation of authority the kolkhoz trade union committee has no right to interfere with the decision of the general meeting. Thus questions of admission to and expulsion from the kolkhoz are outside the jurisdiction of the trade union local. This lack of jurisdiction also holds true with respect to the question of 'incentives, punishment and payment for the collective farmers' labour.' Hence the author, I.F. Shkuratov, a secretary of the ACCTU, advises trade union locals that 'it is hardly expedient to set up a labour disputes commission' in the kolkhoz local because the labour questions are decided by the 'collective agency,' i.e., the management board of the kolkhoz. Besides, 'solving labour disputes is not the committee's greatest concern.'[59] In answer to the question of what the legitimate concern of the kolkhoz local committee should be, aside from the collection of membeship dues and payment of social insurance, Shkuratov argues that attention to mass production work, cultural, and everyday service activities, and labour protection should be the main focus of trade union activity. The Model Stature, if anything, strengthens the position of kolkhoz management vis-à-vis the trade union committee.

---

57 The Collective Farm Statute was adopted by the Second Congress of Collective Farmers in February 1935. It was promulgated by order of the Central Committee of the party and the Council of People's Commissars on 17 February 1935. For the text of the statute see *Izvestiia*, 18 February 1935. See also 'Primernyi Ustav Kolkhoza,' *Pravda*, 30 November 1969.

58 'Profkom kolkhoza-chem emu zanimatsia?' *Trud*, 16 March 1965, p. 2.

59 *Ibid*. See also Ia. Skliarevskii, 'Profkom i pravlenie kolkhoza,' *Sovetskie profsoiuzy*, no 16 (August 1965), pp. 13–15.

The trade union committee has almost no say about the length of the working day, which varies from farm to farm. Although the average working day is about eight hours, it can vary from five-and-a-half to as long as ten hours.[60] And in some sectors the collective farmers, particularly women, have to work as much as '12 to 14 hours a day and go without a day off for years on end.'[61] On the collective farms juvenile labour is still being widely used and it is important to note in this connection that while trade union inspectors exercise some degree of surveillance over labour protection for juveniles in industry, this safeguard hardly exists on collective farms.[62]

In short the trade union committee in the collective farm can recommend measures for consideration by the kolkhoz management board, but its right to demand anything appears to be severely restricted. One chairman of a collective farm, when approached by a trade union committee that took it upon itself to represent an aggrieved worker, received this reply: 'I have been to the chairman of the province committee of the Trade Union of Workers and Employees in Agriculture and Procurement and have told him about your activities. The province committee chairman says you should occupy yourselves with trade union dues and social insurance and stop interfering in other matters.'[63] To this day that is perhaps the best answer to the question of what trade unions in the kolkhozes are supposed to do.

60 T. Zaslavskaia, *Raspredelenie po trudu v kolkhozakh* (Moscow: Ekonomizdat, 1966), p. 104.
61 *Plenum Tsentral'nogo Komiteta Komunisticheskoi Partii Sovetskogo Soiuza 24–26 Marta 1965* (Moscow: Gospolitizdat, 1965), p. 164; see also a letter of milkmaid to *Novyi Mir*, no 1 (1964), p. 91 quoted in R. Conquest, *Agricultural Workers in the USSR* (London: Bodley Head, 1968), p. 98; and *Sel'skaia zhizn'*, 10 October 1965.
62 F.S. Hayenko, *Trade Unions and Labor in the Soviet Union* (Munich: Institute for the Study of the USSR, 1965), p. 75; see also *Sel'skaia zhizn'*, 12 July 1969.
63 'Profkom kolkhoza-chem emu zanimatsia?' *Trud*, 16 March 1965, p. 2. See also 'Profsoiuzy-aktivnye uchastniki vsenarodnoi bor'by za dal'neishii pod'em sel'skogo khoziaistva,' *Sovetskie profsoiuzy*, no 24 (December 1966), pp. 32–3.

6
Social insurance

The evolution of the soviet system of social insurance from the October revolution to the present reflects with extraordinary accuracy the political, social, and economic history of the USSR. Three points are of particular interest for this study: first, the relatively late introduction of programs of social insurance in agriculture; second, the degree to which the evolution of these programs was intimately related to differentiations within the agricultural working force; and finally, the considerable use of social security and insurance schemes for political and economic purposes. During each stage of the Soviet evolution social insurance reforms have been undertaken which affected the scope, financial resources, benefits, and administrative organization of the insurance system. Four periods can be considered: 1922 to 1931, 1931 to 1933, 1933 to 1964, and 1964 to 1970.

1922 – 31

The first phase in the history of Soviet social insurance was one of administration by inter-occupational territorial insurance institutions. These were set up immediately after the promulgation of the Labour Code of 1922, and each of them covered all wage earners working in a specified district, the only exceptions being workers in water and railway transportation, who had their own special funds.

However, from the very beginning there was a close connection between the administration of insurance and the trade unions. Thus, for example, the territorial insurance funds were managed by workers acting in their capacity not as insured persons but as trade unionists. The body competent to select the persons who were assigned administrative duties in the social insurance institutions was the inter-trade union council of a given area. General direction and supervision of the work of these institutions was in the hands of the Central Social Insurance Administration attached to the Commissariat of Labour of the USSR, and of the Insurance Administration of the Commissariat of Labour of the given union republic. At the head of each administration was a chief appointed by the commissariat, in agreement with the trade union council of the republic or, in the case of the Central Social Insurance Administration, with the permission of the ACCTU. These administrations were advised by 'social insurance councils' – one for the Soviet Union and one for each of the republics – consisting of a chairman appointed by the Commissariat of Labour and of representatives of the trade unions, various commissariats, and the Council of National Economy.[1]

Article 175 of the Labour Code of RSFSR adopted on November 1922 provided that:

The social insurance system shall cover all persons employed for remuneration, whether the enterprises, institutions or businesses in which they are employed are state, public, co-operative, established under a concession or lease, of mixed character or private, or whether they are employed by private individuals, and irrespective of the nature and duration of their employment and the method of remuneration.[2]

Although compulsory social insurance was decreed in Russia with the introduction of the NEP, it only began to be adopted in 1923, and the introductory measures were not completed before the end of 1924.[3]

Agricultural workers were brought under the insurance scheme in the spring of 1925.[4] But at the same time the features of the system were modified by the Provisional Rules of 18 April 1925 which removed the obligation to insure their workers from enterprises employing workers only at certain seasons or employing not more than two on a permanent basis. The All-Union Social Insurance Council was instructed to draw up measures for the application of

1 *Polozhenie, utverzhdenoe TsIK i SNK SSSR 6 fevralia 1925g., s izmeneniiami i doplneniiami* (Moscow 1930), p. 8. See also *Sobranie zakonov, SSSR*, no 55 (1932), p. 328.
2 *Sobranie uzakonenii*, RSFSR, no 70 (20 November 1922). See also *Trudovoe pravo: entsyklopedicheskii slovar* (Moscow 1958), p. 184.
3 A circular issued in 1924 exempted from insurance peasants employing only one worker and introduced partial insurance for industrial enterprises employing no more than five workers.
4 *Sobranie zakonov, SSSR*, no 26 (29 April 1925), article 183, paragraph 14.

social insurance to other agricultural undertakings, but it never did follow through on these instructions so that the act of 26 October 1927 should really be considered the first attempt at general legislation adapting the Soviet insurance system to agriculture.

Social insurance had already been introduced in certain agricultural districts in 1925 and 1926 and, according to one source, about 23 per cent of the agricultural workers were insured.[5] But even then official statistics indicate that the classes least affected by social insurance were agricultural workers and domestics.[6] It was openly admitted at the Fourth ACCTU Plenum of June 1926 that, although social insurance had been compulsory for agricultural workers since the spring of 1925, the insurance authorities were experiencing great difficulties in establishing the scheme in the countryside because of the poverty stricken state of small farmers.[7] Indeed, one source noted that in 1926 only 14.5 per cent of all batraks employed in individual farms were insured, while only 2.9 per cent of those employed by village collectives were covered by insurance.[8]

At the end of May 1927 an enlarged Central Committee of the Agricultural and Forestry Workers' Union considered a number of questions related to problems of social insurance and noted that the number of agricultural workers participating in the scheme was still small.[9] In the Urals only 18 per cent of the paid workers on ordinary farms were insured, while the total insurance contribution was equivalent to 5 per cent of the wages earned in cash and kind. In the Ukraine in 1927 only 8 or 10 per cent of the 327,000

---

5 'Novoe v strakhovanii batrachestva,' *Voprosy strakhovaniia*, no 39 (29 September 1927), pp. 5–6; E.K., 'Sotsial'noe strakhovanie lits zaniatykh po naimu v krestianskikh khoziaistvakh,' *ibid.*, no 48 (1 December 1927), pp. 2–3; 'Voprosy strakhovaniia batrakov na IV Plenume TsK sel'khozrabochikh,' *ibid.*, pp. 4–6.
6 See the report of Nemchenko, director of the Social Insurance Department of the Commissariat of Labour of the USSR to the Social Insurance Conference of 16–24 April 1926 and his report at the Fourth ACCTU Plenum of June 1926: 'Vtoroe vsesoiuznoe strakhovoe soveshchanie,' *Voprosy strakhovaniia*, no 16 (22 April 1926), pp. 2–7; *ibid.*, no 17 (29 April 1926), pp. 2–13; 'Doklady na vsesoiuznom strakhovom soveshchanii,' *ibid.*, no 18 (6 May 1926), pp. 3–11; B.G., 'Reshenie vsesoiuznogo strakhovogo soveshchaniia,' *ibid.*, no 19 (13 May 1926), pp. 2–5; V.K-in, 'Chastichnoe strakhovanie i strakhovanie batrakov,' *ibid.*, pp. 5–6; *Trud*, 9 June 1926.
7 *Trud*, 9 June 1926.
8 *Naemnyi trud v sel'skom i lesnom khoziaistve v 1926 g.* (Moscow: Tsentral'noe Statisticheskoe Upravlenie, 1928); 'So strakhovaniem batrachestva neblagopoluchno,' *Trud*, 19 February 1929, p. 2.
9 *Trud*, May 22–2, 1927.

agricultural workers were insured.[10] In industrial farming enterprises, on the other hand, contributions were much higher, sometimes even as much as 20 per cent of wages. These higher contributions, however, covered all risks instead of being limited merely to sickness and accident insurance. Medical assistance was provided for insured agricultural workers in the same manner as for other classes of insured persons, while uninsured agricultural workers had the same access to medical facilities as the rest of the population.[11]

The act of 26 October 1927 attempted to rationalize the social insurance programs.[12] First, it distinguished between industrial and non-industrial enterprises in agriculture. Non-industrial enterprises were those in which the work was entirely performed by the person exploiting the land and by the members of his family or in which paid labour played a secondary part. Industrial enterprises were those that employed three or more workers simultaneously throughout the agricultural season or had a second-class industrial license, a commercial license, or an intermediate license. In these enterprises insurance against all physical risks and against unemployment was compulsory. The industrial farm was required to pay an insurance premium of 10 per cent of wages, 7.5 per cent accruing to the insurance funds and 2.5 per cent to the medical service fund.

The government of the different republics had the right under this act to classify enterprises of a smaller size as industrial. These were to pay a premium of 6 per cent of wages, of which 5 per cent went into the insurance funds and 1 per cent to the medical service fund. The insurance covered temporary disability, total disability, and death resulting from an industrial accident; childbirth; cost of clothing for a new born child in the case of a woman worker; funeral expenses; and medical care.

Workers in non-industrial enterprises had the right to voluntary insurance at reduced rates. In such cases the employer was required to pay for each worker insured about 3 per cent of the average local wage of the corresponding category as fixed at the beginning of each year by the competent insurance fund

10 A. Slavinkov, 'V pote litsa,' *Trud*, 5 July 1927, p. 3; 'Nekotorge itogi provedeniia zakonov otrude v sel'skom khoziaistve,' *Voprosy truda*, nos 7–8 (July-August 1928), p. 31; 'Okhrana truda i strakhovanie batrakov,' *Trud*, 2 December 1928, p. 1; L. Nemchenko, 'O strakhovanii batrakov,' *Trud*, 2 December 1928, p. 2.
11 Medical benefits in kind such as medical and surgical attendance, special, orthopedic and prophylactic treatment, etc., were granted through the public health commissariats of the union republics. Medical assistance for the population as a whole, including insured persons, disabled, and old-age pensioners, and also for the members of their families, was financed by the state and local authorities and the social insurance institutions.
12 'Offitsial'nyi otdel,' *Voprosy strakhovaniia*, no 48 (1 December 1927), pp. 29–32.

in agreement with the ACCTU. These workers were entitled, however, to the same benefits as those granted to persons compulsorily insured and paying a contribution of 6 per cent of their wages.

In districts where social insurance for agricultural workers had not yet come into force, and where the employer was consequently not required to pay social insurance contributions, the following special provisions applied. The employer was required to provide, at his own expense, for the treatment of any worker who fell ill and to pay him full wages for a period not exceeding six weeks. Pregnant women were to be relieved of all work for four weeks before and four weeks after confinement and were to receive full wages. In case of accidents the worker or, in the case of death, his family, was to receive an allowance equal to that which would be paid under the system of social insurance. If agreement was not reached as to the amount of the allowance, the matter was to be referred to the courts. Agricultural workers who were summoned to active military service for training or manoeuvres were to retain their position and were to continue to draw wages or could receive a suitable indemnity in accordance with legislation relating to the privilege of soldiers and their families. The enforcement of social legislation relating to kulaks was handed over to the village soviets and the inspection service. Employers who were guilty of violating labour legislation were liable to prosecution before the courts and to administrative punishment. Again, as previously, questions of details relating to the conditions, period, and amount of benefits were to be settled by instructions from the All-Union Insurance Council.

Nemchenko, an official of the Insurance Council, reported to the Eighth Congress of Trade Unions in December 1928 that the financial position of the social insurance fund remained precarious and in some respects was becoming worse. While at the beginning of the year 1925–6 69 million roubles were available for social insurance, only 48 million roubles at the beginning of 1926–7 and 44 million roubles at the middle of 1927–8 were in the fund. In short, insurance funds had decreased continually so that instead of there being a reserve equal to two months' payments, as at the beginning of 1925–6, in the middle of 1927–8 there was a reserve of only three weeks. In view of this shortage the section on allowances in the overall budget had been subjected to marked reductions. In the case of agricultural workers it was openly admitted that in many cases benefits provided for these workers had no relation to their needs. In addition it was recognized that the program undertaken in 1928 for agricultural workers had given only mediocre results, that their system of insurance was largely imaginary, and that they received in fact only the slightest benefits.[13] Measures to remedy these difficulties were later incor-

13 For example in the Northern Caucasus where in 1928 there was a total of 30,000

porated into the resolutions passed by the congress in 1929, in which the necessity of developing social insurance programs for agricultural workers was particularly stressed.[14]

The All-Russian Conference on the Insurance of Batraks which met in Moscow in February 1929 came to similar conclusions. Liberman, another Social Insurance official, delivered a report to the conference on the state of the social insurance in RSFSR, noting that only 160,000 batraks were covered by insurance in the entire Russian republic, of which 83 per cent were insured voluntarily – a very small number, if one considers that on 1 August 1927 the Russian republic alone had over 1,065,000 batraks.[15] He also pointed out that most of the batraks on rich peasants' farms were not insured.[16]

Some changes in the existing legislation were introduced in the decree of 11 July 1929 of the Commissariat of Labour.[17] In particular, it superseded to some extent the regulations pertaining to non-industrial farms. The decree explicitly stated that the employer on these farms was not required to pay social insurance contributions for workers employed by him. But when an uninsured worker fell ill, the employer had to keep him on for one month if the worker had been employed by him for more than one month, and for two weeks if the worker had been employed by him for less than a month. During these periods the employer had to pay full wages and provide the usual keep. These provisions also applied to pregnant women.[18] When an uninsured worker was maimed or killed in the service of an employer the latter had to pay to the worker or his family a sum equal to that which would be paid in the same circumstances by the social insurance institutions. If agreement over the amount of the sum was not reached the case could be brought before the courts.

batraks covered by insurance, the contributions for the same period totalled only 183,000 roubles. And for the whole year, in only one instance was unemployment compensation paid, amounting to the grand sum of 4 roubles. Most of the labourers did not know about their rights and considered social insurance contributions a waste of money. 'So strakhovaniem batrachestva neblagopoluchno,' *Trud*, 19 February 1929, p. 2; 'Batrak bez medpomoshchi,' *Trud*, 16 February 1929, p. 5.

14 'Rezoliutsii VIII vsesoiuznogo s'ezda profsoiuzov,' *Trud*, 6 January 1929, p. 3.
15 'Osnovnye momenty v rabote strakhovykh organov RSFSR v 1926–27gg. v oblasti obespecheniia zastrakhovanykh,' *Voprosy truda*, nos 7–8 (July–August 1928), pp. 212–24.
16 'Vserossiiskoe soveshchanie po strakhovaniiu batrakov,' *Trud*, 10 February 1929, p. 2; S. Zubkov, 'Kak osushchestvliaetsia sotsial'noe strakhovanie batrachestva,' *Trud*, 17 May 1928, p. 2.
17 *Izvestiia NKT*, nos 34–5 (1929).
18 Compare with K.M. Varshavskii, *Prakticheskii slovar' po trudovomu pravu* (Moscow: Voprosy Truda, 1927), pp. 10–12, 80–1.

A much more significant change in the social insurance system occurred with the promulgation of new rules. The Central Executive Committee of the Council of Peoples' Commissars on 23 October 1929 issued a new regulation relating to the application of social insurance to agricultural wage earners, which was soon supplemented by a decree of 2 January 1930 approved by the Council of Social Insurance of the Peoples' Commissariat of Labour. The new legislation repealed the act of 26 October 1927.

Under the old act insurance was not compulsory except for peasant enterprises of an industrial type. The legislation of 23 October 1929, however, extended compulsory insurance to all wage earners employed in any individual or collective peasant farm except that of a 'peasant cultivator.'[19] Agricultural wage earners continued to be insured by district joint funds; but, in order to adapt the social insurance system for this class of insured persons to the conditions resulting from the agrarian policy pursued by the Soviet Union, the new legislation amended the system of insurance contributions for agricultural workers and fixed the conditions of payment, the period, and the amount of benefits which the act of 1927 had left undetermined.

The new regulation required that the whole cost of insurance contributions be paid by the employers and introduced large increases in the rate of contributions payable by individual enterprises. For individual enterprises of an industrial type the rate of contributions was fixed at 18 per cent of wages.[20] The kulak farm which was not classified as industrial was to contribute 10 per cent of wages. The village or group of peasants employing a shepherd contributed 10 per cent. A group of kulaks, however, had to contribute 22 per cent of wages for shepherds employed by them. On the other hand an individual peasant employer, if he wanted to contribute, paid 30 per cent of wages for the insurance of his employees. He was not compelled to purchase insurance, but he was liable for accidents and the illnesses of his workers.

For kolkhozes the amount of insurance contributions payable was fixed at 6 per cent of wages for agricultural workers.[21] In industrial or semi-industrial enterprises with no more than thirty workers and no less than sixteen (if mechanical power were used), the amount of insurance contributions was 10 per cent of wages. When the number of workers was more than thirty or more than sixteen if the enterprise used mechanical power, the amount of the insurance contribution was the same as that in the industry. Finally, repair

19 The latter was defined as a farm which did not come within the class of kulak farms nor that of agricultural enterprises of an industrial type.
20 An order of 2 January 1930 subsequently raised it to 22 per cent.
21 In this context, the hired labour in the kolkhozes.

shops, sheds for tractors and other agricultural machinery, smithies, etc., had to pay 10 per cent of wages as a social insurance contribution.

The benefits to which insured agricultural workers were entitled were as follows: a / payments for temporary incapacity; b / maternity payments; c / funeral expenses; d / medical aid; e / unemployment benefits; f / death and disability pensions. Payment for temporary incapacity arising from illness or accident was to be granted without any time limit and varied in size from 40 to 320 kopecks a day, according to the wage group to which the insured person belonged. There were twenty-three such groups, the first of which included workers who were earning less than 13 roubles per month and the last those earning more than 95. The payment of the allowance for the first five days was to be only 75 per cent of the full amount in cases in which the incapacity lasted less than two weeks.

Maternity benefits were equal to those for temporary incapacity. They were paid for the total period of eighty-four days; forty-two days before and forty-two days after confinement. In order to be eligible for paid maternity leave, a woman had to prove that in a period of two years immediately before child-birth she had worked for at least six months, and that of these six months she had worked two months immediately before maternity leave. In addition to maternity leave the woman worker was granted a payment for the child's clothing and a bonus for nursing.

The medical aid to which agricultural workers were entitled did not differ from other insured categories of workers, and it was extended to them by the organs of the Commissariat of Public Health in the various republics. Unemployment benefits were only granted to persons who were wholly depen-dent on wages and who had worked for at least twelve months during the two years preceding the beginning of their period of unemployment. The amount of the compensation was 8 roubles per month for workers who were trade union members, and 6 roubles for non-members. Compensation was paid for a maximum of four months a year, not exceeding eight months in all for each period of unemployment.

Finally, the allowance for funeral expenses was set at 10 roubles. Death and incapacity pensions were to be granted under the following conditions. In cases of work-connected incapacity, or because of an occupational disease, the insured worker was entitled to a pension of 4.50 roubles to 15 roubles per month if his wage was 25 roubles per month or less. If the worker's wage was over 25 roubles per month he was entitled to from 5.50 roubles to 64 roubles monthly as incapacity pension. At an invalid's death resulting from work-connected causes the family was entitled to a pension amounting to from 7.50 roubles to 15 roubles a month if his wage did not exceed 35 roubles, or from

7.50 to 47 roubles a month if his wage exceeded that limit. If the permanent incapacity resulted from sickness in general and was not work-connected, the worker was still entitled to a pension but the amount paid to him was smaller. Thus the monthly pension of an invalid who earned less than 25 roubles a month varied from 4.50 to 10 roubles per month. At the same time those who earned more than 25 roubles were entitled to monthly pensions ranging from 5.50 to 42 roubles per month. In the event of the death of an invalid whose monthly wage did not exceed 35 roubles, the family received a pension of from 5 to 10 roubles per month. If the earnings of an invalid were over 35 roubles a month, the pension was anywhere from 5.50 to 28 roubles monthly.[22]

The decree of the Central Executive Committee of the Council of People's Commissars of 3 October 1930 extended the social insurance of wage earners. Henceforth, all peasant farms, individual or collective, were obliged to insure their employees at the insurance office. The differentiated contribution rates were, however, continued. Thus peasant farms falling within the Provisional Rules for hiring additional labour on working farms were obliged to pay insurance premiums at the rate of 6 per cent of the wages of hired workers, male and female. Kulak peasant farms were obliged to pay insurance premiums at the rate of 22 per cent of wages of hired workers. Collective farms were obliged to pay insurance premiums at the rate of 16 per cent of wages of hired workers engaged in the manufacture of farm produce (e.g., in flour mills, cheese factories, distilleries, etc.), in trading enterprises (e.g., warehouses, offices, shops, etc.); for all other hired workers the obligatory insurance premium rate was set at 10 per cent of wages. Agricultural societies and groups of peasant farms collectively hiring shepherds were still obliged to pay insurance premiums for them at the rate of 10 per cent of their wages.

Insurance premiums were to be paid by employers from their own account and no deductions from the wages of the insured were to be made. If the employer failed to pay the insurance premiums when they fell due, the amount, together with a fine, were to be exacted summarily. The insurance covered temporary incapacity, including pregnancy and childbirth, permanent disability with the right to a pension, funeral expenses, and unemployment with the right to unemployment relief. In addition the insured workers and their families had the right to medical attention on the same basis as industrial workers and their families. In the event of the death of a breadwinner his

---

22 'Ob utverzhdenii pravil o sotsial'nom strakhovanii lits zaniatykh po naimu v krestianskikh khoziaistvakh: Postanovlenie soiuznogo soveta sotsial'nogo strakhovaniia pri NKT SSSR ot 2 ianvaria 1930 g.,' *Trud*, 10 February 1930, p. 4; See also *Trud*, 11 February 1930, p. 4; *Trud.*, 13 February 1930, p. 4; *Trud*, 20 February 1930, p. 6.

family had the right to receive payments for funeral expenses and a pension. The procedure for the calculation and payment of insurance premiums and also the conditions, forms, and duration of the relief provided by the insurance office, as well as short-term hire of workers by small farmers in cases where they were not bound to insure these workers, were to be regulated by the All-Union Insurance Council.

The ACCTU Plenum of January 1931 which approved the reorganization and subdivision of the existing trade unions also dealt with the problems of social insurance.[23] The plenum decided on a partial reorganization of insurance funds in order to bring them into accord with the then existing conditions of labour. Greatest attention was paid to such changes in the social insurance as would benefit especially the workers in so-called 'most-important industries,' such as mining, metal-working, engineering, chemicals, and railroads. Changes which encompassed all other categories of workers were also introduced and were designed primarily to combat excessive labour mobility. Because agriculture was especially plagued in this period by the rapid turnover of its labour force, the decisions of the plenum are of particular relevance to this study.

Trade union members who had worked for over two years in one place, and for more than three years altogether, were entitled to an allowance equal to their wages for the whole period of illness. The same benefits were granted to workers and employees who were members of the 'advance guards' irrespective of length of service rendered if they agreed to stay at an enterprise for a total of two or three years. Trade union members in general who worked for over two years in the same enterprise were entitled to three-quarters of their wages during the first twenty days of illness and full wages after that period. Those trade union members who worked less than two years in the same enterprise were entitled to two-thirds of their wages for the whole period of their illness. Workers who were not trade union members received only half of their wages during the first month of illness and two-thirds after that period. Trade union members received priority in the allocation of housing in all new buildings and the use of day nurseries, dining halls, etc. Those who worked for over two years in the same enterprise had priority for admission to sanatoria, rest homes, etc.

1931 – 3

Following the start of the First Five Year Plan in 1928, the territorial organization of social insurance became a target of criticism by party and trade union leaders. As one observer stated:

23 'Rezolutsiia *V* Plenuma VTsSPS po dokladu tov Shvernika,' *Pravda*, 6 February 1931.

The inter-occupational territorial funds were accused of treating all insured persons in the same way and making no distinction between workers whose work was essential to the success of the Plan, such as shock workers, and other workers, of acting bureaucratically without contact with the working masses, and of failing to fight against malingering and the constant changing of their place of work by some insured persons.[24]

The proposal of the Fifth ACCTU Plenum of 1931 to bring insurance institutions 'into closer touch with the mass of insured workers' by the creation of pay centres and occupational insurance funds was converted into law by the decree of the Central Executive Committee and the Council of Peoples' Commissars of 23 June 1931. It provided for the establishment of special funds for various branches of the economy and placed the social insurance institutions at the service of the government's economic plans. This second stage in the history of soviet social insurance lasted two years and was characterized by the coexistence of inter-occupational territorial funds and special funds for certain economic branches, and also by the creation of pay centres in enterprises employing over 1,000 persons. Each centre was directly subordinate to the territorial insurance fund or to the occupational fund for the region or republic. Agricultural workers remained insured with the inter-occupational fund for each republic which was made directly subordinate to the Central Social Insurance Administration for the USSR. At the same time the social insurance directorates and councils for the republics were abolished. Finally the decree also made it compulsory for insurance institutions to keep in close touch with the trade unions. In particular, the institutions had to submit all their rules concerning benefits and their budgets and accounts for review to the trade union organizations.

1933 TO 1964

Exactly two years later the Central Executive Committee reached the important decision to abolish the Commissariat of Labour and the inter-occupational territorial funds and to transfer the administration of social insurance to the ACCTU. The decree of 23 June 1933 initiated a new stage in the development of social insurance in the Soviet Union, and a resolution adopted by the Third ACCTU Plenum (25–30 June 1933) registered agreement with this decision. Finally, a decree of the government was promulgated on 10 September 1933, which was soon supplemented by a decree of the

24 A. Abramson, 'The Reorganization of Social Insurance Institutions in the USSR,' *International Labour Review*, 31 (January–June 1935), pp. 364–82.

ACCTU of 11 September 1933, both relating to the new functions of the trade unions.[25] By virtue of these measures, the ACCTU and the forty-seven central committees of the various trade unions took possession on 15 September 1933 of funds of the social insurance system, and of all its sanatoria, rest homes, research institutes, etc., and also of the funds of the Commissariat of Labour and its local organs. The staff of the Commissariat of Labour and of the social insurance system was attached to the ACCTU and its organs to the central committees of the different unions and their local organs. With some modifications this system exists even now, and before turning to the agricultural workers, let us briefly examine the general duties of central and local trade union organs with respect to the social insurance system.

In September 1933 the ACCTU set up a special insurance office which was responsible for the following tasks: the direction and supervision of all trade union activities related to social insurance; the preparation and submission for government approval of the social insurance budget for the entire USSR, in which the budgets of the different trade unions and inter-trade union bodies of republic, oblast, and krai level, and the special budget of the ACCTU, were combined; the construction and management of sanatoria, rest homes, and other establishments and institutions; the preparation and submission of social insurance rates for government approval; the issue of instructions and regulations for the administration of social insurance.

The central committee of each individual trade union directed and supervised the social insurance activities of all the lower trade union organs, drew up the social insurance budget for the economic branch concerned and approved the budgets for the trade union institutions subordinate to it, issued supplementary instructions concerning social insurance with due reference to the special features of the economic branch with which it had to deal, and was responsible for the construction and management of sanatoria and rest homes. All the resources of the union were at the disposal of its central committee, except those funds which were spent by the enterprises as benefits granted by the pay centres. In accordance with the budgets approved by the government and the ACCTU, each central committee transferred to its lower organs the sums they needed to meet their expenditures on social insurance. The expenditures of the primary insurance institution – the local committee of the union – were covered directly by the enterprises, which deducted the sums they spent on benefits from the contributions they had to pay to the insurance fund.

The inter-trade union councils supervised and directed the activities of the

25 'O poriadke sliianiia Narkomtruda SSSR s VTsSPS: Postanovlenie Sovnarkoma SSSR i VtsSPS ot 10-go sentiabria 1933g.,' *Trud*, 11 September 1933.

insurance institutions in their areas, and in particular of the local committees, and audited the payment of insurance contributions at the local level. The various organs of the trade union from the republic committee down to the oblasts or raion committees directed and supervised the activities of the local committees and approved their budgets. They were also required by law to collect insurance contributions.

At the base of the pyramid were the local committees, which had several duties with respect to social insurance. They determined the right to benefits in cases of temporary incapacity, pregnancy, or nursing and supervised the payment of these benefits by the enterprises. The local committees also managed the granting of sick leave and tried to prevent malingering. In cases of permanent incapacity they received the applications for pensions and checked the documents establishing the pension rights of insured persons and their survivors. They also had to prepare their own insurance budget, submit it for approval to the higher trade union committee, and supervise the payment of contributions by the enterprise.

Let us now turn to the agricultural workers in this period and examine who was included. Social insurance covered all workers (temporary as well as permanent) and salaried employees engaged in sovkhozes and other state agricultural enterprises. But only the following kolkhoz personnel were insured: chairmen, specialists with higher or secondary special education who also worked in their profession, senior bookkeepers, tractor drivers, combine operators, mechanics, lathe operators, metal workers, radio operators, electricians, and other production specialists who were employed as repair and service men.[26] Separate individuals who were not members of a given kolkhoz could be hired to do contract or commission work, but they were not included in the social insurance program. It was therefore, important to determine what was an individual's legal relationship to a given kolkhoz. This was not always easy to decide. Article 27 of the RSFSR Labour Code states that 'a contract of employment shall mean an agreement between two or more persons whereby

26 Decree of Council of Ministers of the USSR of 20 July 1964. 'O gosudarstvennom pensionnom obespechenii i sotsial'nom strakhovanii predsedatelei, spetsialistov i mekhanizatorov kolkhozov' in K. Batygin, Sotsial'noe strakhovanie na sele (Moscow: Profizdat, 1964), p. 6. 'O poriadke peredachi sovkhozam zemel' i obshchestvennogo imushchestva kolkhozov pri preobrazovanii ikh v sovkhozy i o poriadke raschetov s kolkhoznikami: Postanovlenie Soveta Ministrov SSSR i TsK KPSS ot 3 maia 1957 g,' Sotsial'noe obespechenie i strakhovanie v SSSR: Sbornik ofitsial'nykh dokumentov (Moscow: Izdatel'stvo Iuridicheskaia Literatura, 1964), p. 242; 'O dal'neishem razvitii kolkhoznogo stroia i reorganizatsii MTS: postanovlenie TsK KPSS i Soveta Ministrov ot 18 aprelia 1958g.,' Sbornik postanovlenii SSSR, no 7 (1958), article 62.

one party (the employee) places his labour at the disposal of the other party (the employer) [now management, or enterprise] in return for remuneration.' But this formulation no longer sufficed to establish the legal relationship in every case pertaining to social insurance, and the formulation contained in the Draft Labour Legislation of the USSR and Union Republics was more frequently utilized to determine the legal status applicable:

A contract of employment shall mean an agreement between the employee and the enterprise or establishment, under which the employee accepts the obligation to perform work in a given specialty, qualification or position, and the enterprise or establishment undertakes an obligation to pay his wages and to provide conditions of labour provided by labour laws, collective agreements and employment contracts.[27]

Prior to the legislation of October 1964 individual kolkhozniks could be covered by social insurance if they performed tasks requiring that they be paid by an enterprise doing certain contractual work for the kolkhoz. Workers and employees of the trade and procurement apparatus were covered by the state social insurance scheme provided they were permanent employees. In the case of temporary employees, some could be covered by social insurance provided certain conditions were met. For example, temporary workers in slaughter houses and the fur industry were covered by social insurance: a / if their employment was on the basis of a written labour agreement; b / if they were ordered to do such work and did not hold any other job; and c / if in the last two calendar months prior to the month in which the social insurance benefit was to be paid the worker fulfilled his tasks according to the plan.[28] Shepherds and junior shepherds employed by collective groups of citizens were also covered by social insurance as provided by the decree of the ACCTU Secretariat of 24 April 1941.

Some categories of students were also covered by social insurance. These included those who were attending schools or courses in order to raise their qualifications or to requalify if they were in the position of workers or em-

---

27 'Proekt osnov zakonodatel'stva o trude SSSR i soiuznykh respublik,' *Sovetskie profsoiuzy*, no 19, 1959. See also A.E. Pasherstnik, *Teoreticheskie voprosy kodifikatsii obshchesoiuznogo zakonodatel'stva o trude* (Moscow: Akademizdat, 1955); N.H. Aleksandrov, ed., *Novoe v razvitii trudovogo prava v period mezhdu XX i XXII s'ezdami KPSS* (Moscow: MGU, 1961).
28 'O poriadke obespecheniia po sotsial-nomu strakhovaniiu neshtatnykh zaboishchikov skota, neshtatnykh rabochikh pushnopromyslovykh i zverovedcheskikh khoziaistv: postanovlenie sekretariata VTsSPS ot 1 iiulia 1957g,' *Biulleten' VTsSPS*, no 14 (1957).

ployees immediately prior to attending the above schools or courses and students of secondary special scientific establishments (e.g., agricultural tekhnikums) or students of higher scientific establishments, while getting their production experience. However, students in general educational schools, labour reserve schools, and city or village trade schools were not covered.[29]

Persons who did various jobs and provided services for enterprises on a temporary basis were not covered by social insurance unless they fell within the following categories: a / typists working at home on their own typewriters and who possessed a written labour agreement with the enterprise; b / machinists repairing machinery of an enterprise, again on the condition that they had concluded a written labour agreement with the enterprise. Finally, domestics and children's nurses were covered by social insurance, as were some persons employed by religious organizations, but only on condition that their labour agreement was concluded with the help of the trade union.[30]

EXTENSION OF SOCIAL INSURANCE TO KOLKHOZNIKS, 1964 AND 1970

The most significant innovation in the social insurance scheme of this period was contained in an act of the Presidium of the Supreme Soviet of 15 July 1964 which introduced pensions and other benefits for collective farmers. The act entered into force on 1 January 1965 and replaced a previous scheme financed out of collective farm welfare funds by compulsory pension insurance. Provided under this new scheme were old age pensions, disability pensions, survivor's pensions, and maternity benefits.[31]

29 'Polozhenie o proizvodstvennoi rabote i proizvodstvennoi praktike studentov vysshikh uchebnykh zavedenii SSSR: prikaz ministra vysshego i srednego spetsial'nogo obrazovanniia SSSR ot 31 dekabria 1959g,' Sotsial'noe obespechenie, p. 230; 'Instruktsia ob usloviiakh i poriadke oplaty truda uchashchikhsia srednikh spetsial'nykh uchebnykh zavedenii, rabotaiushchikh na predpriiatiiakh, v organizatsiiakh tsekhakh, masterskikh i uchebno-opytnykh khoziaistvakh uchebnykh zavedenii v period obucheniia,' ibid., p. 231; 'Polozhenie o proizvodstvennoi praktike uchashchikhsia srednikh spetsial'nykh uchebnykh zavedenii,' ibid., p. 232.
30 Ibid., p. 239–42.
31 Vedomosti Verkhovnogo Soveta SSSR, no 29 (18 July 1964). An old-age pension was payable to all members of a kolkhoz upon reaching the age of 65 (men) and 60 (women). On the other hand, workers and employees were eligible for pensions five years earlier at the age of 60 for men and 55 for women. The women collective farmers were extended the same privilege only if they had at least five children. The pension was equal to 50 per cent of assessable remuneration up to 50 roubles per month, plus 25 per cent of wages in excess of this figure. The minimum of 12 roubles and the maximum of 102 roubles per month were also set. The payment of the pension was made dependent, however, on the satisfactory work in the collectivized sector.

At the same time an All-Union Social Insurance Fund for Collective Farmers was established. This scheme, it should be pointed out, did not affect the provision in force extending worker's social insurance to chairmen and hired labour (e.g., tractor drivers) in collective farms. But the inequalities among various members of the kolkhoz must have proved irksome, because a new decree of the Supreme Soviet dated 26 September 1967 did slightly improve the social insurance coverage for collective farmers.[32] Of course, the inequality between agricultural workers' benefits and the collective farmers' benefits was not obliterated, because the same decree again improved the position of workers.

In 1970 another serious attempt was made to raise the social insurance of kolkhozniks to the level of the sovkhoz workers, in the form of the unified, comprehensive system of social insurance. This scheme, effective 1 April 1970, was a direct outgrowth of the Third Congress of Collective Farmers of 1969 which recommended its adoption and the setting up of a single Centralized Social Insurance Fund for Collective Farmers.[33] Under it, kolkhozes pay 2.4 per cent of their payroll into the centralized fund, equivalent to roughly 1.5 per cent of their gross income. This, in addition to the pension scheme contributions from kolkhozes (4 per cent of their gross income), raises the total contribution from kolkhozes to about 8.8 per cent of their payrolls, which compares with a combined deduction for industrial enterprises which ranges from 3.7 to 10.7 per cent according to the working conditions of their parent industry.[34]

About 80 per cent of the fund is designated to cover payments for temporary

32 *Vedomosti verkhovnogo soveta SSSR*, no 39 (27 September 1967). The minimum age for an old age pension was reduced by five years, from 65 to 60 for men, and from 60 to 55 for women. Also, for those women who gave birth to five or more children and brought them up to the age of 8 years, the minimum age was reduced from 55 to 50. The provisions concerning old age pensions for persons who became disabled in the course of military service were extended to collective farmers. These individuals were entitled to an old age pension at the age of 55 and after twenty-five years' service for men, or at the age of 50 and after twenty years of service for women. In addition, the kolkhozniks were entitled to a disability pension, even if their disability was classed under category III – i.e., partial fitness for work – and the minimum disability pension sums have been raised. And finally, from 1 January 1968 pensions for kolkhozniks were to be assessed on the basis of average net earnings over any five-year period that the claimant selected within the ten years preceeding the application for pension. *International Labour Review*, vol 97 (1968), pp. 311–12.
33 I. Shkuratov, 'Sotsial'noe strakhovanie kolkhoznikov,' *Ekonomicheskaia gazeta*, no 23 (June 1970), p. 23.
34 A.M. Aleksandrov, *Finansy i kredit* (Moscow 1948), p. 90. This was found to be insufficient and each kolkhoz was ordered to make an additional one-time contribution of 0.2 per cent of the payroll in 1969. Skhuratov, 'Sotsial'noe strakhovanie,' p. 23.

disability, distributed in the following way. All kolkhozniks with an uninterrupted three-year period of employment are eligible to receive 50 per cent of wages. Those with three to five years, 60 per cent; five to eight years, 70 per cent; and those over eight years 90 per cent of wages.[35] Individuals up to eighteen years of age are guaranteed 60 per cent of wages, while invalids of the second world war receive 100 per cent of wages regardless of length of employment.[36] It is hoped that kolkhozniks will henceforth receive a similar level of benefits as workers and employees, although the revised regulations for maternity leave and allowances for female kolkhozniks are distinctly less liberal than those announced in 1964 in the act of the Supreme Soviet.[37]

There are also controls built into this scheme. Thus only those individuals who did not simply leave work on their own and who obtained medical proof of their disability are eligible for temporary disability benefits. The size of the benefits depends on the average wages of the past year, or if a person was employed less than a year on the average wages of the last few months. Again, the benefits are extended first of all to those kolkhozniks who are deemed to have discharged their obligations to the kolkhoz, that is, have worked the appropriate number of calendar days (as calculated by each kolkhoz) for the kolkhoz.[38]

ADMINISTRATION OF THE SOCIAL INSURANCE PROGRAM, 1933–70

In 1933, as has already been noted, the administration of social insurance was transferred from the Commissariat of Labour to the trade unions.[39] Now the insurance of the categories of agricultural workers enumerated above and of kolkhozniks is administered by the Union of Workers in Agriculture and State Procurement. In agriculture as in industry, all the work of the social insurance program at the enterprise level is conducted by primary trade union organizations with the help of union activists. The trade union council of the

35 The industrial workers and the hired labour in kolkhozes are better off in this respect. Thus workers with three years of uninterrupted employment are eligible to receive 50 per cent of wages; those with three to five, 60 per cent; those with five to eight years, 80 per cent; and those with over eight years, 100 per cent of wages. See *Spravochnik profsoiuznogo rabotnika* (Moscow: Profizdat, 1967), p. 297.
36 Shkuratov, 'Sotsial'noe strakhovanie,' p. 23.
37 *Ekonomicheskaia gazeta*, no 35 (1969), p. 15. Compare with: *Vedomosti verkhovnogo soveta SSSR*, no 29 (18 July 1964).
38 Skhuratov, 'Sotsial'noe strakhovanie,' p. 23.
39 'O poriadke sliianiia NKT SSSR s VTsSPS: Postanovlenie SNK SSSR i VTsSPS ot 10 sentiabria 1933g,' *Sobranie Zakonov SSSR*, no 57 (1933), article 333.

oblast, krai, and autonomous or union republic exercises general supervision over the social insurance work conducted by the corresponding organ of the union. At the all-union level the ACCTU is responsible for general supervision of the social insurance activities of the union as a whole.[40]

The primary organization of the union determines all forms of benefits available under the social insurance scheme, controls and supervises the payment of insurance contributions by the enterprises, watches over the disbursement of funds earmarked for the payment of social insurance benefits, together with the medical personnel assigned to the enterprise, oversees the proper administration of medical services for the workers, supervises the distribution of passes to sanatoria and rest homes, supplies assistance to children, and prepares and takes care of the documents necessary for obtaining pensions.[41]

The actual work in each of the union's primary organizations is carried on by a Commission on Social Insurance.[42] These commissions came into existence in 1957 and were organized in enterprises of three hundred or more workers, or in committees uniting that number. Until 1957 the function of social insurance agents were fulfilled by the so-called 'Council of Social Insurance' which was also attached to the union's local committee. The 1962 changes in the legal provisions permitted these commissions in all trade union committees of enterprises with one hundred or more workers.[43] Unlike the elected Council of Social Insurance, the Commission on Social Insurance is an appointive organ, whose members are drawn from among the 'leading workers,' specialists, physicians, and insurance delegates. The size of these commissions is regulated by the union's local committee. In every case the chairman of the trade union committee is the chairman of the Commission on Social Insurance. The commission operates with the help of groups of activists headed by the commission members who are responsible for different

40 'O funktsiiakh profsoiuzov v oblasti sotsial'nogo strakhovaniia: postanovlenie Prezidiuma VTsSPS ot 10 sentiabria 1933g,' *Voprosy strakhovaniia*, nos 7–8 (July–August 1933), as amended by decrees of the Council of Peoples' Commissars of 13 May 1934, article 220 and *Sobranie zakonov, SSSR*, no 22 (1937), article 88.

41 See also 'O pravakh fabrichnogo, zavodskogo, mestnogo komiteta professional'nogo soiuza,' *Pravda*, 16 July 1958, p. 1; 'O razhirenii uchastiia profsoiuzov v reshenii voprosov pensionnogo obespecheniia rabochikh i sluzhashchikh: postanovlenie Soveta Ministrov SSSR i VTsSPS ot 2 ianvaria 1962g,' *Sotsial'noe obespechenie*, p. 22; 'O razshirenii obshchestvennogo kharaktera raboty profsoiuznykh organov po upravleniiu gosudarstvennym sotsial'nym strakhovaniem: Postanovelenie Prezidiuma VTsSPS ot 5 ianvaria 1962 g,' *ibid.*, p. 22.

42 K. Batygin, *Rabota komissii po sotsial'nomu strakhovaniiu* (Moscow: Profizdat, 1960).

43 'Polozhenie o komissii po sotsial'nomu strakhovaniiu: postanovlenie Prezidiuma VTsSPS ot 5 ianvaria 1962g,' *Sotsial'noe obespechenie*, p. 28.

aspects of the commission's work. As a rule the Commissions on Social Insurance seem to be very active indeed. Their activity, in contrast to the passivity apparent in other trade union work, is especially marked in the collective farms, where it is officially encouraged.[44]

In trade union groups, unlike trade union committees, social insurance work is carried on by strakhovye delegaty (social insurance delegates). These agents are elected by means of an open vote by the members of a given group.[45] The number of social insurance delegates for each group is determined by the union's local committee, which considers the requirements of the group.

Each enterprise of one hundred workers or more has the right to organize a Commission on Pension Problems, which is responsible for the preparation of documents needed by the individual worker in order to obtain his pension, ensures that pensions are paid on time, especially for those pensioners who are employed part time, and supervises the placement of invalids.[46] In March 1963 the duties of these commissions were somewhat broadened and now include the task of studying the causes leading to disability in a given enterprise and of working out, together with the administration of the enterprise, such measures as are necessary to remove these causes. As in the case of the Commission on Social Insurance, the Commission on Pensions is composed of whatever number of union members the local committee deems necessary, and it is headed by the chairman of the local committee.

Krai and oblast committees of the union see to it that measures designed to prevent accidents among the workers and employees are observed and operating in all enterprises. It is also their function to supervise, control, and audit the financial activities of the local committees. They confirm the plans for the distribution of sickness passes and tourist tickets and decide questions connected with children's vacations. It is also their responsibility to train social insurance activists, who see that everyone is insured, and to act as clearing houses for all kinds of complaints coming either from individual workers, trade union committees, or management.

The social insurance functions of the union's republic committee vary from republic to republic. In those republics that do not have the oblast or krai administrative subdivisions, the republic committees perform the same func-

44 *Trud*, 16 March, 1965, p. 2.
45 'Polozhenie o strakhovykh delegatakh: postanovlenie Prezidiuma VTsSPS ot 5 ianvaria 1962g,' *Sotsial'noe obespechenie*, p. 31.
46 'Polozhenie o komissii po pensionnym voprosam: postanovlenie Prezidiuma VTsSPS ot 5 ianvaria 1962g,' *ibid.*, p. 27; 'O merakh po snizheniiu invalidnosti sredi trudiashchikhsia i uluchsheniiu vrachebno-trudovoi ekspertizy: postanovlenie Soveta Ministrov RSFSR i VTsSPS ot 11 marta 1963g,' *ibid.*, p. 293.

tion as the krai and oblast committees mentioned above. In republics which do have oblast divisions, the republic committees have very little to do with social insurance. In fact, they are not even vested with the function of confirming the social insurance budgets of the oblast committees, as this comes within the competence of the oblast trade union councils.

The operational tasks of the Central Committee of the Union of Workers in Agriculture and State Procurement consist mainly at the present time of studying the causes of illness and incapacity occurring among the workers and employees in its branch of the economy and, together with the economic and other administrative organs, of taking preventive measures.

The trade union council at the krai, oblast, or republic level exercises both practical guidance and general control of all the social insurance work in its area of competence. It has its own social insurance budget which is part of the general budget of the ACCTU. It controls the work of the health departments and of medical services for workers and employees. It also supervises the work of sanatoria and resorts, launches large-scale undertakings (such as summer camps for children), directs the training of voluntary social insurance functionaries, and assists in the work of all social insurance organizations. The trade union council is organized on an inter-union basis, and at the present time is the strongest regional trade union organ in existence.

General guidance is, of course, given by the ACCTU which issues, with the permission of the Council of Ministers of the USSR, instructions, regulations, and explanations of questions relating to social insurance. The ACCTU submits for the approval of the government legislative bills relating to social insurance, as well as the draft social insurance budget for the USSR as a whole, and reports on the fulfilment of this budget. It approves the social insurance budgets of the trade unions and councils, checks on their fulfilment of its decisions on social insurance, and popularizes advanced experience.

As has been indicated earlier, the social insurance program is financed jointly by the employing organizations and by governmental funds, providing a general pension system with a program of cash benefits for sickness, maternity, and industrial injury and disease. There are no precise data on the size of contribution rates in agriculture at the present time. The United States Social Administration places it at 4.4 per cent of the wages of workers in sovkhozes.[47] The contribution rate of kolkhozniks is fixed at 2.4 per cent of the payroll of the kolkhoz.[48]

The mechanics of collecting contributions are the same in agriculture

47 US Social Security Administration, *A Report on Social Security Programs in the Soviet Union* (Washington, DC: US Government Printing Office, 1960), pp. 76–7.
48 Shkuratov, 'Sotsial'noe strakhovanie,' p. 23.

as they are for all branches of the economy. Each month the enterprise determines the gross amount due by applying the prescribed contribution rate (e.g., 4.4 per cent in sovkhozes) to the total payroll. From this gross contribution there are then deducted cash disbursements made by the establishment to its workers for sickness, maternity leave, industrial injury and disease benefits, and general pensions for those still at work. The net amount of contribution then remaining is transmitted by the employing organization – through a check written on the state bank – to the trade union, which uses part of this money for benefits to the workers, such as sanatorium and rest home care and cultural activities. The remainder of the contribution is then transmitted to the ACCTU, which also uses part of the money for social purposes. What is left of the contribution is transmitted every three months to the Ministry of Social Security of each republic. It is not known whether there is any prescribed or definite method of determining the proportion of the net contributions from the enterprises that the trade unions hold before sending the remainder to the Ministry of Social Security.[49]

Each republic Ministry of Social Security also receives funds from the republic and USSR budgets. The total funds available to the Ministry of Social Security are distributed to the local offices for pension payments.[50] The latter offices receive somewhat more than is estimated to be necessary, so that they may have small reserves available in case their outlays are underestimated. The pension scheme is discussed in more detail below.

As in the past, the Soviet social security program continues to be non-contributory insofar as the workers covered are concerned. In essence this means that although contributions are drawn in the first instance from employing enterprises and general revenue (which is derived principally from

49 Ibid., pp. 76–7.
50 Shortly after the revolution, laws were promulgated making provision for social insurance for wage earners. In the beginning the power to administer social security was vested in the People's Commissariat of Charity (Narkom Prizreniia) and from April 1918 in the People's Commissariat of Social Security (Narkomsobes) of the RSFSR. Following the RSFSR model all other Soviet republics established their own Commissariats of Social Security (presently ministries). The main duties of these ministries are given as being a / the sanctioning and payment of pensions; b / the provision of work for disabled persons partially capable of working; c / to take care of the aged and other needy persons in special institutions (homes for the disabled, for the aged, etc.); d / the management of certain social organizations (the collective farm funds for mutual aid, the associations for the blind, etc.); e / to exercise guidance and control over the Ministries of Social Security in autonomous republics and the Social Security divisions of krai and oblispolkoms in the republics which have these administrative subdivisions, and over the raion social security divisions in the republics without krai or oblast subdivisions. V.A. Vlasov and S.S. Studenikin, Sovetskoe administrativnoe pravo (Moscow: Gosiurizdat, 1959), pp. 500–2; I.N. Ananov, Ministerstva v SSSR (Moscow: Gosiurizdat, 1960), pp. 122–3.

turnover taxes), the costs have ultimately been paid by the Soviet consumer, including the large proportion of the populace living on collective farms that until 1964 was not covered by most of the social security system.

As has already been noted, all Soviet workers may claim sickness benefits, and workers in agriculture are no exception. Yet there are certain peculiarities where some categories of workers in agriculture are concerned. The basic ones lie in the method of calculating temporary benefits for agricultural workers. As is known, a new system of wages was introduced into sovkhozes and a number of other agricultural enterprises in 1962. According to this system, workers do not receive full payment for their labour until the end of the production cycle. During this period, which can extend over several months or even a year, they are paid only a part of their full wages. This also applies to bonuses. In crop-growing and animal-breeding, wages are calculated on the basis of the volume of completed labour, and after the harvest is brought in and the feeding of stock is completed a recalculation of wages due is made and the difference paid to the workers. The benefits of a worker who is temporarily incapacitated prior to such recalculation of wages is based on his factual earnings prior to such incapacity. Later on the benefits are also recalculated. Bonuses established by the existing system of wages and which are paid for a period not exceeding three months can be included in calculating sick benefits.[51]

The method of calculating continuity of service is also important, because continuity affects the size of the benefit rates. Change of work does not necessarily mean discontinuity of service, especially if the worker has volunteered for labour in the sovkhoz or was sent there by an economic, party, Komsomol, or trade union organization. In the case of workers in the countryside who are laid off by an enterprise because of seasonal underemployment or lack of work, benefits for temporary incapacity are granted from the day when such work became available, this being determined by the local trade union committee on the basis of information supplied by the enterprise management.

PENSIONS

Old age, disability, and survivor pensions for wage and salary earners are governed by the 1956 State Pensions Law.[52] Unlike the cash benefits for sickness, maternity, and work injury, which are administered by the trade unions,

51 Batygin, *Sotsial'noe strakhovanie na sele*, p. 42.
52 'Zakon o gossudarstvennykh pensiiakh,' *Vedomosti verkhovnogo soveta SSSR*, no 15 (1956), article 313; 'Polozhenie o poriadke naznacheniia i vyplaty gosudarstvennykh pensii; postanovlenie Soveta Ministrov SSSR ot 4 avgusta 1956g,' *Sotsial'noe obespechenie*, p. 140.

pensions are administered by the government.[53] The role of the trade union is often limited to assisting members in presenting their claims to the pension committee of the local soviet. This assistance is rendered by the Commission of Pensions of the local trade union committee.[54] The executive committee of every local soviet has a social security section which is responsible to the republic Ministry of Social Security. Claims are filed with the local soviet's pension committee and pensions are delivered to pensioners through the mails.

To qualify for an old age pension, men must be sixty years old and must have worked for twenty-five years. Women, on the other hand, can qualify when they are fifty-five years old and have worked for twenty years. For certain categories of workers, primarily those in hazardous occupations, the qualifying age is lower and the length of work shorter, but this does not apply to any category of workers in agriculture. Those who qualify because of age only may retire on a partial pension. Also, service in the armed forces and in partisan detachments during the second world war, as well as study in secondary specialized and higher educational institutions, is taken into consideration in calculating length of service.

There is no forced retirement in the USSR. Workers and employees who continue to work after they have reached retirement age have the right to draw a full or partial old age pension.[55] Under the March 1964 decree, pensioners employed in agriculture are entitled to full pension plus wages.[56] Pensions for long meritorious service for agricultural workers were discontinued in 1962.[57]

Pensions for incapacitation are also regulated by the state pension law of 1956, as amended by a decree of 26 September 1967 and the act of 12 October 1967.[58] These require no qualifying period of employment and pension rates do not depend upon the length of time the worker was employed. The rates are also higher than the rates for disability pensions granted for non-work-connected injuries. Disability pensions are calculated on the basis of average monthly net earnings according to rates established in the 1956 law. The amount of the pension depends on three factors: a / normal net earnings;

53 'Polozhenie o komissii po naznacheniiu pensii pri ispolnitel'nom komitete raionnogo (gorodskogo) soveta deputatov trudiashchikhsia: Postanovlenie Soveta Ministrov RSFSR ot 10 iiulia 1962,' *ibid.*, p. 191.
54 'O zadachakh profsoiuzov v sviazi s priniatiem zakona o gosudarstvennykh pensiiakh: postanovlenie Prezidiuma VTsSPS ot 24 iiuulia 1956g,' *ibid.*, p. 186.
55 *Ibid.*, pp. 129, 179.
56 Batygin, *Sotsial'noe strakhovanie na sele*, p. 47.
57 'O prekrashchenii naznacheniia pensii za vyslugu let rabotnikam sel'skogo khoziastva: Postanovlenie Soveta Ministrov SSR ot 20 dekabria 1962g,' *Sotsial'noe obespechenie*, p. 198.
58 *Vedomosti verkhovnogo soveta SSSR*, no 39 (27 September 1967) and *ibid.*, no 42 (12 October 1967).

b / the disability category (I, II, or III) in which the worker is registered after medical determination of the extent of disability; and c / the degree of hazard in the worker's occupation.

In agriculture, all invalids of disability categories I and II whose wages are 120 roubles per month or less receive the full pension that is established for these categories. Invalids of the category III (those unable to pursue their usual vocation, but who can work under special conditions) who make 120 roubles per month or more receive a pension which when combined with current earnings, equals but does not exceed their prior earnings. All invalids of the category III whose prior earnings were less than 120 roubles per month and are currently less than 120 roubles are entitled to only 50 per cent of the pension set for the category.[59]

Survivor pensions are granted to dependent family members who are unable to work. Children up to sixteen or eighteen are eligible if in school, as are the grandparents of the husband or wife if they are past retirement age or are caring for a child under eight years of age. In cases where death was caused by a non-work-connected injury or illness, the worker's age and length of service determine eligibility for a survivor's pension. The amount of the survivor pension also depends on the number of eligible survivors in each family. In addition a small funeral grant is usually also awarded.

CONCLUSION

On the whole, the Soviet social insurance system works fairly well, considering the inadequately trained personnel who administer it. The gross errors that sometimes occur can be traced directly to this source. Thus, for example,

59 Batygin, *Sotsial'noe strakhovanie na sele*, p. 47. A slightly different provision applies to collective farmers. Beginning 1 January 1968, members of collective farms were entitled to a disability pension, even if their disability was classed under grade III, provided that the disability was the result of an employment accident or occupational disease. In such cases the disability pension was to be paid at a rate of 40 per cent of previous earnings, up to a maximum of 50 roubles per month and 25 per cent of the remaining earnings above this ceiling. Also the minimum disability pension sums have been raised. When the disability results from employment accident or an occupational disease, these sums are increased to 30, 20, and 12 roubles per month respectively, according to whether the disability was classed under category I, II, or III.

Where there was general invalidity the minimum pension sums were increased to 25 and 16 roubles per month respectively, according to whether the disability was classed under category I or II. (Previously the rates did not exceed 18 roubles per month.) Decree of the Presidium of the Supreme Soviet of the USSR of 26 September 1967 approved by the act of 12 October 1967, *Vedomosti Verkhovnogo Soveta SSSR*, no 42 (1967).

during 1957 the Union of Workers in Agriculture and State Procurement wasted eight hundred sanatoria passes by failing to distribute them to needy workers. For the same reason 4,923 kolkhozniks were illegally granted state pensions in 1958 and about 3.5 per cent of all cases tested in Kostroma oblast contained violations of law. However, the majority of these infringements or violations of the laws governing social security have been turned against the state, not the workers. Because of the submission of incorrect length of service and earnings certificates by some managers the state has made considerable overpayments. For example in 1958 in Kuibyshev oblast 571 of 2,062 documents examined (28 per cent) were incorrect, causing overpayments of 147,000 roubles.[60] It may very well be that the newly created 'labour book' for the kolkhozniks is designed to help achieve, first of all, a more efficient administration and distribution of the social insurance benefits.[61]

60 *Sotsial'noe obespechenie*, no 8 (1958), pp. 4–11.
61 See *Primernyi Ustav*, article 3 of chapter 2.

7
Conclusions

The evidence presented in the previous chapters, despite its obvious limitations, allows one to draw certain conclusions, although of necessity they must
be tentative and subject to change on the basis of new evidence.

First and foremost it is necessary to point out that Soviet trade unions
should not be considered identical with those of the Western world. In fact
they differ markedly from trade unions as we know them, and their character
is moulded by the environment in which they operate, which is totally different
from ours. Therefore they should be appraised in the context of their economic,
social, and political system with an understanding of the Communist ideology
of the harmony of interests in production in a so-called 'workers' state,' of
one-party dominance, central planning, strict discipline, and broad emphasis
on public participation in control – from below as well as from above. To the
extent that the ideological precepts are now broadly accepted – and there is no
conclusive evidence that they are not – they change workers' attitudes towards
management and their expectations from the unions.

It would, therefore, be an exaggeration to talk about the real independence of trade unions in such a society. The close watch which is exercised
by the party members active in the unions keeps the latter in line with party
and government policies. This was the case with respect to the relationship
between the party and agricultural unions from the very beginning, much more
so in fact than in the industrial trade unions. Lenin's idea was to organize the
rural labourers as a means of mobilizing the country's peasant masses. This
goal was considered important not least because of concern that the party's
real or potential opponents might themselves assume the initiative. In many
parts of the country, therefore, agricultural trade union affairs were at first

conducted directly by the party and only later transferred to the rudimentary union hierarchy. This close relationship between party and agricultural unions continued after Lenin's death. Stalin himself on several occasions equated the successes and failures of the agricultural unions with those of the party in the latter's attempts to penetrate the village.

The unions played a varying role in the party's agricultural campaigns. They helped prepare the basis for collectivization and participated in setting up the MTS. In 1953 the union was called upon to assist the party in the agricultural reforms culminating in the September Plenum. It also participated in the Virgin Lands campaign and in the 1958 abolition of MTS. More recently, as the July 1970 Plenum of the Central Committee of the CSU indicates, the union has again been called upon to help improve the state of agriculture.

Purges, close party supervision, the appointment of urban workers to the leading posts, continual changes in the distribution of agricultural workers among the various types of unions and in the internal structures of these unions, and tight financial control have been used in the past to prevent union functions from exceeding the limits defined by the 'transmission belt' theory of Soviet trade unionism.

The changes in organizational structure were of two kinds. The first category was directly related to shifts in the state's administrative structure and, specifically, to the proliferation and reduction in the number of ministries and to changes in party's agricultural policies. Thus, with the establishment of the MTS, the workers in these institutions received favoured treatment, and their union was entrusted with increased control functions. Again in 1953 several agricultural unions were amalgamated into one, as a reflection of changes in agricultural policy after Stalin's death. The consolidation of the agricultural unions in 1953 was virtually ignored in the West, and yet it pointed to the agricultural decisions taken later that year by the September Plenum. Similar organizational changes in the future may be equally indicative of future policy shifts.

The second category of changes was an even more direct function of tactical shifts in agricultural policy. The separate organization of the batraks in the 1920s was meant to provide not only a means of mobilizing this widely scattered stratum – whose interests differed from those of the other peasants – but also an additional resource for fomenting 'class war' in the villages. With the dispatch of industrial workers to the countryside in 1927 separate committees were set up for them. Similar measures were adopted on behalf of the new Soviet specialists who began entering the unions in the 1930s and the MTS workers transferred to kolkhozes in the 1950s, the intent in all these cases being to concentrate the impact on agriculture of these presumably more loyal and reliable elements.

This leads to another conclusion: the clear evidence of party manipulation of agricultural trade union membership policy for its own purposes. Lenin's principle that only workers who sold their labour were eligible for union membership was departed from at times in the 1920s for tactical reasons, and the differences among the groups making up the category of 'hired labour' were manipulated by the party. Thus, on the whole, the batraks were the most favoured category in the 1920s and early 1930s, while the poor peasants, initially permitted into the union, were weeded out in the late 1920s. The salaried employees and specialists who were suspected of disloyalty to the regime in the 1920s found their position improved in the 1930s when their ranks were augmented by the Soviet-educated intelligentsia.

The party continues to manipulate membership, as the 1958 reorganization and transfer of MTS workers to the kolkhozes clearly illustrates. Even though, perhaps, this continuing shuffle has other than a political basis, it is clear that the friction thus created was and is exploited by the party for its own purposes.

Membership in the unions, of course, was by no means universal, and their attractiveness to the workers varied with the times. For example, in the 1930s membership was low despite increased political pressures to join trade unions, while in the 1950s incentives to join were much greater and this fact was reflected in the rise of trade union membership as a percentage of the total eligible labour force. The influx of women and war veterans into the unions as a result of the war seems to have had some influence on the broadening of their functions. Furthermore, female workers could apparently criticize conditions in agriculture much more openly than men and may have been a democratizing influence. After the war, and at the present time, the press has continually warned union officials to be mindful of the needs of women workers.

The agricultural unions from the very beginning were financially dependent on state subsidies and very much subject to centralized controls. They accepted this domination because a / complete control of finances by the central organ increased its strength relative to the local branches; b / state subsidies were channelled through the central body, while the branches were excluded from this arrangement and dependent for their administrative expenses solely on the local enterprise; c / centrifugal tendencies were more than counterbalanced by Bolshevik influence within the union, by dependence on the centre for support and maintenance, and by the policy of filling top posts with urban workers; d / since union membership was highly dispersed, collection of dues was difficult and this made the branches even more dependent on the centre. This latter problem was aggravated by the change to voluntary membership during the NEP, the irregularity of wages, and the inflation of the rouble. The adoption, in the early 1930s, of a single budget for all unions, further strengthened the centralizing tendency.

Although the union bureaucracy existed largely on state subsidies, the impecunious local branches nevertheless had to account for the full amount of their members' dues. When the 16 December 1936 decree abolished financial contributions to the unions by enterprises the branches henceforth had to cover expenses entirely from what was left of their dues after obligations to superior union organs had been deducted.

Recently, and especially since 1958, the finances of union branches have greatly improved. They can keep a larger share of dues, and enterprises are again obliged to make payments into union funds. The branches have more say in their budget planning and more autonomy in expending funds for cultural purposes. Even so, however, the power of the central bodies remains unshaken. It is, therefore, premature to expect any real decentralization to take place under these circumstances.

As has already been indicated, there was a very close relationship between the bureaucratic element and the state subsidies, which on the whole operated to the advantage of the bureaucrats. However, the argument for greater financial efficiency and economy was always used in conjunction with actions designed to reduce the number of trade union officials. Since in reality no significant reduction of trade union bureaucrats has occurred, because those removed were replaced by others in short order, the whole procedure can only be viewed as an additional device to excuse, rationalize, and even to camouflage the extensive purging of the trade unions, a suspicion reinforced by the fact that these 'efficiency' campaigns have coincided with periods of purges sweeping the USSR.

In the early years the agricultural unions were unable either to protect the agricultural labour force or to raise its working conditions even to the level attained in industry. This was partly due to the existence of conflicting legal standards. For instance, the employment of batraks was regulated largely by the Provisional Rules, while sovkhoz workers fell under the Labour Code. Furthermore, sovkhoz managers and private employers in the 1920s tended to make every effort to evade whatever legal standards existed. Conditions were made even more difficult because the union leaders, who were usually former urban workers, were unfamiliar with agriculture. Inspectors were few and unenthusiastic about their work. Local soviets were also uninterested and limited their activity to the registration of collective agreements and of any reported violations.

Of course, it would have been unrealistic to expect anything different, in any case, since the law was viewed as a goal rather than a guide. Only in 1927 did the party, as a prelude to the impending collectivization, tell the union and local soviets to apply the provisions of labour legislation in such a way as to put pressure on the richer peasants. Even then, however, the party – consistent with Stalin's objectives – limited itself to pointing out violations without attempting to remedy them. It could thus claim to be a protector of the poorer peasants and still avoid disrupting agricultural production.

Collectivization itself was hardly conducive to the improvement of the trade union's endeavours to upgrade labour conditions, but the war, with its attendant influx of large numbers of female workers and disabled veterans into the agricultural labour force, did have this effect. Attention had to be paid to child care and the special needs of female workers, and this was done by the trade unions and the management of agricultural enterprises. Disabled veterans also often required special working conditions, the organization of which also fell to the unions.

As the party came to realize that labour productivity was a direct function of working conditions it began to redress the balance between management and labour. Thus the reintroduction of the collective agreement was useful from the point of view of the party not only as an information gathering device, or a tool for mobilizing the masses, but also as an important lever for raising productivity by improving conditions of labour. It can be said, therefore, that even such formal arrangements are worthwhile in advancing the welfare of the workers, especially if the party is willing to support their demands. The collective agreements could, perhaps, be considered as a kind of check on management, and to some extent on the union as well. Finally, this arrangement permits the party to act as a mediator or at least to shift the blame either to the management or the union or both for non-performance.

The problem of intolerable working conditions arose again in an acute form with the Virgin Lands campaign of the 1950s and the abolition of the MTS and transfer of its personnel to the kolkhozes in 1958. Dissatisfaction of the Virgin Lands pioneers assumed explosive proportions, and the unions had to be strengthened to cope with it. In the case of the ex-MTS personnel the party and government had to guarantee extension to the kolkhozes of the basic legal provisions governing labour in the MTS. This guarantee was embodied in the special legislation of 1958 – legislation which was, to some extent, the result of unorganized pressure by these very workers.

Although this legislation ameliorated the conditions of other workers in the kolkhozes, the situation of these workers is still inferior to that of the workers in state-owned enterprises. Labour safety lags behind the improvement in mechanization of production, hygienic conditions are on the whole deplorable, and the local union committees have fewer powers in kolkhozes than in sovkhozes. Although the 1958 legislation explicitly extends only to hired labour, by implication it covers ordinary kolkhozniks as well. The vagueness of the legislation on this point, however, permits considerable non-compliance by the kolkhoz management. The situation is unquestionably fraught with tensions, whose resolution will eventually require renewed efforts by the Soviet government (as the speech at the March 1965 Central Committee Plenum of I.S. Gustov, the first secretary of Pskov obkom, seems to indicate).[1]

On the whole, however, the situation is not completely hopeless. At local levels union officers appear now to be increasingly responsible to their membership, even though the influence of party members remains disproportionately strong. And there also seems to be a greater degree of attention to the demands of the workers for improvement of conditions and protection of rights, although those trade union functions intended to promote 'Communist upbringing' and the discipline of the workers are still very much in existence. However, the protective function of unions arise whenever there is a discussion of the increased rights of their primary organs. As far as management-union relations are concerned, a great deal of improvement can be observed, although bureaucratic disregard of workers' rights on the part of management and lack of interest on the part of responsible trade union organs in protecting these rights are still very much in evidence. The result of even these small improvements is that workers are now showing increased confidence in the trade unions.

The rising educational level of workers and their resulting awareness of developments, as well as continuous discontent with the failure of the promises of Communist theory to become reality, may have had some influence on matters. Moreover, the present liberalizing trend may have been dictated by the need of the party and government to obtain the co-operation of the workers in making agriculture operate more efficiently. Therefore, in order to accommodate at least partially changing attitudes and demands of workers, and to meet the need for increased efficiency in production, there appears to be a definite need within the Soviet system for enlarging the scope of trade union activity. This would entail greater opportunities for members to express their views on trade union matters and also greater autonomy for trade unions vis-à-vis their relations with government and management.

Because the pressures from the workers are channelled upward via the existing trade union structure, it becomes more and more possible to view the trade unions not only as organizations exercising control over labour, but also as channels facilitating a greater degree of two-way communication between the leadership and the masses – or at least more so than was the case in the past. This provides a ray of hope from the point of view of the development of pluralism within Soviet society. But only a ray of hope, for surely it is premature to speak in any definite terms of pluralistic tendencies in the USSR. Pluralism, if it ever comes – and there is nothing to suggest that it is inevitable

1 *Plenum Tsentral'nogo Komiteta Kommunisticheskoi Partii Sovetskogo Soiuza 24–26 marta 1965 goda: Stenograficheskii otchet.* (Moscow: Politizdat, 1965), pp. 141–6.

– is a long way off, although one cannot preclude the possibility of evolution in this direction. In any case, this development is probably watched closely by the party leadership, which has the means at its disposal to give it the speed and direction least harmful to the party's interests.

The same could be said with respect to the application of social security and social insurance in agriculture. Not only was insurance introduced relatively late into this sector of the economy, but social insurance schemes were manipulated by the party for political and economic purposes from the very beginning. Thus, for example, all enterprises with no more than two permanent workers, or which employed workers seasonally, were exempted by the Provisional Rules of April 1925 from the Insurance Provisions of the Labour Code. This was the period of 'concessions internally to embryo-capitalist elements,' as the richer peasants were then designated.

On the other hand, the act of 26 October 1927 was aimed not only at systematizing social insurance practices, but also at promoting a 'sharper attack' on the kulak. Further changes along the same lines were made in 1928 and 1929, at which time the kulaks were forced to pay a social insurance premium amounting to 22 per cent of the hired worker's wage, while kolkhozes paid no more than 16 per cent.

Beginning in 1931 changes in social insurance were designed especially with a view towards combatting excessive labour turnover. This practice continues even now. Thus, most social security benefits, particularly paid leave, sick pay, pregnancy and maternity benefits, are scaled according to the length of uninterrupted employment in the same enterprise. These arrangements, combined with such administrative measures as the use of the labour book and the internal passport, constitute a great check on the mobility of the worker, especially if he is an unskilled agricultural labourer.

The workers in sovkhozes as well as in the MTS were covered by social insurance, but most kolkhozniks, with the exception of kolkhoz chairmen, specialists, and senior bookkeepers were not. In recent times, however, the scope for manipulating social security and social insurance has narrowed significantly. Thus, for example, the fear that MTS workers might lose their pension rights and other benefits upon being transferred to the kolkhozes in 1958 was sufficiently widespread to elicit assurances to the contrary from the top leadership. This in turn generated pressures from ordinary kolkhozniks for similar treatment, and the outcome was at first the partial pension scheme for kolkhozniks that went into effect in January 1965 and a unified social security system for kolkhozniks as of April 1970.

Yet even now the fiction of a significant difference between kolkhoz hired labour and kolkhoz members is maintained, the latter being regarded as co-owners. This difference continues to be reflected in provisions for social security and insurance and the protection of ordinary kolkhozniks. Full cover-age of kolkhoz membership added greatly to the government's burden and, perhaps of greater importance, may have reduced the political and economic leverage offered to the government by the previous system. On the other hand, it seems that the cost considerations were outweighed by political or economic ones, such as a desire to stop the 'flight from the land' or to raise productivity of labour in agriculture. For after all, the reverse of the formula 'he who does no work, neither shall he eat,' is probably no less valid. Still, the aim of pro-viding these social security advantages as rewards for those who perform services of value to the system will probably continue.

Where does the extended coverage leave the trade unions? By itself, the fact that the trade unions have been in charge of administering social security programs for those remaining on the job, has not had any particular meaning as far as the growth of their power vis-à-vis the government has been con-cerned. In fact, for a substantial period of time the only legitimate basis for their existence had to do with the performance of their social insurance func-tions. It is not, however, too far-fetched to suggest that in the situation of a changing interpretation of the role of trade unions in the USSR – e.g., a shift in the direction of a greater stress on the defence theory – the expansion of the activities of the union in this sphere might provide them with an additional source of influence and power, which in some instances might be converted into political power. Such a development would be probably long in coming.

Appendices, selected bibliography, index

APPENDIX I

The organizational evolution of Soviet agricultural trade unions

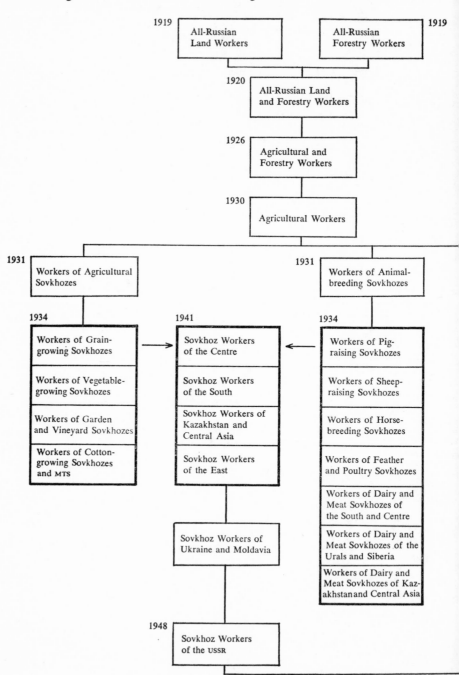

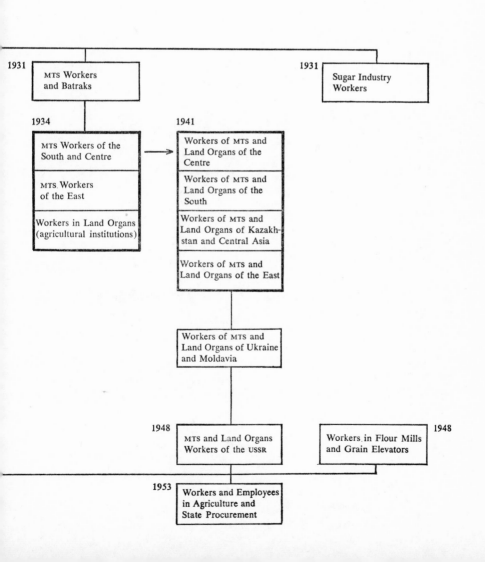

1931 | MTS Workers and Batraks

1931 | Sugar Industry Workers

1934
MTS Workers of the South and Centre
MTS Workers of the East
Workers in Land Organs (agricultural institutions)

1941
Workers of MTS and Land Organs of the Centre
Workers of MTS and Land Organs of the South
Workers of MTS and Land Organs of Kazakhstan and Central Asia
Workers of MTS and Land Organs of the East

Workers of MTS and Land Organs of Ukraine and Moldavia

1948 | MTS and Land Organs Workers of the USSR

1948 | Workers in Flour Mills and Grain Elevators

1953 | Workers and Employees in Agriculture and State Procurement

APPENDIX II

Total membership in agricultural trade unions, 1917–70

Year	Month	Number of members	Source
1917		577	International Labour Office, *The Trade Union Movement in Soviet Russia* (Geneva 1927), p. 67
1918		4,430	*Ibid.*
1919	June	33,594 34,000	*Ibid.* Lev Magaziner, *Chislennost' i sostav professional'nykh soiuzov SSSR* (Moscow: VTsSPS, 1926), p. 49; *Trade Unions in Soviet Russia* (London: Independent Labour party, 1920) p. 80; *Profsoiuz rabochikh sel'skogo khoziaistva: Kratkii istoricheskii ocherk* (Moscow: Profizdat, 1961), p. 5
	July December	48,000 22,936	*Trade Unions in Soviet Russia*, p. 79; *Profsoiuz*, p. 6 *Ibid.*
1920	January June December December	65,000 140,095 230,000 260,018	*Trade Unions in Soviet Russia*, p. 80 ILO, *The Trade Union Movement*, p. 67 *Profsoiuz*, p. 16 ILO, *The Trade Union Movement*, p. 67
1921	June July	658,954 659,000	*Ibid.* *Ibid.*, p. 85; Magaziner, *Chislennost'*, p. 49
1922	January June	566,766 300,000	*Ibid.* *Ibid.*
1922	July October	287,000 283,000	Magaziner, *Chislennost'*, p. 50 *Soviet Union Yearbook* (New York: B. W. Huebsch, 1925) p. 386
1923	January January January October	249,072 253,600 254,000 296,000	*Ibid.*, 1926, p. 437; *ibid.*, 1927, p. 366 *Ibid.*, 1928, p. 452; *ibid.*, 1929, p. 468; *ibid.*, 1930, p. 457 ILO, *The Trade Union Movement*, p. 85 *Soviet Union Review* (Washington, DC: Soviet Union Information Bureau, 1925), p. 386
	October October	297,000 300,000	Magaziner, *Chislennost'*, p. 49 *Industrial and Labour Information*, vol. 8, p. 28

APPENDIX II (*continued*)

Year	Month	Number of members	Source
1924	January	278,805	*Mezhdunarodnoe profdvizhenie, 1923–1924: Otchet Ispolbiuro III-mu Kongressu Profinterna* (Moscow: Izdanie Profinterna, 1924), p. 245
	January	279,000	*Shestoi s'ezd professional'nykh soiuzov SSSR: Stenograficheskii otchet* (Moscow: VTsSPS, 1925), p. 672
	January	280,616	*Soviet Union Yearbook,* 1926, p. 437
	April	297,868	*Soviet Union Review* (January 1926), p. 5; *KPSS o profsoiuzakh* (3rd ed.; Moscow: Profizdat, 1957), p. 201
	July	409,000	*Mezhdunaradnoe profdvizhenie za 1924–27: Otchet Ispolbiuro IV Kongressu Profinterna* (Moscow: Izdanie Profinterna, 1928), p. 232
	October	379,300	Magaziner, *Chislennost'*, p. 49
	November	354,600	*Shestoi s'ezd,* p. 719
1925	January	415,103	*Soviet Union Yearbook,* 1926, p. 437
	April	497,636	*Soviet Union Review* (January 1926), p. 5; VTsSPS, *Otchet VTsSPS k VIII s'ezdu profsoiuzov* (Moscow: Izdatel'stvo VTsSPS, 1928), p. 27; *KPSS o profsoiuzkh,* p. 201
	April	498,000	Magaziner, *Chislennost'*, p. 50
	October	761,526	*Soviet Union Yearbook,* 1926, p. 437, *ibid.,* 1927, p. 366
1926	January	856,925	*Profsoiuz,* p. 47
	January	861,300	*Biulleten' VTsSPS* (12 June 1926), p. 15
	April	922,300	ILO, *The Trade Union Movement,* p. 85
	July	921,868	*The Soviet Union: Facts, Descriptions,* p. 189
	July	1,000,000	*Soviet Union Yearbook,* 1927, p. 366; *ibid.,* 1928, p. 452; *ibid.,* 1930, p. 453
	July	1,003,700	VTsSPS, *Otchet VTsSPS k VIII s'ezdu profsoiuzov,* p. 27
	October	1,094,900	*The Soviet Union,* p. 189
1927	January	1,100,000	*Trud,* 31 July 1927, p. 1
	January	1,108,000	*Soviet Union Yearbook,* 1929, p. 468; *ibid.,* 1930, p. 457
	January	1,108,700	*Ibid.,* 1928, p. 452
	April	1,122,300	*Industrial and Labour Information,* vol. 25, pp. 71–4
	July	1,192,600	VTsSPS, *Otchet VTsSPS k VIII s'ezdu profsoiuzov,* p. 27
	July	1,200,000	*The Soviet Union,* p. 189
	October	1,243,500	*Statistika Truda,* no. 1 (1929), p. 85

APPENDIX II (*continued*)

Year	Month	Number of members	Source
1928	January	1,300,000	*Industrial and Labour Information*, vol. 43, pp. 65–75
	January	1,309,000	VTsSPS, *Materialy k otchetu IX s'ezdu, profsoiuzov* (Moscow: Profizdat, 1932), p. 27
	July	1,359,100	*Statistika Truda*, no. 1 (1929), p. 85
	July	1,362,000	*Trud*, 28 November 1928
	July	1,367,500	VTsSPS, *Otchet VTsSPS k VIII s'ezdu*, p. 27
	December	1,362,187	*Profsoiuz*, p. 47
1929		1,260,300	*Soviet Union Yearbook*, 1930, p. 457
		1,632,500	VTsSPS, *Materialy k otchetu IX s'ezdu*, p. 28
1930		559,000 (in sovkhozes only)	*Profsoiuz*, p. 58
	January	1,500,000	*Ibid.*
	August	1,715,000	*Piatyi Kongress Profinterna: Stenograficheskii otchet* (Moscow: Izdatel'stvo Profinterna, 1930), p. 528
	August	1,717,000	*Istoriia profdvizheniia V SSSR* (Moscow: Profizdat, 1961), p. 282. Of the 1,717,000 workers 700,000 were batraks. *Ibid.*, p. 283
	August	1,829,000	VTsSPS, *Materialy k otchetu IX s'ezdu*, p. 28
1931		2,049,600	*Ibid.*, p. 28
1932		2,040,000	*Industrial and Labour Information*, vol 43, pp. 65–75
1934	April	1,554,000	*Trud*, September 1934, p. 2
1936	January	1,455,000	*Industrial and Labour Information*, vol 60, pp. 249–50
	June	1,500,000	*Profsoiuz*, p. 79
1947	January	1,400,000	*Istoriia profdvizheniia V SSSR*, p. 427
1948		1,000,000 (in sovkhozes only)	*Ibid.*, p. 125
1949		2,400,000 (in 3 unions of agriculture)	*Istoriia profdvizheniia V SSSR*, p. 408

APPENDIX II (*continued*)

Year	Month	Number of members	Source
1950	January	2,000,000	*Ibid.,* p. 427
1951		1,600,000 (MTS and Land Organs)	*Ibid.,* p. 129
1953	October	3,700,000	*Ibid.,* p. 427
1954		4,800,000	*Ibid.,* p. 150
1956	March	5,159,000	*Ibid.,* p. 158; *Trud,* 31 March 1956, p. 2
1958	April	6,000,000	*Profsoiuz,* p. 164
1960		Over 6,000,000	International Labour Office, *The Trade Union Situation in the USSR: Report of a Mission From the International Labour Office* (Geneva 1960), p. 98
	March	7,000,000	*Trud,* 1 April 1960, p. 2
1963	February	11,000,000 10,105,000	*Trud,* 19 February 1963, p. 2 *Spravochnaia kniga o profsoiuzskh* (Moscow: Profizdat, 1968), p. 348
1964	July	10,575,000	*Spravochnaia kniga o professional'nykh soiuzakh SSSR* (Moscow: Profizdat, 1965), p. 305
1966	June	11,000,000	*Sovetskie profsoiuzy,* no 12 (June 1966), p. 1
1967	January	13,864,000	*Spravochnaia kniga o profsoiuzakh* (2nd ed., Moscow: Profizdat, 1968), p.348
1968	January	Over 14,000,000	*Sel'skaia zhizn',* 19 January 1968, p. 1
1970	March	Over 15,000,000	*Sovetskie profsoiuzy,* no 5 (March 1970), p. 11

APPENDIX III

Jurisdiction of Soviet agricultural trade union in 1921[1]

---

1 Workers in agricultural enterprises under the jurisdiction of the Commissariat of Agriculture and its local organs, in lease farms, in co-operative farms and in concessions, in addition, workers attached to the following farms:

a / grain growing farms
b / gardens
c / dairies
d / hothouses and greenhouses
e / animal-breeding farms (cattle-breeding, horse-breeding, poultry-breeding, rabbit-breeding, sheep-breeding, fisheries, beekeeping)
f / plantations of fibrous cultures and industrial crops, flax growing, cotton-growing, etc., and also hop-growing, tobacco-growing, and sugar-beet growing plantations

2 Workers in agricultural communes and artels operating either under the union or the normal statute of communes and artels

3 Workers in experimental and seed stations, agricultural meteorological stations, and living stations found within the jurisdiction of the Commissariat of Agriculture

4 Workers in repair stations (agriculture machinery) within the jurisdiction of Commissariat of Agriculture or its organs

5 Workers in tractor detachments within the jurisdiction of the Commissariat of Agriculture

6 Workers in mills and flour mills within the jurisdiction of the Commissariat of Agriculture

7 Workers in forestry, forest cultivation, forest conservation and forest protection services within the jurisdiction of the Commissariat of Agriculture (i.e., foresters, instructors in forest cultivation, inspectors, superintendents, assessors, workers in forestry organizations, workers and employees in lumbering

8 Workers in land conservation, agricultural and forest melioration within the jurisdiction of the Commissariat of Agriculture. Land surveyors, technicians, meliorators, hydrotechnicians, and workers employed in irrigation works

9 Members of the Learned Committee of the Commissariat of Agriculture

10 Employees of the Commissariat of Agriculture and its local organs

---

1 Vsesoiuznyi Tsentral'nyi Sovet Professional'nykh Soiuzov, Iugo Vostochnoe Biuro, *Sbornik po organizatsionnomu stroitel'stvu profsoiuzov* (Rostov na Donu 1921), p. 101.

APPENDIX IV

Jurisdiction of Soviet agricultural trade unions in 1920[1]

Institutions and enterprises whose workers were members of the Agricultural and Forestry Workers' Union.

Institutions and enterprises in agriculture:
1 Sovkhozes, sel'khoses and grain growing farms, animal-breeding farms, seed farms, combination farms, special crop farms, e.g., vineyards, flax, tobacco, sugar-beets, etc., regardless of what administration or branch of industry they belonged to
2 Agricultural plantations for special crops, e.g., cotton, tobacco, sugar-beets, vineyards, rice, tea, medicinal herbs, potatoes, etc., regardless of what administration or branch of industry they belonged to
3 Horse-breeding enterprises, stables
4 Apiaries
5 Transportation, grain-cleaning, sorting and pairing yards
6 Seed farms, hot-beds
7 Repair stations of agricultural machinery of the land, public and co-operative organizations in rural areas
8 Tractor detachments
9 Fisheries
10 Hunting and trapping industries
11 Fodder stations and hay pressing stations
12 Oblast, gubernia, and raion experimental stations
13 Experimental fields of general and special designations, i.e., meadows, potatoes, flax, use of fertilizers, etc.
14 Experimental stations and laboratories of special designation, i.e., silk-worm, wine-making, apiaries, fisheries (excluding those directly attached to other industries), medicinal herbs, orchards, sugar-beets, etc.
15 Selective-genetic stations
16 Agro-meteorological stations and bureaus
17 Bacterio-agronomic stations
18 Moscow's Soil Committee and its laboratories
19 Agricultural museums of practical and educational importance
20 Botanical gardens
21 Agronomic stations
22 O.Z.R.A. stations (defence of plants from parasites)

1 G. Melnichanskii, ed., *Spravochnik profrabotnika: Sbornik rukovodiashchikh materialov po professional'nomu dvizheniiu* (Moscow: VTsSPS, 1927), pp. 267–70; 'Postanovlenie Prezidiuma VTsSPS, 6.X.1926,' *Ibid.*, p. 37.

23 Enochemical laboratories
24 Seeding stations
25 The organization of land exploitation network
26 Colonization groups and expeditions
27 Experimental meliorative enterprises and irrigation and irrigation and drainage works
28 Hydrotechnical organizations involved in agricultural melioration works
29 Migration stations (excluding medical personnel), Water Works in Central Asia (repair workers and employees of the Central Asiatic Waterworks were members of Construction Workers' Union)
30 The central and local hydrological stations and bureaus, and hydromodular laboratories
31 Forestries of general economic importance, regardless of the branch of industry to which they belonged. Experimental forestries that used hired labour
32 Forestry meliorative works
33 Seeding stations
34 Timber enterprises: felling of timber, chopping, sowing, lumbering, floating, regardless of what administrative or economic organ was responsible for the work. Exceptions: a / forest sections of the trusts remained within the union which united workers of a given trust; b / workers of the trusts of the wood-working industry (members of the trade union of woodworking) who were temporarily assigned to procurement bureaus retained membership in their union
35 Forest bureaus directly in charge of timbering
36 Workers in charcoal enterprises (however, if charcoal production was concentrated on the territory of some enterprise, the workers then became members of one union of a given enterprise)
37 Batraks in individual and public peasant farms employed in agricultural works, shepherds, wet nurses, etc.
38 Drivers of cattle attached to cattle-transport bureaus
39 Hired labour in agricultural artels, communes, labour associations (agritural, machine, meliorative, etc.)
40 Artisan association and artels and their unions in rural areas (spoon makers, tanners, tar sprayers, weavers, furriers, etc.)
41 Peoples' Commissariat of Agriculture and its local organs, with the exception of the veterinary administration
42 Higher Geodetical Administration and its local organs
43 Oblast and gubernia agricultural trusts
44 Workers and employees of fishing industries and fisheries and also workers and employees of fish conservation working directly in rivers

and seas, workers and employees of ichthiological laboratories, etc.
Exception: workers of fish trusts charged with fish conservation were
members of the Food Workers' Union

45 The lower network of agricultural, forestry, and integrated co-operatives
in rural areas

46 Workers of agricultural and forestry co-operatives temporarily remained
within the Agricultural and Forestry Workers' Union with the exception
of workers in banks and credit institutions in the cities, and commercial
enterprises (magazines and warehouses) who were members of the
Soviet Trade Workers' Union. The employees of Vsekokhotsoiuz,
Vsekopromrybaksoiuz and association of hunters and fishers also remained members of the union on a temporary basis.

47 Agricultural and forestry associations

48 Employees of the peasant home in rural areas on the oblast and raion
level

49 Hired workers in peasant organizations: e.g., Koshchi, Komnezams Zharli,
Khamnachitov, and peasant self-reliance associations and their uezd and
gubernia organs

APPENDIX V

Jurisdiction of Soviet agricultural trade unions in 1931[1]

I The union of workers of agricultural sovkhozes united workers and employees of:

1 Grain and rice sovkhozes (grain sovkhozes)
2 Seed farms
3 Vegetable and fruit, and all suburban sovkhozes of the Tsentrozoius
4 Sovkhozes of technical industrial crops (of L'nokonoplevodtrest, Novlub-trest, Kauchukonos, Tabaksoiuz, Chai Gruzii, Lektekhsyria) [Workers of these sovkhozes were members of this union until 1934. *Trud*, 10 September 1934, p. 2.]
5 Cotton sovkhozes
6 Mulberry tree sovkhozes with nurseries
7 Combined sovkhozes
8 Sovkhozes which were part of the OMPK system and the trusts of volatile and vegetable oils
9 Enterprises located on the territory of a given sovkhoz and belonging together with the sovkhoz to the same economic association
10 Construction works in the sovkhozes
11 Experimental fields of general and special purpose (field crop cultivation, cultivation of meadows)
12 Krai zone stations (with raion experimental fields) of plant growing and soil science
13 Agro-meteorological, selective, seed-controlling governmental stations
14 The apparatus of the Commissariat of Agriculture and its local land organs and agricultural enterprises with the exception of the raizo [raion land departments]
15 Editorial offices of the union periodicals
16 Scientific and research institutes (e.g., the Lenin Academy) of agricultural sovkhozes
17 Vine and chemical laboratories responsible for experimenting with vines
18 Students of agricultural schools (grain, industrial crops, field conservation, etc.)

1 'Profkarta profsoiuzov SSSR,' *Trud*, 9 August 1931, p. 4.

II The Union of Workers of Animal-breeding Sovkhozes united workers and employees in:

1 Sovkhozes of the trusts: Skotovod, Svinovod, Ovtsevod, Maslotrest, Ptitsetrest, Molokoovoschchtrest, Ukrmolokotrest, Belseltrest, and republic, krai, and oblast cattle-breeding trusts and sovkhozes and those of them attached to separate organizations
2 State stud farms and hippodromes of the konevodtrest
3 Rabbit-breeding, reindeer-breeding, and fur-breeding farms, preserve nurseries of small animals and birds of industrial importance
4 Silkworm farms, silkworm breeding sovkhozes, and apiaries
5 Cattle-feeding stations, cattle yards, quarantine stations, and also cattle drivers
6 Attached enterprises and enterprises of the produce processing industry such as butter manufacturing, cheese making, alcohol, and other factories located within sovkhozes
7 Construction works in the sovkhozes
8 Selective-genetic stations and krai zone stations of cattle-breeding
9 Veterinary, medical and prophylactic enterprises in sovkhozes, veterinary institutes, veterinary tekhnikums
10 Veterinary, protective, quarantine and export-import stations, stations combatting rabies, the veterinary network in the cities, horse and cow market sites, disinfecting stations for milk produce if these stations were in the system of the Commissariat of Agriculture
11 Factories and laboratories producing biological preparations and warehouses supplying veterinary stations, and also shops manufacturing veterinary instruments and apparatus
12 Management of cattle-breeding trusts and experimental stations
13 Editorial offices of the union publishing houses
14 Students of Vuzes and tekhnikums that are under the jurisdiction of the administration of cattle-breeding sovkhozes
15 Scientific and research institutes administered by cattle-breeding sovkhozes

III The Trade Union of MTS Workers and Batraks united workers and employees in:

1 MTS
2 Repair factories and repair shops of Traktorotsentr
3 Repair shops of collective-co-operative and other organizations (dealing with agricultural tools)
4 Hired labour in individual sectors of agriculture, batraks, shepherd, and nannies

5 Hired labour in the artels, communes, collective farms, working associations, industrial, handicrafts, and co-operative artels, etc.
6 Experimental land-reclamation organizations and hydrotechnical organizations carrying out work in agriculture land reclamation
7 Land exploitation
8 Agricultural plants and stations
9 Seed controlling stations
10 Agricultural pest control sections, central and local organs
11 Bacteriological stations in plant growing
12 Construction projects in MTS and kolkhozes directed by the director or management of kolkhozes
13 Administration of Electrotechnical Structures
14 Economic agencies in MTS, organizations of land exploitation, melioration, kolkhozes, and agricultural co-operatives both in the centre and in localities, and raion land organs
15 Editorial offices of the union publishing houses
16 Scientific and research institutes administered by economic agencies that are united with the Union of MTS Workers and Batraks
17 Students in technical colleges, institutions of higher education, technicums administered by economic agencies that are united with the Union of MTS Workers and Batraks

IV Trade Union of Sugar Industry united workers and employees in enterprises and institutions of the sugar industry:

1 In sugar sand factories and beet-root drying factories
2 In sugar refineries
3 In sovkhozes, agricultural bases, selection stations within the system of Soiuzsakhar
4 In construction work in sovkhozes and current factory repair work
5 In seeding stations, seed plots (hot-beds), agricultural stations, fattening stations, milk farms, cattle-breeding enterprises, agricultural workshops, agricultural repair stations within the system of Siouzsakhar
6 In attached enterprises: repair shops, railroad lines, mills, etc.
7 In the economic organs and sugar industry
8 In scientific and research institutes administered by economic organs of the sugar industry
9 In editorial offices
10 Students in VTUZ, technicums, educational kombinats, raion schools of FZU (industrial training schools), SKHU (agricultural training schools) administered by economic organs of the sugar industry

APPENDIX VI

Jurisdiction of Soviet agricultural trade union in 1968[1]

It unites workers and employees of sovkhozes; institutions of 'sel'khoz-tekhnika' granaries; grain elevators; mills; groats and mixed feed factories; inter-kolkhoz organizations; water economy; administrative institutions in agriculture; scientific and experimental stations; faculty administration and student body of agricultural institutes; and specialists and machine operators who work in kolkhozes.

1 *Spravochnaia kniga o professional'nykh soiuzakh SSSR* (Moscow: Profizdat, 1965), p. 305; *Spravochnaia kniga o profsoiuzakh* (2nd ed., Moscow: Profizdat, 1968), p. 346.

APPENDIX VII

Distribution of the Group of the 25,000 according to sex, age, party membership, and years as hired workers, 1928-9

Regions	Number sent into villages	Sex		Age				Party membership			Years as hired worker		
		Male	Female	up to 22	23–29	30–39	40 and over	Party members and candidates	Komsomol	Non-party	up to 5	5–12	over 12
Severnyi krai	234	80.4	19.6	12.9	38.9	37.6	10.6	56.9	8.9	34.2	18.1	33.1	48.8
Leningrad oblast	4,614	91.0	9.0	9.3	47.7	31.2	11.8	75.5	8.2	16.3	9.1	57.4	33.5
Moscow oblast	5,565	89.8	10.2	8.9	50.5	30.4	10.2	76.2	7.0	16.8	13.6	30.8	55.6
Zapadnaia oblast	317	93.1	6.9	3.9	33.3	47.1	15.7	61.9	10.7	27.4	11.7	31.4	56.9
Ivanovsk oblast	1,445	87.4	12.6	9.9	48.8	31.7	9.6	83.0	4.0	13.0	16.0	45.1	38.9
Central Blackearth oblast	284	96.9	3.1	6.6	44.8	30.9	17.7	77.9	5.6	16.5	9.9	43.1	47.0
Ural oblast	251	94.9	5.1	12.8	42.3	33.8	11.1	66.2	8.7	25.1	5.5	48.3	46.2
Boskiriia	113	93.0	7.0	10.6	48.7	30.1	11.1	71.7	9.7	18.6	10.6	41.6	47.8
Middle-Volga oblast	241	94.2	5.8	5.8	39.0	41.1	14.1	66.4	5.3	28.3	15.3	36.1	48.6
Lower-Volga oblast	1,021	90.3	9.7	7.6	40.5	37.3	14.6	74.1	5.4	20.5	16.0	38.6	45.4
Crimea	200	n.d.	n.d.	n.d.	n.d.	n.d.	n.d.	64.0	14.0	22.0	n.d.	n.d.	n.d.
Northern Caucasus	272	90.5	9.1	2.2	56.6	32.7	8.5	76.5	5.5	18.0	12.8	48.2	39.0
Far East	331	96.4	3.6	10.2	26.3	32.9	30.6	68.6	9.6	21.8	22.0	25.7	52.3
Byelorussia	934	89.0	11.0	9.9	43.6	34.8	11.7	81.1	7.6	11.3	8.0	43.6	48.4
Ukraine	7,397	96.1	3.9	n.d.	n.d.	n.d.	n.d.	57.6	11.3	31.1	17.1	7.1	75.8
Armenia	54	88.9	11.1	11.1	42.6	37.1	9.2	70.4	7.4	22.2	27.7	40.8	31.5
Azerbaidzhan	348	98.9	1.1	8.9	41.5	39.7	9.9	74.2	10.6	15.2	1.4	52.6	46.0
Uzbekistan	197	95.4	4.6	10.6	40.7	31.9	16.8	66.5	9.6	23.9	21.7	44.1	34.2
TOTAL	23.409	92.3	7.7	9.0	47.1	32.1	11.8	69.9	8.6	21.5	13.0	39.0	48.0

SOURCE: *Politicheskii i trudovoi pod'em rabochego klassa SSSR, 1928–1929 gg* (Moscow: Gospolitizdat, 1956), pp. 544-5.

APPENDIX VIII

Distribution of new members of selected agricultural trade unions in various republics according to nationality, July – December 1931

Republic	Union	Total number in sample	Percentage distribution of the total by nationality								
			Russians	Ukrainians	Byelo-russians	Jews	Uzbeks	Kazakhs	Poles	Tartars	Others
Ukrainian SSR	Agricultural workers	284	12.0	53.5		21.5					13.0
Byelorussian SSR	Agricultural workers	1750	4.7		82.1	5.3			3.4		5.5
	Agricultural Sovkhozes	835	3.3		83.8	3.8			2.6		6.5
	Animal-breeding Sovkhozes	614	5.3		85.0	2.6			1.8		5.2
Uzbek SSR	Agricultural Sovkhozes	5796	54.1				27.1				18.8
Kazakh SSR	Agricultural workers	3736	30.7	10.5				23.6			15.2
	Agricultural Sovkhozes	2812	53.2	10.0				18.2			18.6
	Animal-breeding Sovkhozes	702	40.2	12.3				44.7			2.8
	MTS and Batraks	222	52.2	11.7				25.2			10.9
Tatar ASSR	Agricultural workers	1598	79.0							19.5	1.5

SOURCE: VTsSPS, *Sostav novykh millionov chlenov profsoiuzov* (Moscow: Profizdat, 1933), pp. 100–1.

APPENDIX IX

Characteristics of agricultural trade union membership in selected republics, based upon sample data, July – December 1931

Republic	Union	Nationality	Number in sample	Percentage of women	Percent distribution by age				Percentage distribution by social origin			
					to 17	18–23	24–29	Over 30	Workers	Peasants	Salaried employees	Artisans
Ukrainian SSR	Agricultural workers	Ukrainians	152	22.4	26.9	68.4	4.7		40.0	51.1	8.9	
Uzbek SSR	Agricultural Sovkhozes	Uzbeks	1575	2.9	6.8	33.3	39.0	20.9	24.7	68.9	2.7	0.6
		Russians	3132	31.6	4.9	37.2	26.4	31.5	12.3	80.7	3.8	0.2
Byelo-russian SSR	Agricultural Sovkhozes	Byelo-russians	700	32.1	10.9	49.8	16.8	22.5	20.8	77.6	0.8	0.8
	Animal-breeding Sovkhozes	Byelo-russians	522	22.8	12.9	46.5	18.2	22.4	18.8	78.9	1.6	0.5
Tatar ASSR	Agricultural workers	Tatars	311	6.4	8.6	32.5	19.6	39.3	8.1	91.1		0.8
		Russians	1263	26.3	12.5	37.6	20.1	29.8	14.6	82.6	1.1	1.7
Kazakh SSR	Agricultural workers	Russians	1896	44.1	13.5	44.6	17.2	24.7	14.7	77.0	3.0	4.4
		Ukrainians	393	42.7	12.7	38.6	16.6	32.1	14.4	80.7	1.9	2.7
	Agricultural Sovkhozes	Kazakhs	512	9.4	3.7	36.1	22.8	37.4	14.2	82.5	0.4	2.4
		Russians	1498	48.3	14.7	45.9	17.3	22.1	13.7	79.5	2.1	3.6
		Ukrainians	281	43.4	14.5	36.0	16.7	32.8	13.7	82.5	0.8	2.6
	Animal-breeding Sovkhozes	Kazakhs	314	5.8		22.6	28.3	49.1	19.6	77.6	2.8	
		Russians	282	28.1	8.6	42.9	14.5	34.0	20.1	68.0	3.5	8.4
	MTS and Batraks	Russians	116	28.4	10.3	32.8	21.5	35.4	15.7	65.0	13.1	6.2

NOTE: Data may not always total 100 per cent because of some omitted categories.
SOURCE: VTsSPS *Sostav novykh millionov chlenov profsoiuzov* (Moscow: Profizdat, 1933), pp. 102–11.

APPENDIX IX (*continued*)

Republic	Union	Nationality	Number in sample	Agricultural connection		Party membership		
				Per cent connected with agriculture	Per cent with an agricultural connection who are collective farmers	Per cent who are party members or candidates	Per cent who belong to Komosomol	Per cent who are illiterate
Ukrainian SSR	Agricultural workers	Ukrainians	152	50.8	92.6	1.9	46.1	
Uzbek SSR	Agricultural Sovknozes	Uzbeks	1575	2.5	7.6	2.2	4.6	61.0
		Russians	3132	47.6	0.2	0.3	5.3	9.3
Byelorussian SSR	Agricultural Sovkhozes	Byelorussians	700	53.9	55.2	0.9	12.4	15.1
	Animal-breeding Sovkhozes	Byelorussians	522	67.1	51.5	1.9	16.5	7.5
Tatar ASSR	Agricultural workers	Tatars	311	75.4	67.2	6.4	10.9	20.5
		Russians	1263	60.1	56.6	0.7	8.0	9.3
Kazakh SSR	Agricultural workers	Russians	1896	39.4	88.9	1.5	6.8	17.0
		Ukrainians	393	38.0	83.6	2.0	6.1	19.8
		Kazakhs	512	25.6	90.6	1.4	7.0	53.8
	Agricultural Sovkhozes	Russians	1498	43.5	88.5	1.2	7.2	19.5
		Ukrainians	281	37.0	78.4	0.3	5.3	22.3
	Animal-breeding Sovkhozes	Kazakhs	314	40.6	96.9	3.1	4.8	42.6
		Russians	282	25.0	89.9	1.7	5.7	11.1
	MTS and Batraks	Russians	116	24.2	96.4	4.3	5.1	11.6

APPENDIX IX (*continued*)

Republic	Union	Nationality	Number in sample	Last job before entering sovkhozes								
				Non-hired labourers (percentage of sample)				Hired-labourers (percentage of sample)				
				All non-hired labourers	Arti-sans	Own farms	Stu-dents	All hired labourers	Agri-cultural	Forest	Fac-tories	Trans-port
Ukrainian SSR	Agricultural workers	Ukrainians	152	88.9		11.0	77.2	11.1	7.5		2.8	
Uzbek SSR	Agricultural	Uzbeks	1575	22.8	2.3	13.9	5.0	77.2	57.7	5.0	3.5	3.2
	Sovkhozes	Russians	3132	37.0		18.4	3.5	63.0	27.9	7.4	2.6	
Byelorussian SSR	Agricultural Sovkhozes	Byelorussians	700	65.6	1.1	45.8	3.7	44.4	24.9	6.9	3.8	2.5
	Animal-breeding Sovkhozes	Byelorussians	522	67.4	1.0	56.6	5.9	32.6	20.9	9.9	3.2	
Tatar ASSR	Agricultural workers	Tatars	311	74.3	0.6	63.7	6.2	25.7	7.7	3.8	4.5	0.8
		Russians	1263	64.7	3.6	47.6	5.4	35.3	11.0	3.6	4.0	
Kazakh SSR	Agricultural workers	Russians	1896	49.3	0.2	31.5	4.3	50.7	28.1	5.5	1.4	1.6
		Ukrainians	393	46.7	1.9	35.8	3.1	53.3	28.7	8.2	1.1	0.6
	Agricultural Sovkhozes	Kazakhs	512	35.2	1.0	24.6	3.1	64.8	57.0	1.3	0.5	1.0
		Russians	1498	59.4	1.3	34.9	3.6	46.6				
		Ukrainians	281	55.6	1.6	43.9	2.8	44.4	28.2	1.6	1.7	0.8
	Animal-breeding Sovkhozes	Kazakhs	314	10.9	0.3	8.5	1.0	89.1	61.8	24.8		1.1
		Russians	282	29.6	4.4	18.9	4.5	70.4	36.6	20.8	1.7	
	MTS and Batraks	Russians	116	50.8	6.8	24.3	11.2	49.2	19.0	4.3		0.9

APPENDIX X

Membership in the Agricultural and Forestry Workers' Union in various
Central Asian republics, 1 April 1925

	Europeans			Natives			Total
	Male	Female	Total	Male	Female	Total	
UZBEKISTAN	6742	1180	7922	11312	187	11499	19421
TURKMENISTAN	877	69	946	491	0	491	1437
KARA-KIRGIZIIA	1189	31	1220	220	8	228	1448
CENTRAL ASIAN REPUBLICS	8808	1280	10088	12023	195	12218	22306

SOURCE: VTsSPS, Sredne Aziatskoe Biuro, *Professional'nye soiuzy v Srednei Azii, 1924–1925*
(Tashkent 1925), pp. 50–1.

Selected bibliography

BOOKS

ABRIUTINA, M.S. *Sel'skoe khoziaistvo v sisteme balansa narodnogo khoziaistva.* Moscow 1965

AIMBEIOV, A., M. BAIMAKHANOV, and M. IMASHEV *Problemy sovershenstvovaniia organizatsii i deiatel'nosti mestnykh sovetov.* Alma Ata 1967

ALEKSANDROV, N.G., ed. *Sovetskoe gosudarstvo i profsoiuzy.* Moscow 1965

ANOKHINA, L.A. and N.N. SHMELEVA *Kul'tura-byt kolkhoznikov kalininskoi oblasti.* Moscow 1964

ARMSTRONG, JOHN A. *Ideology, Politics, and Government in the Soviet Union: An Introduction.* New York 1962

ARUTIUNIAN, IU.V. *Sovetskoe krestianstvo v gody velikoi otechestvennoi voiny.* Moscow 1963

BAGDAGIULIAN, V.O. *Stimulakh i rukovodstve sel'skokhoziaisivennogo proizvodstva.* Erevan 1967

BAIKOVA, V.G., A.S. DUCHAL, and A.A. SEMTSOV *Svobodnoe vremia i vsestoronnee razvitie lichnosti.* Moscow 1965

BAKHTIN, M.I. *Soiuz rabochikh i krestian v gody vosstanovleniia narodnogo khoziaistva, 1921–1925.* Moscow 1961

BASHMOKOV, G.S. *Pravovoe regulirovanie vnutrennego rasporiadka v kolkhozakh.* Moscow 1960

BATYGIN, K. *Rabota kommissii po sotsial'nomu strakhovaniiu.* Moscow 1960
– *Sotsial'noe strakhovanie na sele.* Moscow 1964

BELKIN, V.B. *Professional'noe razdelenie truda i podgotovka rabochikh kadrov v SSSR.* Moscow 1966

BELOV, FEDOR *The History of a Soviet Collective Farm.* New York 1955

BERGSON, A. *The Real National Income of Soviet Russia Since 1928.* Cambridge, Mass. 1944

– *The Structure of Soviet Wages,* Cambridge, Mass. 1944

– ed. *Soviet Economic Growth.* Evanston and New York 1953

BERGSON, A. and S. KUZNETS, eds. *Economic Trends in the Soviet Union.* Cambridge, Mass. 1963

BETEREV, M.M. and M.M. BOL'SHOV, eds. *Spravochnik po okhrane truda v sel'skom khoziaistve.* Moscow 1961

BOL'SHOV, M.M. and A.I. PODOPRIGORA *Sbornik zakonodatel'nykh aktov po okhrane truda v kolkhozakh.* Moscow 1963

BOETTCHER, ERIK, *et al.,* eds. *Bilanz Der Aera Chruschtschow.* Stuttgart, Berlin, Koeln, Mainz, 1966

BORISOV, IS.S. *Podgotovka proizvodstvennykh kadrov sel'skogo khoziaistva SSSR v rekonstruktivnyi period.* Moscow 1960

BORODANOV, N.M. and I.S. CHERNIAK *Otvety na voprosy kolkhoznikov, rabochikh i sluzhashchikh po priusadebnomu zemlepol'zovaniiu.* Moscow 1960

BRODERSEN, ARVID *The Soviet Worker.* New York 1966

BROWN, E.C. *Soviet Trade Unions and Labor Relations.* Cambridge, Mass. 1966

BRUMBERG, ABRAHAM *Russia Under Khrushchev: An Anthology from Problems of Communism.* New York 1963

BYKHOVSKI, A.B. *Vserossiiskii sovet krestianskikh deputatov 1917 goda.* Moscow 1929

CHAPMAN, J.G. *Real Wages in Soviet Russia Since 1928.* Cambridge, Mass., 1963

Chetvertyi (ob'edinitel'nyi) s'ezd RSDRP–aprel'1906 goda: Protokoly. Moscow 1959

CHOMBART DE LAUWE, J. *Les Paysans sovietiques.* Paris 1961

CHUGUNOV, T.K. *Derevnia Na Golgofe.* Munich 1968

CZUGUNOW, T.K. *Die Staatliche Leibeigenschaft.* Munich 1964

DANILOVA, IE.S. *Sotsial'nye problemy truda zhenshchiny-rabotnitsy.* Moscow 1968

DEGRAS, J. and A. NOVE, eds. *Soviet Planning: Essays in Honour of Naum Jasny.* Oxford 1964

DE PAUW, J.W. *Measures of Agricultural Employment in the USSR, 1950–1966.* Washington 1969

DEUTSCHER, I. *Soviet Trade Unions.* London and New York 1950

DEWAR, MARGARET. *Labour Policy in the USSR, 1917–1928.* London 1956

Direktivy KPSS i sovetskogo pravitel'stva po khoziaistvennym voprosam: Sbornik dokumentov. I–IV. Moscow 1957/58

DIACHKOV, G.V. *Obshchestvennoe i lichnoe v kolkhozakh.* Moscow 1968

DMITRASHKO, I.I. *Vnutrikolkhoznye ekonomicheskie otnosheniia.* Moscow 1966

DMITRIEV, V.V., comp. *Opyt oplaty truda v kolkhozakh.* Moscow 1956

DODGE, N.T. *Women in the Soviet Economy: Their Role in Economic, Scientific, and Technical Development*. Baltimore 1966

Dostizheniia sovetskoi vlasti za sorok let v tsifrakh: Statisticheskii Sbornik. Moscow 1957

DUMONT, RENÉ *Sovkhoz, kolkhoz ou le problèmatique communisme*. Paris 1964

DUNN, ST P and E. DUNN *The Peasants of Central Russia*. New York 1967

XXIII S'ezd kommunisticheskoi Partii Sovetskogo Soiuza, 29 marta–8 aprelia 1966 goda: Stenograficheskii otchet. I–II. Moscow 1966

XXII S'ezd kommunisticheskoi Partii Sovetskogo Soiuza: Stenograficheskii otchet. Moscow 1962

XII S'ezd professional'nykh soiuzov SSSR 23–27 marta 1959: Stenograficheskii otchet. Moscow 1959

EASON, W.W. *The Population of the Soviet Union*. Washington Council for Economic and Industrial Research 1955

– *Soviet Manpower: The Population and Labor Force of the USSR*. New York 1959

EISENDRAHT, E. *Das Bevoelkerungspotential Der Sowjetunion*. Berlin 1960

Ekonomika sotsialisticheskogo sel'skogo khoziaistva. Moscow 1965

EMEL'IANOV, A.M. *Metodologicheskie problemy nakopleniia i rentabel'nosti v kolkhozakh*. Moscow 1965

EREMINA, N.M. and V.P. MARSHALOVA *Statistika truda*. Moscow 1965

ERLICH, A. *The Soviet Industrialization Debate, 1924–1928*. Cambridge, Mass. 1960

EVREINOV, N. *O svoeobraznom krizise profsoiuzov i ob ikh novykh zadachakh*. Moscow 1936

FAINSOD, M. *How Russia is Ruled*. Rev. ed. Cambridge 1964

FESHBACH, M. *The Soviet Statistical System: Labor Force Recordkeeping and Reporting since 1957*. Washington 1962

GAISINSKII, M. *Bor'ba bol'shevikov za Krestianstvo 1917: Vserosiiskie s'ezdy sovetov Krestianikikh deputatov*. Moscow 1963

GALENSON, W. *Labor Productivity in Soviet and American Industry*. New York 1955

GENKIN, D.M. and A.A. RUSKO *Kolkhoznoe pravo*. Moscow 1947

GORBUNOV, A. *Sotsial'noe strakhovanie v SSSR*. Moscow 1945

GRANICK, D. *The Red Executive*. New York 1960

GUSEINOV, K.A. and M.I. NAIDEL *Ocherki istorii profdvizheniia v Azerbaidzhane*. Baku 1966

– *Profsoiuzy sovetskogo Azerbaidzhana*. Moscow 1962

HAMMOND, THOMAS T. *Lenin on Trade Unions and Revolution, 1893–1917*. New York 1957

HASTRICH, A. *Alltag und Recht der UdSSR im Spielgel der Sowjetpresse*. Koeln 1967

HAYENKO, F.S. *Trade Unions and Labor in the Soviet Union.* Munich 1965

HAZARD, JOHN N. *The Soviet System of Government.* 2nd ed. rev. Chicago 1960

HAZARD, J.N., I. SHAPIRO and P.R. MAGGS *The Soviet Legal System: Contemporary Documentation and Historical Commentary.* New York 1969

IGNATOVSKII, P.A. *Sotsial'no-ekonomicheskie izmeneniia v sovetskoi derevne.* Moscow 1966

ILEBAEV, U. *Prava i obiazannosti kolkhoznikov: Po materialam Kirgizskoi SSR.* Frunze 1966

INKELES, A. and R.A. BAUER *The Soviet Citizen: Daily Life in a Totalitarian Society.* Cambridge, Mass. 1959

INTERNATIONAL LABOUR OFFICE *The Trade Union Movement in Soviet Russia.* Geneva 1927

– *The Trade Union Situation in the USSR: Report of a Mission from the International Labour office.* Geneva 1960

INKELES, A. *Social Change in Soviet Russia.* Cambridge, Mass. 1968

Ispol'zovanie trudovykh resursov v sel'skom khoziaisive Kirgizskoi SSSR. Frunze 1968

Ispol'zovanie trudovykh resursov v sel'skom khoziaisive SSSR. Moscow 1964

Itogi vsesoiuznoi perepsi naseleniia 1959 goda, SSSR: Svodnyi tom. Moscow 1962

Istoriia profdvizheniia v SSSR. 2nd ed. Moscow 1961

IVANOV, G.V. *Chlenstvo v kolkhoze.* Moscow 1960

Izmenenie soisial'noi struktury soistalisticheskogo obshchestva: Materialy k vsessoiuznoi teoreticheskoi konferentsii v Minske. Sverdlovsk 1965

Izmenenie sotsial'noi struktury sovetskogo obshchestva: Besedy po aktual'nym Problemam nauki. Moscow 1962

Izmeneniia sotsial'noi struktury sovetskogo krestianstva: Tezisy dokladov i vystuplenii po nauchnoi konferentsii 'Izmenenie sotsial'noi struktury sovetskogo obshchestva.' Minsk 1965

JASNY, NAUM *The Socialized Agriculture of the USSR: Plans and Performance.* Stanford 1949

– *The Soviet Economy during the Plan Era.* Stanford 1967

KARCZ, J.F., ed. *Soviet and East European Agriculture.* Berkeley 1967

KASSIROV, L.N. *Planovye pokazateli i khozraschetnye stimuly proizvodstva v kolkhozakh i sovkhozakh.* Moscow 1966

KAZACHKIN, V.G. *Pravovoe polozhenie mekhanizatorov kolkhozov.* Moscow 1959

Khoziaistvennyi rashchet v kolkhozakh i sovkhozakh. Moscow 1967

Khozrashchet i stimulirovanie v sel'skom khoziaistve. Moscow 1968

KHRUSHCHEV, N.S. *Otchetnyi doklad Tsentral'nogo Komiteta Kommunisticheskoi. Partii Sovetskogo Soiuza XX s'ezdu.* Moscow, 1959

– *Stroitel'stvo kommunizma v SSR i razvitie sel'skogo khoziaistva.* Moscow 1962

KISELEV, Ia.L. *Osnovy trudovogo zakonodatel'stva SSSR.* Moscow 1964

KOCHIN, I.N. *Preodolenie sotsial'no-ekonomicheskikh razlichii mezhdu gorodom i derevnei.* Moscow 1964

Kolkhoz-shkola kommunizma dlia krestianstva: Kompleksnoe sotsial'noe issledovanie kolkhoza 'Rossiia.' Moscow 1965

Kolkhoznoe pravo. Moscow 1962

Kolkhozy vesnoi 1931 Goda: Statisticheskaia rozrabotka otchetov kolkhozov ob itogakh vesennogo seva 1931g. Moscow-Leningrad 1932

KON'KOV, V. and F. LIUTIKOV *Kak organizovat' rabotu profsoiuznogo komiteta v sovkhoze.* Moscow 1962

Konkretno-sotsiologicheskie issledovanniia v pravovoi nauke. Materialy nauchnoi Konferentsii, Kiev, 26–27 Oktiabia 1965g. Kiev 1967

Konstitutsiia (Osnovnoi Zakon) Soiuza Sovetskikh Sotsialisticheskikh Respublik. Moscow 1958

KOTLIAR, A.F. *Rabochaia sila v SSSR.* Moscow 1967

KOTOV, G.G. *Rezervy povysheniia proizvoditel'nosti truda v sel'skom khoziaistve.* Moscow 1966.

KPSS o profsoiuzakh. 3rd ed. Moscow 1957

KPSS o profsoiuzakh, 1956–1962. Moscow 1963

KPSS o profsoiuzakh. Moscow 1967

KPSS v rezoliutsiiakh i resheniiakh s'ezdov, konferentsii i plenumov TsK. 7th ed. Moscow 1954

KUGEL', S.A. *Zakonomernosti izmeneniia sotsial'noi struktury obshchestva pri perekhode k kommunizmu.* Moscow 1963

KULIEV, T.A. *Problema interesov v sotsialisticheskom obshchestve.* Moscow 1967

LAGUTIN, N.S. *Problemy sblizheniia urovnia zhizni rabochikh i kolkhoznikov.* Moscow 1965

LAIRD, ROY D. *Collective Farming in Russia: A Political Study of the Kolkhoz.* Lawrence, Kansas 1958

– *The Rise and Fall of the MTS as an Instrument of Soviet Rule.* Lawrence, Kansas 1960

Lenin o profsoiuzakh, 1895–1923. Moscow 1957

LENIN, V.I. *Sochineniia.* 4th ed. Moscow 1941–50

LEWYTZKYJ, B. *Die Gewerkschaften in der Sowjetunion.* Frankfurt am Main 1970

– *Die Kommunistische Partei der Sowjetunion.* Stuttgart 1967

LORIMER, F. *The Population of the Soviet Union.* Geneva 1946

LUDAT, H., et al., eds. *Agrar-, Wirtschafts- und Sozialprobleme, Mittel- und Osteuropas in Geschichte und Gegenwart.* Wiesbaden 1965

MAGAZINER, LEV *Chislennost' i sostav professional'nykh soiuzov SSSR.* Moscow 1926

MAMAEVA, K.I. *Sel'skaia intelligentsiia v period perekhoda ot sotsializma k kommunizmu (auto-referat dissertatsii).* Moscow/Riga 1966

Materialy XIV s'ezda professional'nykh soiuzov SSSR. Moscow 1968

Materialy dekabr'skogo (1957 goda) plenuma TsK KPSS. Moscow 1957

Materialy ob rabote politotdelov MTS za 1933. Moscow-Leningrad 1934

MEISSNER, B., ed. *Sowjetgesellschaft im Wandel – Russlands Weg zur Industrie-gesellschaft.* Stuttgart 1966

MEL'NIKOV, M. *Delegatskie sobraniia v sovkhozakh na plantatsiiakh i v selakh.* Moscow 1928

MIKHAILOV, A.M. *Profsoiuzy Belorussii v bor'be za vypolnenie chetvertoi piatiletki v oblasti promyshlennosti.* Minsk 1961

MITROFANOVA, A.V. *Rabochii klass sovetskogo soiuza v pervyi period velikoi otechestvennoi voiny.* Moscow 1960.

MOROZOV, V.A. *Trudoden': Den'gi i torgovlia na sele.* Moscow 1965

MUSATOV, I.M. *Sotsial'nye problemy trudovykh resursov v SSSR.* Moscow 1967

Naemnyi trud v sel'skom i lesnom khoziaisive v 1926g. Moscow 1928

Narodne hospodarstvo Ukrains'koi RSR v 1965 rotsi: Statystychnyi shchorichnyk. Kiev 1966

Narodnoe khoziaistvo SSSR: Statisticheskii sbornik. Moscow 1956

Narodnoe khoziaistvo SSSR v 1956 godu: Statisticheskii ezhegodnik. Moscow 1957, 1959, 1960, 1961, 1962, 1963, 1964, 1965, 1966.

New Directions in the Soviet Economy: Studies Prepared for the Subcommittee on Foreign Economic Policy of the Joint Economic Committee, Congress of the United States. Washington 1966

NIMITZ, N. *Farm Employment in the Soviet Union, 1928–1963.* Santa Monica, Calif. 1965

NOVE, A. *The Soviet Economy.* New York 1961

– *Economic Rationality and Soviet Politics.* New York 1964

Obshchestvennye fondy kolkhozov i raspredelenie kolkhoznykh dokhodov. Moscow 1961

OSTROVSKII, V.B. *Kolkhoznoe krestianstvo SSSR: Politika partii v derevne i ee sotsial'no-ekonomicheskie rezul'taty.* Saratov 1967

PANOVA, E.A. *Pravovoe regulirovanie truda v sovkhozakh.* Moscow 1960

PASHAVER, I.S. *Balans trudovykh resursov kolkhozov: Voprosy metodologii, metodiki i analiza.* Kiev 1961

– *Razvitie kolkhoznoi demokratii v period razvernutogo stroitel'stva kommu-nizma.* Moscow 1962

Piatyi Kongres Profinterna 15–30 Augusta 1930: Stenograficheskii otchet. Moscow 1930

PIPES, R., ed. *The Russian Intelligentsia.* New York 1961

Plenum Tsentral'nogo Komiteta KPSS, 24–26 Marta 1965 goda: Stenograficheskii otchet. Moscow 1965

PLOSS, SIDNEY I. *Conflict and Decision Making in Soviet Russia: A Case Study of Agricultural Policy, 1953–1963.* Princeton, New Jersey 1965

Polozhenie, utverzhdenoe Tslk i SNK SSSR 6 fevralia 1925g., s izmeneniiami i doplneneniiami. Moscow 1930

POPOV-CHERKASOV, I.N. *Zarabotnaia plata rabotnikov sfery obsluzhivaniia.* Moscow 1967

Postanovleniia iiul'skogo plenuma TsK Kommunisticheskoi Partii Sovetskogo Soiuza 1955 goda. Moscow 1955

Postanovleniia plenumov VTsSPS deviatogo sozyva. Moscow 1949

Postanovleniia plenumov VTsSPS odinadtsatogo sozyva, 1954–1958. Moscow 1961

Problems of Leninism. 4th ed. Moscow 1928

Problemy filosofii i sotsiologii. Leningrad 1968

Problemy izmeneniia soisial'noi struktury sovetskogo obshchestva. Moscow 1968

Problemy proizvoditel'nosti truda i narodnogo potrebleniia v period razvernutogo stroitel'stva kommunizma. Moscow 1965

Profsoiuz rabochikh sel'skogo khoziaistva: Kratkii istoricheskii ocherk. Moscow 1961

Profsoiuznaia rabota na sele. Moscow 1965

Profsoiuzy i narodnyi kontrol, 1917–1965: Dokumenty i materialy. Moscow 1965

Profsoiuzy i piatiletka. Moscow 1968

Programma Komunisticheskoi Partii Sovetskogo Soiuza priniataia XXII s'ezdom KPSS. Moscow 1961

Puti povysheniia proizvoditel'nosti truda v sel'skom khoziaistve SSSR. Moscow 1964

Rabochii klass SSSR, 1951–1965gg. Moscow 1969

Rabota profsoiuznogo aktiva po sotsial'nomu strakhovaniiu. Moscow 1965

RADKEY, OLIVER H. *The Sickle Under The Hammer: The Russian Socialist Revolutionaries in the Early Months of Soviet Rule.* New York 1963

Raionnoe zveno. Moscow 1966

RIGBY, T.H. *Communist Party Membership in the U.S.S.R., 1917–1967.* Princeton, New Jersey 1968

RITVO, H. *The New Soviet Society.* New York 1962

RUBAN, MARIA-ELISABETH *Die Entwicklung des Lebensstandards in der Sowjetunion unter dem Einfluss der Sowjetischen Wirtschafts politik und Wirtschaftsplanung.* Berlin 1965

SAIBEKOV, K.A. *Pravovye formy oplaty truda v kolkhozakh.* Moscow 1963

SAZANSKII, Ia.I. *Normirovanie truda v sel'skom khoziaistve.* Moscow 1964

Sbornik polozhenii po oplate truda rabotnikov gosudarstvennykh sel'skokhoziaistvennykh predpriiatii. Moscow 1965

Sbornik postanovlenii i rasporiazhenii po trudu dlia rabotnikov sel'skogo khoziaistva. Moscow 1958

Sbornik reshenii po sel'skomu khoziaistvu. Moscow 1963

Sbornik zakonodatel'nykh aktov o trude. Moscow 1960

SCHILLER, O. *Das Agrarsystem der Sowjetunion.* Tuebingen 1960

SCHWARZ, S.M. *Labor in Soviet Russia.* New York 1952

Sel'skoe khoziaistvo SSSR: Statisticheskii sbornik. Moscow 1960

SEMENOV, A.A. *Trud i ekonomika.* Moscow 1966

SENIAVSKII, S.L. *Rost rabochego klassa SSSR, 1951–1965gg.* Moscow 1966

SHMELEV, G.I. *Raspredelenie i ispol'zovanie truda v kolkhozakh.* Moscow 1964

SLUTSKY, A. and V. SYDORENKO. *Profsoiuzy Ukrainy posle pobedy velikogo oktiabria.* Moscow 1961

SNIGIREVA, I.O. and L.S. IAVICH. *Gosudarstvo i profsoiuzy.* Moscow 1967

SOSNOVY, T. *The Housing Problem in the Soviet Union.* New York 1954

Sotsial'no-ekonomicheskie preobrazovaniia v voronezhskoi derevne, 1917–1967. Voronezh 1967

Sotsial'noe obespechenie i strakhovanie v SSSR: Sbornik ofitsial'nykh dokumentov. Moscow 1964

Sotsiologicheskie issledovaniia: Voprosy metodologii i metodiki. Novosibirsk 1966

Sotsiologiia v SSSR. I–II. Moscow 1965

Sovetskoe gosudarstvo i profsoiuzy. Moscow 1965

Sovetskoe pensionnoe obespechenie. Moscow 1966

Spravochnaia kniga o profsoiuzakh. Moscow 1968

Spravochnik bukhgal'tera kolkhoza. 2nd ed. Moscow 1964

Spravochnik ekonomista po planirovaniiu v kolkhozakh i sovkhozakh. Kishinev 1967

Spravochnik partiinogo rabotnika. Moscow 1930

Spravochnik partiinogo rabotnika. Moscow 1959

Spravochnik partiinogo rabotnika. Moscow 1967

Spravochnik po okhrane truda v sel'skom khoziaistve. Moscow 1961

Spravochnik po oplate truda v sovkhozakh i drugikh gosudarstvennykh sel'skokhoziaistvennykh predpriiatiakh. 2nd ed. Moscow 1963

Spravochnik profsoiuznogo rabotnika. Moscow 1962

Spravochnik profsoiuznogo rabotnika. Moscow 1964

Spravochnik profsoiuznogo rabotnika. Moscow 1969

SSSR v tsifrakh: Statisticheskii sbornik. Moscow 1958

STALIN, I.V. *Works.* Moscow 1952–5

Strana sovetov za 50 let: Sbornik statisticheskikh materialov. Moscow 1967

Stroitel'stvo kommunizma i razvitie obshchestvennykh otnoshenii. I–V. Moscow 1966

Stroitel'stvo kommunizma i sotsial'nye imeniia v krestianstve Belorussii. Minsk 1966

SUKHAREV, A.I. *Sel'skaia intelligentsiia i ee rol' v stroitel'stve kommunizma.* Moscow 1963

SUSLOV, I.F. *Ekonomicheskie problemy razvitiia kolkhozov.* Moscow 1967
SUVOROVA, L. *Oplata truda v sovkhozakh i kolkhozakh.* Moscow 1961
The Soviet Union in Facts and Figures. London, Soviet News, ND
The Soviet Union Yearbook. New York 1926
TOLKUNOVA, V.N. *Pravo zhenshchin na trud i ego garantii.* Moscow 1967
Trade Unions in Soviet Russia. London 1920
Trud i zarabotnaia plata v SSSR. Moscow 1968
Trud v SSSR. Moscow 1968
TSOGOEV, N.V. *Statistika sebestoimosti sel'skogo khoziaistva.* Moscow 1963
URZHINSKII, K.P. *Trudoustroistvo grazhdan v SSSR.* Moscow 1967
US Congress, Joint Economics Committee. *Dimensions of Soviet Economic Power.* Washington, DC, 1962
US Social Security Administration. *A Report on Social Security Programs in the Soviet Union.* Washington, DC, 1960
Ustav Professional'nykh Soiuzov SSSR. Moscow 1954
Ustav Professional'nykh Soiuzov SSSR. Moscow 1959
Ustav Professional'nykh Soiuzov SSSR. Moscow 1963
VARSHAVSKII, K.M. *Prakticheskii slovar' po trudovomu pravu.* Moscow 1927
Vazhneishie resheniia po sel'skomu khoziaistvu za, 1938–1946gg. Moscow 1948
VERBIN, ANDREI *Soviet Trade Unions.* London 1958
Vnutriklassovye izmeneniia krestianstva. Minsk 1966
VOLKOV, V.F. and A.K. MALAKHOV *Oplata truda v sovkhozakh.* Moscow 1962
VOLOSHIN, N.P. *Pravo lichnoi sobstvennosti kolkhoznogo dvora.* Moscow 1961
Voprosy profsoiuznoi raboty. 3rd ed. Moscow 1965
Voprosy truda. Moscow 1958
XVIII s'ezd VKP (B). Moscow 1939
VOVK, IU.A. *Novoe v oplate truda kolkhoznikov.* Moscow 1963
VSEROSIISKII TSENTRAL'NYI SOVET PROFESSIONAL'NYKH SOIUZOV *Otchet za 1919 god.* Moscow 1920
– *X s'ezd Professional'nykh Soiuzov SSSR: Stenograficheskii otchet.* Moscow 1949
– *XI s'ezd Professional'nykh Soiuzov.* Moscow 1954
– *Kratkii otchet VTsSPS IX s'ezdu.* Moscow 1932
– *Materialy k otchetu VTsSPS k IX s'ezdu profsoiuzov.* Moscow 1932
– *Otchet VTsSPS k VIII soiuzov.* Moscow 1928
– *Otchet VTsSPS k VI s'ezdu professional'nykh soiuzov.* Moscow 1924
– *Professionalnoe dvizhenie SSSR, 1917–1927.* Moscow 1927
– Sredne-aziatskoe biuro. *Professional'nye soiuzy v Srednei Azii, 1924–1925* Tashkent 1925
– *Tretii s'ezd profsoiuzov: Stenograficheskii otchet.* Moscow 1920
– *Vtoroi s'ezd profsoiuzov: Stenograficheskii otchet.* Moscow 1919
– Zakavkazskoe Biuro. *Pervyi zakavkazskii s'ezd professional'nykh soiuzov 6–9 marta, 1922.* Tiflis 1922

VSESOIUZNYI TSENTRAL'NYI SOVET PROFSOIUZOV *Otchet VTsSPS k VII s'ezdu profsoiuzov.* Moscow 1926

VUCINIC, ALEXANDER *Soviet Economic Institutions: The Social Structure of Production Units.* Stanford 1952

WAEDEKIN, KARL-EUGEN *Fuerungskraefte im Sowjetischen Dorf.* Berlin 1969
– *Privatproduzenten in der Sowjetischen Landwirtschaft.* Koeln 1967

ZAIONCHKOVSKAIA, zh.a. and v.i. PEREVEDENTSEV *Sovremennaia migratsiia naseleniia krasnoiarskogo kraia.* Novosibirsk 1964

Zakonodatel'stvo o pensiiakh i posobiiakh chlenam kolkhoza: Sbornik ofitsial'nykh materialov. 2nd ed. Moscow 1966

ZASLAVSKAIA, T.I. *Raspredelenie po trudu v kolkhozakh.* Moscow 1966

ARTICLES

ABDULLAEV, N. 'Mozhet li profsoiuz ob'ediniat' kolkhoznykh mekhanizatorov,' *Trud,* 20 March 1958

ABRAMSON, A. 'The Reorganization of Social Insurance Institutions in the USSR,' *International Labour Review,* XXXI (January–June 1925)

ADAMS, A.A. 'Informal Education in Soviet Agriculture,' *Comparative Education Review,* no 2 (June 1967

AHLBERG, R. 'Die Socialstruktur der UdSSR,' *Osteuropa,* no 5/6 (1968)

AITOV, N.A. 'Nekotorye osobennosti izmeneniia klassovoi struktury v SSSR,' *Voprosy filosofii,* no 3 (1965)

AIMETDINOV, A. and v. PETROV 'Trebovaniia vremeni-v ustav kolkhoza,' *Ekonomika sel'skogo khoziaistva,* no 1 (1966).

AKOPIAN, A. 'Na uroven' novykh zadach,' *Trud,* 7 May 1957

'Aktual'nye zadachi profsoiuzov,' *Pravda,* 8 January 1970

ALEKSANDROV, N. 'Ekzamen na zrelost,' *Sovetskie profsoiuzy,* no 2 (1966)

ALTMOROV, V. 'Piatiletie leningradskogo gubotdela Vserabotzemlesa,' *Trud,* 27 March 1924

ANDREEV, V. 'V nadezhde na tsirkular: Tisiachi rabochikh sela eshche ne vovlecheny v profsoiuz,' *Trud,* 5 June 1951, p. 2

ANNENKO, M. 'Pervye shagi raboty po novomu,' *Trud,* 3 March 1958, p. 1.

ANTIPOV, M.G. 'Kolkhoznoe proizvodstvo i demokratiia,' *Sovetskoe gosudarstvo i pravo,* no 3 (1967)

ANTSELOVICH, N. 'Nuzhno delo,' *Trud,* 1 June 1923

ARKHIPOV, A. 'Razvitie obshchestvennykh fondov potrebleniia v kolkhozakh,' *Voprosy ekonomiki,* no 12 (1965)

ARUTIUNIAN, F. 'V dve smeny,' *Sovetskie profsoiuzy,* no 16 (1966)

ARUTIUNIAN, IU. V. 'Iz opyta sotsiologicheskikh issledovanii sela v dvadt satye gody,' *Voprosy istorii KPSS,* no 3 (1966)
– 'Konkretno-sotsial'noe issledovanie sela,' *Voprosy filosofii,* no 10 (1966)

– 'Podvizhnost' sotsial'noi struktury sela,' *Vestnik Moskovskogo Untversiteta, seriia ekonomika*, no 3 (1966)
– 'Sotsial'naia struktura sel'skogo naseleniia,' *Voprosy filosofii*, no 5 (1966)
– 'Sotsial'nye aspekty kul'turnogo rosta sel'skogo naseleniia,' *Voprosy filosofii*, no 9 (1968)
ASTRAUSKAS, V. 'Povyshat' boevitost' sel'skikh partorganizatsii,' *Partiinaia zhizn'*, no 7 (1966)
'Avangard rabochego klasa v derevne: Desiat let soiuza S.Kh. i Lesnykh Rabochikh,' *Trud*, 15 June 1929
BABAEV, M. 'Nakanune mezhsoiuznoi konferentsii,' *Trud*, 22 October 1948
BAIKALOV, I. 'Sviaz s massami osnovnoe uslovie uspekha v rabote profsoiuznykh organizatsii,' *Trud*, 15 September 1940, p. I.
BALLARD, A. B. Jr. 'Problems of State Farm Administration,' *Soviet Studies*, no 3 (January 1966)
– 'Sovkhoz Kuban,' *Survey*, no 48 (July 1963)
BALTIANS'KYI, M. 'Vysoka vidpovidal'nist,' *Robitnycha hazeta*, 26 February 1970
BARTON, PAUL 'The Current Status of the Soviet Worker,' *Problems of Communism* IX (July–August 1960)
BASHKIRTSEV, A. 'Rabochaia odezhda-spros i predlozhenie,' *Sovetskie profsoiuzy*, no 4 (1966)
BASHMAKOV, G.S. 'Pravovye voprosy oplaty truda v kolkhozakh,' *Sovetskoe gosudarstvo i pravo*, no 5 (1957)
– 'Teoreticheskaia konferentsiia po pravovym problemam nauki upravleniia,' *Sovetskoe gosudarstvo i pravo*, no 6 (1966)
'Batrachestvo na Ukraine,' *Trud*, 26 September 1923
'Batrak bez medpomoshchi,' *Trud*, 16 February 1929
'Batrakov v kolkhozy,' *Trud*, 26 January 1930
BELIAEVA, A.S. 'Garantii ukrepleniia sotsialisticheskoi zakonnosti v kolkhozakh,' *Sovetskaia iustitsiia*, no 24 (1966)
BELIAEVA, A.S. and M.I. KOZYR 'Razvitie khoziaistvennoi deiatel'nosti kolkhozov,' *Sovetskoe gosudarstvo i pravo*, no 12 (1967)
BELOUSOVA, E. and V. STESHENKO 'O nekotorykh problemakh demograficheskogo prognozirovaniia,' *Ekonomika sovetskoi Ukrainy*, no 1 (1967)
BEREZHNOT, N. M. and S. I. OVCHINNIKOV 'Opyt issledovaniia izmenenii v strukture svobodnogo vremeni kolkhoznikov,' *Filosofskie nauki*, no 5 (1966)
BERGMAN, S. 'Stalin i profsoiuzy,' *Trud*, 23 December 1939
'Blazhennoi son u podnozhzhia surama,' *Trud*, 22 March 1933
BLOK, V. 'Rost batrachestva – taktika Vserabotzemlesa,' *Trud*, 19 October 1923
'Boevaia programma v deistvii,' *Sovetskie profsoiuzy*, no 2 (January 1963)
'Bol'shaia zhatva,' *Trud*, 11 July 1958
'Bol'she vnimaniia koldogovoram v MTS,' *Trud*, 24 March 1949

'Bol'shie zadachi sel'skikh kommunistov,' *Partiinaiaia zhizn'*, no 2 (1966)

BORNYCHEVA, V. 'Nash semeinyi biudzhet,' *Novyi mir*, no 4 (1968)

BREUS, F. 'Kurs vernyi, za nami delo ne stanet-reportazh s sobraniia mekhaniza-torov MTS,' *Trud*, 11 March 1958

BROWN, EMILY C. 'The Local Union in Soviet Industry: Its Relations with Members of the Party and Management,' *Industrial and Labor Relations Review*, XIII (January 1960)

CHERNOV, I. 'Voprosy plenuma,' *Trud*, 1 June 1923

'Chetvertyi vsesoiuznyi s'ezd Sel'khozlesrabochikh,' *Trud*, 1 December 1928

CHIRKOV, I. 'Tak sozdavalsia profsoiuz zemli,' *Trud*, 7 July 1959

CHURAKOV, V. 'Problemy ispol'zovaniia trudovykh resursov sela,' *Voprosy Eko-nomiki*, no 1 (1968)

DEMIANENKO, V.N. 'Gosudarstvennoe rukovodstvo i kolkhoznaia demokratiia,' *Sovetskaia iustitsiia*, no 7 (1966)

– 'Sovershenstvovanie pravovogo regulirovaniia vzaimootnoshenii kolkhozov s organami gosudarstvennogo upravleniia,' *Sovetskoe gosudarstvo i pravo*, no 5 (1966)

DENISENKOV, I. 'Rezervy kolkhoznogo proizvodstva,' *Kommunist*, no 4 (1967)

DENISKINA, E.V. 'Svoeobrazie otraslei neproizvodstvennoi sfery na sele,' *Vestnik Moskovskogo Universiteta, seriia ekonomika*, no 6 (1966)

DEREVIANKIN, T. 'Poslevoennoe vosstanovlenie stosialisticheskogo khoziaistva Ukrainy,' *Ekonomika sovetskoi Ukrainy*, no 1 (1967)

DMITRASHKO, I. 'Ekonomicheskaia effektivnost' novykh form organizatsii truda v kolkhozakh,' *Voprosy Ekonomiki*, no 11 (1962)

DMITRUK, M. 'Profsoiuzy i podem sel'skogo khoziaistva,' *Professional'nye soiuzy*, no 8 (1949)

'Dobit' nepmana-v gorode, kulaka-v derevne,' *Trud*, 1 June 1929

'Doklad tov. Dogadova,' *Trud*, 13 December 1928

DOLOTKAZIN, A. 'O sel'skikh profsoiuznykh aktivistakh,' *Trud*, 22 September 1948

DOVHAL, S. 'Rebellion of Young People in Temir-Tau,' *Problems of the Peoples of the USSR*, no 6 (1960)

EDE, I. 'Soiuz na sele,' *Trud*, 4 December 1928

EFIMOV, V. 'Kolkhoznoe sobranie-kollektivnyi ekonomist i organizator,' *Kommunist*, no 1 (1968)

EFIMOV, V. and K. KARPOV 'Sovkhozam-polnyi khozraschet,' *Kommunist*, no 15 (1966)

EGURAZDOV, S.V. 'O profsoiuznykh organizatsiiakh na sele,' *Trud*, 26 March 1958

EMEL'IANOV, A. 'Ekonomicheskie stimuly i upravlenie sel'skim khoziaistvom,' *Planovoe khoziaistvo*, no 1 (1966)

– 'Neobkhodimyi produkt i oplata truda v kolkhozakh,' *Voprosy ekonomiki*, no 3 (1966)

FISCHER, G. 'The Number of Soviet Party Executives,' *Soviet Studies*, no 3 (January 1965)

FISHEVSKII, IU. 'Sotsiologicheskie issledovaniia v ideologicheskoi rabote,' *Partiinaia zhizn*', no 18 (1966)

GAPONENKO, G. 'O demokraticheskom tsentralizme v planirovanii sel'skogo khoziaistva,' *Planovoe khoziaistvo*, no 1 (1965)

GLADKOV, M. 'Davaite podumaem i ob etom,' *Trud*, 27 March 1958

– 'Novoe v zhizni sel'skikh profsoiuzov,' *Trud*, 3 August 1958

GLADKOVSKII, O., B. LEONOV and A. NAGAITSEV 'Dela i problemy sela,' *Trud*, 19 January 1968

– 'Dela i problemy sela,' *Trud*, 20 January 1968

GLEZERMAN, G. 'Sotsial'naia struktura sotsialisticheskogo obshchestva,' *Kommunist*, no 13 (1968)

GLIKSMAN, J. 'Recent Trends in Soviet Labor Policy,' *Problems of Communism*, no 4 (July–August 1956)

GLUKHOV, N. 'Profkom-pomoshchnik pravleniia,' *Sovetskie profsoiuzy*, no 13 (1969)

GOLIAEV, A. and A. NAGAITSEV 'Neotlozhnye zadachi sel'skikh profsoiuzov,' *Trud*, 20 June 1970

GOLOVKO, G. 'Avtoritet raikoma,' *Sovetskie profsoiuzy*, no 6 (1969)

GORSHKOV, A. 'Obedinit' 'profsoiuznye organizatsii sela,' *Trud*, 21 May 1941

– 'Polozhit' konets rasobshchennosti,' *Trud*, 19 April 1957

GRAFOV, I.I. 'Neobkhodim vykhod,' *Trud*, 14 December 1923

GROSSMAN, G. 'Economic Reforms: A Balance Sheet,' *Problems of Communism*, no 6 (November/December 1966)

GUDKOV, I. 'Sozdaetsia profgruppa,' *Sovetskie profsoiuzy*, no 20 (1969)

HINGLEY, R. 'Home Truths on the Farm: The Literary Mirror,' *Problems of Communism*, no 3 (May/June 1965)

HOLLANDER, P. 'The Dilemmas of Soviet Sociology,' *Problems of Communism*, no 6 (1965)

HOUGH, J. F. 'The Soviet Concept of the Relationship between the Lower Party Organs and the State Administration,' *Slavic Review*, no 2 (1965)

IANCHUK, V.Z. 'Teoreticheskie predposylki sovershenstvovaniia kolkhoznogo zakonodatel'stva,' *Sovetskoe gosudarstvo i pravo*, no 5 (1968)

IAROSLAVSKII, B. 'Profsoiuznaia organizatsiia sovnarkhoza,' *Na rubezhakh semiletki*. Moscow 1959

IASINSKII, G.M. 'Sobliudat' zakonnost' v kolkhoznykh pravootnosheniiakh,' *Sovetskoe gosudarstvo i pravo*, no 6 (1966)

IGNATOVSKII, P. 'Rost kul'turno-tekhnicheskogo urovnia krest'ianstva,' *Ekonomika sel'skogo khoziaistva*, no 11 (1967)

'Instruktsiia o provedenii vyborov profsoiuznykh organov,' *Trud*, 8 February 1947

'Iskrivlenie klassovoi linii,' *Trud*, 1 June 1929

IVIN, I. and A. KHRAMOVA 'Sovershenstvovat' oplatu truda rukovoditelei i spetsialistov kolkhozov,' *Ekonomika sel'skogo khoziaistva*, no 12 (1964)

JASNY, N. 'The Failure of the Soviet Animal Industry,' *Soviet Studies*, no 2, (October 1963)

KABANOV, M. 'Podderzhivaiu predlozhenie mekhanizatorov enbekshi-kazakhskoi MTS,' *Trud*, 8 March 1958

'Kak osushchestvliaetsia Sotsial'noe strakhovanie batrachestva,' *Trud*, 17 May 1928

'Kakoi dolzhna byt' struktura profapparata posle likvidatsii okruzhnykh zvenev,' *Trud*, 18 July 1930

KALANDADZE, A.M. 'O pravovom polozhenii dolzhnostnykh lits kolkhozov,' *Sovetskoe gosudarstvo i pravo*, no 3 (1966)

KARAVAEV, V.V. 'Ob okhrane truda v kolkhozakh,' *Trud*, 19 March 1958

– 'Razvitie pensionnogo zakonodatel'stva v SSSR, *Sovetskoe gosudarstvo i pravo*, no 7 (1966)

KARNAUKHOVA, E.S. 'Obespechit' polnuiu zaniatnost' kolkhoznikov v techenie goda,' *Kolkhozno-sovkhoznoe proizvodstvo*, no 1 (1965)

KAZAKOV, A. 'Batrachestvo i novye organizatsionnye zadachi Vserabotzemlesa,' *Trud*, 2 December 1923

KAZAKOV, P. 'Vyshe uroven' organizatsionno-massovoi raboty. K itogam soveshchaniia zaveduiushchikh orgotdelami Ts. K. profsoiuzov,' *Trud*, 31 July 1945

KAZ'MIN, I.F. 'Usilit' okhranu imushchestvennykh prav kolkhoznikov,' *Sovetskaia iustitsiia*, no 9 (1966)

– 'Organizatsiia i oplata truda kolkhoznikov,' *Sovetskoe gosudarstvo i pravo*, no 4 (1966)

KEDER, A. 'Vserabotzemles na Ukraine,' *Trud*, 26 September 1923

KEKHN, M. 'Kollektivnye dogovory soiuza Rabzemlesa,' *Trud*, 25 Auguist 1923

KHARATISHVILI, G. G. 'K voprosu o prave chlenstva v kolkhoze,' *Vestnik Leningradskogo Universiteta, Ekonomika, Filosofiia, Pravo*, no 4 (1968)

KHOMIAKOV, A. 'Profkom pravleniiu pomoshchnik,' *Sovetskie profsoiuzy*, no 10 (1968)

KHRUSHCHEV, N.S. 'O dal'neishem razvitii kolkhoznogo stroia i reorganizatsii MTS,' *Trud*, 28 March 1958

– 'O dal'neishem uvelichenii proizvodstva zerna v strane i ob usvoenii tselinnykh i zalezhnykh zemel'," *Pravda*, (February 1954)

KIKIN, B. 'O metodakh upravleniia proizvodstvom v MTS,' *Sotsialisticheskoe sel'skoe khoziaistvo*, no 3 (1947)

'Klassovoi vrag u sovkhoznoi molotilki,' *Trud*, 3 January 1933

KOLBASOV, J.S. 'Konferentsiia po teoreticheskim probleman budushchego primer-nogo ustava sel'skokhoziaistvennoi arteli,' *Sovetskoe gosudarstvo i pravo*, no 3 (1966)

KOLOD'KO, B.O. 'Krugovaia poruka,' *Trud*, 8 January 1938

'Konflikt mestnogo znacheniia,' *Sovetskie profsoiuzy*, no 23 (1966)

KONOTOP, V. 'Resheniia martovskogo plenuma TsK KPSS v deistvii,' *Kommunist*, no 3 (1966)

'Konveier predrabochkomov,' *Trud*, 17 May 1933

KOTOV, G. 'MTS reshaiushchaia sila v dal'neishem pod'eme sel'skogo khoziaistva,' *Trud*, 5 June 1954

KOVAL', L. 'Normirovanie truda v sovkhozakh pod obshchestvennyi kontrol,' *Sovetskie profsoiuzy*, no 16 (1968)

KOVGAN, S. 'V soiuze Vserabotzemles,' *Trud*, 26 April 1922

KOVTUN, K. 'Ia ne soglasen s bogorodskimi mekhanizatorami,' *Trud*, 18 March 1958

KOZHANOV, N. 'Uporiadochit' shtaty TsK profsoiuzov,' *Trud*, 26 January 1940

KOZLOV, A. 'Partiinye organizatsii i kolkhoznaia demokratiia,' *Partiinaia zhizn'*, no 15 (1966)

KOZLOVSKII, A. 'Glavnoe-bor'ba za pod'em ekonomiki,' *Sovetskie profsoiuzy*, no 3 (1966)

KOZYR, M. 'Kakim dolzhen byt' novyi primernyi ustav kolkhoza,' *Sovetskaia iustitsiia*, no 1 (1966)

KRAVCHENKO, I.I. and E.T. FADDEEV 'O sotsial'noi strukture sovetskogo obsh-chestva,' *Voprosy ekonomiki*, no 5 (1966)

KRIVOKOBYL'SKII, I., MARTYNIUK, S. 'Predlozhenie k novomu ustavu kolkhoza,' *Ekonomika sel'skogo khoziaistva*, no 2 (1966)

'Krupneishii etap,' *Trud*, 6 September 1934

'Kto rukovodit rabochkomami zernosovkhozov v ikh bor'be za khleb,' *Trud*, 4 January 1933

KUIDIN, I. 'Sotsial'noe strakhovanie v kolkhoze,' *Sovetskie profsoiuzy*, no 20 (1966)

KULIKOV, V. 'Sel'skii raikom partii segodnia,' *Kommunist*, no 11 (1965)

– 'Sovetskoe krestianstvo,' *Kommunist*, no 4 (1966)

KUROPATKIN, O. 'O prevrashchenii sel'skokhziaistvennogo truda v raznovidnost' truda industrial'nogo,' *Bol'shevik*, no 5 (1949)

LADENKOV, V. 'Sotsial'no-ekonomicheskie usloviia vosproizvodstva kvalifitsirovan-nykh kadrov sel'skogo khoziaistva,' *Voprosy ekonomiki*, no 1 (1967)

LAGUTIN, N. 'Povyshenie material'nogo blagosostoianiia i kul'tury truzhenikov sela,' *Ekonomika sel'skogo khoziaistva*, no 3 (1967)

LAIRD, R.D. 'Some Observations on the Impact of Politics on Soviet Agriculture,' *Osteuropa-wirtschaft*, no 4 (1968)

LAZUTKIN, E. 'Nauchnye mezhzonal'nye seminary po ekonomike sel'skogo khoziaistva,' *Voprosy ekonomiki*, no 3 (1966)

'Lenin ob organizatsii batrachestva,' *Trud*, 27 March 1924

LEWYTZKYJ, B. 'Die Gegenwaertige Lage in den Gewerkschaften der UdSSR,' *Osteuropa*, no 2 (1961)

– 'Die Nomenklatur-ein wichtiges Instrument Sowjetischer Kaderpolitik,' *Osteuropa*, no 6 (1961)

– 'Die Sowjetischen Gewerkschaften im Zeitalter des Technischen Fortschritts,' *Gewerkschaftliche Monatshefte*, no 11 (November 1962)

– 'Zur Territorial en Verteilung der Sowjetischen Arbeitskraeftereserven,' *Osteuropa*, no 5 (1964)

LEZHNEV-FIN'KOVSKII, P. 'Rabota v derevne i rol' Vserabotzemlesa,' *Trud*, 4 February 1924

LIBERMANN, O.G. 'Reforma zdiisniuetsia. Iak zhe poznachaet'sia na zhytti suspil'stva,' *Nauka i suspil'stvo*, no 3 (1970)

LININ, S. 'Batrak Ukrainy,' *Trud*, 5 July 1927

LISHANSKI, M. and D. ZAKERZHAEV 'Dagestanskaia ekonomicheskaia konferentsiia,' *Ekonomika sel'skogo khoziaistva*, no 7 (1967)

LOBOV, A. 'Ne tol'ko dengami no i naturoi,' *Kolkhozno-sovkhoznoe proizvodstvo*, no 1 (1965)

LOGVINOV, V. 'Kraikom profsoiuza bez predsedatelia,' *Trud*, 23 March 1940

LOZA, G. 'Problemy nauchnoi organizatsii upravleniia v kolkhozakh i sovkhozakh,' *Ekonomika sel'skogo khoziaistva*, no 12 (1966)

LUBKOV, A. and M. TSITVER 'Za obshchimi pokazateliami,' *Sovetskie profsoiuzy*, no 22 (1966)

L'VOV, V. 'Rabochii den' sel'skokhoziaistvennykh rabochikh,' *Trud*, 6 September 1923

– 'Zarabotnaia plata rabochikh sovkhozov,' *Trud*, 24 August 1923

'MTS nuzhny krepkie predrabochkomy,' *Trud*, 16 September 1933

MAKAROV, D. 'Profsoiuznye gruppy v kolkhozakh,' *Trud*, 18 June 1958

MAKHNOV, M. 'K priemu mekhanizatorov gotovy,' *Trud*, 6 March 1958

MATSKEVICH, V. 'Sel'skomu khoziaistvu-vysokie ustoichivye tempy razvittia,' *Ekonomika sel'skogo khoziaistva*, no 5 (1966)

MAZHAROV, V. 'Vedushchaia rol' sovkhozov v peredelke sel'skogo khoziaistva trebuet perestroiki raboty proforganizatsii,' *Trud*, 29 October 1931

MCAULEY, A.N.D. 'Kolkhoz Problems in Recent Literary Magazines,' *Soviet Studies*, no 3 (January 1964)

MEISSNER, B. 'Die sociale Struktur der KPdSU,' *Osteuropa*, no 9 (1966)

– 'Chruschtschowismus Ohne Chruschtschow' (11, 111), *Osteuropa*, no 3 (1965)

– 'Machtelite und Inteligenz in der Sowjetgesellschaft,' *Europa Archiv*, no 20 (1967)

MEL'NIKOV, I. 'Po nakazam delegatov,' *Sovetskie profsoiuzy*, no 15 (1968)
MIKHAILOV, A. 'Slovo kolkhoznogo agronoma,' *Trud*, 22 March 1958
MIKHALKEVICH, W. 'Pensionnoe obespechenie kolkhoznikov i ego organizatsionnoe sovershenstvovanie,' *Sotsial'noe obespechenie*, no 3 (1969)
MILLER, R.F. 'A Good Kolkhoz,' *Survey*, no 51 (April 1964)
MISHCHENKO, F. 'Chto ogorchilo starykh khleborobov,' *Partiinaia zhizn'*, no 21, (1966)
'Misto i suchasni zavdannia sela,' *Robitnycha hazeta*, 7 April 1970
'Mnozhit' riady stakhanovskikh sovkhozov,' *Trud*, 26 March 1949
'Moskovskie profsoiuzy vyskazyvaiutsia za raiprofsovety,' *Trud*, 21 July 1930
'Naivazhlyvishi zavdannnia profspilok,' *Robitnycha hazeta*, 30 January 1970
'Na konferentsiiakh i s'ezdakh profsoiuzov,' *Trud*, 29 March 1951
'Na plenumakh Ts. K. profsoiuzov,' *Trud*, 10 April 1954
'Na pomoshch Vserabotzemlesu,' *Trud*, 19 May 1922
'Na s'ezdakh rabochikh MTS i batrakov,' *Trud*, 17 May 1931
NASH, E. 'Extension of Trade Union Functions in the Soviet Union,' *Monthly Labour Review*, LXXXI (December 1958)
'Nasushchnye zadachi profsoiuzov,' *Sovetskie profsoiuzy*, no 5 (1970)
'Nekotorye ekonomicheskie problemy kolkhoznoi derevni (Obzor pisem, zametok i statei, postupivshikh v redaktsiiu),' *Kommunist*, no 8 (1961).
NEMCHENKO, L. 'O strakhovanii batrakov,' *Trud*, 2 December 1928)
NIKITUSHKIN, N. and N. BELIAEV 'Uverennym shagom: S'ezd profsoiuza rabochikh i sluzhashchikh sel'skogo khoziaistva i zagotovok,' *Trud*, 10 April 1958
NIZHEGORODTSEV, A. 'Voprosy razmezhevaniia v soiuze Vserabotzemlesa v turkestane,' *Trud*, 14 November 1923
'Novoe v instruktsii o poriadke priema profsoiuznykhh vznosov,' *Sovetskie profsoiuzy*, no 21 (1968)
'Novoe v izuchenii pravovykh voprosov upravleniia sel'skim khoziaistvom,' *Sovetskoe gosudarstvo i pravo*, no 1 (1965)
'Novye rubezhi sela, *Sovetskie profsoiuzy*, no. 5 (1970)
'O dal'neishem razvitii kolkhoznogo stroia i reorganizatsii mashinno traktornykh stantsii,' *Trud*, 18 April 1958
'O funktsiiakh profsoiuzov v oblasti sotsial'nogo strakhovaniia. Postanovlenie prezidiuma VTsSPS ot 10 Sentiabria 1933,' *Voprosy strakhovaniia*, nos 7/8 (1933)
'O perestroike profsoiuzov,' *Trud*, 6 September 1934
'O perestroike profsoiuzov,' *Trud*, 9 September 1934.
'O perevyborakh fabzavmestkomov: Postanovlenie prezidiuma VTsSPS O strokakh perevybornoi kampanii V FZMK po soiuzam,' *Trud*, 23 November 1932
'O poriadke obespecheniia po sotsial'nomu strakhovaniiu neshtatnykh zaboish-chikov skota, neshtatnykh rabochikh pushno-promyslovykh i zverovedcheskikh

khoziaistv: Postanovlenie sekretariata VTsSPS ot 1 Iulia 1957g,' *Biulleten' VTsSPS*, no 14 (1957)

'O poriadke sliianiia Narkomtruda SSSR s VTsSPS,' *Trud*, 11 September 1933

'O pravakh fabrichnogo, zavodskogo, mestnogo komiteta professional'nogo soiuza,' *Pravda*, 16 July 1958

'O razgranichenii funktsii proizvodstvennykh soiuzov i mezhsoiuznykh organov: Postanovlenie prezidiuma VTsSPS,' *Trud*, 2 August 1931

'O reorganizatsii narodnogo kommissariata zernovykh i zhivotnovedecheskikh sovkhozov,' *Trud*, 29 November 1935

'O reorganiztsii Narkomsovkhozov SSR i ego mestnykh organov. Postanovlenie Ts. I. K. SNKSSR,' *Trud*, 24 April 1934

'O trudovom zakonodatel'stve i partiinoi distsipline,' *Partiinaia zhizn'*, no 16 (1966)

'O zadachakh profsoiuznykh organizatsii v sviazi s postanovleniem Ts. K. KPSS i Soveta Ministrov SSSR: O dal'neishem razvitii kolkhoznogo stroia i reorganizatsii MTS,' *Trud*, 8 June 1958

'Ob uchastii profsoiuznykh organizatsii v obsuzhdenii tezisov doklada N.S. Khrushcheva: Postanovlenie prezidiuma VTsSPS,' *Trud*, 11 March 1958

'Ob ukreplenii starykh sovkhozov: Iz postanovleniia T.S.K. VKP (B),' *Trud*, 30 June 1929

'Ob ustranenii nekotorykh nedostatkov v profsoiuznom apparate i uluchshenii raboty profsoiuznykh organov,' *Trud*, 27 August 1940

'Obedinenie profsoiuzov rabochikh MTS s profsoiuzom rabochikh zemel'nykh organov,' *Trud*, 2 February 1941

'Obedinenie soiuzov sakharnoi promyshlennosti i rabochikh sveklosovkhozov: Postanovlenie prezidiuma VTsSPS ot 8 Maia,' *Trud*, 11 May 1941

'Okhrana truda i strakhovanie batrakov,' *Trud*, 2 December 1928

'Okhrana truda v derevne,' *Trud*, 5 February 1924

'Opyt massovoi raboty politotdelov vsem rabochkomam MTS i sovkhozam,' *Trud*, 24 April 1934

'Organizatorskaia rabota na sele,' *Pravda*, 2 March 1970

'Organizatsiia territorial'nykh profsoiuzov rabochikh sovkhozov,' *Trud*, 28 March 1941

ORLOV, I. 'Na perednem krae,' *Sovetskie profsoiuzy*, no 3 (1966)

OSIPOV, G. and M.T. YOVCHUK 'Some Principles of Theory, Problems and Methods of Research in Sociology in the USSR,' *American Sociological Review*, no 4 (1963)

'Otchety i vybory profsoiuznykh organov,' *Sovetskie profsoiuzy*, no 23 (1966)

'Otkrylsia s'ezd rabochikh zemledel'cheskikh sovkhozov,' *Trud*, 29 May 1931

' Ot Pontia k Pilatu,' *Trud*, 8 July 1934

PAKHOMOV, A. 'Uprostit' strukturu, sokratit' upravlencheskii personal v sovkhozakh,' *Finansy SSSR*, no 6 (1967)

PAKHOMOV, IU. 'O material'nykh stimulakh v sovkhozakh,' *Ekonomika Sovetskoi Ukrainy*, no. 10 (1966)

PALYVODA, N. and V. GULEVSKII 'Traktor v konnoi upriazhke,' *Pravda*, 30 January 1970

PARAMONOV, I. and F. RASPORKIN 'Govoriat khoziaeva zemli,' *Trud*, 1 April 1960

'Partiinye i profsoiuznye gruppy,' *Partiinaia zhin'*, no 3 (1969)

'Partkom i obshchestvennye organizatsii,' *Partiinaia zhizn' Kazakhstana*, no 1 (1969)

PASHERSTNIK, A.E. 'O sfere deistviia i printsipakh sovetskogo trudovogo prava,' *Sovetskoe gosudarstvo i pravo*, no 10 (1957)

PAVLOV, I.V. 'Novyi etap razvitiia kolkhoznoi demokratii,' *Sovetskie profsoiuzy*, no 18 (1969)

– 'O printsipakh novogo primernogo ustava kolkhozov,' *Sovetskoe gosudarstvo i pravo*, no 2 (1966)

'Pered bol'shoi zhatvoi,' *Trud*, 18 June 1958

PERELYGIN, S., and P.N. ROSLOV 'Sistema organov upravleniia v kolkhozakh,' *Sovetskoe gosudarstvo i pravo*, no 10 (1966)

PEROV-TERENT'EV, N. 'Na sele nuzhny mezhsoiuznye proforgany,' *Trud*, 26 May 1954

PERSHITS, N. 'Garantirovannaia oplata truda v kolkhozakh,' *Sovetskie profsoiuzy*, no 21 (1966)

'Pervostepennaia zadacha profsoiuznykh organizatsii,' *Trud*, 3 October 1941

PERVUSHIN, A. and N. SINITSYN 'Prava i obiazannosti kolkhoznikov i garantii ikh osushchestvleniia,' *Sovetskaia iustitsiia*, no 3 (1966)

PIKOREVICH, I. 'V dni zhatvy,' *Trud*, 8 July 1958

PIKUL'KIN, A. and I. SATIN 'Polnee ispol'zovat' trudovye resursy kolkhozov,' *Ekonomika sel'skogo khoziaistva*, no 8 (1966)

'Plenum TsK profsoiuza rabochikh i sluzhashchikh sel'skogo khoziaistva i zagotovok,' *Trud*, 19 April 1953

'Plenum TsK sakharnikov za sliianie s soiuzom sel'khozlesrabochikh,' *Trud*, 20 July 1930

'Plenum TsK sel'khozles-rabochikh,' *Trud*, 21 January 1930

'Plenum TsK Vserabotzemlesa,' *Trud*, 24 February 1924

'Plenum TsK Vserabotzemlesa,' *Trud*, 29 February 1924

'Plenum TsK Vserabotzemlesa,' *Trud*, 5 June 1923

'Plenum VTsSPS,' *Pravda*, 28, 29 January 1970

PLOSS, S.I. 'Politische Diskussion und Entscheidung im Sowjetsystem: Der Streit um die Kolchosverbaende,' *Osteuropa*, no 8/9 (1968)

'Po voprosu o strukture i metodakh raboty VTsSPS: Postanovlenie prezidiuma VTsSPS ot 8 ianvaria 1930 goda,' *Trud*, 25 January 1930

'Pochemu eti raisofprofy ne avtoritetny,' *Trud*, 5 December 1932

'Pochemu slaba zashchita naemnogo truda v derevne,' *Trud*, 4 December 1968

POPOV, N. 'Mnozhit' uspekhi v trude,' *Sel'skaia zhizn'*, 20 January 1968

– 'Za dostoinyi vklad v piatiletku,' *Sel'skaia zhin'*, 19 January 1968

– 'Raisovprof-organizator perestroiki derevni,' *Trud*, 24 September 1930

POPOVA, N.V. 'O rabote s profsoiuznym aktivom,' *Trud*, 20 January 1948

'Posle s'ezda profsoiuza,' *Trud*, 30 December 1939

'Postanovleniia XVI plenuma,' *Trud*, 11 May 1947

'Postanovlenie prezidiuma VTsSPS o deiatel'nosti TsK soiuza sel'khoz i lesnykh rabochikh SSR,' *Trud*, 2 September 1927

'Postanovlenie prezidiuma VTsSPS o meropriiatiiakh v sviazi s likvidatsiei okrugov ot 8 augusta, 1930 goda,' *Trud*, 26 September 1930.

'Postanovlenie prezidiuma VTsSPS o strukture apparata VTsSPS,' *Trud*, 28 August 1932

'Postanovlenie prezidiuma VTsSPS ot 25 marta 1935 goda po dokladu TsK soiuza miaso molochnykh sovkhozov Urala i zapadnoi Sibiri,' *Trud*, 3 April 1935

'Postavovlenie VIII plenuma VTsSPS ot 28 aprelia 1939,' *Trud*, 18 May 1939

POTASHNIKOV, F. 'Zhilishchno bytovaia rabota profsoiuznogo komiteta,' *Trud*, 26 May 1954

POZHIDAEV, V. 'Ukrepliat' kolkhoznuiu demkratiiu,' *Sovetskie profsoiuzy*, no 14 (1966)

'Preniia po otchetnomu dokladu TsK soiuza,' *Trud*, 28 December 1937

'Primernyi Ustav Kolkhoza,' *Pravda*, 30 November 1969.

'Privedem v deistvie use rezervy: Pervyi s'ezd rabochikh i sluzhashchikh sel'skogo khoziaistva i zagotovok,' *Trud*, 8 April 1954

'Pro sotsial'ne strakhuvannia chleniv kolhospiv,' *Robitnycha hazeta*, 14 April 1970

'Profgruppa v stepi,' *Trud*, 26 March 1940

'Profkom kolkhoza,' *Sel'skaia zhizn'*, 18 January 1968

'Profrabota na sele,' *Trud*, 8 February 1923

'Profsoiuz truzhevnikov derevni,' *Sel'skaia zhizn'*, 18 January 1968

'Profsoiuznaia gruppa kolkhoza,' *Trud*, 12 January 1968

'Profsoiuzy-aktivnye uchastniki vsenarodnoi bor'by za dal'neishii pod'em sel'skogo khoziaistva,' *Sovetskie profsoiuzy*, no 24 (1966)

'Profsoiuznye gruppy v kolkhozakh,' *Trud*, 1 July 1958

'Profsoiuzy posle s'ezdov,' *Trud*, 8 January 1948

PROKHOROV, V. 'Profsoiuzy na novom etape,' *Sovetskie profsoiuzy*, VI, no 18

PRONIN, I. 'Ekonomicheskaia podgotovka kadrov v Kuibyshevskoi oblasti,' *Ekonomika sel'skogo khoziaistva*, no 5 (1966)

– 'Podgotovka kvalifitsirovannykh kadrov v sel'skom khoziaistve SSSR,' *Ekonomika sel'skogo khoziaistva*, no 6 (1967)

'Protiv opportunizma, za leninskuiu vyderzhannost' v profsoiuzakh,' *Trud*, 9 June 1929

PROTSENKO, K. 'Novoe v oformlenii del po naznacheniiu pensii i posobii,' *Sotsial'noe obespechenie*, no 4 (1969)

PRUTOVYKH, P. 'Rezervy proizvoditel'nosti-v deistvie,' *Sovetskie profsoiuzy*, no 1 (1966)

'Rabota sredi batrakov na Ukraine: Beseda s predsedatelem iuzhbiuro Vserabotszemlesa t. Keder,' *Trud*, 10 February 1923

'Rabota sredi sel'khozrabochikh,' *Trud*, 31 July 1927

RAPOPORT, A. 'Byt batraka,' *Trud*, 2 September 1923

RASPORKIN, F. 'Kak eto nachalos',' *Trud*, 25 July 1958

'Reorganizatsiia profsoiiuzov Latvii,' *Trud*, 24 November 1940

REPP, K. and M. TAMM 'Analiz struktury rabochego vremeni brigadirov i upravliaiushchikh,' *Ekonomika sel'skogo khoziaistva*, no 5 (1967)

'Resheniia IX s'ezda eshche ne doshli do rabochkomov zernosovkhozov,' *Trud*, 23 September 1932

'Reshitel'no uluchshit' bytovye usloviia rabochikh sovkhozov,' *Trud*, 16 May 1933

'Rezoliutsii VIII s'ezda profsoiuzov,' *Trud*, 6 January 1929

ROZOV, K. 'Pravil'nyi put: K 10-letiiu 1-go vserossiiskogo s'ezda soiuza S. K. rabochikh,' *Trud*, 22 June 1929

RUBEL', I. 'Batrachestvo na Ukraine,' *Trud*, 26 September 1923.

RUSKOL, A.A. 'Demokratizatsiia printsipov upravleniia v kolkhozakh,' *Sovetskoe gosudarstvo i pravo*, no 11 (1967)

– 'Sotsial'noe obespechenie kolkhoznikov,' *Sovetskoe gosudarstvo i pravo*, no 4 (1966)

RUTKEVICH, M.N. 'O poniatii intelligentsii kak sotsial'nogo sloia sotsialisticheskogo obshchestva,' *Filosofskie Nauki*, no 4 (1966)

– 'Sotsial'nye istochniki popolneniia sovetskoi intelligentsii,' *Voprosy filosofii*, no 6 (1967)

S.R., 'Rukovoditeli bez klasovogo chut'ia,' *Trud*, 4 January 1930

'S etim miritsia nel'zia,' *Sovetskie profsoiuzy*, no 4 (1966)

SAKOFF, A.N. 'Production Brigades: Organizational Basis of Farm Work in the U.S.S.R.,' *Monthly Bulletin of Agricultural Economics and Statistics*, no 1 (January 1968)

'Samarskii gubotdel, rabota za 1921 god,' *Trud*, 9 March 1922

SARKISIAN, G. 'Povyshenie zhiznennogo urovnia kolkhoznikov,' *Ekonomika sel'skogo khoziaistva*, no 12 (1964)

SAVENKOV, N.T. 'O povyshenii roli raionnykh sovetskikh organov,' *Sovetskoe gosudarstvo i pravo*, no. 9 (1965)

SAVICHEV, K. 'Ne porali obnovit' polozhenie o raspredelenii molodykh spetsialistov,' *Sovetskaia iustitsiia*, no 12 (1966)

SCHINKE, E. 'Aussichten und Tendenzen der Sowjetischen Landwirtschaft,' *Osteuropa*, no 5/6 (1968)

– 'Zwischenbetriebliche Kolchosunternehmen in der Sowjetunion,' *Osteuropa Wirtschaft*, no. 2 (1967)
SCHWARTZ, SOLOMON M. 'Trade Unions in the Soviet State,' *Current History* (August 1969)
SDOBNOV, S. 'Sushchestvennye razlichiia mezhdu gorodom i derevnei i korennye voprosy ikh preodoleniia,' *Ekonomika sel'skogo khoziaistva*, no 1 (1967)
'XVII plenum VTsSPS,' *Trud*, 27 December 1947
'S'ezd profsoiuza rabochikh i sluzhashchikh sel'skogo khoziaistva i zagotovok,' *Trud*, 29 March 1960
'S'ezd rabochikh i sluzhashchikh MTS i zemorganov,' *Trud*, 6 March 1949
'XVI plenum, *Trud*, 20 April 1947
'Shestoi vsesoiuznyi s'ezd sel'khozlesrabochikh: Okhrana truda, strakhovanie batrakov,' *Trud*, 2 December 1928
SHKURATOV, I. 'K sevu: vysokuiu gotovnost',' *Trud*, 17 March 1970
– 'Rasshiriat' demokraticheskie osnovy rukovodstva sovkhozami,' *Ekonomika sel'skogo khoziaistva*, no 1 (1966)
– 'Sotsial'noe strakhovanie kolkhoznikov,' *Ekonomicheskaia gazeta*, no 23 (June 1970)
– 'Vysokii dolg profsoiuzov sela,' *Sovetskie profsoiuzy*, no 12 (1966)
SHLAEN, R. 'Politicheskaia ucheba profsoiuznykh kadrov,' *Trud*, 28 August 1938
SHUBKIN, V.N. 'Molodezh vstupaet v zhin' po materialam sotsiologicheskogo issledovaniia problem trudoustroistva i vybora professii,' *Voprosy filosofii*, no 5 (1965)
– 'Vybor professii v usloviiakh kommunisticheskogo stroitel'stva,' *Voprosy filosofii*, no 8 (1964)
SHVERNIK, M. 'Zadachi profsoiuzov v rekonstruktivnyi period,' *Trud*, 14 July 1930
SIMONENKO, G. 'Pensionnoe obespechenie v SSSR,' *Sovetskie profsoiuzy*, no. 19 (1968)
– 'Posobiia po sotsial'nomu strakhovaniiu,' *Sovetskie profsoiuzy*, no 15 (1968)
– 'Posobiia rabotnikam sel'skogo khoziaistva po wremennoi netrudosposobnosti,' *Sovetskie profsoiuzy*, no 6 (1966)
SINITSYN, V. 'Pereustroistvo byta derevni,' *Kommunist*, no 3 (1965)
SIRC, I. 'Economics of Collectivization,' *Soviet Studies*, no 3 (January 1967)
SKLIAREVSKII, IA. 'Profkom i pravlenie kolkhoza,' *Sovetskie profsoiuzy*, no 16 (1965)
SLAVINKOV, A. 'V pote litsa,' *Trud*, 5 July 1927
'Slovo delegata s'ezda' *Trud*, 18 January 1968
SMUGLYI, S. 'Neiasnye roziasneniia,' *Trud*, 16 January 1937
SOLOVEV, I. 'Sovetskii rabochii klass,' *Pravda*, 5 March 1970
'So strakhovaniem batrachestva neblagopoluchno,' *Trud*, 19 February 1929
'Sokrashchenie chisla chlenov soiuza sel'sko-khoziaistvennykh rabochikh,' *Trud*,

11 August 1928

'Soveshchanie po organizatsionno-massovoi rabote profsoiuzov,' *Trud*, 12–13 July 1945

'Sovety kolkhozov,' *Pravda*, 7 March 1970

'Sozdaetsia edinyi soiuz rabochikh lesnoi i lesoobrabatuvaiushchei promyshlennosti: Postlanovlenie prezidiuma VTsSPS ot 16 sentiabria,' *Trud*, 29 September 1930

'Sroki sozyva vsesoiuznykh s'ezdov professional'nykh soiuzov: Postanovlenie VTsSPS,' *Trud*, 12 March 1931

'Struktura gorodskikh i raionnykh sovetov professional'nykh soiuzov,' *Trud*, 28 August 1932

SYRODOEV, N. 'O roli raionnogo zvena v rukovodstve sel'skokhoziaistvennym proizvodstvom,' *Sovetskaia iustitsiia*, no 12 (1966)

'Tak sozdavalsia profsoiuz rabotnikov zemli,' *Trud*, 7 July 1959

TAKTAMYSOV, S. 'Sovershenstvovat' profsoiuznuiu rabotu,' *Trud*, 27 March 1958

'Ten' predrabochkoma v kolyshleiskoi MTS,' *Trud*, 25 March 1933

'Territorial'naia partorganizatstia,' *Partiinaia zhizn'*, no 24 (1966)

'Tipovaia struktura soiuznykh organov na predpriiatii: Postanovlenie prezidiuma VTsSPS,' *Trud*, 28 August 1932

TITOV, M. and T. SOVERSHENSTVOV 'Kolkhoznoe zakonodatel'stvo na nauchnoi osnove,' *Sovetskaia iustitsiia*, no 17 (1966)

TIUMENBAEV, A. 'Bez lishnikh zvenev,' *Trud*, 28 August 1932

TOTSKII, I. 'Dolzhniki,' *Pravda*, 24 January 1970

TOVKUN, V. 'Sovershenstvovat' uchet migratsii naseleniia,' *Ekonomika sovetskoi Ukrainy*, no 2 (1966)

'Trem soiuzam v lesu tesno,' *Trud*, 7 August 1930

'Trudiahchiiesia sovetuiut,' *Trud*, 20 April 1957

TRUFANOVA, N. 'O rabote na sele,' *Trud*, 8 March 1924

'TsK soiuza sel'khoz-lesrabochikh za sliianie s sakharnikami,' *Trud*, 11 August 1930

'Tseli i zadachi politicheskikh otdelov MTS i sovkhozov: Rezolutsiia obedinennogo plenuma TsK i TsK VKP (B) po dokladu tov. Kaganovicha priniataia 11 ianuaria 1933 goda,' *Trud*, 14 January 1933

TSOGOEV, NV. and M. TKALENKO 'Pochemu ukhodiat kolkhozniki,' *Ekonomika sel'skogo khoziatstva*, no 3 (1965)

'U rabochikh sovkhozov iuga,' *Trud*, 28 November 1947

'U rabotnikov sela,' *Trud*, 18 March 1951

'Uchastie profsoiuzov v rabote po pod'emu sel'skogo khoziaistva,' *Trud*, 18 April 1954

'Ukrepim politicheskoe i khoziaistvennoe znachenie raiona,' *Trud*, 18 July 1930

'Ukrepim profsovety sel'skikh raionov,' *Trud*, 5 January 1933

'Ukreplenie soiuza sel'khozlesrabochikh,' *Trud*, 2 September 1927

'Uporno borot'sia za usvoenie novykh metodov rukovodstva,' *Trud*, 10 September 1934

'Uralobkom soiuza zemsovkhozov ne vozglavil bor'bu za bol'shevitskuiu uborku urozhaia,' Trud, 24 August 1933

'Uroki rabochkoma luchanskogo sovkhoza,' *Trud*, 4 February 1933

'Usilit' rabotu profsoiuzov na zagotovkakh,' *Trud*, 15 August 1945

'V bor'be za vysokie urozhai: Na s'ezdakh profsoiuzov rabotnikov sel'skogo khoziaistva,' *Trud*, 7 January 1948

'V kakom zhe, nakonets, my profsoiuze,' *Trud*, 12 June 1935

'V MTS I MTM Odesskoi oblasti zaseli kulaki, pianitsy, vory,' *Trud*, 1 November 1933

'V obstanovke bol'shego pod'ema: Na s'ezde profsoiuza rabochikh i sluzhashchikh sel'skogo khoziaistva i zagotovok,' *Trud*, 8 April 1958

'V Petrozavodskom gubotdele Vserabotzemlesa,' *Trud*, 15 February 1931

'V prezidiume VTsSPS: Organizatsiia teritorial'nykh profsoiuzov rabochikh sovkozov,' *Trud*, 28 March 1941

'V sel'skikh profsoiuznykh organizatsiiakh,' *Sovetskie profsoiuzy*, no 4 (1966)

'V. I. Lenin o roli profsoiuzov v osushchestvlenii sotsial'nykh trebovanii trudiashchikhsia,' *Sovetskie profsoiuzy*, no 5 (1969)

'V VTsSPS: O poriadke provedeniia oblastnykh, kraevykh, respublikanskikh, dorozhnykh, baseinovykh konferentsii i s'ezdov profsoiuzov,' *Trud*, 11 February 1947

'V VTsSPS: Profsoiuznye organizatsii v bor'be za vysokii urozhai,' *Trud*, 2 April 1946

v-ov, p. 'Batraki govoriat: Iz kraevoi konferentsii batrachestva i bednoty,' *Trud*, 6 February 1929

VARENTSOVA, V. 'Sobliudat' zakonodatel'stvo o trude molodykh spetsialistov,' *Sovetskaia iustitsiia*, no 2 (1966)

'Vchera na s'ezdakh: U rabotnikov sela,' *Trud*, 7 April 1954

VILENSKII, I. 'Pristanishche dlia temnykh elementov,' *Trud*, 24 March 1937

VOINOV, K. 'V nadezhde na rozshirenie shtatov Pochemu ne nalazhivaetsia profrabota v novykh sovkhozakh,' *Trud*, 10 May 1954

VOL'CHIKHIN, V. 'Sel'skie mekhanizatory rabotaiut kruglyi god.' *Trud*, 29 March 1956

VOLKONSKII, A. 'Iz opyta raboty po pod'emu ekonomicheski slabykh kolkhozov,' *Voprosy ekonomiki*, no 11 (1963)

VOLKOV, A.I. 'Vsemerno okhraniat' prava kolkhoza i kolkhoznikov,' *Sovetskaia iustitsiia*, n 10 (1966)

– 'Pravovye voprosy sel'skokhoziaistvennogo pereseleniia v SSSR,' *Sovetskoe gosudarstvo i pravo*, no 9 (1967)

'Voprosy material'nogo stimulirovaniia sel'skokhoziaistvennogo proizvodstva-obzor statei i pisem postupivshykh v redaktsiiu,' *Voprosy ekonomiki*, no 3 (1966)

VORKUNOV, S. 'O sblizhenii uslovii zhizni naseleniia derevni i goroda,' *Ekonomika sel'skogo khoziaistva*, no 5 (1966)

VOROSHILIN, M. 'Dogovornaia praktika v soiuze vserabotsemles,' *Trud*, 31 January 1923

'Vosemdesiat sem tsirkuliarov,' *Trud*, 9 December 1947

VOSKRESENSKAIA, M. 'Splochennye voedino,' *Sovetskie profsoiuzy*, no. 5 (1969)

'Vserosiiskaia konferentsia Vserabotzemlesa,' *Trud*, 25 September 1923

'Vserossiiskii s'ezd rabotnikov zemli i lesa,' *Trud*, 21 December 1922

'Vserossiskoe soveshchanio po strakhovaniiu batrakov,' *Trud*, 10 February 1929

VSEVOLODOV, M. 'Rabota ot sluchaia k sluchaiu,' *Trud*, 5 June 1929

'Vyshe uroven raboty na sele,' *Trud*, 6 April 1955

WAEDEKIN, K.E. 'Betriebsleiter und Funktionaere, die Kolchosvorsitzenden in ihrem Verhaeltnis zu Uebergeordneten Instanzen gegen Ende der Chruschtschow-aera,' *Osteuropa*, no 19 (1966)

– 'Die Expansion des Sovchoz-sektors in der Sowjetischen Landwirtschaft,' *Osteuropa Wirtschaft*, no 1 (1968)

– 'Fuehrt der Weg zur Agrostadt,' *Sowjetstudien*, no 24 (1968)

– 'Internal Migration and the Flight from the Land in the USSSR, 1929–1959,' *Soviet Studies*, no 2 (October 1966)

– 'Landwirtschaftliche Bevoelkerung und Arbeitskraefte der Sowjetunion in Zahlen,' *Osteuropa Wirtschaft*, no 1 (1967)

– 'Manpower in Soviet Agriculture: Some Post-Khrushchev Developments and Problems,' *Soviet Studies*, no 3 (January 1969)

– 'Nicht-Agrarische Beschaeftigte in Sowjetischen Doerfern,' *Osteuropa Wirtschaft*, no 3 (1968).

– 'Sowjetische Doerfer-Gestern, Heute, Morgen,' *Osteuropa*, no 8/9 (1968)

– 'Sozialstruktur und Klassen, Sowjetische Soziologen diskutieren die Rinordnung von Intelligenzia und Kolchosbauern in das Klassenschema des Sozialismus,' *Osteuropa*, no 1 (1968)

– 'Zur Sozialschichtung der Sowjetgesellschaft,' *Osteuropa*, no 5 (1965)

'What Should Trade Unions Do on a Collective Farm,' *Current Digest of the Soviet Press*, XVII, no 12 (1965)

'Za dal'neishuiu perestroiku professional'nykh soiuzov,' *Trud*, 5 September 1934

ZABELYSHENSKII, A. 'Usilit' okhranu prav kolkhoznikov i ikh rol' v upravlenii delami kolkhoza,' *Sovetskaia iustitsiia*, no 4 (1966)

'Zabota o cheloveke zakon nashego obshchestva,' *Trud*, 19 June 1954

'Zashchita intersov sel'khozrabochikh,' *Trud*, 29 May 1929

'Zavodskii profaktiv v dni voiny,' *Trud*, 3 October 1941

ZEKULIN, G. 'Aspects of Peasant Life as Portrayed in Contemporary Soviet Literature,' *Canadian Slavonic Studies*, no 4 (1967)

ZEN'KO, K. and L. SEMENOVA 'Rabotu profsoiuzov na uroven' novykh zadach,' *Trud*, 11 June 1957

ZHUKOV, D. 'Neustanno rastit' i vospityvat' profsoiuznye kadry,' *Trud*, 10 October 1958

ZHURIKOV, V. and V. MIKHAILOV 'Pravil'no organizovat' garantirovannuiu oplatu truda v kolkhozakh., *Ekonomika sel'skogo khoziaistva*, no 9 (1966)

ZOERB, C.R. 'From the Promise of Land and Bread to the Reality of the State Farm,' *Studies on the Soviet Union (New Series)*, no 4 (1967)

ZVORYKIN, A.A. 'Structural Analysis of Publications in the Field of Social Studies in the Soviet Union, 1960–1965,' *Social Research*, no 4 (1966)

Index

Abdullaev, N. (Uzbek Republic Committee), 86

Antselovich, V. (AFWU), 151

Agricultural Code, 149

Agricultural and Forestry Workers' Union, 9; membership in, 16, 19, 47, 77–112; and Communist party, 16, 22–29, 47; and working conditions, 17, 23, 149–58; and batraks, 18, 25, 29, 47, 49, 98–101; finances of 19, 135–42; and collectivization, 31; in Central Asia, 47, 48, 51; structure of 50–3; becomes Agricultural Workers' Union (1930), 54–5; and seasonal labourers, 104; and social insurance; *see also* Agricultural unions

Agricultural unions: early attempts to organize, 3–4; struggle for control of, 7–12; All-Russian Agricultural Workers' Union established, 8–12; becomes Agricultural and Forestry Workers' Union (1926), 9n; as transmission belt, 9, 14, 17, 53, 194; and Communist party, 7–12, 13, 21, 28, 29, 34–5, 54, 56, 66, 67, 193, 194; and finances, 19, 69, 132–48, 195, 196; membership in, 12–13, 22–3, 29, 54–7, 86–8; and NEP, 14–23, 45–53, 98–108, 135–42; and collectivization, 22–33, 109–10, 194; failures of, 24, 27, 28, 30, 79, 150–2, 194; becomes Agricultural Workers' Union (1930), 54–5; split into four unions, 1931, 31, 58–63, 112, 142–7; reorganization of 1934, 31, 32, 63–75, 114–22, 142–7; production function of, 33; defence function of 33, 108, 151–3, 155, 157, 161, 198; in Central Asia, 47–50; and purges, 62, 67, 69, 70–1; 194; elections in, 70, 92–3; amalgamation into five territorial unions, 1941, 75–9; effects of war on, 77–8, 122–4; amalgamation into two unions, 1948, 78–81; post-Stalin period in, 33–44; becomes Union of Workers and Employees in Agriculture and State Procurement (1953), 35–9, 81–4, 194; and Virgin Lands campaign, 35, 40, 82, 83, 163, 194, 197; new structure of,

1962, 89–90; commissions of, 93–4;
and social insurance, 168–9; and
working conditions, 42, 149–67;
see also individual unions

Agricultural Workers' Union: structure of 45–6, 56–7; membership in,
57; split into four unions, 1931, 58,
112; *see also* Agricultural unions

All-Russian (Union) Central Council
of Trade Unions (ACCTU): and agricultural unions' membership, 9, 10,
48–51, 101, 110, 118, 122; and
struggle for control of agricultural
unions, 10–12, 29; and agricultural
unions' finances, 19, 71, 133–5,
139, 142, 144, 145, 147; role in
collectivization, 26, 27, 29; reorganized (1930), 55; and union
reorganization of 1931, 31, 58–60,
158; and powers of unions, 36; and
federalism, 37; and union reorganization of 1934, 60–1; and purges,
62, 70–2; and union bureaucracy,
69, 73–4, 137; further union reorganizations, 1933–9, 71; 72; and
reorganization of 1941, 75–6; cri-
ticizes union leadership, 78; and
Virgin Lands campaign, 35, 82; and
reorganization of 1953, 81; on
failures of unions, 87; new structure
of, 89–90; and MTS, 128; and working conditions, 152, 160, 161; and
social insurance, 169, 170, 177–82,
185–9
– Plenums: Fifth (1931), 31, 177–8;
Thirteenth (1954), 35–6; Fifth
(1955), 36; Sixth (1957), 38;
Tenth (1940), 69; Sixth (1937),
69; Seventh (1938), 70, 71, 145,
160; Eighth (1939), 72; Tenth
(1940), 73–4; Sixteenth (1947),
78, 161; Thirteenth (1954), 82;
Third (1960), 87; Second (1925),
101; Third (1926), 101, 139, 152;
Third (1929), 110; Eighteenth
(1939), 118; Seventeenth (1947),
122; Fourth (1926), 170; Third
(1933), 178

All-Union Social Insurance Council,
169, 172

All-Union Social Insurance Fund for
Colective Farmers, 183

Babinskii, S. Ia. (Central Committee
of Union), 11

Baltic States, 74, 121

Batraks, relations with agricultural
unions: recruitment of, 19, 24, 25,
27, 48, 97, 194; education of, 26,
28, 29; and Co-operative Movement,
26; and collectivization, 30, 31, 108,
110, 111, 114–16; and kulaks, 46;
in Central Asia, 47, 101; and ACCTU,
48–50; under NEP, 99–108; and
finances, 136; and Provisional Rules,
196; and social insurance, 170–3

Belorussia, 7, 13, 136

Bolsheviks, relations with agricultural
unions: struggle for control of,
7–12; and expansion of union,
12–14; Lenin on role of in NEP,
14–15; Stalin and offensive of, 30;
and economic reconstruction policies, 98; and finances, 133; influence
in union, 194; *see also* Communist
party

Brumberg, I.N. (ACCTU), 10

Bureaucracy, in union: size of, 51, 64,
68–9, 73; in raisovprofs, 56; volunteers in, 57, 74; and social welfare
agencies, 64; and purges, 67, 70–1;

in commissariats, 63–4, 68; and Virgin Lands campaign, 83; and elected officials, 106; and finances, 135, 137–41, 144; and corruption, 138–41, 146; union domination of, 195–6

Central Administration of Social Insurance, 26, 169
Central Asia, 47–50, 51, 101
Civil War, 14, 98
Class: Lenin on, 6, 14; Stalin on, 17; struggle in countryside, 23, 25, 27
Collective Farm Statute, 95, 166
Collectivization, 23–33, 158; results of, 58, 114–22; and union membership, 106, 108–14; role of unions in, 110, 111, 194; and conditions of labour, 158, 197
Commissariat of Agriculture, 63–4
Commissariat of Education, 26
Commissariat of Health, 26
Commissariat for Grain and Live-stock-farming Sovkhozes, 67–8
Commissariat of Labour, 26; amalgamated with ACCTU, 31, 144, 158; and social insurance, 169, 173, 178–9, 184
Commissariat of State Farms, 64
Commission of Social Insurance, 185
Communist party: and membership in agricultural unions, 11, 14, 29, 108, 117, 193, 195; and control of union, 12, 21, 28, 29, 34–5, 39, 54, 56, 66, 67, 193, 194; and NEP, 14–15, 16; and role of unions in agriculture, 16, 18, 74; Stalin on role of, 17, 20–1; on failure of agricultural unions, 18, 22, 24–5, 27, 36, 150; and finances of union, 19, 27, 134; and union bureaucracy, 19, 27; and

collectivization, 23–33; 106, 110, 111; and Virgin Lands campaign, 35, 82; and MTS, 34–5, 124; and Seven Year Plan, 43; on reorganization of unions, 1934, 64, 114; and hired labour, 17, 149; and defence theory of unions, 31, 33, 152–3, 158; and productivity, 131, 163; and social insurance program, 178, 199
– Conferences and congresses: Tenth Congress (March 1921), 15–16; Tenth Conference (May 1921), 16; Eleventh Congress (March–April 1922), 16–17, 20; Eleventh Conference (December 1921), 16; Twelfth Congress (April 1923), 17–18, 19; Twelfth Conference (August 1922), 18; Thirteenth Congress (May 1924), 18, 22; Thirteenth Conference (January 1924), 18; Fourteenth Congress (December 1925), 21–2, 24, 27, 139, 150; Fourteenth Conference (April 1925), 20; Fifteenth Congress (December 1927), 23–4, 28, 106, 152, 158; Sixteenth Congress (June–July 1930), 30; Sixteenth Conference (April 1929), 27, 58; Seventeenth Congress (January-February 1934), 31–2, 114; Eighteenth Congress (1939), 32, 74, 117; Twentieth Congress (February–March 1956), 36, 83, 163
Co-operative Movement, 26

Defence (protective) theory of unions, 31, 33, 198, 200
Dvadtsiatipiatitisiachniki, 29, 30, 31, 111

Education, of proletariat, 26, 28, 55, 74, 107, 198
Egurazdov, S.V. (UWEASP), 85, 123
Elections, in unions, 70,73, 92–3
Engineering and Technical Sections (ITS), 57

Federalism, within unions, 23, 37
Finances, of union, 69, 110, 132–49; centralized administration of, 132–3; early period, 133–5; and NEP, 135–42; collection of, 135–6, 139, 147; expenditures, 136–7; and membership, 139; reorganization of, 142; after 1933, 142–7; and bureaucracy, 135, 137–41, 144–5, 146; after 1958, 147–8; of social insurance program, 172, 174–5, 176, 183–4, 187–8; party control over, 19, 27, 134, 194, 195, 196
Five Year Plans: First, 23, 177–8; Second, 80
Forestry Workers' Union, 54–5, 97
Functional principle, 63, 65

Gladkov, M. (Krasnodar Trade Union Council), 85–6, 127
Golubev, F. (ACCTU), 10
Gosovprofs, 55
Grupporg, 57
Grupprabochkoms (territorial), 46–7
Gubotdel, 46
Gubernias, 3–4, 11, 12–13
Gustov, I.S., 198

Hired workers, 6, 9, 17, 57; and union membership, 96–7, 107, 108, 128, 129; and Agricultural Code, 149–50; and Provisional Rules, 150; and Labour Code, 149, 150; and conditions of labour, 149, 197; on violation of codes, 152; benefits of, 155–6; regulations for employment of, 157; and living conditions, 158; prohibited, 159; defined, 166; and social insurance, 169, 174; significance of term, 199–200

Iachmennikova, N. (AFWU), 111
Illison, L. (Estonian Trade Union Council), 37
Immigrants, European, 13, 48
Inter-trade Union Bureau of Engineers (MBIT), 57
Iotko, M.E. (Union of MTS and Land Organs Workers), 81, 117

Kalanov, M. (Institute of Marxism-Leninism), 126–7
Kaplan, S. (Commissariat of Labour), 152
Katorgin, I. (Union of MTS Workers of the East), 117
Kazakhstan, 107n, 162, 164
Kerimov, Kh., 37
Khrushchev, N.S., on crisis in agriculture, 34; on failure of unions, 36; and MTS, 41n; on raising agricultural productivity, 43–4; on liquidation of MTS, 124, 125; and Virgin Lands Campaign, 162
KKOV, relations with union, 26
KNS, relations with union, 26
Kolkhoz Statute, 40
Kolkhoz Union, 44
Kolkhozes: and collectivization, 30, 31; labour participation in management of, 40; and social insurance, 44, 174, 180–4, 187, 199–200; and raikom, 56; and raisovprof, 56; and rabochkoms, 57; and MTS workers, 84–8, 162, 194, 195, 197; and union,

95, 166–7; and membership, 110, 124–31

Kolkhozniks, 111, 120; *see also* Kholkhozes

Kombedy, 7n, 17

Komsomol, and union, 13, 14; in sovkhozes, 26; members in Virgin Lands campaign, 35, 162–3; and war, 160

Koshchi, 13, 26, 48–50

Kulaks: Stalin on, 17, 18, 20–1, 25; and batraks, 24, 25, 46; liquidation of, 26, 27, 30, 114, 158, 199; and union membership, 107; and conditions of labour, 155–6; and social insurance, 174, 176

Labour Code (1922), 96, 127; enforcement of, 24, 26, 149, 150, 152, 156; reaffirmed, 154–5; and social insurance, 168, 169, 180–2; and sovkhoz workers, 196; and seasonal workers, 199

Labour, conditions of, 9, 17, 42, 149–67; under NEP, 149; length of work day, 150–2, 153–4, 155, 157, 161, 167; and Agricultural Code, 149, 150; and Labour Code, 149, 150, 152, 155, 156; pre-collectivization, 149–58; and hired workers, 150, 152, 154, 157, 159; in sovkhozes, 150, 152, 163; and Provisional Rules, 150, 153, 154, 157; and collective agreements, 152, 161; and agricultural unions, 152, 157, 163, 164, 166; and temporary workers, 153; housing, 154, 155, 164; post-collectivization, 158–60; wages and insurance, 158, 165; postwar, 160–7; enforcement of regulations re, 153–4; and women

workers, 154, 157, 160, 161, 167; and kulaks, 155, 156; and labour inspectors, 154, 160; and Communist party, 158; and Commissariat of Labour, 158; and social welfare benefits, 159; and workers grievances, 159; and war, 160–1; and Komsomol, 160, 162; and MTS, 60, 162, 163; and kolkhozes, 162, 166–7; and Virgin Lands campaign, 162, 163, 197; and production conferences, 163, 197; and Model Statute, 165; and Collective Farm Statute, 166

Labour Inspectorate, 152, 154, 160, 165

Latvia, 3, 5, 75

Laws, Soviet, 18, 33

Lenin, V.I.: on dictatorship of the proletariat and peasantry, 4–5, 14; on organizing village proletariat, 5–6, 8, 193; definition of hired workers, 6; on agricultural unions as transmission belt, 9, 14; on classes, 6, 14; on NEP, 14–15; theses, 16–17; and federalism in unions, 37

Leningrad, 20, 31

Lespromkhoz, 111

Levman, G. (ACCTU), 10

Lewytzkyj, B., 165

Liberman, M., 173

Local Committees (FMZK), 50, 61

MTM, 119, 121

Machine Tractor Stations (MTS), 57, 58, 194, 195; and agricultural production, 34; and tractor drivers in, 34, 40; and Communist party, 34–5; and Virgin Lands campaign, 35; reorganization of 1958, 40–2, 84–8; politotdels in, 62, 67; zampolits

appointed in, 67; and union membership, 109, 118, 119–22; batraks and,
111; abolition of, 124–31, 197; and
social insurance, 199
Maksimov, M.T., 146
Medical and Sanitation Workers'
Union, 54
Medium Machine-building Workers'
Union, 121
Membership, 96–131; in early period,
96–99; and hired labour, 96, 107,
129; and Labour Code, 96–7; and
batraks, 97, 99–108, 110, 111, 114;
in sovkhozes, 97, 107, 108, 109,
111, 118; and NEP, 98, 99–108; and
women, 98; in Ukraine, 100; in
Central Asia, 101; and seasonal
labourers, 104, 108, 119; and purges,
106; and collectivization, 106, 108–
22; and kulaks, 107, 114; and MTS,
109, 111, 112–14, 118, 119–25,
128–9; in kolkholzes, 110, 111,
124–31; and reorganization of 1931,
112–14; postwar, 122–4; and Kolkhoz Statute, 126
Mensheviks, 4, 5, 7–12 passim
Mestkoms, 46, 56
Mikhailov, A., 86
Model Statute, 40, 95, 96; and role of
union, 165; and kolkhozes, 166
Moscow, 3, 13, 31, 55, 183
Moscow Landowners' Union, 8
Murashkin, F.I., 72

Nemchenko, I. (Insurance Council),
172
New Economic Policy (NEP), 14–23;
organization of unions under,
45–54; effect on union membership,
98; and recruitment of batraks,
99–108; finances under, 135–42;

and status of agricultural workers,
149; and social insurance under,
169
Nikolaev: strike in, 40
North Caucasus, 12, 31
Novocherkassk: strike in, 40

Odessa, 12; strike in, 40
Obkom, 57, 71, 87
Oblast, 23, 50
Okrugs, 55
Okruzhotdel, 50, 51

The Peasant Question, 20
People's Commissariat of State Farms,
63–4
Pensions, 40, 143, 182; problems of,
186; Commission on Pensions, 186;
and Ministry of Social Security,
188; and State Pensions Law,
189–91; and unions, 190
Petrograd Gubernia Agricultural
Union, 3, 13; dominated by Bolshe-
viks, 7; Agricultural Workers'
Union formed, 8; congress of, 8, 9;
refuses to send delegates to First
All-Russian Congress of Agricul-
tural Workers, 11
Petrovskii, A. (MTS Workers), 72
Politburo. See Communist party
Politotdels, 62, 67
Popova, N.V., 122
Presidium of the ACCTU. See All-
Russian Central Council of Trade
Unions
Pripisnye sovkhozes, 99
Production principle, of unions, 33,
37; basis of 1934 reorganization, 66,
75; and reamalgamation proposed,
72; and reorganization of MTS, 85,
121; and party apparatus, 89

Profgruppa, 61
Proletariat: Lenin on, 6, 14–15; and party congress on, 16, 19; Stalin on, 17–18, 20–1; and union membership, 22; and collectivization, 23–33; living conditions of, 25; *see also* Hired labour, Seasonal labour, Temporary labour, Women labourers
Promyshlenno-podsobnye enterprises, 108
Provisional Rules: and conditions of labour, 150, 153, 154–5, 157; and social insurance, 176; and batraks, 196, and seasonal workers, 199
Purges: effects of, 32, 44, 62, 70, 106, 114, 194, 196

Rabkors, 26
Rabachkoms, 53; relations with batraks, 46; subordinated, 58; and Virgin Lands campaign, 35; structure of, 62; and purges, 62; failures of, 79; election of, 92; commissions of, 93
Raikoms, 51, 56; duties of, 55; and union membership, 57; and transformation of agriculture, 58; failures of, 79
Raiotdels, 51
Raipravleniia, 55
Raiprofbiuro, 51
Raiprofsovets, 58
Raisovprofs, 51, 55, 61
Raisekretariats, 51, 55
Repair Tractor Stations (RTS), 84–8, 129
Republican Committees, 50, 51–3, 71
Revolution: February 1917, 3, 4; October 1917, 6, 7
Revizionnaia Kommissiia, 92
Rozov, K.L. (secretary of Central

Committee of Unions), 11
Russian Social-Democratic Labour party (RSDLP), 5

Seasonal labourers: and union, 22, 23, 54, 104, 108, 119, 135; and Provisional Rules, 199; and Labour Code, 199
Second world war, effects on unions, 32, 122–4, 197; effect on working conditions, 160–1
Sel'koms: organized for batraks, 46, 50, 58
Sel'rabochkoms, 53, 57
Seven Year Plan, 43
Shefstvo associations: importance of, 24, 28, 30; membership in, 20, 31; and collectivization, 27, 31; and Virgin Lands campaign, 35; and Section for Work in the Villages, 55
Shock brigades, 31
Shkuratov, I.F. (ACCTU), 166
Shmidt, G. (Commissar of Labour), 9
Shvernik, M., 54; on need to control unions, 66; on bureaucracy, 69, 73; on 1937–8 union elections, 70; on batraks in kolkhozes, 110; accused of ignoring agricultural unions, 145–6; on conditions of labour, 158, 160
Siberia: outside Bolshevik control, 7, 12; Lenin on union in, 14; union organization in, 51; and union dues, 136
Socialist Revolutionary party, 4, 5; struggle for control of agricultural unions, 7–12; strength in villages, 15n
Sotsstrakh. *See* Social insurance
Social insurance, 24, 168–92, 199; administration of, 40, 64, 74, 184–9;

pensions, 43, 182, 186, 189–91; financing of, 110, 171, 172, 174; inequalities in, 130; extension to kolkhozes, 131, 174; rates of, 138; and ACCTU, 144; 1922–31 period of, 168–77; role of union in administration of, 168–9, 184–9; participation in, 170–1, 180–2; 1931–3 period, 177–82; death benefits, 171, 175–6, 182; accident benefits, 171, 175, 182; maternity benefits, 172, 173, 175, 176, 182; and kulaks, 172, 174; and unemployment, 175, 176; abuses, 192

Sovkhozes: workers in, 19; conditions of labour, 25, 150; and union, 26, 90–4; and collectivization, 31; and Virgin Lands campaign, 35, 163; and Communist party, 54; administration of, 55–7, 99; and NEP, 98; and union membership, 107, 108, 109, 114, 118–9; and social insurance, 180, 187, 189, 199; and Labour Code, 196

Sovprofs, 13, 23, 37–9

Stalin, Joseph: on role of party in union, 17–18, 21, 194; on leadership of agricultural union, 19; on weakness of party in villages, 20; *The Peasant Question*, 20; on kulaks, 20–1; on collectivization, 23–4, 30, 31; calls for liquidation of kulaks, 25; "Dizziness from Success," 30

Students, 143, 181–2

Temporary workers, 153; in MTS, 120, 123; and social insurance, 180–2

Territorial principle, 66, 75–6, 89

Tikhonov, K.A., 145

Tomsky, M.P., 7; ejected from politburo, 30, 108; and union member- ship under NEP, 98–9; on financial corruption, 141; on working conditions, 150; on defence principle, 152

Trade Union Statute, 42n, 127, 130, 143, 166

Trade unions: as transmisison belts, 26, 28, 34, 53; role in collectivization, 30; defence theory of, 31, 33, 165; crisis of, 32; production theory of, 33, 37; and Virgin Lands campaign, 35, 82; powers of, 36; role in society, 37–9, 40; on role of batraks, 48; and purges, 62, 67, 69, 70; and agricultural unions, 76; postwar congresses of, 78–9; finances, 132–3, 136; and social insurance, 168–9, 178–9; and pensions, 189–90; compared to Western unions, 193

– Congresses: First, 132; Second, 132, 133; Third, 133; Sixth, 136, 138; Seventh, 53, 133; Eighth, 28, 31, 53, 139, 142, 154; Ninth, 60; Tenth, 81, 161; Eleventh, 35–6, 165; Twelfth, 43, 165; Sixth All-Union, 51; First All-Russian, 7; Second All-Russian, 7; Third All-Russian, 14; Third All-Russian Conference, 5

Transport Workers' Union, 54

Tsekh, 74

Tselevoi profsoiuznyi upolnomochenyi, 57

Tsentral'noe pravlenie, 51–3

Turkmen SSSR, 51–3, 107n

Tver gubernia, 4, 7, 13

Transmission belt theory, 9, 14, 17, 26, 28, 34, 53, 194

Uchastkom, 57

Uezd, 14

Uezdotdels, 46, 47, 51

Ukraine: outside Bolshevik control, 7, 12; union in, 13, 14, 18; union organization in, 51, 58; union membership in, 100; and social insurance in, 170

Union of Education Workers, 54

Union of Foresters, 9, 10, 55, 99

Union of Gardeners, 3

Union of Land Organs Employees, 117

Union of Land Surveyors, 3, 8

Union of MTS and Land Organs Workers of the USSR, 79–81, 120, 122–3

Union of MTS Workers, 32

Union of MTS Workers and Batraks, 58, 60, 61; split, 65, 66; and 1931 reorganization, 60, 112; membership of, 114, 120; *see also* agricultural unions

Union of Metal Workers, 141

Union of Soviet Trade Workers, 55

Union of Sovkhoz Workers of Kazakhstan and Central Asia, 76

Union of Sovkhoz Workers of the Centre, 76

Union of Sovkhoz Workers of the East, 76

Union of Sovkhoz Workers of the South, 76

Union of Sovkhoz Workers of Ukraine and Moldavia, 76

Union of Sovkhoz Workers of USSR, 79–81, 123

Union for Workers of Agricultural Sovkhozes, 58; split according to production principle, 65; membership of, 114; amalgamated, 123

Union of Workers and Employees in Agriculture and State Procurement: First Congress of 35, powers of 36, 38; working conditions in, 42, 163;

formed, 82–3; organization of 88–95; membership in, 123; and administration of social insurance, 184–92

Union of Workers of Cotton-growing Sovkhozes and MTS, 65, 117, 146

Union of Workers of Dairy and Meat Sovkhozes of Kazakhstan and Central Asia, 65, 71, 72

Union of Workers of Dairy and Meat Sovkhozes of the South and Centre, 65, 70–1, 72

Union of Workers of Dairy and Meat Sovkhozes of the Urals and Siberia, 65, 72

Union of Workers in Animal-breeding Sovkhozes, 58, 65, 114, 123

Union of Workers of Feather and Poultry Sovkhozes, 65, 68–9, 70, 117

Union of Workers in Flour Mills and Grain Elevators, 82, 123

Union of Workers of Garden and Vineyard Sovkhozes, 65, 116

Union of Workers of Grain-growing Sovkhozes, 65, 116, 117, 146

Union of Workers of Horse-breeding Sovkhozes, 65, 72, 118

Union of Workers in Land Organs, 66, 70, 75, 117, 120, 123, 146

Union of Workers of MTS and Land Organs of the Centre, 75

Union of Workers of MTS and Land Organs of the East, 75

Union of Workers of MTS and Land Organs of Kazakhstan and Central Asia, 75

Union of Workers of MTS and Land Organs of the South, 75

Union of Workers of MTS and Land Organs of the Ukraine, 75

Union of MTS Workers of the South and Centre, 66, 71, 75, 117, 120
Union of MTS Workers of the East, 66, 75, 120, 145
Union of Workers of Pig-raising Sovkhozes, 65, 72
Union of Workers of Sheep-raising Sovkhozes, 72, 116, 117
Union for Workers in the Sugar Industry, 54, 58, 110, 112
Union of Workers of Vegetable-growing Sovkhozes, 65, 117
Upolnomochenyi, 57
Uprofbiuro, 47
Urals, 31, 153, 170
Uzbek SSSR, 51–3, 107n, 117

Virgin Lands campaign, 35, 40, 82, 83, 194; and conditions of labour, 162–3, 197
Vladimir gubernia, 4, 7, 12
Volga, 7, 12, 18
Volosti, 16

Volsekretariats, 46, 47, 50
Vsesoiuzsel'khoztekhnika, 88

Wages: union control over, 56, 72, 74; inequalities in, 130; and working conditions, 150, 156
Western Belorussia, 74, 121
Western Ukraine, 74, 121
Women: effects of on unions, 17, 20, 23, 160–1, 195, 196, 197; education of, 26, 28, 107; and union membership, 98, 122; dues for, 143; conditions of labour of 154; social insurance for, 171, 172, 173
Woodworkers Union, 54, 112
Work in the Village Section, 26, 27, 28, 55
Workers and Peasants Inspection, 31

Zampolits, 67
Zemliacheastva, 19
Zhdanov, A., 55–6, 74